A DICTIONARY OF THE VEDIC RITUALS

A DICTIONARY OF THE VEDIC RITUALS

BASED ON THE ŚRAUTA AND GRHYA SŪTRAS

CHITRABHANU SEN

CONCEPT PUBLISHING COMPANY
DELHI

Reprint *1982, 2001*

First edition 1978

Chitrabhanu Sen (*b.* 1927)

Published and Printed by
Ashok Kumar Mittal
Concept Publishing Company
A/15-16, Commercial Block, Mohan Garden
New Delhi-110059 (India)
Phones: 5648039, 5649024
Fax: 091–(11)–5648053
E-mail: publishing@conceptpub.com

TO
THE MEMORY OF MY FATHER
ARUN SEN, B.A. (CANTAB), BARRISTER-AT-LAW
ACADEMICIAN AND LINGUIST
WHO TAUGHT ME TO UNDERSTAND
INDIA AND HER PEOPLE
THROUGH THE CLASSICS

CONTENTS

CONTENTS

INTRODUCTION

Our knowledge of the vedic ritual is derived with a varying degree of accuracy from three sources: the Saṁhitās, the Brāhmaṇas, the Śrauta and Gṛhyasūtras. But none of these books can be taken as the starting point of the vedic ritual. The earliest form of the vedic ritual remains unrecorded.

But the earliest reference to the vedic ritual is found in the Ṛgvedasaṁhitā. The names of sacrificial objects are mentioned: *yūpa, idhma, samidh, juhū, grāvāṇaḥ, droṇa, camasa* etc. The three *savanas* of the *Soma* sacrifice have been mentioned. The Ṛgveda also knew the existence of at least seven priests: *Hotṛ, Potṛ, Neṣṭṛ, Agnīdh, Praśāstṛ, Adhvaryu* and *Brahman.*[1] A stage was reached when the hymns, as a poet claims, could only be understood by means of a sacrifice.[2] It is certain therefore that in the Ṛgvedic period the ritual was fairly extensive.

There are, on the other hand, a large number of hymns in the Ṛgveda which have no sacrificial use. The Ṛgvedasaṁhitā was not a book of ritual. Āśvalāyana could not maintain the order of the hymns in his sūtra. Sāyaṇa, who was brought up in the orthodox ritualistic tradition, believed that the Ṛgvedasaṁhitā was a book of ritual. He took pains to prove that there was no anomaly when Āśvalāyana in his Śrautasūtra could not employ the first verse of the saṁhitā in the first sacrifice, *Darśapūrṇamāsa* he described.[3]

There are instances that the meaning and purpose of the hymns were disregarded or arbitrarily altered when a hymn was employed in a rite. The word *kasmai,*[4] an interrogative pronoun, meaning to whom, when used in a rite was turned to a deity. Ka became Prajāpati.[5] Max Müller comments: But soon a new adjective was formed, and not only the hymns, but sacrifice also, offered to the god, were called Kāya or who-ish.[6] In course of time the word *kāya* was legitimatized, and Pāṇini had to frame a rule to form the word.[7] In the sacrificial practice the Ṛgvedasaṁhitā has been assigned to the *Hotṛ*, one of the principal priests, whose duty it is to recite certain hymns called *śastras*, distinctly with proper accent.

The Atharvavedasaṁhitā, which contains popular spells, has no practical use in the *śrauta* rites. Consequently, the *Brahman* priest to whom the saṁhitā has been assigned remains silent most of the time during the service. His duty it is to supervise the sacrifice. Keith observes: A deliberate attempt was later made to bring the Atharvaveda into the circle of the three orthodox Vedas by the addition to the collection of book XX which contains the hymns to be used by the *Brāhmaṇācchaṁsin* priest in the ritual of the *Soma* sacrifice.[8] But despite the attempts it remained beyond the pale of orthodoxy. In many *gṛhya* rites, however, a large number of the verses of the Atharvaveda have been used.[9]

But the case with the saṁhitās of Yajurveda and Sāmaveda is quite different. In the very arrangement of these later saṁhitās the ritualistic bias can easily be seen. The *Adhvaryu* and his assistants who carried out the manual operations of the sacrifice required a special type of formulas. These formulas consisting of prose and verse were collected in a separate saṁhitā called Yajurveda, and the formulas were called the *yajus*. This was obviously a priestly creation.

The saṁhitā of Yajurveda which has been preserved in two schools, *śukla* (white or pure) and *kṛṣṇa* (black)[10], in five recensions, were created exclusively for the ceremonial purpose. The verses of the Yajurvedasaṁhitās are mostly borrowed from the Ṛgvedasaṁhitā for the sacrificial purpose of the *Adhvaryu*, in many cases without any real propriety and with deliberate alterations to adapt them to the ritual.[11]

In the ritual application of the verses a significant change occurred. The accentuation of the verses is entirely ignored. The *Adhvaryu* simply mutters the verses in accentless tone, and no one at a distance can hear or understand him. This mode of pronunciation is called *upāṁśu*. Evidently, the system of accentuation which was an integral part of the text lost its force in the ritual. So is the case of all other hymns when used as *mantra*. It is enjoined that all *mantras* except *japa* etc. are to be pronounced in *ekaśruti* (q. v.), monotone. The grammarians were, however, sticklers for the use of accents, and they insisted on it. As a note of warning to the delinquents Patañjali quotes a verse in his Mahābhāṣya : *duṣṭaḥ śabdaḥ svarato varṇato vā mithyāprayukto na tamarthamāha. sa vāgvajro yajamānaṁ hinasti yathendraśatruḥ svarato' parādhāt.*[12] An interesting legend is repeatedly cited to show what would befall a person who put a wrong accent on a wrong place. Vṛtra performed a sacrifice to punish Indra who desicrated his sacrifice by forcibly drinking *soma* juice without being invited. The *mantra* was *indraśatrurvaradhasva,* "O Agni, the foe of Indra," prosper, and the word *indraśatru* being a *tatpuruṣa* compound should have acute accent on its last syllable. But Vṛtra pronounced the *mantra* with a misplaced acute accent on the first syllable of *Indraśatru*, and as a result the word became a *bahuvrīhi* compound, meaning having Indra as a foe prosper. Vṛtra himself was killed.[13]

In spite of the views of the grammarians a fundamental change occurred, and the *mantras* had lost the accents. It follows therefore that the *Adhvaryu* who is the most important functionary in the manual operations of the sacrifice did not have to learn the accents of his prayer book. With a penchant for variety the priests introduced another method of pronunciation which is said to be a little louder than *upāṁśu*. This is called *dhvāna*, murmur, in which vowels and consonants can be distinguished but as a whole the letters cannot be distinguished. It is certainly a sign of decay.

The Sāmavedasaṁhitā is also a liturgical collection. But by no means it is an original one. It is almost entirely a verbatim copy of the Ṛgvedasaṁhitā. Of the total 1810 verses or 1549 verses (261 verses are repetitions) contained in *ārcika* and the *uttarārcika* all but 75 are found in the 8th and 9th *maṇḍalas* of the Ṛgvedasaṁhitā. The Sāmavedasṁhitā has been assigned to the *Udgātṛ* priests who chant the verses called *stotras* set to a melody called *sāman* chiefly in the *Soma* sacrifice. The *Udgātṛ* priests have hardly any role in the sacrifice apart from chanting the *stotras*. While the *Adhvaryu* priests have discarded the accent of the Yajurvedasaṁhitā, the *Udgātṛ* priests adopt a peculiar fashion in chanting the *stotras*. The verse is broken up in various parts called *prastāva*, *udgītha*, *pratihāra*, *upadrava* and *nidhana*, and then by repetition of the *pādas* (see *stoma*) and interpolations of syllables (see *stobha*), the chant assumes a bizarre form. It is so intricate that it is almost impossible to determine its exact nature.[14] A stage of stagnation has been reached when no new literary piece can be created, and the technicalities of recitation or chanting are the primary aims.

It is a very fond practice of the priests to render a word unintelligible by a peculiar process of permutation and combination. Thus the summons *śaṁsāva*, let us praise, becomes *soṁsāvom* or *śoṣoṁsāvom* or *śoṁsāvo* (see *āhāva & partigara*). It becomes a meaningless jargon.

It is no wonder therefore that long before the Buddha there grew a strong resentment against the ritual practice : Then the seers, the kāvaṣeyas, knowing this, say, 'To what end shall we repeat the veda, to what end shall we sacrifice? For we sacrifice breath in speech, or in breath speech'.[15] Or again : People say, Hymn,Hymn. The hymn is indeed the earth. For from it all that exists springs.[16]

Apart from the technicalities which were constantly developed, changed and added, the sacrifice itself suffered a considerable transformation. The sacrifice once represented the social activity of the worshippers. It was a web of practices, emanating from the social thinking and emphasizing particular aspects of life. But with the decay of the society and the change in the social life the sacrifice, in abstraction, drifted to its natural death. We shall find that within a sacrifice various rites have been combined indiscriminately. They have no logical bearing on the sacrifice in which they are included. Keith observes : As a result of the constant development of the ritual, the festivals of the *śrauta* type are full of details which are of no consequence with regard to the meaning of the sacrifice : practically in no case is an important rite addressed to one god only : the effort on the contrary was clearly to find as much room as possible for as many gods as possible.[17]

The proliferation and transformation of the vedic sacrifice that took place have been confirmed by the ritualists. Some sacrifices are considered models and called *prakṛti*. These sacrifices form the basis of other rites which are looked upon as modifications and called *vikṛti*. Only the *prakṛti* form of a sacrifice is described in detail in the Sūtras. Thus it is held that the *Darśapūrṇamāsa* is a model of all other sacrifices known as *Iṣṭi*, and so is the *Agniṣṭoma* of all other *Soma* sacrifices.

Oldenberg has pointed out : It shows how much system there is in the Indian sacrifices, and how fully and minutely that system must have been elaborated, before it assumed that form in which we find it in the Brāhmaṇas and Sūtras.[18] On account of the detailed exposition of the *prakṛti* class of sacrifices it must not be supposed, however, that these sacrifices are historically the most ancient.[19]

It is held that the animal sacrifice belonging to the *Soma* sacrifice the *agnīṣomīya* or *saumya* is a model of all other animal sacrifices. Therefore the so called independent animal sacrifice known as the *Nirūḍhapaśubandha* is termed as *nirmita*, made (see *Paśu*). But the *Nirūḍhapaśubandha* itself becomes the *prakṛti* of all other animal sacrifices other than the *savanīya* and *anubandhyāpaśu*. Similarly, the *Pravargya* is really an independent rite but incorporated into the *Soma* sacrifice. Āpastamba treats it separately,[20] and does not consider it as an essential part of the *Agniṣṭoma*.[21]

According to the sacrificial theory some rites within a sacrifice are marked as *pradhāna*, main and the others as *aṅga*, limb. These minor *aṅga* rites may recur in various other sacrifices as ancillary rites. The *aṅga* rites are called the web of a sacrifice (see *tantra*).

But the most significant change in the arrangement of the sacrifice that occurred in the recorded period was the interpolation of the *dīkṣā* rite in the *Soma* sacrifice. The central feature of the rite is the ritual rebirth of the sacrificer. The idea of rebirth has been vividly emphasized in the Brāhmaṇas. The sacrificer becomes an embryo. He closes his fists like a foetus in the womb, which is represented by the shed for the initiate (*dīkṣitavimita*); he gets a piece of cloth, a covering which stands for the placenta. He mimics stammering (*parihvāla*).[22] The Śatapatha Brāhmaṇa says : he who is consecrated becomes an embryo.[23]

The etymology of the word *dīkṣā* has drawn much more attention of the scholars[24] than the nature of the rite itself. The *dīkṣā* rite has obvious affinities with the ceremony of initiation practised by the primitive people all over the world. In the hunting stage of economy of the primitive society the birth of a child, specially a male child, was a very important event. A male child would augment the food supply by hunting. It is no wonder therefore that so much emphasis has been laid on the domestic rites relating to the child birth: *Sīmantonnayana, Puṁsavana, Jātakarman.*

Far more important is the event in the tribal life when the boy is an adolescent. He is now ready to accept his share of social and economic responsibilities of the society. In the tribal belief every stage of the physical change is the death and the rebirth of the novice. The initiation rite by which the novice is ushered into the next stage of life is a drama of life and death.[25]

The initiation rite was so important that even when the vedic society had moved forward from the tribal life the vedic ritual could not discard it altogether. As a relic of the past it found its place in the preparatory rite which consecrates the sacrificer to the *Soma* sacrifice.

In the same light is to be seen the domestic rite of *Upanayana.* The Śatapatha Brāhmaṇa says that it is a rebirth of the novice.[26] As in the *dīkṣā* the novice wears ths skin of a black deer, a girdle, and holds a staff. Later, however, the *Upanayana* was associated with the studentship. Keith comments: The case of the initiation of the boys of the people is the most striking instance of the peculiar character given to a rite by the influence of the priests.[27]

But the most important transformation that occurred in the patriarchal vedic society is the exclusion of women from the sacrifices. She has precious little to do in the sacrifice (see *patnī*). In the Ṛgvedasaṁhitā a *patnī* is a proprietress, owner or wife RV. III. 61.4; VII. 75.4; X.85.39, etc. Yet it is interesting to note that according to Pāṇini the word *patnī* means a wife who takes part in the sacrifice of her husband (*patyurno yajñasaṁyoge* IV. 1.33). The nature and extent of her participation are however not known from this *sūtra.* Even a more drastic change took place in the position of the sacrificer himself. He is supposed to be the central figure of a sacrifice as implied by the word *yajamāna* (q. v.). Although he is patronizingly called the *svāmin* (chief or master) of the sacrifice, he is merely a donor, or institutor of a sacrifice. He has no prominent part to play. He engages priests for a fee, and performs some minor acts as instructed by the *Adhvaryu,* who has now become the central figure of the sacrifice. The sacrificer has been hopelessly abondoned in the hands of the priests. The sacrifice has become a priestly affair. The sacrifices have been described in the Brāhmaṇas and codified in the Sūtras from the point of view of the priests. With the proliferation of the sacrificial rules and the amplification of the list of absurd expiations (*prāyaścitta*) it is impossible for a sacrificer to perform any *śrauta* sacrifice on his own.

In the performance of a sacrifice the community does not participate. The vedic sacrifice as described in the Brāhmaṇas is a personal affair. It is performed by the priests for the benefit of the institutor, *yajamāna.* The only exception is the *Vrātyastoma* in which all the *vrātya*s take part.

The sacrificial fee, *dakṣiṇā,* is a very important element in a sacrifice. No sacrifice can be performed without the fee. It has been cleverly argued why a sacrificer should pay the fees to the priest. The sacrifice goes to heaven, and the fee follows it. The only way for the sacrificer to go to heaven is to cling to the fee he pays to the priest.[28]

Over a long period the transformation of the vedic ritual continued with the change in the society itself. It took a standard form with certain variations among different priestly schools in the Brāhmaṇa texts. The main purpose of these texts was to describe the sacrifices in detail, to set rules for the performance, and to provide a rationale with their rather queer sacrificial doctrines. An atmosphere of sterility has already closed in. In style they are moribund. The sacrifice they describe is no more primitive than their own language. As a manual of sacrifice they are clumsy. Of the Brāhmaṇas, Max Müller says : The general character of these works is marked by shallow and insipid grandiloquence, by priestly conceit and antiquarian pedantry. It is most important to the historian that he should know how soon the fresh and healthy growth of a nation can be blighted by priestcraft and superstition. It is most important that we should know that nations are liable to these epidemics in their youth as well as in their dotage. These works deserve to be studied as the physician studies the twaddle of idiots, and the raving of mad men.[29]

As a remedy a systematic and business-like code was called for, and this led to the composition of the Śrautasūtras. The sūtras presuppose the *Saṁhitās* and the Brāhmaṇas. But unlike the Brāhmaṇas the Śrautasūtras, shorn of all clumsy doctrines of the Brāhmaṇas, give a succinct account of the sacrifices. From the ritualistic point of view the importance of the sūtras is so great that one can perform the sacrifices without the vedas, simply with the help of the sūtras. But without the help of the sūtras no one can learn the rituals from the hymns and the Brāhmaṇas.[30]

The Śrautasūtra is a functional manual of the priests, and it follows faithfully its own Brāhmaṇa. As a manual it has taken only those terms of the Brāhmaṇa which are essential in the operation of a sacrifice.

Like the *śrauta* rites the domestic rites underwent the stages of transformation. Many of the hymns of the Ṛgvedasaṁhitā which are employed as *mantra*s at the domestic ceremonies have no bearing on the ceremonies.[31] Moreover, the Ṛgveda verses which accompany the funeral and wedding rites are found in the 10th *maṇḍala* which is of late origin. The claim that there was another set of *mantra*s as old as the rites themselves may probably be true, but no such *mantras* are found in the Saṁhitās.[32] On the other hand, the Atharvavedasaṁhitā is one of the main sources of *mantra*s for many domestic rites.[33] There are two Gṛhyasūtras : Āpastamba and Gobhila which have separate books for the *mantra*s they employ : the *Mantrapāṭha* and the Mantrabrāhmaṇa. These *mantra*s do not occur in any Saṁhitā.[34]

The Gṛhyasūtras have no extant Brāhmaṇa to provide them with a sacrificial doctrine. The terms and names of the domestic rites are, however, found in the Saṁhitās and the Brāhmaṇas without any exposition of the rites.[35]

The domestic rites are as old as the *śrauta* sacrifices, and they have a common origin. In course of time the domestic rites were developed in a different stream. In orthodox view the *śrauta* sacrifice was known by revelation (*śruti*) in contrast to the domestic rite which was derived from memory (*smṛti*).

In manner and form the Gṛhyasūtras depend on and presuppose their respective Śrautasūtras. In the manner of writing the Gṛhyasūtras the authors the-imitate the Śrautasūtras and they try to make the Gṛhyasūtras as respectable as the Śrautasūtras. It is also claimed that the domestic ritual is based on the Brāhmaṇa texts (see brāhmaṇāveksa).There is an obvious tendency to bring in as many gods as possible in the domestic rites. Śāṅkhāyana admits that there are deities for whom no *mantra* could be provided. These deities are called ***anāmnātamantras*** (see *āmnātamantra*) and they are to be propitiated by uttering svāhā only ŚGṛ. I. 9.18.

The Gṛhyasūtras are less rigid than the Śrautasūtras, and contain less technical terms.

The Gṛhyasūtras have recognized the popular rites. It is enjoined that the custom prevailing in the village community is to be observed at the funeral and the wedding, because the village is the authority on these matters.[36]

The present work is mainly based on the following sūtras for the *Śrauta* rites :

(i) Āśvalāyana which belongs to the Aitareya Brāhmaṇa (Ṛgveda), and the ritual code of the *Hotṛ* priest.

(ii) Baudhāyana, Bhāradvāja and Āpastamba of the Taittirīya Bnāhmaṇa (Kṛṣṇa Yajurveda) which are the code books of the *Adhvaryu* priest, and

(iii) Kātyāyana of the Śatapatha Brāhmaṇa (Śukla Yajurveda) which is the code book of the *Adhvaryu* priest.

Of all Śrautasūtras the Baudhāyana is recognized by scholars as the oldest. Its antiquity is confirmed by the style and the language of the sūtra. It is called a *pravacana,* meaning traditional doctrine (literally, sayings) or sacred writing. Baudhāyana follows a style of narrative akin to the Brāhmaṇas. It can hardly be called a *sūtra.* Chronologically, Bhāradvāja comes next to Baudhāyana. Bhāradvāja Śrautasūtra did not attain the perfection of the *sūtra* style. Āpastamba is a very extensive work written in the *sūtra* style, and so is Kātyayāna which belongs to a different school. But wherever necessary other *sūtra*s have been used.

For the domestic rites the following Gṛhyasūtras have been mainly used : Āśvalāyana, Kāṭhaka, Baudhāyana, Bhāradvāja, Āpastamba, Hiraṇyakeśin Pāraskara, Gobhila and Kauśika.

A dictionary has its obvious disadvantage. The terms belonging to a single concept get dispersed throughout the book owing to the alphabetical arrangement.But only a general description will not help a scholar in understanding the different aspects of a sacrifice.Besides,the sacrificial terms without explanation are baffling. The dictionary will help the scholars in understanding the exact purport of a term, its different usages, and its correlation with other sacrificial concepts. It is always difficult to draw a distinction between the sacrificial and the non-sacrificial terms. As the purpose of the dictionary is to show how an object was used in a sacrifice, how a particular action was performed or how a person behaved in a given ritual context,only those terms have been selected which are useful in understanding the nature of the vedic sacrifice. It is not claimed that the dictionary is exhaustive. But every attempt has been made to include all significant terms of the sacrifice that occur in the sūtra.

In India, as far as is known, scholars have not given much attention to the study of the vedic ritual in its social background. Scholars have not sought an answer to the questions : What in the vedic ritual is characteristically "Vedic" ? A serious study of the ritual is essential for a proper understanding of the vedic literature. It is a study of the society which no longer exists. "What a people does in relation to its gods must always be one clue, and perhaps the safest, to what it thinks."[37]

REFERENCES

1. RV II. 1. 2.
2. *Yajñena vācaḥ padavīyamāyan* RV X.71.3,
3. Sāyaṇa's introduction to the Ṛgvedasaṁhitā. Poona p. 25-26.
4. *Kasmai devāya haviṣā vidhema* RV.X.121.1.

5. ŚBr I.1.1.13.
6. Max Müller HASL 228.
7. *Kasyet*, Pāṇ IV.2.25.
8. Keith RPV 18.
9. Ram Gopal : India of vedic kalpasūtras 16.
10. for the explanation of the words *śukla* and *kṛṣṇa*, see Max Müller HASL 90-91.
11. Keith RPV 17, Winternitz I, 177.
12. Mbh : paspaśāhnika.
13. ŚBr I.6.3.8.
14. H. Dh II(2), 1169-71.
15. *etaddha sma vai tadvidvāṁsa āhurṛṣayaḥ kāvaṣeyāḥ kimarthā vayamadhyeṣyāmahe kimarthā vayaṁ yakṣyāmahe. vaci hi prāṇaṁ juhumaḥ, praṇe vā vācam.* A. Ār III.2.6. & Keith ib 257.
16. *ukthamukthamiti vai prajā vadanti tadidamevokthamiyameva pṛthivīto hīdaṁ sarvamuttiṣṭhati yadidaṁ kiṁca.* ib II.1.2. & 201.
17. Keith RPV 313.
18. Oldenberg SBE XXX, 346.
19. ib.
20. Āp. Śr. XV. 5-12.
21. ib. XIII. 4. 3-5.
22. ABr I.3.
23. ŚBr. III. 3.3.12.
24. Keith RPV 302.
25. Cf. Themis 13-29; Thomson SAGS 45-49.
26. ŚBr. XI. 5.4.12.
27. Keith RPV 377.
28. ŚBr. I.9.3.1. See also *ṛtvij* and *dakṣiṇā*.
29. Max Müller HASL 204.
30. Cf. Max Müller HASL 97; Ram Gopal : India of vedic kalpasūtras 1.
31. Oldenberg SBE XXX, x.
32. ib. x-xi,
33. Ram Gopal : India of vedic kalpasūtras 37.
34. Winternitz I, 276-77,
35. Ram Gopal : India of vedic kalpasūtras 16-18; Oldenberg SBE XXX, xviii
36. PGṛ I.8.11-13; AśvGṛ. I.7.1.
37. Harrison, Jane Ellen : Prolegomena to the study of Greek religion,vii. (Meridian Books). New York, 1957.

ACKNOWLEDGEMENTS

In compiling this dictionary, I had to rifle and plunder various books. In particular, I am indebted to the excellent dictionary of Louis Renou : Vocabulaire du rituel vedique. I have often drawn on this book.

I am indebted to two of my friends : Mr. Haridas Sinha Roy, Assistant Professor in Sanskrit, Chandernagore Government College (Hooghly) and Mrs. Santi Acharya, Senior Lecturer in Sanskrit, Sarojini Naidu College (Dum Dum) who helped me very much by suggesting many improvements upon my work and giving me encourgement. I also received constant support and advice from my wife Renuka Sen, Lecturer in Sanskrit, Siliguri College.

I am grateful to Mr. Nirmal Bhattacharya, Lecturer in Geography, Siliguri College, who drew the plans for me. Mr. J. N. Ganguli, Deputy Controller of Examinations of the North Bengal University, took keen interest in my work and read through the typescript.

I acknowledge with thanks the service and co-operation received from the members of the Library and Office Staff of the Asiatic Society, Calcutta, and the members of the Library Staff of the North Bengal University.

I desire to express my thanks to Mr. Naurang Rai, of Concept Publishing Company, who took a keen interest in bringing out this book. It gives me much pleasure to acknowledge the services of Dr. Mantrini Prasad, who took great pains in dealing with the proofs.

In a work like this, however, the possibility of errors remaining in the book persists. For such errors I take the entire responsibility.

CHITRABHANU SEN

Raja Rammohunpur,
North Bengal University
Dt. Darjeeling.

ABBREVIATIONS

abbrev—abbreviation
ABr—Aitareya Brāhmaṇa
Ādhāna or *Ādheya*—Agnyādhāna or Agnyādheya
adj—adjective
ĀpDh—Āpastamba Dharmasūtra
ĀpGṛ—Āpastamba Gṛhyasūtra
ĀpŚr—Āpastamba Śrautasūtra
ĀpŚulb—Āpastamba Śulbasūtra
Aśva—Aśvamedha
ĀśvGṛ—Aśvalāyana Gṛhyasūtra
ĀśvŚr—Āśvalāyana Śrautasūtra
AV—Atharvaveda Saṁhitā (śaunaka)
BGr—Baudhāyana Gṛhyasūtra
BhGṛ—Bhāradvāja Gṛhyasūtra
BhPar—Bhāradvāja Pariśiṣṭa
BhPi—Bhāradvāja Pitṛmedhasūtra
Bh Śr—Bhāradvāja Śrautasūtra
BPi—Baudhāyana Pitṛmedhasūtra
Brough Gotra—Early brahmanical system of gotra and pravara, by John Brough
BṛUp—Bṛhadāraṇyaka Upaniṣad
BŚr—Baudhāyana Śrautasūtra
BŚulb—Baudhāyana Śulbasūtra
ca—circa
Caland PBr—Pañcaviṁśa Brāhmaṇa; tr. & ed. by W. Caland
Cātur—Cāturmāsya
caus—causative
Cayana—Agnicayana
C. H.—L'Agniṣṭoma, by W. Caland & V. Henry
Chinna—Yajñatattvaprakāśaḥ, by A. Chinnaswami Sastri
comm—commentary
Darśa—Darśapūrṇamāsa
du—dual
Dumont L'Agni—L'Agnihotra, by P. E. Dumont
Dumont L'Aśva—L'Aśvamedha, by P. E. Dumont
Eggeling SBE—Śatapatha Brāhmaṇa; tr. & ed. by Julius Eggeling (Sacred books of the east, vols. XII,XXVI.XLI,XLIV)
ERE—Encyclopaedia of religion and ethics; ed. by James Hastings
f- feminine

GGṛ—Gobhila Gṛhyasūtra
Gonda Sava—Savayajñas : Kauśikasūtras, 60-68; tr. & ed. by J. Gonda
H.Dh—History of dharmaśāstra, by P. V. Kane
Heesterman—Ancient Indian royal consecration, by J. C. Heesterman
HGṛ—Hiraṇyakeśī Gṛhyasūtra
Hoogt—The vedic chant studied in its textual and melodic form, by J. M. Van der Hoogt
HSṛ—Hiraṇyakeṣī Śrautaśūtra
ind—indeclinable
Jaim Br—Jaiminīya Brāhmaṇa of the Sāmaveda
KāGṛ—Kāṭhaka Gṛhyasūtra
Kauś S—Kauśikasūtra
KBr—Kauṣītaki Brāhmaṇa
Keith Drama—Sanskrit drama, by A. B. Keith
Keith RPV—Religion and philosophy of the veda and upanishads, by A. B. Keith
Keith RVBr—Rigveda Brahmanas : Aitareya & Kauṣītaki Brāhmaṇas of the Rigveda; tr. by A. B. Keith
KhGṛ—Khādira Gṛhyasūtra
KŚṛ—Kātyāyana Srautasūtra
LŚṛ—Lāṭyāyana Śrautasūtra
m—masculine
Max Müller HASL—History of ancient Sanskrit literature, by F. Max Müller
Mbh—Mahābhāṣya of Patañjali
MGṛ—Mānava Gṛhyasūtra
Mī—Pūrvamīmāṁsāsūtra of Jaimini
Mn—Manusmṛti
MSṛ—Mānava Śrautasūtra
MW—Sanskrit-English dictionary, by M. Monier-Williams
n—notes ; neuter gender after entry words
Nid—Nidānasūtra
nom—nominative
NVO—Das altindisches Neu-und Vollmondsopfer, by A. Hillebrandt
Oldenberg SBE— Gṛhyasūtra ; tr. & ed. by Herman Oldenberg (Sacred books of the east, vols. XXIX, XXX).
Pāṇ—Aṣṭādhyāyī of Pāṇini
Paśu—Paśubandha or Nirūḍhapaśubandha
PBr—Pañcaviṁśa Brāhmaṇa
PGṛ—Pāraskara Gṛhyasūtra
pl—plural
Puṣpa—Puṣpasūtra (or Phullasūtra)
Rāja—Rājasūya
Renou Vocabulaire—Vocabulaire du rituel vedique, by Louis Renou
rpt—reprint (ed)
RV—Ṛgveda Saṁhitā
Śab—Śabarasvāmin

Śāṅ Br —Śāṅkhāyana Brāhmaṇa
SBE—Sacred books of the east; ed. by F. Max Müller
ŚBr—Śatapatha Brāhmaṇa
sg—singular
SG NTCA—Native tribes of central Australia, by Baldwin Spencer and F. J. Gillen
ŚGṛ—Śāṅkhāyana Gṛhyasūtra
Simon Pañcavi—Pañcavidhasūtra; ed. by Richard Simon
Smith Semites—Religion of the Semites, by W. Robertson Smith
Soma—Soma sacrifice or sacrifices
Śr(K)E—Śrautakośa, English section
Śr(K)S—Śrautakośa, Sanskrit section
ŚŚr—Śāṅkhāyana Śrautasūtra
SV—Sāmaveda Saṁhitā
SW—Sanskrit Wörterbuch, by Otto Böhtlingk & Rudolph Roth
TĀr—Taittirīya Āraṇyaka
TBr—Taittirīya Brāhmaṇa
Themis—Themis, a study of the social origin of Greek religion, by Jane Ellen Harrison
Thomson SAGS—Studies in ancient Greek society, the pre-historic Aegean, by George Thomson
Todten—Altindischen Todten-und Bestattungsgebräuche, by W. Caland
TS—Taittirīya Saṁhitā
Upasak Monastic terms—Dictionary of early Buddhist monastic terms, by C. S. Upasak
VādhŚr—Über das Vādhula Śrautasūtra; ed. by W. Caland
VaiŚr.—Vaikhānasa Śrautasūtra
Vāja—Vājapeya
VasDh—Vasiṣṭha Dharmasūtra
V. I. —Vedic index, by A. A. Macdonell & A. B. Keith
V R.—Vedic religion, by Abel Bergaigne
VS—Vājasaneyi Saṁhitā
VtŚr.—Vaitāna Śrautasūtra
Whitney Grammar—Sanskrit grammar, by William Dwight Whitney
Whitney Roots—Roots, verb—forms and primary derivatives of the Sanskrit language, by William Dwight Whitney
Winternitz—History of Indian literature, by Maurice Winternitz
WR—Wörterbuch zum RigVeda, by Hermann Grassmann
YV—Yajurveda Saṁhitās

LIST OF WORKS AND AUTHORS

1. Saṁhitās

Atharvaveda Saṁhitā (śaunaka), with Sāyaṇa commentary; ed. by Viśvabandhu ; 4 vols; Hoshiarpur, 1960-62.

Kapiṣṭhala Saṁhitā; ed. by Raghu Vira; Lahore, 1932.

Kāṭhaka Saṁhitā: ed. by Leopold von Schröder; 4 vols; Wiesbaden, 1970-72 rpt.

Maitrāyaṇī, Saṁhitā; ed. by Leopold von Schröder; 4 vols; Wiesbaden, 1970-72 rpt.

Ṛgveda Saṁhitā, with Sāyaṇa commentary; 5 vols; Poona, Vaidic saṁshodhan mandal, 1933-1951.

Sāmaveda Saṁhitā; ed. by Th. Benfey; Leipzig , 1848.

Taittirīya Saṁhitā; ed. by A. Weber; Berlin, 1871-72.

Vājasaneyi Saṁhitā with Uvaṭa & Mahīdhara bhāṣya; Bombay, 1926.

2. Brāhmaṇas, Āraṇyakas & Upaniṣads

Aitareya Brāhmaṇa; with Sāyaṇa commentary; Poona, Anandasrama.

Gopatha Brāhmaṇa; ed. by D. Gaastra; Leiden, 1919.

Jaiminīya Brāhmaṇa of the Sāmaveda; ed. by Raghu Vira & Lokesh Chandra; Nagpur, 1954.

Pañcaviṁśa Brāhmaṇa; ed. by A. Chinnaswami Shastri; Varanasi, 1935.

Śāṅkhāyana Brāhmaṇa; tr. into Bengali & ed. by Harinarayan Bhattacharya; Calcutta, Sanskrit College, 1970.

Śatapatha Brāhmaṇa; ed. by Albrecht Weber; Varanasi, Chowkhamba, 1964 rpt.

Taittirīya Brāhmaṇa with Sāyaṇa commentary; 2 vols; Poona, Anandasrama 1934-38.

Aitareya Āraṇyaka; ed. & tr. by A. B. Keith; Oxford, 1969 rpt.

Taittirīya Āraṇyaka; Poona, Anandasrama.

Bṛhadāraṇyaka Upaniṣad, with the commentary of Śaṅkaracarya and Ānandagiri; ed. & Bengali tr. by Durgācaraṇa Sāṁkhyavedāntatīrtha; 4 vols; Calcutta, Deb Sahitya Kutir, 1958-65.

Chhāndogya Upaniṣad with Śaṅkara commentary; ed. by Durgācaraṇa Vedāntatīrtha; Calcutta, 1956.

3. Śrauta & Gṛhyasūtras

Āpastamba Dharmasūtra; ed. by George Bühler; Bombay, 1932.

Āpastamba Gṛhyasūtra, with Haradatta & Sudarśana commentaries; Varanasi, 1928.

Āpastamba Śrautasūtra; ed. by Richard Garbe; 3 vols; Calcutta, 1882-1902 (B. I. series).

Āpastamba Śulbasūtra, with the commentaries of Kapardisvāmin, Karavinda and Sundararāja; ed. by Satya Prakash & Ram Swarup Sharma; tr. into English by Satya Prakash; New Delhi, 1968.

Āśvalāyana Gṛhyasūtra with Nārāyana commentary; Poona, Anandasrama, 1936.

Āśvalāyana Śrautasūtra with Nārāyana vṛtti; Poona, Anandasrama, 1917,

Baudhāyana Gṛhyasūtra; ed. by Sham Sastri; Mysore, 1920.
Baudhāyana Pitṛmedhasūtra :
(1) praśna I, ed. by W. Caland. 1896
(2) praśna II & III; ed. by C. H. Raabe. 1911
(3) text printed in BGṛ. Mysore, 1920
(4) text printed in ŚrK(S) I.
Baudhāyana Śrautasūtra; ed. by W. Caland; 3 vols; Calcutta, 1904-23 (B. I. series).
Baudhāyana Śulbasūtra; ed. by Satya Prakash & Ram Swarup Sharma; New Delhi, 1968.
Bhāradvāja Gṛhyasūtra; ed. by Henriette J. W. Salomons; Leiden, 1913.
Bhāradvāja Śrautasūtra, including Paitṛmedha & Pariśeṣa; ed. & tr. by C. G. Kashikar; 2 vols; Poona, 1964.
Gobhila Gṛhyasūtra; ed. by Mukunda Jha Bakshi; Varansi, 1936.
Hiraṇyakeśī Gṛhyasūtra with Mātṛdatta commentary; ed. by J. Kirste; Vienna, 1889.
Hiraṇyakeśī Śrautasūtra; Poona, Anandasrama, 1907-22.
Kāṭhaka Gṛhyasūtra; ed. by W. Caland; Lahore, 1925.
Kātyāyana Śrautasūtra, with extracts from the commentaries of Karka & Yājñikadeva; ed. by Albrecht Weber; Varanasi, 1972 rpt.
Kauśika Sūtra of Atharvaveda; ed. by Maurice Bloomfield; Delhi, 1972 rpt.
Kauthuma Gṛhyasūtra; ed. by Suryakanta; Calcutta, 1956 (B. I. series).
Khādira Gṛhyasūtra, with Rudraskanda commentary; Mysore, 1913.
Lāṭyāyana Śrautasūtra, with Agnisvāmin commentary; ed. by Ananda Chandra; Calcutta, 1872 (B. I. series).
Mānava Gṛhyasūtra, Aṣṭāvakra commentary; Baroda, 1926 (Gaekwad oriental series).
Mānava Śrautasūtra; ed. by F. Knauer (books I-V). St. Petersburg, 1900-03; by J. M. Van Gelder (book VI); Leiden, 1921.
Nidānasūtra of Patañjali; ed. by K. N. Bhatnagar; Delhi, 1971.
Pañcavidha Sūtra; ed. by Richard Simon; Breslau, 1913.
Pāraskara Gṛhyasūtra, with Harihara commentary; Bombay, 1911.
Puṣpasūtra (or Phullasūtra)—10 prapāṭhakas in Usā (jl); Calcutta, 1890.
Sāṅkhāyana Gṛhyasūtra; ed. by S. R. Sehgal; Delhi, 1960.
Sāṅkhāyana Śrautasūtra; ed. by A. Hillebrandt; Calcutta, 1886-89 (B. I. series).
Śrautakośa, English section; vol. I parts 1 & 2; vol. II part 1; Poona, 1958-73.
Śrautakośa, Sanskrit section; vol. I, vol. II part 1; Poona, 1958-70.
Vādhula Śrautasūtra; ed. & tr. by W. Caland in A (cta) O (rientalia), vols. I, II, IV, VI.
Vaikhānasa Gṛhyasūtra; ed. by W. Caland; Calcutta, 1927 (B. I. series).
Vaikhānasa Śrautasūtra; ed. by W. Caland; Calcutta, 1941 (B. I. series).
Vaitāna Śrautasūtra; ed. by Richard Garbe; London, 1878.
Vārāha Śrautasūtra; ed. by W. Caland & Raghu Vira; Delhi, 1971.
Vasiṣṭha Dharmasūtra; ed. by A. A. Führer; Bombay, 1930.

4. Dictionaries

Böhtlingk, Otto & Roth, Rudolph: Sanskrit Wörterbuch; 7 vols; Wiesbaden, 1966 rpt.

Grassmann, Hermann: Wörterbuch zum RigVeda; 4th ed; Wiesbaden, 1964 rpt.
Joshi, Viśvanātha Śāstrī: Śrautapadārthanirvacanam (in Sanskrit); Varanasi, 1919.
Monier-Williams, M: Sanskrit-English dictionary; Oxford; 1963 rpt.
Ṛenou, Louis: Vocabulaire du rituel vedique; Paris, 1954.
Upasak, C. S: Dictionary of early Buddhist monastic terms; Varanasi, 1975.

5. Other texts

Manusmṛti, with Kullūkabhaṭṭa's commentary; ed. by Gopala Śāstrī Nene; Varanasi, 1970.
Medhātithi's commentary on Manusmṛti; tr. into Bengali by Bhūtanātha Saptatīrtha; 4 vols; Calcutta, Sanskrit College, 1954.
Pāṇini: Aṣṭādhyāyī, with Siddhāntakaumudī of Bhaṭṭoji Dīkṣita and Bālamanoramā,
Tattvabodhinī commentaries; Varanasi, 1970.
Patañjali: Mahābhāṣya, with the commentaries of Kaiyaṭa and Nāgeśabhaṭṭa; 3 vols; Delhi, 1967.
Pūrvamīmāṁsā sūtra of Jaimini with Śabarasyāmī bhāṣya; Poona, Anandasrama.
Yāska: Nirukta, with Durgācārya commentary; ed. by V. K. Rajvade; 2 vols; Poona, Anandasrama, 1921.
Vāmana & Jayāditya Kāśikā; Varanasi, 1952.

6. Modern works

Agrawala, V. S: India as known to Pāṇini; Lucknow, 1953.
Apte, V. M: Social and religious life in the grihya sutras; Bombay, 1954,
Bergaigne, Abel: Vedic religion according to the hymns of the Ṛgveda; tr. by V. G. Paranjpe; 4 vols; Poona, 1969-72.
Bloomfield, Maurice: Atharvaveda and the Gopatha Brahmana; Varanasi, 1975 rpt.
–: Religion of the veda; New York, 1908.
Brough, John: Early brahmanical system of gotra and pravara, a translation of the Gotrapravaramañjarī of Puruṣottama; Cambridge, 1953.
Caland, W: Altindischen Todten und Bestattungsgebräuche; Amsterdam, 1896.
–: Altindischer Ahnencult; Leiden, 1893.
–: Altindisches Zauberritual; Amsterdam, 1900.
–: Pañcaviṁśa Brāhmaṇa; Calcutta, 1931 (B. I. series).
Caland, W. & Henry, V: L' Agniṣṭoma; 2 vols; Paris, 1925.
Dumont, P. E., ed. & tr: L' Agnihotra, description de l'agnihotra dans le rituel védique d'après śrautasūtras; Baltimore. 1939.
–: ed & tr: L' Aśvamedha; Paris, 1927.
Eggeling, Julius ed. & tr: Śatapatha Brāhmaṇa (SBE, XII, XXVI, XLI & XLIV).
Encyclopaedia of religion and ethics; ed. by James Hastings; 13 vols; Edinburgh, 1967 rpt.
Ferreira, John V: Totemism in India; Bombay, Oxford Univ. Press, 1965.
Fick, R: Social organization in north-east India in Buddha's time; tr. by S. K. Maitra; Calcutta, 1920.
Gonda, J., ed. & tr: Savayajñas: Kauśikasūtras, 60-68; Amsterdam, 1965.

Harrison, Jane Ellen: Themis, a study of the social origin of Greek religion; London, Merlin Press, 1963 rpt.

—: Prolegomena to the study of Greek religion; New york, Meridian Books, 1957 rpt.

Heesterman, J. C: Ancient Indian royal consecration; The Hague, 1957

Hillebrandt, A: Altindisches Neu-und Vollmondsopfer; Jena, 1879.

—: Ritualliteratur, vedische Opfer und Zauber. Strassburg, 1897.

—: Vedische Mythologie. Breslau, 1891.

Jayaswal, K. P: Hindu polity; Bangalore, 1943 rpt.

Kane, P. V: History of dharmaśāstra; 5 vols. (7 parts). Poona, 1930-62.

Keith, A. B: Religion and philosophy of the veda and upanishads; 2 Pts; Delhi, 1970 rpt (HOS 31 & 32).

—: Rigveda Brāhmaṇas : Aitareya & Kauṣītaki Brāhmaṇas of the Rigveda; Delhi, 1971 (HOS 25).

—: Sanskrit drama in its origin, development theory & practice; Oxford, 1954.

—: Taittirīya Saṁhitā; Delhi, 1967 (HOS 18 & 19).

Levi, S: La doctrine du sacrifice dans les Brāhmaṇas; Paris, 1898.

Macdonell, A. A: Vedic mythology; Varanasi, 1963 rpt.

Macdonell, A. A. & Keith, A. B: Vedic index of names and subjects; 2 vols. Delhi, 1958 rpt.

Max-Müller, F: History of ancient Sanskrit literature; Allahabad, Bhuvaneshwari ashrama, 1926.

Oldenberg, Herman: Religion des Veda; Berlin, 1894.

—: Grihyasūtras (SBE XXIX, XXX).

Potdar, K. R: Sacrifice in the Ṛgveda; Bombay, 1953.

Ram Gopal: India of vedic kalpasūtras; Delhi, 1959.

Sacred books of the east; ed. by F. Max-Müller; 50 vols. Delhi, Motilal Banarsidass, 1962-64 rpt.

Sastri, A. Chinnaswami: Yajñatattvaprakāśaḥ (in Sanskrit); Madras, 1953.

Schwab, J: Altindische Thieropfer mit benutzung handschriftlicher Quellen dargestelt; Erlangen, 1886.

Shende, N. J: Religion and philosophy of the Atharvaveda; Poona, 1952.

Smith, W. Robertson: Religion of the Semites: New York, Meridian library, 1957 rpt.

Spencer, Baldwin & Gillen, F. J: Native tribes of central Australia; New York, Dover publ., 1968 rpt.

Thomson, George: Studies in ancient Greek society, the prehistoric Aegean; London, 1954.

Van der Hoogt, J. M: Vedic chant studied in its textual and melodic form; Wageningen, 1929.

Weber, A: Zur Kenntnis des vedischen opferrituals, Indische Studien X, 321-96; XIII, 217-92.

Whitney, William Dwight: Roots, verb-forms and primary derivatives of the Sanskrit language, Leipzig, 1945 rpt.

—: Sanskrit grammar; Cambridge, Harvard, 1955 rpt.

Winternitz, Maurice: History of Indian literature; 2 vols. (Eng tr.); Delhi, 1972 rpt.

—: Mantrapāṭha, or the prayer book of the Āpastambins. Oxford, 1897.

TRANSLITERATION AND ORDER

OF THE NĀGARĪ LETTERS

vowels : a, ā, i, ī, u, ū, ṛ, ḷ, e, ai, o, au

anusvāra : ṁ (true anusvāra or symbol of nasal)

visarga : ḥ

consonants : k, kh, g, gh, ṅ

c, ch, j, jh, ñ

ṭ, ṭh, ḍ, ḍh, ṇ

t, th, d, dh, n

p, ph, b, bh, m

y, r, l, v

ś, ṣ, s, h

THE ARRANGEMENTS OF ENTRIES

The *śrauta* and *gṛhya* terms are arranged in alphabetical order of the Devanāgarī letters in two separate sections.

Under the main entries the combination terms and the derivatives follow the alphabetical order. The headword is not fully transcribed before or after the sub-entry. The headword is indicated by a circle, as at *dadhi*—°*graha*, °*gharma* etc., under *tīrtha*—*pitṛ*°, *mṛga*°.

Similarly, within most entries a word is abbreviated by the first letter of the word and a circle *e.g.*, *barhis*—B°.

The source of reference has been given fully once, and for the immediately succeeding references from the same source only the relevant portions are given, as at *patnī*— Āp.Śr I.6.12, for *Puroḍāśa* 7.5(*i.e.*, ĀpŚr I.7.5),for *soma* stalks X.15.13(*i.e.*, ĀpŚr).

Under the entry the name of the sacrifice or the rite with which the term is associated is given within the first bracket and the first letter is capitalized, *e. g.* (*Soma*), (*Darśa*), (*Vivāha*) etc.

MEASUREMENTS

Akṣa	104 *aṅgula*	
Aratni	24 ,,	=2 *Prādeśa*
Īśā	88 ,,	
Kṣudrapāda (small *pāda*)	10 ,,	
Jānu	32 ,,	
Pada	15 ,,	
Puruṣa	120 ,,	=5 *Aratni*
Pṛtha (=*Uttarayuga*)	13 ,,	
Prakrama	30 ,,	=2 *Pada*
Prādeśa	12 ,,	=1 *Span*
Yuga	86 ,,	
Vyā(yā)ma	96 or 120 *aṅgula*=4 or 5 *Aratni*	
Śamyā (=*Bāhu*)	36 *aṅgula*	

Baudhāyana Śulbasūtra I. 1

PART ONE : SRAUTA SECTION

अ A

अंशु *Aṁśu* m. stalks of *soma*, which, soaked in water, are deposited on a board (*adhiṣavaṇa-phalaka*) for being pressed and thrashed for extraction of juice from them Āp. Śr. XII. 9.10; 10.5. Six of these stalks are mentioned separately ib; thirteen Vādh.Śr. (AO. VI. 215); also the cup into which juice is poured after pressing Bh. Śr. XIII. 8.17; *alpān aṁśūn* stalks from which juice flows feebly K. Śr. IX. 4.20.

°*graha* (*aṁśu* in abbrev.) name of the first drawing *soma*na (optional) Āp. Śr. XII. 7.17; 8.5.

°*grahaṇa* a dish for measuring the *soma* stalks B. Śr. VI.10.

अंस *Aṁsa* m. "shoulders" of the *vedi* (*uttara-vedi*); the 2 corners on the eastern side: *uttara*° or the northeastern corner and *dakṣiṇa*° or the southeastern corner Āp. Śr. VII.5.5; of the *mahāvedi* XI.4.13. Cf. *śroṇi*. Also said of the corners of *khara* Āp. Śr. XII. 1.7. For measurements Āp. Śulb. I.2.5.

अक्ष *Akṣa* m. nut of *vibhīdaka* (Terminalia be-lerica) which is used as die in the game of dice, played at the consecration of the *sabhya* (*Ādheya*); in the *Rāja* Āp. Śr. V.19.2; XVIII. 18.16; B. Śr. II.8 mentions 49 dice; also axle of a cart; a measurement, 104 *aṅgula*s, the length of the north-south line on the west of the altar of *Paśu* Āp. Śr. VII.3.8. Cf. B. Śulb. I.1.

°*dhur* f. pole fixed to the axle of the *havir-dhāna* cart, anointed by the sacrificer's wife Āp. Śr. XI.6.5,7.

°*pāli* f. edge of the axle B. Śr. I.4

°*abhihoma* m. oblation with the dice (*Ādheya*) L. Śr. IV.12.13.

°*āvāpa* m. superintendent of the game of dice, one of the dignitaries of *Rāja* Āp. Śr. XVIII.18.15; those who play or, according to some, keep the dice K. Śr. XV.3.17 comm.

°*upāñjana* n. act of anointing the axle of *havirdhāna* cart with earth mixed with clari-fied butter Bh. Śr. X.15.19.

अक्ष्णया *Akṣṇayā* ind. diagonally Bh. Śr. XII. 4.18 (measurement of the *mahāvedi*).

अग्नि *Agni* m. sacrificial fire; in pl. three fires: *āhavanīya, gārhapatya; dakṣiṇa*; in du.: *āhava-nīya* and *gārhapatya*. Sometimes five fires (cf *sabhya* and *āvasathya*) are mentioned; cf. *vitāna, vihāra, vistāra* (*agnīnām*). In abbrev. also designates the fire-altar or its construc-tion. See *Agnicayana*.

अग्निक्षेत्र *Agnikṣetra* n. "site of fire", situated on the eastern side of the *mahāvedi* where the fire-altar is constructed in the form of a bird (*śyena*) K. Śr. XVI.7.31 comm. The normal form is *saptavidha*, i.e. *saptapuruṣa* : the sum of 7 human (sacrificer's) length, 3 *puruṣa*s north-south and 4 *puruṣa*s east-west Āp. Śr. XVI. 17.9. The size, in certain cases, can be doubled (*caturdaśavidha*) or trebled (*ekaviṁśavidha*), as in *Aśvamedha* K. Śr. XX. 4.15. In abbrev. *agni, agnivimāna*. Cf. Dumont L'Aśva 73; see *Agnicayana*.

अग्निचयन *Agnicayana* n. rite of piling the fire altar, included in the soma sacrifices, in 5 layers with bricks, on the *uttaravedi* for set-ting up the *āhavanīya*; it is represented in ŚBr. as a human imitation of the construc-tion of the cosmic world of the Prajāpati. The heads of 5 animals are built up into the altar, and the trunks are thrown into water. Bricks of the altar are prepared with this water. Ant-hill clay is mixed with the earth of a pit, and the first brick called *aṣāḍhā* is prepared by the sacrificer's wife. The sacrificer prepares a fire pan (*ukhā*), and 3 *viśvajyoti* bricks. On the *ukhā* the bricks and pan are burnt. There-after other bricks are made and burnt. After the *dīkṣā*, the building of the altar begins. The altar may be of several shapes, *e.g.* *suparṇa* (eagle), *śyena* (hawk), *droṇa* (trough) etc. K. Śr. XVI.5.9. The bricks have different shapes: triangular, oblong, square etc. The bricks also bear different names *yajuṣmatī, aṣāḍhā, svayamātṛṇṇā, retaḥsic, lokampṛṇā, citriṇī, vālakhilyā*. The bricks are laid accom-panied with *mantra*s, and in a definite pattern, for which a knowledge of geometry is required. Of the 5 layers, the 1st, 3rd and 5th layers are of the same pattern while the

2nd and the 4th follow a different pattern. See plan 1 & 2.

The ground on which the altar is erected is measured with a rope, and ploughed K. Śr. XVI.8.

At the lowest level a golden figure of a man is placed. The total number of bricks for all the 5 layers is 10,800 (K. Śr. XVII.7.21-23); each layer is covered with thick mud (*purīṣa*). A living tortoise is placed on a layer (Āp. Śr. XVI.25.1). Various other materials, *e.g.* a mortar and a pestle, an *ukhā*, a *śūrpa* are placed in different positions. The view on the time taken for piling varies: 8 months for the first 4 layers and 4 months for the last; or only five consecutive days Āp. Śr. XVI.35.9; XVII.1.1, 11; 2.8; 3.1. The performance of A° is obligatory, at least theoretically, only in certain cases. The main authority on the rite is ŚBr. which devotes 5 out of its 14 kāṇḍas: VI—X, more than one third of the entire text. For the theory and significance of this rite Eggeling SBE XLIII, introduction, Āp. Śr. XVI-XVII, K. Śr. XVI-XVIII; Keith TS. 18. cxxv—cxxxi TS. IV.1-6.

In abbrev. *Cayana* or *Agni*. *Agnicit* is a person who has offered A° Āp. Śr. XVI. 10.6.

अग्निदीक्षणीया *Agnidīkṣaṇīyā* (*iṣṭi*) f. oblation introducing the *dīkṣā* belonging to *Cayana* B. Śr. XV. 3.

°*paristaraṇa* n. act of strewing *darbha* grass called *paribhojanīya* round the fire (*Darśa*) Āp. Śr. I.14.12.

°*praṇayana* n. rite of carrying the *āhavanīya* fire in a ceremonial procession to the *uttaravedi* at the time of animal sacrifice in the *Agniṣṭoma* Āp. Śr. XI. 5.9-10, B. Śr. VI.24, C.H. 78.

°*manthana* n. production of fire by friction (churning) Āśv. Śr. IV.5.2. Cf. *araṇi*.

°*yojana* n. "yoking" of the fire-altar which consists of touching the three logs (*paridhi*) accompanied with the muttering of three formulas at the end of consecration of the altar Āp. Śr. XVII.23.1, K. Śr. XVIII.6.16(*Cayana*)

°*vimocana* n. rite of "unyoking", the opposite of °*yojana*, consisting of touching the *paridhis* at 2 western points where 2 logs touch the third one by muttering 2 *mantras* K. Śr. XVIII. 6.17; *agner vimokam juhotī* Āp. Śr. XVII. 23.10.

अग्निष्टुत् *Agniṣṭut* m. name of an *ekāha* of the *Agniṣṭoma* type Āp. Śr.XII.6.15.

अग्निष्टोम *Agniṣṭoma* m. "praise of Agni"; a *Soma* sacrifice, the first of the 7 *saṁsthās* and a model of *Soma* Āp. Śr. X.2.3; closely related to *Jyotiṣṭoma* (cf. Bh. Śr. X—XV). It derives its name, like all other *Soma*, from a *stotra* (the last one) called a°, chanted in the rite. Although it takes only one day to perform the core of the rite (*sutyā*, day of pressing and libation) and is classified as *ekāha* this rite lasts 5 days, and is performed annually in the spring. The first day: sending *somapravāka*s to the priests and choosing the priests, *madhuparka*, *dīkṣā* of the sacrificer, *dīkṣaṇīyeṣṭi*, construction of the *prācīnavaṁśa*, *vrataśrapaṇāgāra*.

The second day: *prāyaṇīyeṣṭi*, *somakrayaṇa* (purchase of *Soma* stalks from a °*vikrayin*), *ātithyeṣṭi* (reception of *Soma*), *pravargya* (also considered an independent rite according to some), and *upasad* ("homage or investment") both performed twice, morning and evening. On this day *Soma* after having been purchased is led ceremoniously in a cart to the *prācīnavaṁśa*, accompanied with the *subrahmaṇyā* litany and placed on the *āsandī*, followed by the rite of *āpyāyana* and *avāntaradīkṣā*.

The third day: *pravargya* and *upasad* (both twice), followed by the construction of the *mahāvedi* and the *uttaravedi* (which remains covered).

The fourth day: *pravargya* and *upasad* (both twice) followed by the transfer of fire from the *āhavanīya* to the *nābhi* of the *uttaravedi*. On this day the *sadas* with its *dhiṣṇya*s, the *mārjālīya* shed and the *havirdhānamaṇḍapa* are constructed, the *uparava*s are dug and the *audumbarī* post is raised. An animal sacrifice (*agnīṣomīya paśu*) is performed, and *agnīṣomapraṇayana* is done. The fifth day (the last), called *sutyā* has 3 *savanas*: *prātaḥ*, *mādhyandina* and *tṛtīya*. Preparation begins long before dawn; all utensils: *droṇakalaśa*, *daśāpavitra*, *ādhavanīya*, *pūtabhṛt* etc. are arranged. After the recitation of *prātaranuvāka*, begins the pressing of *Soma* stalks (*abhiṣavana*) which is done in all the *savanas*. In all the 3 *savanas stotras* (q.v.) are chanted and *śastras* (q.v.) are recited. Before reciting the *bahiṣpavamāna* the priests perform a creeping movement (*prasarpaṇa*). The pressing is followed by libations (*graha*) of *Soma*, also of cakes, a hot mixture of milk and sour milk etc. Then follow the drinking of *Soma* and another sacrifice of a goat.

The climax is reached at the *mādhyandina*° which follows the pattern of the *prātaḥ*°. Sacrificial fees are distributed. Immediately after the *mādhyandina*° the *tṛtīya*° follows. The rite closes with a sacrificial bath (*avabhṛtha*).

For details cf. C.H; general description H.Dh. II(2), 1133-1203. See plan of the arena of Soma sacrifice (plan 3). Āp. Śr. X—XIII; XIV. 8-12, B. Śr. VI—X, K. Śr. VII—XI.

°*stotra* n. the last *stotra* of A°, also called *yajñāyajñīya* Āp. Śr. XIII.15.3 (C.H. 368); it is an *ekaviṁśastoma* cf. Śr. K(S). II(1), 453-4. All priests who participate in the chant and the choristers cover their heads together with the ears (optional according to Āp. Śr. XIII.15.5).

अग्निष्ठ *Agniṣṭha* m. (1) name of the middle post (out of 11 or 21) which is placed near the *vedi* in front of the *āhavanīya* fire (*Ekādaśinī* or *Aśva*) Āp. Śr. XVII.14.6; XX.9.6; made of *rajjudāla* wood K. Śr. XX. 4.17.

(2) adj. name of a cart for utensils, considered as "sitting near the fire" (*Darśa*) Āp. Śr.I.2. 10; commonly known as *śakaṭa* cf. Āp. Śr. 1.17.5.

अग्निसंयोजनीया *Agnisaṁyojanīyā* (*iṣṭi*) f. an oblation at *Agnicayana* B. Śr. XXIII.9.

अग्निहोत्र *Agnihotra* n. rite of offering cow s milk into the fire, performed daily in the evening and early in the morning. It begins with the setting up of the sacrificial fires. The precise time of offering is a matter of controversy, whether just before or a little after the setting of the sun both for the evening and morning services Āp. Śr. VI.4.7-9. Cf. ABr. XXIV. 4—6.

The question whether one should maintain all the three fires permanently or only one has been debated in the sūtras, (3 fires, K. Śr. IV.13.5, the *gārhapatya* only Āp. Śr. VI. 2.13). Therefore one has to establish the *āhavanīya* and *dakṣiṇa* out of the *gārhapatya* for the a° offerings. Only fuel is to be added, in case one has maintained all the 3 fires.

Generally, cow's milk is milked from the *agnihotra* cow by a śūdra Āp. Śr. VI.3.11—14 or a brahmin B. Śr. III.4; śūdra is categorically debarred from milking K. Śr. IV. 14.1. The milk is heated over the burning embers drawn from the *gārhapatya*, allowed to cool, and a portion of the milk in the a° ladle is offered in the evening first to Agni, then to Prajāpati.

In the morning the first oblation is offered to Sūrya, the second to Prajāpati. After the oblation, the *Adhvaryu* wipes the milk sticking to the ladle with his hand and *darbha*. He should drink the residue of the a° milk in the ladle.

Then after the a° oblations the sacrificer offers prayer (*agnyupasthāna*), in the evening to the *āhavanīya*, cattle, home, night, and thereafter to the *gārhapatya*. Āp. Śr. VI, B. Śr. III.4-9, Śr. K(E).I(1), 85—198. H.Dh. II (2), 998—1008. For details Dumont L 'Agni. a° is also the name of the oblation Āśv. Śr. II.2.16. Cf. *pretāgnihotra*.

°*sthālī* f. an earthen pot with a straight brim containing a° milk (*prasṛtākṛti*, *ūrdhva kapāla*) Āp. Śr. VI.3.7, Vai. Śr. XI.9. cf. *āryakṛtā*; neither made by a śūdra nor turned on a potter's wheel (*acakravartā* Bh. Śr. VI.8.14) H. Śr. III.7.15.

°*havaṇī* f. a spoon with a long handle, made of *vikaṅkata* wood, used in the rite; one's arm or 1 *aratni* in length Āp. Śr. VI.3.6, K. Śr. I.3. 36 comm.

agnihotrī f. the cow which provides milk for A° Āp. Śr. VI.3.8. Cf. *gavīḍā*.

अग्निहोत्रोच्छेषण *Agnihotroccheṣaṇa* n. remnant of a° milk, poured over curds Bh. Śr. I.14.6 (*Darśa*).

अग्नीध् *Agnīdh*=*āgnīdhra* Vādh. Śr. (AO. 11.155), the priest who kindles fire; *agnīdh* in RV. II. 1.2; X. 41.3; 91.10.

The word occurs in Āp. Śr. either in a *praiṣa* or in a mantra II.12.10; 15.2; elsewhere *āgnīdhra*.

अग्नीषोमप्रणयन *Agnīṣomapraṇayana* n. ceremonial procession with the fire (taken from the old *āhavanīya*) and the *Soma* stalks. The *Adhvaryu* puts *idhma* into the *śālāmukhīya* (old *āhavanīya*) and carries the fire with the help of *upayamanī* earth. The sacrificer holds the *Adhvaryu*, and the wife holds her husband. The wife is held by her sons, sons by grandsons and so on. The transfer takes place on the day before the *sutyā*; with the fire of the āhavanīya the *āgnīdhrīya* is kindled. The *soma* stalks are placed in the *havirdhānamaṇḍapa* on the *sutyā* day.

Now they offer the *vaisarjana* oblations B. Śr. VI.30, Āp. Śr. XI.16. 12—15. They go out of the *prācīnavaṁśa*; the *Brahman* carries *Soma*; the other vessels are loaded into a cart. They reach the *āgnīdhrīya* shed where the hearth is kindled and the *Brahman* hands over *Soma* to the *Pratiprasthātṛ*. From there the fire is carried to the new *āhavanīya* (of *mahāvedi*), and the *Soma* stalks are deposited on the *havirdhāna* cart Āp. Śr. XI.17.4—10, C.H. 109—115. There is a great controversy as to who carries *Soma* ib. 109 n. Cf. *agnipraṇayana*.

agnīṣomīya (*paśu*) relating to Agni and Soma; but specially referred to the animal sacrifice performed in the *Agniṣṭoma*; offered to Agni and Soma on the last day of the *upasad* (the 4th day) Āp. Śr. XI. 5. 11-6. 2, B. Śr. VI 24. This rite is considered as the archetype (*prakṛti*) of all animal sacrifices. The word may also mean the victim itself, a goat XII.3.3. C.H. 78-79. see also *kratupaśu*, *anubandhyā*.

अग्न्यगार *Agnyagāra* m. a shed where 3 fires are preserved; =*śālā* Āp. Śr. I.2.10; K. Śr, IV. 2.11 mentions 2.

अग्न्यवभृथ *Agnyavabhṛtha* m. see *avabhṛtha*.

अग्न्याधेय *Agnyādheya* or *ādhāna* n. rite of establishment of sacrificial fires; a sacrifice of the *iṣṭi* type, which like the *Darśapūrṇamāsa*, requires 4 priests (cf. *ṛtvij*). A° requires 2 days : the first day, called *upasad*, for the preliminaries, and the second for the main rite. The fire may be established on the newmoon or fullmoon day, but the season may vary according to the caste of the sacrificer Āp. Śr. V.3. 17—20.

Several days before setting up the fires, the *araṇis* and other implements are prepared. The sacrificer chooses the priests, and honours them with the *madhuparka*. The *devayajana*, sacrificial ground, is prepared. The sacrificer and his wife get themselves ready by taking a bath, pairing nails etc.

In the afternoon or when the sun is on the tree top the *Adhvaryu* fetches fire from the *aupāsana* fire. This is called the *brahmaudana* fire on which 4 platefuls of rice are cooked (*brahmaudana*) and clarified butter poured over it, and finally consumed by all the priests. On the day preceding the setting up of fire, a game of dice is played by the sacrificer with his wife and sons, while a cow remains tied to a stake. The cow is immolated (*Gopitṛyajña*) B. Śr. II.8—11; V; XV; XX.16; XXIV. 12-13; her omentum is offered into the fire. A goat may be substituted for the cow.

All the fire places are cleaned. The *Adhvaryu* churns out fire by putting the upper *araṇi* upon the lower one after the midnight has passed. The *Udgātṛ* sings various *sāmans* or, in his absence, the *Brahman* recites the *ṛks*.

The fire thus churned is collected in a vessel and the *gārhapatya* hearth is formally set up, and from this hearth the *Adhvaryu* gets some fuel stick lighted, and carrying it in a pan proceeds to the east for setting up the *āhavanīya*. Later on, the *sabhya*, *āvasathya* are set up from the *āhavanīya*. The *Āgnīdhra* brings the *gārhapatya* fire or churns out fire, and sets up the *dakṣiṇāgni*.

The *anvāhāryapacana* is set up from the *gārhapatya*. While the *Adhvaryu* proceeds to set the *āhavanīya* a horse is made to tread on certain materials deposited on the *āhavanīya* fire-place.

After setting up the fires, various kinds of grains and fuel sticks are offered into them. An oblation with a full spoon (*sruc*) is offered (*pūrṇāhuti*) K. Śr. IV. 10.5 comm. H.Dh. II (2), 986—998, Śr. K(E). I(1), 1—78.

The re-establishment of fire is prescribed for one who gets benefit from the A°; it is done in the same way as before Āp. Śr. V.26. 2-3. Cf. *āhita*, *anvādhāna*, *pretādhāna*, *punarādhāna*.

अग्न्युपस्थान *Agnyupasthāna* n. adoration of fires: *āhavanīya*, then *gārhapatya*, lastly a new *āhavanīya* along with the worship of the cow of *Agnihotra*, and some other rites at the end of the *Agnihotra* Āp. Śr. VI.16—29. Cf. *upasthāna*.

अघोदक *Aghodaka* n. water libation for the deceased during the period of impurity (*agha*), to be offered daily for 3 or 6 or 12 days or a year B. Pi: Śr. K(S). I, 807 ¶ 9 (*Antyeṣṭi*). see *Udakakriyā*.

अङ्ग *Aṅga* n. "limb", a subordinate rite; thus the *Paśubandha* is a "limb" of the Soma sacrifice Āp. Śr. XI.16.3; the *aṅga* is associated with the principal rite (*pradhāna*) XXIV.

2.31, 39; thus it becomes the *tantra* of a sacrifice XIV. 5.3. *Yajñāṅga* means the sacrificial utensils XXIV.2.13. Some of the *aṅgas*, e.g. *prayājas* etc. which are part of *Darśa* (which itself yields reward) do not yield a reward K. Śr. I.2.4; cf. Mī IV. 4.35.

अङ्गार *Aṅgāra* m. burning embers of the sacrificial fire, removed from the *gārhapatya* fire with a stick (*upaveṣa* or *dhṛṣṭi*) Bh. Śr. I.12.11 (*Darśa*), and the embers are placed round a sacrificial object ib. 13; XI.8.2.

°*nivapana* n. transport of fuel logs on the hearths (*dhiṣṇya*) and lighting them; *aṅgārān nivapati* K. Śr. IX. 7.6 (*Soma*) or *agnīn nivapati* Āp. Śr. XII.8. 1-4. cf. C.H. 184.

अचक्रवर्ता *Acakravartā* f. "not turned on a potter's wheel", said of the *agnihotrasthālī* (q.v.).

अच्छावाक *Acchāvāka* m. "inviter"; a subordinate priest of the *Hotṛ* group Āp. Śr. X. 1.9; he joins the *Soma* drinking ritual in the *Soma* sacrifice when all other priests had already consumed their shares in the first pressing. He recites a verse RV. V.25. 1-3 which begins with the word "*acchā*" (whence probably the name), and is allowed to have his share of the *Soma* juice and the cake C.H. 220, Āp. Śr. XII.26.1—8. He also recites the 3rd *ājyaśastra* C.H. 262 (the first pressing), Āśv. Śr. V. 10.28.

अजगाव *Ajagāva* n. a sacrificial vessel dedicated to Mitra and Varuṇa (*Soma*) and is ornamented with nipple-like designs Āp. Śr. XII.1.11 & comm.

Variant form : *ajakāva* K. Śr. IX.2.6.

अज *Aja* m. goat, whose flesh is cooked with barley grains, and eaten after the cremation Bh. Pi. I.12. 4-5.

ajā f. she-goat, a unit of price for soma Bh. Śr. X.17.4: its milk is used in the *pravargya* XI.2.10; tied to a peg (*śaṅku*) out side the western gate of the *prācīnavaṁśa* XI. 6.10.

अजिन *Ajina* n. see *kṛṣṇājina*.

अञ्जन *Añjana* n. act of anointing an object, specially with clarified butter.

āñjana n. one of the materials for *Darśa*, an ointment for the eyes Āp. Śr. 1.8.2; *abhyañjana* ointment for the body, *samañjana* unction with 2 mixed waters Āp. Śr. XII. 6.3 (C.H. 143) cf. *upāñjana* B. Śr. VI. 24; *avāñjana* = *ślakṣṇapeṣaṇa* B. Śr. X.13.

अञ्जलि *Añjali* m. a cavity formed by joining both the palms, in prayer Bh. Śr. II. 13.1, for holding water in libation and offering other things into the fire VI. 14.3.

अञ्जःसव *Añjaḥsava* m. variety of *Rāja*. B. XXVI. 3

°*kārīra* variety of *Kārīrīṣṭi* B. Śr. XIII. 40.

अतिग्राह्य *Atigrāhya* m. name of the three "extra" libations for Agni, Indra and Sūrya which are included in the *Agniṣṭoma* Āp. Śr. XII.15.9, Bh. Śr. XIII.16.1; cf. Eggeling SBE XXVI, 402; XLI, 6; also the name of the cups.

अतिथि *Atithi* m. a guest to whom a shelter is offered, by a person (as his vow, *vrata*) while setting up the fires Bh. Śr. V.16.11, 14.

°*gavī* f. a cow for the *ātithya* rite B. Śr. XXV.4.

अतिरात्र *Atirātra* m. prepared or performed overnight RV. VII.103. 7; the 5th *saṁsthā* of the *Soma*, performed during a day and overnight with 29 *śastras* and 29 *stotras*; some of the additional *śastras* and *stotras* are recited in 4 *prayāyas* Āp. Śr. XIV.3. 8—16; details XIV.3.8—4. 11. This is one of the optional forms of the *Jyotiṣṭoma*, taking place on the third day of pressing in the *Aśva*. Cf. Dumont L' Aśva 215, Eggeling SBE XLI, xvii—xx ; Sab. on Mī. II.4.26.

अतीकाश *Atīkāśa* m. opening in the *śālā*, directed to every cardinal point B. Śr. IX.11 (comm : *avakāśa*); cf. *dīkṣvatīkāśa* B. Śr. VI.1; these openings are differentiated from the doors Caland on Āp. Śr. X.5.3; synonyms: *atīroka*, *āroka*.

अतीमोक्ष *Atīmokṣa* m. name of formulas in which the gods who are destroyers of sacrifice are propitiated Bh. Śr. IV.22.1 (*Darśa*); Āp. Śr. XIII.25.1, 2 : the sacrificer sits within the altar, holding the *veda* in his lap and mutters the formulas.

अत्यग्निष्टोम *Atyagniṣṭoma* m. the 5th Soma *saṁsthā*, a variety of *Agniṣṭoma* obtained by adding a *ṣoḍaśistotra* as well as a libation called *ṣoḍaśin* and an additional victim to

Indra Āp. Śr. XIV.2.10 comm., K. Śr. X. 9.28. Name of the second of the seven modifications of the *Jyotiṣṭoma*. Also the verse recited at the close of that ceremony.

अत्यन्तप्रदेश *Atyantapradeśa* m. a direction which crosses the limit, i.e. a general rule for the performance of rites Āp. Śr. XII.7.12, Bh. Śr. I.1.9.

अत्सरुक *Atsaruka* mfn. See *tsaru*.

अदाभ्य (ग्रह) *Adābhya* mfn. (*graha* m.) name of an optional libation of *Soma* in a cup, as an alternative to *aṁśugraha* Āp. Śr. XII. 7.17.

°*pātra* n. the cup for taking the juice Bh. Śr. XIII. 9.1;=*aṁśvadābhyagrahaṇapātra*, made of *udumbara* wood K. Śr. I.3.36 comm.

अद्रि *Adri* m. stone for crushing *Soma* stalks; *grāvan* K. Śr. XI. 1.5 (comm.: *abhiṣavārthapāṣāṇa*).

अधिदेवन *Adhidevana* n. space dug and levelled with a *sphya*, used as a site for a game of dice Āp. Sr. V.19.2 (*Ādhāna*); XVIII. 18.16 (*Rāja*); situated between the *sabhya* and *āvasathya* Bh. Śr. V.12.4.

अधिनिर्णेजनीय *Adhinirṇejānīya* mfn. name of a *khara* on which utensils are cleansed=*ucchiṣṭa* (*khara*) M. Śr. IV.2.3.

अधिमन्थन *Adhimanthana* n. a piece of wood used as the lower portion of the *araṇi* (*adharāraṇi*) and with which the spindle is engaged Āp. Śr. VII.3.3 (it is a *śakala*; it is a chip of wood obtained at the time when the *yūpa* is cut off a trunk). Cf. *svaru*.

अधिषवण *Adhiṣavaṇa* (*adhi-√su*, cl. 5 "to press out, over") n.

°*carman* a piece of raw hide of a red ox, cut round, and having four folds (*puṭa*) to hold the pressing stones; on this hide *Soma* stalks are measured, and it is placed over the planks for pressing and extracting juice Āp. Śr. XII.2.14.

°*phalaka* n. the two wooden pressing boards (*adhiṣavaṇe phalake*), made of *udumbara* or *kārṣmarya* or *palāśa* wood, in front rounded off like the rim of a wheel (*pradhimukhe*) and at the back cut straight, they are dovetailed by means of a peg (in the *Soma* other than the *ekāhas*), and placed over the *uparava* Āp. Śr. XI.13. 1-2, B. Śr. VI.28, C.H. 102. On these boards are placed the pressing skin, and the *Soma* stalks are pounded for extracting juice K. Śr. VIII.5.25. See also *abhiṣava*.

अधीवास *Adhīvāsa* m. a kind of carpet (*vistārikā*), used at *Rāja* B. Sr. XII.14 (also *adhi*°), spread under the horse at *Aśva* K. Śr. XX. 6. 10. It also designates an upper garment, used as sacrificial fee for the priest Bh. Śr. XIII. 8.16 (*Soma*).

अध्यर्धकार *Adhyardhakāra* (mfn.) m. having an additional half; one and a half. A method of recitation of the *aponaptrīyā* verses (RV. X.30. 1—9&11) by the *Hotṛ*: the 1st stanza fully and ended with *03m*, and without taking breath the 1st half of the stanza, pause. The 2nd half, terminated by *03m*; and again without taking breath the entire stanza, terminated by *03m* Āśv. Śr. V.1.5; I. 2.19. C.H. 140.

अध्यवसान *Adhyavasāna* (*adhi-ava-√so*, cl. 4 "to unharness on") n. ceremonial entry and installation of the sacrificer and the priests in the *prācīnavaṁśa*; literally, "the act of unyoking on a chosen spot" Āp. Śr. X.3.3(*Soma*). C.H. 9.

अध्यास *Adhyāsa* (*adhi-√ās*, cl. 2 "to sit down upon") m. substitution of a *pāda* similar to the previous *pāda* in a stanza Āśv. Śr. VIII. 8.6 & comm.

अध्यूध्नी *Adhyūdhnī* f. a tubular vessel above the udder of a victim Āp. Śr. VII. 22.6 (*Paśu*) =*adhyuddhi* Bh. Śr. VII. 19.11.

अध्रिगु *Adhrigu* (mfn.) m. "possessing irresistible rays"; a formula ABr. VI.6-7, TBr. III. 6.6, of *praiṣa* or *nigada* type, recited by the *Hotṛ* at the beginning of the slaughter of a victim. An invocation to divine and human slaughterer Āśv. Śr. III.3.1. According to the limbs, deities and number of victims, the formula is modified (*ūha*) III.2. 11—30. A° is actually the name of the initial *mantra*. cf. Dumont L'Aśva 170, H.Dh. II(2), 1121-2.

अध्वर *Adhvara* (√*dhvṛ*, cl. 1 "to injure") m. sacrifice (not injuring), in *saumya* a° animal offering is integrated in the Soma sacrifice Āp. Śr. VII.2.17.

अध्वर्यु *Adhvaryu* m. the priest who performs an *adhvara* (?). A° is one of the principal priests as distinguished from the *Hotṛ*, the *Udgātṛ* and the *Brahman*. He is the central figure of the sacrifice so far as the manual operations are concerned. He measures sacrificial ground, builds altars, prepares utensils, cooks sacrificial oblation, fetches water and wood, kindles fire, brings animals to be slaughtered, and probably kills it himself. He repeats the *yajus mantras*; and the YV is said to belong to him. As he is constantly on the move he has no specific seat in the sacrificial arena. He is assisted by 3 assistant priests: *Pratiprasthātṛ*, *Neṣṭṛ* and *Unnetṛ*; whence they are called *adhvaryavaḥ* Āp. Śr. X.29.7, K. Śr. I.8.29. Not less than 36 A° are mentioned in *Aśva* Āp. Śr. XX. 10.5. cf. *ṛtvij*.

°*patha* the space between the *havirdhāna-maṇḍapa* and the *āgnīdhrīya* Āśv. Śr. VIII. 13.24 & comm.

अनद्धापुरुष *Anaddhāpuruṣa* m. designation of an individual, useless to the gods, manes and men, whom the *Adhvaryu* should look at while the latter utters a certain formula K. Śr. XVI.2.13. (*Cayana*). This part is played by a *dveṣya* Āp. Śr. XVI.2.6.

अनशन *Anaśana* n. fasting as a mark of mourning, to be undertaken by the relatives of the deceased, who studied the vedas, for 2 or 3 or 6 or 12 days Bh. Pi. I.8.10, but the wife (*pretapatnī*) is exempted ib. 13. see also *patnī*.

अनस् *Anas* n. a cart for carrying *Soma*, provided with rails (*phalakas*), surrounded by mats or similar things and covered with a sheet (*chadis*) Āp. Śr. X.24.2 & comm. The word is generally explained as *śakaṭa* (q.v.).

अनालम्भुका *Anālambhukā* f. "intangible"; a woman in her menstrual courses. A sacrifice is to be carried on by the sacrificer himself, debarring his wife who becomes "untouchable" on the day of the sacrifice Āp. Śr. IX. 2.1.

अनिरुक्त *Anirukta* mfn. (*gāna* n.) "not uttered"; a way of singing the stotra in which every syllable of the part of the verse, to be sung by the *Udgātṛ*, is replaced by the syllable O. The *Udgātṛ* transforms the *prastāva: upāsmai gāyatā narom* by his *udgītha: om o202000 002 000000 1212*. He says this in mind (*manasā*) L. Śr. VII.10.20, Āp. Śr. XXII.7 2, C. H. 180. see *sāman*; also said of a rite (*upahavya* q.v.) in which the names of gods are concealed XXII.9.8; also the appertaining *sāman*, *āniruktya* L. Śr. VIII. 9.1 comm.

अनुकम्पन *Anukampana* n. shaking of the *nārāśaṁsa* goblets by the *camasādhvaryus* (at the first pressing, *Soma*) Bh. Śr. XIII.32.1. See *camasa*.

अनुख्या *Anukhyā* f. authoritative passage equivalent to the *Brāhamaṇa* or *śruti* B. Śr. XX. 16; XXI. 22.

अनुचर *Anucara* m. "a follower" (1) the triplet which follows the *pratipad* in the recitation of a *śastra* Āśv. Śr. V. 10.13; this is the second portion of a *śastra* where the *āhāva* is to be uttered. (2) follower, as the *Neṣṭṛ* is the a° of the *Adhvaryu* Vt. Śr. XIV. 8.

अनुतुन्न *Anutunna* mfn. (°*toda* m.) "repeated blow" in the *sāman* singing, e.g. repetition of the syllable "*e*" at the end of *prastāva* Caland on PBr. XII.9.17, L. Śr. VII.7.30 comm; °*toda* Nid. III.12.

अनुदेश *Anudeśa* m. (*anu-√diś*, cl. 6 "to point out after") supplementary formulas with which the different objects like *āhavanīya*, *cātvāla* etc. are addressed by the *Adhvaryu* Āp. Śr. XI. 14.10-15; *anudiśati* K. Śr. VIII.6.23. C.H. 106.

अनु-द्रु *Anu-√dru* (cl. 1 "to run after") to recite in "a run" a series of consecutive verses (*daśahotṛ*) Āp. Śr. V. 22.10 (*Ādheya*).

अनुनिर्वाप्या *Anunirvāpyā* (*iṣṭi*) f. offering which follows the *tanuhavis* (*Ādheya*) Āp. Śr. V. 22. 8, Mī. XII.3.3; literally, "to get admitted to a principal rite".

अनुप्रसर्पक *Anuprasarpaka* m. (√*sṛp*, cl. 1 "to creep") a group of 90 brahmins who appear in addition to 10 *camasins* in the *Daśapeya* rite of the *Rāja* for drinking *Soma* L. Śr. IX.1. 19 comm; cf. *-sarpayeyuḥ* Āśv. Śr. IX. 3.19.

Special qualifications mentioned: their 10 ancestors, both paternal and maternal, must have been vedic scholars, and have performed holy functions, and had no sexual relation with the non-brahmins Āśv. Śr. IX.3. 20. But Āp. Śr. XVIII.21. 3-4 says that the 10 ancestors of the 10 *camasins* must have been *Soma* drinkers; but see also *prasarpakas* who are just spectators.

अनुबन्ध्या *Anu(ū)bandhyā* f. a sterile cow, immolated and offered after the *udayanīyā* rite at the close of the *Soma*; it is an animal sacrifice belonging to *Soma* and it follows the pattern of *Paśu* Āp. Śr. XIII. 23.6-7 (also explained as the cow which is immolated after the sacrifice ib. comm), 9 a° to Sūrya or 21 are sacrificed at *Aśva* Āp. Śr. XX. 22.10, K. Śr. XX. 8.23. A° in *Soma* C.H. 407.

अनुमन्त्रण *Anumantraṇa* n. recitation of a mantra which comes at the end of a sacrificial act S. Śr. VII.2.15; it is pronounced in *svarita* (Āśv. Śr. 1.1.20), and indicates participation of the sacrificer in the sacrifice Āp. Śr. IV.1.3.

°*mantray* to follow with eyes while pronouncing a secret formula (*abhimantraṇa*) Āp. Śr. X. 22.10; C.H. 36.

अनुयाज *Anuyāja* n. "after-offering"; series of three supplementary oblations subsequent to the principal offerings, offered mainly to the *barhis, Narāśaṁsa, Sviṣṭakṛt* (*Darśa*) Ś. Śr. I. 1.40 (variant: *anū*° Āp. Śr. II. 9.8); sometimes the number of a° is 9 as in the *Cātur* Āp. Śr. VIII.6.18; it is 11 in *savanīyapaśu* K. Śr. X. 7.10.

°*anu-yaj* to recite the *anuvaṣaṭkāra* Āp. Śr. VIII. 3.10 (*Cātur*); see also *prayāja*.

अनुरूप *Anurūpa* m. (antistrophe) a triplet, recited by a *hotraka* at the beginning of the *śastra*, and its metre, number of syllables, characteristics and deities correspond to the preceding *stotriya* (strophe) Āśv. Śr. V. 10.26.

अनुलोम *Anuloma* mfn.ind. "in the direction of the hair", *i.e.* in the natural direction (opposite of *pratiloma*, q.v.): gradually lowering the *dhruva vessel* downwards while decanting *soma* from it into the *Hotṛ*'s cup (*camasa*) Bh. Śr. XIV.15.2 (*Soma*); said of a ladle with its handle turned towards the offerer of oblation at the *Pitṛmedha* Bh. Pi. I.12.2.

अनुवाक्या *Anuvākyā* f. (*anu-√vac*, cl. 3 "to say after") also called *puro'nuvākyā* (q.v.); it is a call of invitation to the deity, pronounced by the *Hotṛ* while he sits for the *ājyabhāga*, *āvāpa* etc. It is pronounced in monotone (*aikaśrutya* Āśv. Śr. I. 10.1. comm.) before *soma* libation with the final *om* prolated. The *Adhvaryu* urges the *Hotṛ* by saying: *amuṣmā anubrū 3hi*, pronounce a° for such person K. Śr. I.9.13 (this is called *anuvācana* K. Śr. ib). At the rite to the manes: *anu svadhā* Āp. Śr. VIII.15.8; a° is recited by the *Hotṛ* before he utters his *yājyā*.

अनुस्तरणी *Anustaraṇī* f. (√*stṛ*, cl. 9 "to spread") an old cow, killed at the funeral rite, dissected, and its limbs are spread on the dead body Śr.K (S). I, 806; its flesh is also cooked Bh. Pi. I.5.1,4,5. also called *rājagavī*. See *Antyeṣṭi*.

अनूचान *Anūcāna* m(fn.) the priest who has not forsaken his vedic studies, i.e. learned Bh. Śr. X.1.1; *mārgād anupeta* Bh. Par. 133.

अन्तर्धान (कट) *Antardhāna* (*kaṭa*) m. a dish, made of *varaṇa* wood, semicircular in shape K. Śr. I. 3.36 comm.

अन्तर्याम (ग्रह) *Antaryāma* (*graha*) m. drawing of *soma* with the retention of breath during the *soma* libation (the second), accompanied by a mantra in which occur the words: ***antar yaccha***, "stop the *soma* in the flow". It is performed while *soma* is in continuous flow from the cup of the *Hotṛ* into the cup called *antaryāmapātra*, which is held in hand by the *Adhvaryu* Āp. Śr. XII.13.5; for description C.H. 161.

अन्तर्वर्त *Antarvarta* m. a mat (*kaṭa*) of split bamboos which covers the "space between" the roof of 2 *havirdhāna* carts (TS. VI. 2.10.7) Āp. Śr. XI.8.3 (*Soma*); also *tṛṇavarta* ib. comm.

अन्तःपात्य (शङ्कु) *Antaḥpātya* (*śaṅku* m.) a peg (*śaṅku*) which is driven in the middle of the sacrificial ground; fixed at a distance of 3 (K. Śr. VIII.3.7) or 6 (B. Śr. VI.22) *prakrama*s to the east from the eastern post (middle of the eastern door) of the *prācīnavaṁśa*, also called *śālāmukhīya*; one of the many pegs used for marking out the area of the *mahāvedi*. *antaḥ patati śālādvārasya ca vedeśca* K. Śr. ib. comm. see also *śaṅku*.

अन्त्येष्टि *Antyeṣṭi* f. the last rite of a man, a part of the *Pitṛmedha* rites. The deadbody is taken out of the fire hall. Hair on his head and face are shaved, nails pared. The corpse is washed and adorned with new clothes, a garland of *nalada* flowers put round the head. The deadbody is laid on an *udumbara āsandī* (couch) and tied to it, and covered with a new cloth. The belly of the corpse is cut open and the entrails are taken out, the faeces are squeezed out of the entrails, which is filled with *sarpis* and replaced in the belly. This strange rite which is optional can be also performed at the cremation ground (Bh. Pi. I.4.1-2). The deadbody can be carried either by men or in a cart drawn by oxen. All the sacrificial implements and other things and the sacred fires are carried to the cremation ground. The funeral procession stops at 3 or 2 places. The carriers, who are servants or old men, lay down the deadbody, place cooked rice on crushed clods (or kill a goat without a knife); the wives and kinsmen ruffle their hair, clap their right thighs, and fanning the corpse with the skirt of their garments they go round it 3 times in *prasavya* direction. This is done at each halt. The *anustaraṇī* cow tied at the left forefoot is led to *śmaśāna*, which may even be selected and prepared before the person is dead (Bh. Pi. I. 2-3). On the pyre the wife is made to lie (optionally, by the side of her dead husband); and the wife is raised up (see *patnī*). The corpse is laid upon the pyre together with the *āsandī*. The sacrificial implements filled with *pṛṣadājya* are placed on various limbs. The earthen utensils are disposed of. The limbs of the immolated *anustaraṇī* are cut off and placed on the corpse limb by limb. *Āmikṣā* is placed upon his hands. With the skin of the cow the dead body is covered. An oblation of flesh of the cow is offered. The pyre is now lighted. All the members of the family sprinkle themselves with the water contained in three furrows, and bathe in the water. They are to offer water libations thrice from *añjali*, mentioning the name of the deceased. They return home and observe a vow for 3 or 6 or 12 days or one year B. Pi. I.1-9; II.1, 6, 7, Bh. Pi. I.1-8. For *Pitṛmedha* Śr. K(E), I(2), 1033—1132. The word A° does not occur in the sūtras. Cf. Hillebrandt : Death and disposal of the dead ERE IV, 475-9.

अन्त्र *Antra* n. intestines of the deceased which, according to the Śāṭyāyanaka Brāhmaṇa(?) are taken out by cutting open the belly of the corpse; faeces are squeezed out, a° are reinserted into the belly after filling them with *sarpis* Bh. Pi. I.4.1.

अन्नहोम *Annahoma* m. oblation of nourishment, made of clarified butter, grains and powder of barley and grains of pounded rice; offered, just before sunrise, one by one, by the *Adhvaryu* at a soma rite in the *Aśva*. cf. Dumont L' Aśva 126-130; oblatory materials differ Āp. Śr. XX.10.5; performed in the *Vāja* XVIII. 6.5.

अन्वाधान *Anvādhāna* (*anu-ā-√dhā*, cl. 3 "to add by placing upon") n. act of offering fuel logs into the sacrificial fire (*agnyanvādhāna*) Āp. Śr. IV.2.8.

अन्वाधि *Anvādhi* m. end of a *mantra* Āp. Śr. XIV.12.3.

अन्वारभ् (*anu-ā-√rabh*, cl. 1 "to seize someone from behind," by shoulder, by a flap of garment), specially in a processional march in which the priests participate B. Śr. X. 10, Āp. Śr. IV.9.5. Also said of the objects taken hold of from behind Āp. Śr. VII.15.7. *Anvārambhaṇa* (elsewhere) is the duty, mainly, of the sacrificer K. Śr. I.10.12. *Samanvārambhaṇa* act of touching one another : the sacrificer touches the *Adhvaryu*, the wife touches the sacrificer, and other relatives touch the wife Bh. Śr. XII.16.13. see *Agniṣṭoma*.

अन्वारम्भणीया (इष्टि) *Anvārambhaṇīyā (iṣṭi)* f. introductory rite of the *Darśa* Āp. Śr. V.23. 4-9 & comm. Literally, "that which is to be attached to the introduction".

In this rite gruel (*caru*), cooked on 11 potsherds, is offered to Agni and Viṣṇu, on 12 potsherds to Sarasvatī, and on 8 potsherds to Agni bhagin B. Śr. II.21 (*anvārambha*).

अन्वाहार्य *Anvāhārya* (*anu-ā-√hṛ*, cl. 1 "to supply") m. rice meant for sacrificial fee-for the priests (literally, rice which is supplemented) Āp. Śr. III.3.12, K. Śr. II.5.27 (*Darśa*).

°*pacana* m. another name of the *dakṣiṇāgni* on which a° rice is cooked Āp. Śr. I.1.4. Cf. *Ādheya*.

°*sthālī* f. a dish on which the said rice is cooked Āp. Śr. I.15.9, Vai. Śr.XI.9.

अपगर *Apagara* m. abuse, hurled by the participants at the priests during the *Mahāvrata* rite K. Śr. XIII.3.6 (*Gavāmayana*). See *abhigara*.

अपघाटलिका *Apaghāṭalikā* f. a sort of lute (comm.) Āp. Śr. XXI.17.16=*apaghāṭilā* P Br. V.6.8. (*Mahāvrata*).

अपप्लवन *Apaplavana* (*apa-√plu*, cl. 1. "to immerse") n. immersion of utensils and other materials : *yoktra*, *kṛṣṇājina* etc. which have been "smeared" with *soma* (*somalipta*), C.H. 399, at the end of *Agniṣṭoma*. Cf *prāsyati* K. Śr. X.9. 5; *pravidhyati* Āp. Śr. XIII.20.12; *praplāvayanti* B. Śr.VIII.20.

अपरा *Aparā* f. the second ("other") *viṣṭuti* of performing the *pañcadaśastoma* : *aaa b c*, *abc*, *a bbb ccc* Eggeling SBE XXVI, 308.

अपराग्नी *Aparāgnī*(du) m. the *gārhapatya* and *dakṣiṇa*, the fires of the west and the south K. Śr. II.1.11.

अप-व्या-हृ (*apa-vi-ā-√hṛ*, cl. 1. "to speak wrongly") one who pronounces profane words during a rite Āp. Śr. II.16.1. cf K. Śr. III.3.13.

अपस्या *Apasyā* f. = *pariśrit* B. Śr.X.19.

अपस्राव *Apasrāva* m. = *ava°* Āp. Śr. XVIII. 18.5.

अपाकरण *Apākaraṇa* n. (*apa-ā-√kṛ*, cl. 8 "to drive away") rite of driving out the calves, 6 in number, from their mothers with *darbha* blades Āp. Śr. I.2.3. (*Darśa*), Bh. Śr. VIII. 1.10 (*Vaiśvadeva*); 5.4 (*Varuṇapraghāsa*).

अपामार्ग (होम) *Apāmārga* (*homa*) m. oblation of the fruit of the a° (literally, cleansing) plant (Achyranthes aspera), offered by the *Adhvaryu* with a *sruva* in order to drive out the demons. The *Adhvaryu*, taking a firebrand from the *dakṣiṇa* fire, leaves the fire-hut and makes fire in another place Āp. Śr. XVIII.9.5-20 (preliminaries of the *Rāja*). Cf. Heesterman 32.

अपालम्ब *Apālamba* m. B. Śr. VII.15, 17, K. Śr. VII. 9.15.=*avā°*.

अपिधान *Apidhāna* n. a lid, made of iron or wood, but not clay, for the jar into which milk for *Darśa* is collected Bh. Śr. I.14.9; 15.1.

अपिपक्ष *Apipakṣa* m. meeting point of the side and the base of the altar (*Cayana*) Āp. Śr. XVII.12.11.

अपूप *Apūpa* m. a cake of barley or rice, baked on the domestic fire in the *Ādheya* Āp. Śr. V. 4.15.

अपोनप्त्रीया *Aponaptrīyā* f. an *iṣṭi*; oblation prepared by mixing the *vasatīvarī* and *ekadhanā* water in a bowl of the *Hotṛ* L. Śr. X 17.1; a drink dedicated to *Apāṁ Napāt* Ś. Śr. XIII 29.12; *aponaptrīyā* stanzas (RV.X. 30), recited by the *Hotṛ* at the time of fetching water for preparation of *soma* C.H. 139.

अप्तोर्याम *Aptoryāma* m. the 7th *Soma* (*saṁsthā*), a further development of the *Atirātra*, requiring 4 additional *stotras* and *śastras* (33 of each in total); one can obtain (√*āp*) by performing this rite whatever one desires, whence the name PBr. XX.3.4-5. Cf. K. Śr. XXIII.1.19, Āp. Śr. XXII.13.19; XIV.4. 12—16, SBE XLI, xx-xxiii

अप्यय *Apyaya* m. joint of the wings and the tail of the *Agnikṣetra* K. Śr. XVI.8.20. (*Cayana*).

अप्रचरणीय *Apracaraṇīya* mfn. anything not being in actual use, kept in reserve; said of the two *mahāvīras* Āp. Śr. XV. 6.11. see *mahāvīra*.

अभिगर *Abhigara* (*abhi-√gṛ*, cl. 9. "to sing towards") m. name of an assistant of the *Sadasya* who reminds the call of *partigara* B. Śr. II.3; one who praises the sacrificer participating in a *sattra* L. Śr. IV.3.1 (comm: *abhiṣṭauti*).

अभिघारण *Abhighāraṇa* (*abhi-√ghṛ*, cl. 3 "to sprinkle over") n. (1) act of sprinkling clarified butter over an oblation in a continuous flow B. Śr. VI.18, as distinguished from *upaghāraṇa*, *upastaraṇa*; done twice K. Śr. I. 9.10, Mī. IV.1.33. (2) pouring out *soma* juice into 9 *camasas* at the *camasonnayana* rite: *soma* juice taken from the *pūtabhṛt* is poured in partly filled *camasas* (with the juice), and again *soma* taken from the *droṇakalaśa* is poured into them Bh. Śr. XIII.23.8. Cf. *upastaraṇa*.

(*praty*) *abhighāraṇa* n. sprinkling on a portion of the oblation which has already been cut up K. Śr. I.9.11.

अभि-चर् (*abhi-√car*, cl. 1) to practise exorcism; as a charm the noose of an immolated animal is tied to a piece of wood or a bunch of grass Bh. Śr. VII.13.8, either to a tree or the trunk of a tree or a pillar (*stambha*) Āp. Śr. VII. 17.7 (*Paśu*).

अभिज्वालन *Abhijvālana* n. straw used for lighting up the oblation Vt. Śr. VII. 3. cf. *avajvalay* Āśv. Śr. II. 3.3, *avajyotay* K. Śr. IV. 14 5.

अभिद्योतन *Abhidyotana* n. as above B. Śr. III 4. Cf. *abhitāpana* M. Śr. I. 6. 1. 24.

अभिधानी *Abhidhānī* f. a rope for tying a calf accompanying the cow, which supplies milk for the *Darśa* Āp. Śr. 1.12.7; another rope for cow supplying the *gharma* XV.5.20= *raśanā* 9.3; a cord binding the yoke to the pole, X. 28.1, of the cart by which soma is carried, or according to some : *śirobandhana*.

अभिप्लव *Abhiplava* (*ṣaḍaha*) m. name of *Soma* ceremony lasting six days in the *Gavāmayana*, and in the *sattra*, consisting of 4 *Ukthya*s preceded and followed by an *Agniṣṭoma*, with the succession of *Bṛhat* and *Rathaṁtara sāman* Āp. Śr. XXI. 15.10. Cf. Eggeling SBE XXVI, 403.

अभिमन्त्रण *Abhimantraṇa* n. addressing a *mantra* over an object (*e.g.* soma) Āp. Śr. XII. 9.10; in presence of a similar object I. 2.8 comm. This is done to consecrate a sacrificial object by means of a *mantra*.

अभिमर्शन *Abhimarśana* n. rite of touching an object by pronouncing a *mantra* B. Śr.VII. 2,5; name of a *mantra* recited when the pillars of the *sadas* are touched Āśv. Śr. IV.13.5 comm; the rite occurs on various occasions : at the *havirdhāna* shed Āp. Śr. XI.8.11, the top of the *uparava*s 11.4 (opposite : *āmarśana*, act of touching at the bottom of *uparava*s) C.H. 91, 102, 137.

अभिवान्या *Abhivānyā* f. a cow whose calf is dead but who suckles an adopted calf, and yields milk for the porridge Āp. Śr. VIII.14.14. See *mantha*.

अभिषव (ण) *Abhiṣava* (*ṇa*) m., n. (*abhi-√su*, cl. 5 "to press out") act of pressing *soma* stalks with stones for extracting juice. There are 2 kinds of pressing, the little pressing (*kṣullakābhiṣava*) also called the pressing of the *upāṁśugraha* and the great pressing called *mahābhiṣava*. The *Adhvaryu* takes a few *Soma* stalks, places them on the *upara* stones (also called *upāṁśusavana*), pours *nigrābhya* water over them, beats the stalks in 3 turns, each turn consisting of 8,11 and 12 single beatings. Extracted juice is filled in a cup Āp. Śr. XII. 9, C.H. 149-55. The *mahā*° is done in 3 turns after a large portion of the stalks have been placed on the *adhiṣavaṇacarman*, and sprinkled with *nigrābhya* water by the *Adhvaryu* and other priests Āp. Śr. XII. 12.1-13, C.H. 157-9. Cf. also Eggeling SBE XXVI, 244-5.

अभिषेक *Abhiṣeka* (*abhi-√sic*, cl. 6 "to pour out towards") m. unction rite of the *Rājasūya* in which water, drawn from various places, and purified, is poured over the sacrificer (king). The unction water is distributed in 4 vessels of *palāśa*, *udumbara*, *nyagrodha* and *aśvattha*. The sacrificer, donning a turban, a *tārpya* dress, and a mantle (*pāṇḍva*), K. Śr. XV. 5.7-11, gets hold of a bow and arrows, recites the *āvid* formulas Āp. Śr. XVIII. 14. 10. He treads on a piece of lead and pushes it off. The sacrificer with his raised arm takes steps to the directions. The *Adhvaryu* first pours out water on him, then the other priests follow K. Śr. XV.5.30-6.9, Āp. Śr. XVIII. 15.10-16.8. A° is the culmination of the *Abhiṣecanīya* rite. See *Rāja*. Heesterman 114-22. A° at *Cayana* Āp. Śr. XVII. 19.5, at *Vāja* XVIII. 6.6, at *Aśva* XX. 19.11.

अभिषेचनीय *Abhiṣecanīya* m. consecration rite of the *Rāja* of which it is the core; a Soma rite of *Ukthya* type, lasting 5 days consisting of 1 *dīkṣā*, 3 *upasad* and 1 *sutyā* days K. Śr. XV.4. 2; a year long *dīkṣā* prescribed in Āp. Śr. XVIII.12. Cf. Heesterman 63-8.

अभ्यञ्जन *Abhyañjana* n. See *añjana*.

अभ्यारोहणीय *Abhyārohaṇīya* m. a *Soma* ceremony, also called *Pavitra*, *Prāyaṇīya*, of *Agniṣṭoma* type, performed before the *Rāja* Āp. Śr. XVIII.8.3. Cf. Heesterman 12-14.

अभ्यूह *Abhyūha* (*abhi-√ūh*, cl. 1 "to remove towards") m. a sort of broom, made of reeds, used for separating symbolically 100 princes, who are engaged for protecting the sacrificial horse, into two groups, and for pushing water towards the horse B. Śr. XV. 1,6=*udūha* Āp. Śr. Cf. Dumont L' Aśva 294, 300-1.

अभ्रि *Abhri* (*ī*) f. a spade, 1 *aratni* or *prādeśa* long, used for digging up the site of the *audumbarī* (AO. VI. 226) or of the *ukhā* (*Cayana*) Āp. Śr. XVI.1.7. It is made of spotted (*kalmāṣī*) bamboo (*vaiṇavī*) having one or two blades (*ubhayataḥkṣṇut*, *anyataḥkṣṇut*) ŚBr. VI.3.1.30-34 used by the *Adhvaryu* for digging around the line drawn with a *sphya* for making the altar Bh. Śr.VII.3.3 (*Paśu*).

अमात्य *Amātya* m. persons belonging to the same house (*amā́* at home RV. X.63.16, together Pāṇ III.1.122); relatives of the sacrificer who are called to join the animal sacrifice Bh. Śr.XII.16.12 (*Soma*); on the death of an *āhitāgni* they should wear the sacred cords in the *prācīnāvītin* fashion, ruffle hair and pour dust on themselves (obviously as a mark of mourning) Bh.Pi. I.1.15.

अमावास्या *Amāvāsyā* (*amā* "in the house", √*vas* "to dwell": to dwell together) f. the night when the sun and the moon "dwell together" =*darśa* (seen by the sun only); Āp. Śr. I.7.1. It is the *tithi* on which both the sun and the moon are the nearest to each other.

अम्भृण *Ambhṛṇa* m. a common name of 4 washing tubs : *ādhavaniya*, *pūtabhṛt*, the vessel for rinsing mouth, and for washing dishes B.Śr. VI.34.

अरणी *Araṇī* (du) f. two pieces of wood used for churning fire, made of *aśvattha* wood covered by or grown on a *śamī* tree Āśv. Śr. II. 1.17, Āp. Śr. V.1.2; 10.7. Two pieces are cut off, planed, dried and shaped rectangle; each 16 *aṅgulas* in length, 12 in breadth and 4 in thickness B. Śr. II. 6; but cf. Vai. Śr. I. 1. The lower piece is called *adharāraṇi* having a hole in its centre (*yoni* or *deva*°) on which the upper piece *uttarāraṇi* is not directly mounted. A spindle (*pramantha*) connects them. By rotating the spindle fire is generated B Śr ib., Vai. Śr. ib. The operation is called *agnim manthati* Āp. Śr. VII.12.10.

अरण्येऽनुवाक्य *Araṇye'nuvākya* mfn. *mantras* preserved in a section of the *Āraṇyaka* Āp. Śr. XVII. 16.6. to be studied in the forest (on account of their obscure character), as distinguished from *grāme'nuvākya* XVII.17.1. There are 61 *araṇye'nūcya* libations in *Aśva* (its *mantras* are to be used in forest owing to its esoteric nature) Eggeling SBE XLIV, 336-7, Dumont L' Aśva 205.

अरत्नि *Aratni* m. a measurement, the 5th part of a *puruṣa* (the sacrificer's height) K. Śr. XVI. 8.21, B. Śulb I.1.

अर्थवाद *Arthavāda* m. explanatory words or statements which illustrate a '*vidhi*' (rule) of a sacrifice. The Brāhmaṇa texts contain, apart from *vidhi*, such statements; a° consists of *nindā*, *praśaṁsā*, *purākalpa* (traditions), *parakṛti* (story, action of others)—these help to clarify a rule Āp. Śr. XXIV.1.33; those passages or *mantras* do not refer to anything special in the sacrifice and therefore remain unchanged 3.51. Cf. Oldenberg SBE XXX, 324, 351 comm; Medhātithi on Mn. I.3; II.6.

अर्धिन् *Ardhin* mfn. one who gets a half share in the sacrificial fee; a designation of that group of priests, the first assistants, who receives a half of what the principal priests get Āp. Śr. XXI.2.17; also called *dvitīyin*. Cf. *ṛtvij*.

अलङ्करण *Alaṁkaraṇa* n. decoration of mourners which consists of shaving etc. (*nāpitakarmāṇi*) Bh. Pi. I.12. 7-8, application of collyrium to eyes by the women 11.14.

°*kāla* the time when *upastaraṇa* takes place Āp. Śr. VIII. 2.10.

अलङ्कार *Alaṁkāra* m. cleansing of the hearths; sweeping round the place with hand (*parisamūhanena*) Āp. Śr. VI.3.1.

अवकाश *Avakāśa* m. (*caraṇa*) rite of reciting *mantras* (TS. III. 2.3) while the sacrificer is made to look at *soma* and different cups B. Śr. VII. 8 (*avakāśaiścarati*) C.H.183. Cf. Eggeling SBE XXVI, 409. K. Śr. IX. 7.9: *grahān avekṣyati*.

अवट *Avaṭa* m. a hole in the ground for fixing the sacrificial post (=*yūpāvaṭa*) B. Śr. VI.26; Āp. Śr. VII. 9.9; a hole for *ukhā* XV. 3.20, also designates *uparava* XI. 12.5.

अव-तम् *Ava*-√*tam* (cl. 4) to withhold breathing after pronouncing *om* (*praṇava*) at the end of a *mantra* until breath is exhausted Āp. Śr. VIII.18.9.

अवदान *Avadāna* (*ava*-√*dā/do*, cl. 6? "to cut off") n. act of cutting up the offerings, specially the cakes, and also the portion thus cut off K. Śr. I.9.6. The size of the cut off portion is that of the first joint of the thumb (*aṅguṣṭhaparvamātra*) Āp. Śr. II.18.9; it is pinched off the middle of the cake with 3 fingers, the middle, the third, and the thumb, but using only the fleshy portions not the nails 10. A° consists of the portions cut off the heart, tongue and lungs of animal at the *Paśu*.

anavadānīya portions of flesh not cut off B. Śr. XI.5. Cf. *catur*, *pañca* and *ṣaḍavatta*; see also *aupabhṛta*, *jauhava*.

nir° cutting up of *iḍā* into portions for offering Āp. Sr. XII.25.8.

sam-ava-√*dā* to cut off simultaneously from two substances Āp. Śr. II.20.3.

adhyavadānīya what is to be cut up B. Śr. X.59.

अवनर्दन *Avanardana* (*ava*-√*nard*, cl. 1. "to bellow out") n. stretching of musical tone by inserting an intermediary tone (*anusvarati*, Sāyaṇa). Cf. Caland on PBr. (VII.1.2), 132, C.H. 466, L.Śr. VII. 10.22.

अवनेजन *Avanejana* (*ava-√nij*, cl. 3 "to wash off") n. rite of washing hands with appropriate *mantras* when the *agnihotra* milk has been placed over the fire or when it is being taken up into the *agnihotra* ladle Bh. Śr. VI.3.11.

अवभृथ *Avabhṛtha* (*ava-√bhṛ*, cl. 3 "to push down") m. literally, carrying off or descent into the water; the final purificatory bath which marks the end of a sacrifice. This is an *iṣṭi* connected with Varuṇa, consists of bathing of the sacrificer, his wife and priests either in a flowing river or in a reservoir (K. Śr. X.8.19), and disposal of various sacrificial utensils smeared with *soma* into water, and objects like the antelope skin, *yoktra* in the *cātvāla* Āp. Śr. XIII.19.8-9; 21.12, K. Śr. X.8.24. The accompanying rite is called *avabhṛtheṣṭi* B. Śr. VIII.19-20, Āp. Śr. XIII. 20.6-7. The *sāman* is called °*sāman* L. Śr. II.12.1 chanted by the *Prastotṛ*. The rite is to take place in water and not in fire Mī. XI. 2.28. In other rites : *Cātur* Āp. Śr. VIII.7. 14—8.12, *Sautrāmaṇī* XIX. 4.6, *Aśva* XX. 22.5. For A° in the *Agniṣṭoma* C.H. 393-405.

(*agny*) *avabhṛtha* a rite consisting of throwing the fire of the dead into water before the A° Āp. Śr. XIV.21.8.

अवस्राव *Avasrāva* m. drainage of water from the *śālā* B. Śr.XII. 4.

अवहनन *Avahanana* n. pounding of grains in a mortar for husking K. Śr. V.8.14.

avahantrī f. thresher, a woman, of grains B. Śr. I.6.

अवान्तरदीक्षा *Avāntaradīkṣā* f. an intermediate consecration Eggeling SBE XXVI, 97. See *dīkṣā*.

अवान्तरेडा *Avāntareḍā*.See *iḍā*.

अवालम्ब *Avālamba* m. point of support of the *havirdhāna* cart, a stick hanging down from the rear axle. used as a sort of brake Āp. Śr. XII.25.27=*apālamba* B. Śr. VII.15, K. Śr. VII.9.15 comm.

अविवाक्य *Avivākya* mfn. literally, "the day when no indication is to be given" (by a participant as to a fault committed by another person); name of the eleventh day of *Dvādaśāha* (=the tenth of the period of ten days) Āp. Śr. XXI.9.1.

अवेक्षण *Avekṣaṇa* n. rite of "looking at" the beverage : the *Adhvaryu* looks at his own image in the liquid butter poured into the hot drink of *caru* Āp. Śr. XIII.14.2, C.H. 364.

अवेष्टि *Aveṣṭi* f. a propitiatory offering to the quarters (*diśām*) in attenuation for mounting the quarters (*diśo vyāsthāpayati* Āp. Śr. XVIII. 14.17) 21.8 (*Rāja*). It is an *iṣṭi*. Cf. Heesterman 196-9. Also considered an independent rite Mī. II. 3.3.

अशन *Aśana* n. partaking of food before or after the assumption of vow Āp. Śr. IV.2.8, Bh. Śr. IV.3.2 (*Darśa* : duties of the sacrificer).

अश्मन् *Aśman* m. stone for pounding grains on the mill stone, Āp. Śr.I.20.2; name of four or, according to some, five stones, each 1 span long, narrower at the upper end, used for thrashing *soma* XII.2.15. Also said of the four stones placed along with the bricks XVII.9.5 (*Cayana*).

अश्वपदिक *Aśvapadika* m. fire kindled on the place where the horse puts its foot B. Śr. II.7.

अश्वमेध *Aśvamedha* m. horse sacrifice, recorded in the RV.I.162 & 163, to be performed by a sovereign (*sārvabhauma*) or a crowned king though not yet sovereign Āp. Śr. XX. 1.1. It takes place in March-April (*caitra*) ib. 4, but time varies K. Śr. XX. 1.2-3.

It is a *Soma* and lasts 3 days (the core) but the preparatory rites extend over a year or even two. Actually it is a combination of animal sacrifices, *Soma* and various other popular features. Participants are, besides the king, his 4 wives, 400 attendants and 4 priests. After the preliminary rites, a horse of a particular specification is selected K. Śr. XX.1.29-35, bathed, sprinkled and let off to wander over the country for a year (during which he is not allowed to mate) under the protection of 400 armed guards which include 100 princes (Cf. *talpya*). During this time the king is entertained with laudatory hymns composed in his honour and the *pāriplava* legends, and several *iṣṭis* are performed.

At the end of the year the horse returns, and then the principal rites begin: an animal sacrifice, *dīkṣā* lasting 12 days, measuring of the altars, 12 *upasad* days and followed by the 3 *sutyā* days. The first day of pressing is an ordinary *Agniṣṭoma*. The second day is the most interesting : the horse is led to a pond, anointed by the queens and adorned with 101 golden beads. Then the great animal sacrifice is performed. The horse is strangled to death. The queens go round the carcase, fanning it with their garments, and loosening their hair they beat their left thighs with the left hands (as the mourners do Bh. Pi.I.2.15 cf. *Antyeṣṭi*). The chief queen lies down beside the dead horse and under the cover of a mantle she simulates sexual copulation with it and abuses it Āp. Śr. XX.18.3-4, K. Śr. XX.6.15-17; the priests and women exchange an obscene dialogue 18. Thereafter a dialogue in riddles (*brahmodya*) follows between the priests and the sacrificer. The horse and other victims are cut up and offered. The third day of pressing is an *Atirātra*. The *avabhṛtha* marks the end of A°. The amount of sacrificial fee is so big as 48,000 cows for each of the 4 principal priests L. Śr. IX.10.15-11.4. cf. K. Śr. XX.4.27-28. On the account of A° in the Mahābhārata, Kane comments : "the author does not depict what he has seen but only what he has heard or read" H. Dh.II (2), 1238. B. Śr. XV, Āp. Śr. XX. 1—23, K. Śr. XX. 1—8. For details Dumont L' Aśva

अष्टका *Aṣṭakā* f. the eighth day after every fullmoon; see the domestic rite. A° par excellence (*ekāṣṭakā*) is the eighth day after the fullmoon of *māgha*, undoubtedly the eighth day before the new year Āp. Śr.VI.30.7; three *vyaṣṭakā* are the first three days of the dark half of a month L. Śr. IX. 3.8; also AV. XV.16.2.

अष्टम *Aṣṭama* mfn. name of a small basket, "the eighth", for the offerings of grains B. Śr. XV.16.

अष्टरात्र *Aṣṭarātra* mfn. an *ahīna* type of *Soma* lasting "eight nights", which includes 2 *Agniṣṭomas* Āp. Śr. XXII.23.7, Mī. XII.3.1.

अष्टापृष् *Aṣṭāpruṣ* n. a kind of golden coin having marks similar to "eight drops", used as fee for *Adhvaryu* Āp. Śr. IX. 19.1.

°*pṛḍaka*, Vādh. Śr. (AO. II. 158 comm).

°*pilaka* or *pulaka* B. Śr.XXVI.8.

अष्टाश्रि *Aṣṭāśri* mfn. "eight cornered", said of the octagonal shape of the *yūpa* at the top Bh. Śr. VII. 2.8 (*Paśu*).

असिद *Asida* m. sickle for cutting the *barhis* Āp. Śr. I.3.1.

अस्तु श्रौ३षट् *Astu śrau 3 ṣaṭ* the reply of the *Āgnīdhra*. See *pratyāśrāvaṇa*.

अस्थिसंचयन *Asthisaṁcayana* n. rite of collecting the charred bones of a cremated person (or only *saṁcayana*). Views differ greatly on the date of gathering of the bones : on the next day after cremation, or after 3 or 5 or 7 or 9 or 11 or odd number of nights have passed or even after a year B.Pi.I.11-13.

The cremation site is sprinkled either by the *Adhvaryu* Bh. Pi. I.9.2 or the performer. The bones are sprinkled by women, and the first wife standing upon a stone collects the bones piece by piece in a definite order and puts them in a jar. The jar is placed into a pit B. Pi., or on a *śamī* tree or at the root of a *palāśa* tree, and all take bath into the furrows (*karṣū*) Bh. Pi. I.9.13. Todten 90. see also *Antyeṣṭi*.

अहर्गण *Ahargaṇa* m. name of rites from the *dvirātra* to the *śatarātra* Mī. VIII.1.17, *i.e.* the *ahīnas* and the *sattras* Āp. Śr.XXIV. 4.4.

अहीन *Ahīna* mfn. "lasting several days" Pāṇ VI.4.145; the name of a class of *Soma* rite in which the pressing days last 2 to 12 days, and always end with an *Atirātra*; and together with *dīkṣā* and *upasad* days it must not extend beyond a month Āp. Śr. XXII. 14.1, *e.g.* *Gargatrirātra* (3 days), *Pañcarātra* (5), *Ṣaḍah* (6) etc. *Dvādaśāha* is both an a° and a *sattra* Āśv. Śr. X. 5.2. for a° & s° Mī. X. 6. 59-61.

आ Ā

आक्रमण *Ākramaṇa* (*ā*-√*kram*, cl. 1 "to step or tread upon", RV. X.166.5) n. crossing the *prastara* in front of the *dhruvā* Bh. Śr.II. 13. 7; also *praty*° recrossing II.14.2 (*Darśa*).

आखर *Ākhara* m. *khara* Vādh. Śr. (AO. I.10).

आख्यान *Ākhyāna* n. "legends"; see *pāriplava*.

आगुः *Āguḥ* (*ā*-√*gur*, cl. 6 "to greet") f. technical name of the words: *ye 3 yajāmahe* at the beginning of the *yājyā*, uttered by the *Hotṛ* indicating his "agreement". The formula is followed by *vaṣaṭ* Āśv.Śr. I.5.4-5 (*Darśa*). Cf. Keith TS 18, 94. Also name of the formula: (*agnim*) *yaja*, by which the *Adhvaryu* urges the *Hotṛ* to recite (modified to *hotā yakṣat* in *Soma*), uttered by the *Maitrāvaruṇa*. The formula *ye* etc. is replaced by *ye svadhāmahe* in a rite to the *pitṛs* Āp. Śr. VIII.15.11. *āgūrtin* mfn. pronouncer of the ā° formula; or a person who has had the formula uttered for him. cf. Eggeling SBE XLIV, 32.

आग्निमारुतशस्त्र *Āgnimārutaśastra* n. name of a ś° dedicated to Agni and the Maruts; the 2nd ś° in the *tṛtīyasavana* (and the last one in the *Agniṣṭoma*) B. Śr. VIII.15, Āp. Śr. XIII.15.12—14; text Śr. K(S). II(1), 457—64. Cf. C.H. 372—9.

आग्नीध्र *Āgnīdhra* m. (1) lighter of the fire, name of an assistant of the *Brahman* (actually of the *Adhvaryu*), whose main function is to pronounce the formula: *astu śrauṣaṭ* in response to the *āśrāvaṇa* of the *Adhvaryu*; moreover, he kindles the *dhiṣṇyas* (*Soma*) Āp. Śr. XII.18. 1—4, C.H. 184, and usually maintains the fires; finally, he gives a recital about the wives of the gods B. Śr.VI.20, Āp. Śr. XI.3.13-14, C.H. 71. He holds fast the *sphya* in hand turned towards the south. See *ṛtvij*. (2) n. a small shed in which the *dhiṣṇya* of Ā° is constructed Āp. Śr. XI.9.4; also called *āgnīdhrāgāra* B. Śr.VI.27; situated half inside and half outside the *mahāvedi*, 6 *prakramas* to the west of the *utkara*, supported by 4 beams (west to east) built on 4 posts; a square of 5 x 5 *aratnis*, having a door on the south and covered with mats on all sides. Cf. K. Śr. VIII.6.13, C.H. 99. See plan 3.

āgnīdhrīya m. one of the *dhiṣṇyas*, a circular hearth situated in the above shed, 1 *aratni* in diameter, meant for the *Āgnīdhra* priest Āp. Śr.XI.14.2; a square hearth built of bricks K. Śr. XVIII. 6.8 (*Cayana*).

आग्रयण *Āgrayaṇa* m. This is an agricultural rite of the *iṣṭi* type which an *āhitāgni* should perform in order to be able to make use of his harvest Āp. Śr. VI. 29.2. It is explained as a rite in which the first fruits (*agra*) are first employed (eaten) (*ayana*) Āśv. Śr.II.9.1 comm. It follows the procedure of the *Darśeṣṭi*, and may be performed either on the new moon or fullmoon (*parvan*) day.

In the rainy season, the ripe *śyāmāka* grains cooked either in milk or in water, are offeres. to Soma. In the autumn, a cake, made of the newly harvested paddy, on 12 *kapālas*, is offered to Indra-Agni, Āp. Śr. VI. 29.10, or a cake, made of old paddy on 8 *kapālas* is offered to Agni as an additional deity, ib. 6, *caru* to Viśve Devāḥ, a cake on one *kapāla* to Dyāvāpṛthivī. In the spring, when barley has ripened, offerings of barley are to be made.
If one has not performed the Ā°, he may make the *agnihotra* cow eat new grains, and offer the *Agnihotra* with her milk in *homa* on the Ā° day K. Śr. IV.6.11, Āśv. Śr. II.9.4. There are 17 *sāmidhenī* verses Bh. Śr. VI.15.3. The domestic Ā° rite follows closely the *śrauta* rite. B. Śr. III.12, Āp. Śr. VI.29.2—31.14, Āśv. Sr. II.9, K. Śr. IV. 6, Bh. Śr. VI. 15—18. H.Dh. II(2), 1106, Śr. K(E). I(1), 502—515.
°*graha* m. the first drawing of *soma* in the 3rd pressing, in 4 streams (*dhārā*), by 4 priests together Āp. Śr. XIII.10.11-12, B. Śr. VIII.10. Cf. C.H. 335.

°*sthālī* f. a vessel for receiving the drawing Āp. Śr. XII. 1.14.

आघार *Āghāra* (*ā*-√*ghṛ*, cl. 3 "to sprinkle") m. libation (pouring) of clarified butter (*ājya*). 2 in number, offered by the *Adhvaryu* on the *āhavanīya* always to the east K. Śr.I.8.42, (*Darśa*).

The first ā°, offered to Prajāpati with a *sruva* (*srauva°* or *prājāpatya°*) by the *Adhvaryu*, sitting on the northern side of the fire, in a continuous line from the west to the east and the second ā° by the same priest in a standing position from the southern side, west to east again, Eggeling SBE XII, 124, with a *sruc* or *juhū* (*sraucya°* or *jauhava°*) Āp. Śr. II.19.9; 12.7; 14.1. Also the libation of *soma*, drawn by the *Adhvaryu* with the *pariplavā* from the *droṇakalaśa* XII.20.20, Bh. Śr. XIII. 22.5 (*Soma*).

आचाम *Ācāma* m. water into which rice or barley has been boiled K. Śr. XIX.1.20. see also (distillation of) *surā*.

आच्छेदन *Ācchedana* n. stubbs=*ālava* B. Śr. I.2. *ācchedanī* f. the name of a *mantra* (TBr : *ācchettā vo mā riṣaṃ, jīvāni śaradaḥ śatam* etc. III.7.4.9-10, used at the time of cutting *darbha* grass Āp. Śr. I.5.5 (*Darśa*).

आज्य *Ājya* n. melted butter, one of the essential materials for oblation; poured into a pot (*sthālī*) covered with 2 *pavitra*s, melted on the burning embers of the *gārhapatya*, again 2 *pavitra*s are moved backwards and forwards over it Āp. Śr. II.6.1-7 (*Darśa*). The word ā° means *ghṛta* K. Śr. I.8.36 & comm. When no other material is mentioned, ā° is the only oblatory material 38. For offering of ā° see *homa*.

°*graha* m. a ladleful of clarified butter Āp. Śr. XII.7.9.

°*bhāga* m. two libations of clarified butter preceding the principal oblation in *Darśa*, belonging to Agni and Soma; ā° is drawn 4 or, according to some, 5 times with a *sruva* into a *juhū* preceded by *āśrāvaṇa*, *pratyā,°* and accompanied with the *yājyā* recital Āp. Śr. II.18.1-8. H.Dh. II(2), 1060, NVO. 102.
°*śastra* n. 4 recitations in the first pressing of the *Agniṣṭoma*; the first by *Hotṛ*, the second by *Maitrāvaruṇa*, the third by *Brāhmaṇācchaṃsin*, the fourth by *Acchāvāka* B. Śr. VII.17; XIV.9-10, Āp. Śr. XII.27.11-17, C.H. 231-4. Śr. K(S). II(1), 323-7; see *śastra*.

°*stotra* n. 4 chants corresponding to ā° *śastra* (also called *kṣullakavaiśvadevasya stotra*, chanted during the morning pressing near the *audumbarī* post (see plan 3) by the 3 priests : *Prastotṛ*, *Udgātṛ* and *Pratihartṛ*; see *sāman*, *stotra*. The 1st is RV. VI. 16.10-12, the 2nd, III.62.16-18, the 3rd, VIII.17.1-3. the 4th, III. 12.1-3. C.H. 236, 243, 247, 261; also called *dhurya* (q.v.).

°*sthālī* f. the pot in which ā° is poured Āp. Śr. I.7.5.

आज्येडा *Ājyeḍā* f. cake sprinkled with ā° Bh. Śr. IV.19.6 (*Darśa*).

आञ्जन *Āñjana* n. See *añjana*.

आतञ्चन *Ātañcana* (*ā-√tañc* or *tac*, cl. 7 "to cause coagulation") n. milk, milked on the preceding day of the sacrifice, and used as a curdling agent for fresh hot milk. The curd is used as oblation (*Darśa*) Bh. Śr.I. 1.2-3. If this curdling substance is not available, grains can be used 14.8.

आतिथ्य *Ātithya* n. rite for the reception of the *soma* stalks, which are brought into the *prācīnavaṃśa* on a cart, laid over the royal seat (*rājāsandī*). The *soma* is considered as a king, and as a guest is offered *madhuparka*, a cow etc. Āp. Śr. X.30.1-31, 31.6-7. An *iṣṭi* called *ātithyeṣṭi* (guest offering, also called *ātithya* ŚBr. III. 4 1.1) is performed B. Śr.VI. 18, Āp. Śr. X. 31.8-16, the first phase of which is an ordinary *iṣṭi* followed by the principal offering of a cake to Viṣṇu C.H.53-60.

आत्मन् *Ātman* m. "the self"; the main body (trunk) of the fire-altar, as distinguished from its tail (*puccha*) and wing (*pakṣa*) Āp. Śr. XVI.17.11 (*Cayana*).

आद्यर्त्विज् *Ādyartvij* m. K. Śr. XX.1.5. See *ṛtvij*.

आधवनीय *Ādhavanīya* (*ā-√dhu*, cl. 5 "to stir thoroughly") m. an earthen tub (which contains water) in which the wet and pounded *soma* stalks are laid, stirred before the juice, thus extracted, is to be poured through a strainer into various cups and *droṇakalaśa* Āp. Śr. XII.2.12, K Śr. IX.5.6, 15. Cf. H.Dh. I I(2), 1164-5; *ādhavanān aṃśūn* "stirred stalks" Āp. Śr. XII. 8.4.

आधान *Ādhāna* or *Ādheya*. See *Agnyādheya*.

आप्यायन *Āpyāyana* (*ā-√pyā/pyai*, cl.4 "to swell, make swell") n. rite of causing the *soma* stalks "to swell" either by touching them accompanied with the muttering of a *mantra*: from stalk to stalk increase (swell), O god Soma, or by sprinkling water over them Āp. Śr. XI. 1.11, B. Śr.VI.19; the *mantra* is to be uttered in a low voice Āśv. Śr.I.1.20. This rite is performed before the juice is extracted. After drinking **soma** juice in their own goblets the goblet holding (*camasin*) priests perform this rite over their goblets by uttering a *mantra* (RV.I.91.16).

This is the "swelling" of goblets (*camasa*) Ś Br. VII. 15, Āp. Śr. XII. 25, 24-27 (*Agniṣṭoma*), C.H. 219-20. Ā° is also performed in *Paśu* in which *prāṇa* or breath of the dead animal is caused to "swell" (strengthen) by the sacrificer's wife and the *Adhvaryu* who pours water over it Āp. Śr.VII.18.6-7.

आप्री *Āprī* (*ā*-√*prī*, cl. 9 "to propitiate" or, according to ŚBr. III.8.1.2, √*pṛ*, cl 3 "to fill") f. name of the "propitiating or fulfilling verses, which are *yājyās*' to be recited according to the *gotra* of the sacrificer by the *Hotṛ* at the time of pouring oblations at the *prayāja* (*Paśu*). There are 10 ā° *sūktas* (hymns) in RV. in which these verses occur, each prescribed for the members of a different *gotra* : RV.I. 13 (Medhātithi Kāṇva), I.142 (Dīrghatamas Aucathya, an Āṅgiras), I.188 (Agastya), II.3 (Gṛtsamada, a Śaunaka), III. 4 (Viśvāmitra), V.5 (Atri), VII.2 (Vasiṣṭha), IX.5 (Kāśyapa), X.70 (Vadhryaśva), X.110 (Jamadagni) Āśv. Śr. III.2.5-9. Cf. Dumont L'Aśva 165. For composition of the ā° hymns in consonance with 11 *prayājas* in *Paśu* Caland PBr. 413-14, H.Dh. II(2), 1118-19. Ā° might have been the songs for reconciliation between the priestly families Max Müller HASL. 247.

आमात्य *Āmātya* m. domestic fire (*amā*=house) said of the *āvasathya* fire B. Śr.II.8.

आमिक्षा *Āmikṣā* f. a mixture of coagulated milk and fresh hot milk. It is the solid portion of the mixture, obtained by pouring the fresh, hot milk over the coagulated milk of the previous day (*sāyaṁ doha*) Āp. Śr.VIII. 2.5-6, K. Śr.IV 3.10. Śab. on Mī. II.2.23; IV. 1.22 mentions : milk and curd remain in ā°. See also *vājina* (K. Śr. IV.4.9. comm).

आयतन *Āyatana* n. site, of fire (places) Bh. Śr. I.6.14, of the altar where ladles are to be kept II.16.11.

आरम्भणीया (इष्टि) *Ārambhaṇīyā* (*iṣṭi*) f. an introductory oblation at *Darśa* (=*anvārambhaṇīyā*) Mī. XII 2.19. *ārambhaṇīyam* "an initial day of the *Gavāmayana*, following the *prāyaṇīya*" Āp. Śr. XXI.15.8.

आरोक *Āroka* (*ā*-√*ruc*, cl. 1 "to shine towards") m. openings at the 4 corners of the *prācīnavaṁśa* Āp. Śr. X.5.3. Cf. *atīkāśa*, *atīroka*.

आर्भवपवमान (स्तोत्र) *Ārbhavapavamāna* (*stotra*) n. name of the first "purifying" *stotra* belonging to the Ṛbhus, also called *tṛtīya p*°, chanted at the third pressing. It is composed of 11 verses but raised to 17 by repetition (*saptadaśastoma*) C.H. 339, Eggeling SBE XXVI, 315. ŚrK (S). II(1), 420—31.

आर्यकृता *Āryakṛtā* f. "made by an *ārya*" said of the *agnihotrasthālī* Bh. Śr. VI.8.14.

आर्षेय *Ārṣeya* mfn. relating or belonging to a *ṛṣi*; used as a substantive RV.IX. 97.51 : may we acquire wealth and ā° resembling Jamadagni's; in AV. XI.1.16, 25-26, 32-23, 35 etc. ā° means descendants of the sages or belonging to them. The officiating priests must belong to a *ṛṣi*, *i.e.* they must have a *ṛṣi* ancestor who was associated with Agni in conducting a sacrifice. Synonym of ā° is *pravara* Bh. Śr.II.15.8, 11 (*Darśa*). For details H.Dh. II (1), 482-500.

आलम्भन *Ālambhana* (*ā*-√*labh*, cl. 1 "to take") n. act of tying an animal for killing it K. Śr. VIII.8.15; of slaughtering it (*paśvā*°) XX.4.21.; of touching an object IX.3.19.

आलव *Ālava* m. cut up *darbha* grass which constitutes the *muṣṭis* Āp. Śr I.4.8 (comm: *yeṣu kāṇḍeṣv ālūnā darbhāḥ*).

आवपन *Āvapana* (*ā*-√*vap*, cl 1 "to scatter into") n. act of pouring out grains for the oblation into a mortar Bh. Śr. I 21.5; the relating formula, °*mantra* XIII. 18.10.
See also *avahanana*, *udvapana*, *niṣpavana*.

आवसथ्य *Āvasathya* m. hearth, situated to the east of the *sabhya* in a hut called *āvasatha* ("dwelling place, night's lodging" AV. IX. 6.7) Āp. Śr. IV.2.1; according to V.17.1 comm. some are against its establishment while others hold it optional, and installed with the fire brought from the domestic or *gārhapatya* hearth or by churning. It is a triangular hearth of 25 *aṅgulis* in length on the 3 sides Vai. Śr. I.3.

The word *āvasatha* is explained as *atithīnāṁ vāsabhūmiḥ*, residence of guests Āp. Śr.V. 4.8 comm.

आवाप *Āvāpa* (*ā-√vap*, cl. 1 "to scatter into, insert") m. "insertion", a part of the rite which takes place within the framework (*tantra*) of a sacrifice; various principal offerings taking place between (or only after) the 2 *ājyabhāgas* and the *Sviṣṭakṛt*, *e.g.* milking of cows, arranging of potsherds etc. B. Śr. XXIV. 3. Ś. Śr. I.16.3-4. *āvāpika* mfn. in which an insertion is required Āp. Śr. XIX. 16.4.

°*sthāna* portion of a *paryāya* consisting of an insertion of chanted verses (called *āvāpika*); the ā° has a second position in the first *paryāya* L. Śr. VI.5.2. The opposite of ā° is *udvāpa* rejection of *sāmans* Mī. X.4.21.

आवाहन *Āvāhana* n. invitation to the gods Āśv. Śr. III. 1.12; particularly, to Agni who sends for the gods to take part in the offerings (*āvaha devān*) V.3.7 : *paricodana* I.3.17 comm.

आवीत *Āvīta* mfn. see *upavīta*; *āvītin* m. See *prācīnāvītin*.

आवृत् *Āvṛt* f. (1) procedure of a sacrificial act (comm. *kriyā, saṁskāra*) Āp. Śr. VII.8.6.

(2) part of the *udgītha* L. Śr. VII.10.21, *e.g. pavamānāyendave abhi devāṁ iyakṣate* are divided into 3 ā° : *pā* 2 *vā* 2 *mānāyendāvā* 2/ *abhi devāṁ iyā 1212*/ *kṣāte*.

ā-√vṛt (cl 1) to repeat a *mantra* or a sacrificial act Āp. Śr. I.4.6; also in caus. II.9.4.

आवेदन *Āvedana* n. proclamation by the *Adhvaryu* that the sacrificer has been consecrated (*dīkṣā*) Āp. Śr. X.11.5-6 (*āveday*). Cf. C.H. 20.

आशिर् *Āśir* (*ā-√śrī/śṛ*, cl.9. "to mix, boil") f. sour milk, whisked, warmed and mixed with *soma* juice in the *pūtabhṛt* (third pressing) Āp. Śr.XIII.10.8–10 (*āśiram avanayati*). Cf. C.H. 336.

आशिस् *Āśis* (*ā-√śās*, cl. 2 "to pray for") f. benediction, pronounced by the *Hotṛ* saying: this sacrificer desires long life Āp. Śr.III.7.1; *pratygāśis* prayers, muttered by a sacrificer for himself (*ātmagāmin* and *uttamapuruṣavācin*, comm.) IV.1.3.

आश्रावण *Āśrāvaṇa* (*ā-√śru*, cl 5 "to listen to") n. this is a call "to cause to listen to" given by the *Adhvaryu* to the *Āgnīdhra* with the consent of the *Brahman*. The call consists of any of the following : *āśrāvaya*, *ośrāvaya* or *śrāvaya* or finally, *om āśrāvaya* Āp. Śr.II.16.2; the first 2 syllables, each being prolated (Pāṇ VIII. 2.92), *e.g.* *ā3, o3, śrā3 vaya* TS. I. 6.11.1, are used in the announcement of the *pravara* (q.v.). The following procedure is adopted in ā° : The *Adhvaryu* addresses the *Brahman*, "*O Brahman*, I shall cause the *Āgnīdhra* to announce for the *pravara*"; with his consent the *Adhvaryu* causes the *Āgnīdhra* to announce with the above call: "do thou announce". It is pronounced in the raised pitch Āp. Śr. XXIV. 1.10; in the rite to the manes *ā svadhā* is used as ā° VIII.15.10; *āśruta* is a synonym of ā° II.15.6 The reply given by the *Āgnīdhra* is called *pratyāśrāvaṇa* (q.v.).

आश्विन (ग्रह) *Āśvina* (*graha*) m. drawing of *soma* for the Aśvins at the 1st pressing B. Śr. VII.8. C.H.182.

°*pātra* n. cup used at the drawing, having 2 corners shaped like a lip B. Śr. VII. 2, Āp. Śr. XIX. 4.9. C.H.136.

आसन्दी *Āsandī* f. stool, made of *udumbara* wood, with boards and side bars as support, each 1 *aratni* long, and with the legs reaching upto navel-height ; all tied and woven with the cord of *muñja*. A black antelope's skin is spread over it, and on this *soma* stalks are laid; called *rājā°* (seat of the king) Āp. Śr.X. 29.7; 31.3-5. Similar stool for *ukhya* (*Cayana*) XVI. 10.16; for *gharma* (*pravargya*) XV. 5.7 (called *samrāḍ°*); for sacrificer (*Vājapeya*) XVIII. 6.3; in the *Rāja* XVIII. 15.5; for the *Udgātṛ* (*Mahāvrata*) XXI.17.12. Also a couch on which a dead body is carried Bh. Pi. I. 2.1, Todten 15.

आस्ताव *Āstāva* (√*stu*, cl.2 "to praise") m. name of the place where the chanters sit and chant the *bahiṣpavamānastotra* (*bahiṣpavamānāstāva* Āp. Śr.XI.14.10); situated outside the *sadas*, within the *mahāvedi*, to the south of the *cātvāla* C.H.106n. In *Aśva* K. Śr. XX.5.7.

आहवनीय *Āhavanīya* m. "oblatory": one of the 3 principal sacrificial fires. It is a square mound situated on the eastern part of the *prācīnavaṁśa*. The hearth is kindled by fire brought from the *gārhapatya* K.Śr. IV.9.10, and *homa* is performed on it; cooking may also be done on it K. Śr. I.8.35, 44, Ś. Śr. III. 19.4. In *Paśu* and *Soma* the fire of ā° is transferred to the navel of the *uttaravedi*, and the latter is called ā° Āp. Śr.VII. 7.3; and the original ā° is then called *gārhapatya*, *śālāmukhīya* or *śālādvārya* (*Soma*) XI. 5.9-10. C.H. 78 ā° is also called *samedhanīya* B Śr. X.21; See plan 3-6. For measurements Āp. Śulb. II.4.6-8.

°*agāra* n. a shed for ā° constructed with its door on the east, and beams directed to the east or north K. Śr.IV.7.8-10. There is no partition between it and the shed for the *gārhapatya*. Cf. Dumont L' Aśva 2,35.

आहार्य *Āhārya* (*ā-√hṛ*, cl 1 "to gather") m fn. name of the fire, not obtained by churning, but set by borrowing from another fire Āśv. Śr. VI.10.9 (*aupāsana*, comm.).

आहाव *Āhāva* (*ā-√hū* or *hvā*, cl 4 "to call, to summon") m. technical name of a formula of the summons, pronounced loudly by the *Hotṛ* before he starts reciting his *śastra*. The ā° formula is: *śoṁ3sāvom* or *śoṁsāvo3* (a corrupt form of *śaṁsāva*), "let us both praise", to which the *Adhvaryu* replies with a formula called *pratigara* (q.v.) Ś. Śr. VII 9.1, Āśv. Śr. V.9.1-2. The ā° is required (and there are several ā°) in course of the *śastra* recitation; 4 at the *śastras* of the *prātaḥsavana* and the third *savana*, 5 at the midday Āśv. Śr.V.10. 10—12, and varieties recorded as *adhvaryo śoṁ3sāvo3m* at the beginning of all *śastras* in the midday pressing 14.3; *adhvaryo śośoṁ3sāvo3m* in the third pressing 18.4; or further varieties, in the first pressing, *śoṁsāvo3*; in the midday *adhvaryo śoṁ°* Ś. Śr. VII.19.6; VIII. 3.5, C.H. 232-3.

आहिताग्नि *Āhitāgni* m.(fn.). one who has laid the fire, *i.e.* performed an *Agnyādheya* Āp. Sr. V. 25.15 (also *anvā°* IX. 1.8, *anā°* I.10.17), has some privileges, and at his death he is burnt in his fires along with the sacrificial utensils Śab. on Mī. XI.3.34. *Nityadhṛts* are differentiated—those who constantly carry the fires Ś. Śr.II.6.4.

आहुति *Āhuti* (*√hu*, cl 3 "to sacrifice") f. offering of a ladleful (*sruc*) of clarified butter into the fire Āp. Śr. II.14.7. The procedure is described as follows: butter is taken in a pot, melted over the *gārhapatya*, purified by dipping 2 *darbha* strainers (*pavitra*). The *Adhvaryu* fills the *juhū* with liquid butter by means of a *sruva*, gets hold of a *samidh*, walks to the north of the *āhavanīya*, strews grass round the ā° and puts *samidh* into it; bending his knees he pours butter contained in the *juhū* into the fire by uttering *svāhā*, followed by a *mantra* uttered by the sacrificer H.Dh. II(2), 997.

pūrṇa° a full spoon offering of butter K. Śr. IV.10.5 (*pūrṇayā srucā*, comm.). See also *juhoti*, *homa*.

इ I

इज्या *Ijyā* (*√yaj*, cl.1 "to offer"; cf. Pāṇ III. 3.98) f. (1) performance of an *iṣṭi* as an expiatory rite Āp. Śr.IX.1.3. (2) substitution of the name of a god in a *yājyā* Āśv. Śr. II.8.10 comm.

इडसून *Iḍasūna* (*√sīv*, cl 4. "to sew") m.n. mat of reeds on which the omentum of a victim is laid B. Śr. XV. 31 (*baidalī phalakā* comm.). A board for cutting the animal organs, Kashikar on Bh. Pi. I.7.7.

इडा *Iḍā* f. portions cut up from all oblatory materials, 4 or often 5 times, sprinkled with *ājya* and consumed by all the participants together Āp. Śr. III.1.1. Also the appellation of the goddess Iḍā and the rite. The offering of i° takes place between the *sviṣṭakṛt* and *anuyāja* in *Darśa*. Cf. *avadāna*. In abbrev. i° means *iḍāhvāna*. In *Paśu* cut up portions of the limbs of a sacrificial victim is called i° Āp. Śr. VIII. 7.3. For the legend of deluge of Manu and his daughter Iḍā ŚBr. I.8.1.

avāntareḍā "intermediary" *iḍā*, a portion cut off the *iḍā*, held by the *Hotṛ* in his left hand, by the *Adhvaryu*, and another portion cut off by the *Hotṛ* himself with his thumb and forefinger Āp. Śr. III. 2.5-6, Āśv. Śr. I.7.3-5. Ś. Śr.I 10.4 mentions *uttareḷā*. In *Paśu* the *Adhvaryu* puts a portion of the victim's flesh called *avāntareḍā* consisiting of fat in the *Hotṛ*'s hand Bh. Śr. VII.21.1.

°*pātra* or *pātrī* (also called *dārupātrī*, *iḍācamasa, iḍopahavana* B.Śr.I. 18) or *samavattadhānī* f. a vessel made of *aśvattha* wood, as long as the foot of the sacrificer, having a rod of 4 *aṅgula*s in breadth (Vai. Śr. XI. 8) or having a hole of 4 *aṅgula*s in breadth K. Śr. I. 3.36. comm, used for holding the *iḍā* Āp. Śr. I.15.7.

°*hvāna* or °*upahvāna* or *iḷopa*—invocation to i° as well as to the goddess I°. The rite which follows the cutting up of the i° is supposed to induce the goddess to succour the sacrificer Āśv. Śr. I. 7.7.

इध्म *Idhma* m. wood sticks used for kindling fire, made of *palāśa* or *khadira* wood, 21 in number. Out of these, 15 are thrown into fire at the time of *sāmidhenī* verses, 3 are used as *paridhi*, 2 for the 2 *āghāras*, 1 for *anuyāja* Āp. Śr. I.5.6 & comm. But the number of i° varies : 17 or 23 at *Paśu*, 22 at *ātithya*, 23 at *Cātur*.

°*pravraścana* m. splinters obtained when *paridhi*s are planed Āp. Śr. I.6.3, used as a special oblation (*Darśa*) III. 9.12.

°*saṁnahana* n. cord for tying up the logs II.13.1.

idhmabarhirāharaṇa n. rite consisting of fetching i° and b° at (*Darśa*) = śulba Bh. Śr. I.5.11-13.

इन्द्रतुरीय *Indraturīya* n. name of an *iṣṭi* in which "one fourth" of the 4 fold parts is dedicated to Indra, performed at the beginning of *Rāja* Āp. Śr. XVIII. 9.6. cf Heesterman 34-7.

इन्द्रानस् *Indrānas* n. chariot (*anas*) of Indra, having 4 wheels B. Śr. XV.14 (*Aśva*). Cf. Dumont L'Aśva 312, 320.

इष्टका *Iṣṭakā* f. bricks, generally, made of clay, used at *Cayana* for constructing the altar, of various size and form, as long as sacrificer's foot and having 3 lines drawn on them, burnt red Āp.Śr. XVI.13.6-7, 10. Bricks are named, the first one is called *aṣāḍhā* (manufactured by the sacrificer's wife); others are *yajuṣmatī, lokaṁpṛṇā, vālakhilyā, svayamātṛṇṇā, citriṇī* etc. Total number of i° required for the five layers is 10,800.

Bricks are also required for constructing a mound over the remains of charred bones at the cremation ground Bh. Pi.II.4.3-4. cf. *asthisaṁcayana*; each measuring 1/24th of the *citi* or one human foot ib 5.

°*paśu* m. animal sacrifice at the beginning of the *Cayana* in which the heads of 5 victims smeared with blood are used as bricks. Cf. Mahīdhara on VS. XXVII. 29.

इष्टर्ग *Iṣṭarga* m. of doubtful meaning; comm. as, *darvī*, *aṅgārakarṣaṇārthaṁ kāṣṭham, ulmukam* B. Śr.XIV.4.

इष्टि *Iṣṭi* (√*yaj*, cl. 1 "to sacrifice") f. oblation of *havis*, offered by the *Adhvaryu* in a standing position to the south of the altar accompanied by *vaṣaṭ* and *yājyānuvākyā* K.Śr. I. 2.6; 9.18. The term is distinguished from *āhuti* and *homa*. The so-called class of rite, of which *Darśa* is the model (*prakṛti*), requiring 4 priests : *Adhavaryu*, *Āgnīdhra*, *Hotṛ* and *Brahman*, helped and sponsored by the sacrificer and his wife B. Śr.II.3.

इष्टयन *Iṣṭyayana* n. a group of rites comprising *Cāturmāsya*, *Turāyaṇa* and other similar rites Āśv. Śr. II. 14.1. (*iṣṭibhirayanaṁ gamanaṁ yeṣu karmasu*, comm.).

ई Ī

ईषा *Īṣā* f. shafts (poles) of the cart for rice; there are 2, one on the right and the other on the left (*Darśa*) Āp. Śr. I. 7.5; of the cart for carrying soma stalks Bh. Śr. X.19.15; XIII. 3.10; also a measurement 88 fingers, the length (west—east) of the altar of *Paśu* Āp. Śr. VII. 3.8 & comm. see also *akṣa*. cf B. Sulb. I.1.

ईषीका *Īṣikā* f. brush of *śara* or *darbha* grass with which collyrium is applied to the eyes of the sacrificer Bh. Śr. X. 4.13 (*Soma*). Cf. *śareṣikā*.

उ U

उक्थ *Uktha* n. recitation in general (=*śastra*), forming one of the 4 parts (actually the principal one) of the *śastras*. Cf °*mukha*.

bṛhad°/mahad° the great litany; a series of verses in triplets, also consisting of prose formulas, recited by the *Hotṛ* at the midday pressing, in response to the *mahāvratasāman*, in the *Mahāvrata* day of the *Gavāmayana* Eggeling SBE XLIII, 110-11.

°*pātra* n. a vessel in which the remnant of libation is poured after each *śastra* Āśv. Śr. V 9.26. cf. Eggeling ib XXVI, 293.

°***mukha*** **n.** "the face of u°", the main part of a *śastra*, *e.g.* the third part of the *ājya-śastra* Ś. Śr. VII. 11.3 (*mukhīya* XI.14.3) of the *Brāhmaṇācchaṁsin* (RV. VIII.17.7-13) C.H. 248.

°***vīrya*** **n.** "the strength of the praise", the last part of a *śastra* (*ājya°*), consisting of a formula : *ukthaṁ vāci* etc. and followed by some other words as necessary at different *śastras* Ś. Śr. VII.9.6. C.H. 233=*śastvā japa* Āśv. Śr V. 10.22-24. Synonym *ukthasampad* Vt. Śr. XX. 21.

°*śas* mfn; m. "singer of praise", *i.e. Hotṛ*; the word is pronounced in vocative by the *Adhvaryu* when he urges the former to recite Āp. Śr. XII. 27.19.

उक्थ्य *Ukthya* m. (or *uktha*) a *Soma* sacrifice (one of the *saṁsthās*), in which there are 15 *stotras* and as many *śastras* (by adding 3 more of each to the 12 *stotras* and 12 *śastras* of *Agniṣṭoma*). The last 3 are called *uktha*, one for each *hotraka*. There is also an additional animal sacrifice : a goat for Indra and Agni (besides that of the *Agniṣṭoma*) Āśv. Śr. VI. 1.1-3, Āp.Śr. XVI. 1. cf. Eggeling SBE XLI, xiv-xvi.

°***graha*** **m. name of a *soma* libation at the morning and midday pressings** B. Śr.VII.18, **Āp. Śr. XII.28.11-13,** belonging to Mitra **and Varuṇa C.H 242.** °*pātra* and °*sthālī* are **the necessary utensils** Āp. Śr. XII.1.14. cf. Eggeling SBE XXVI, 293.

उखा *Ukhā* f. earthen pot (RV. I.162.15) for *sāṁnāyya* (=*kumbhī* Āp. Śr.) Bh. Śr. VII.6.8; also used at the *pravargya* Āp. Śr. XV.2.7; specially at *Cayana*, shaped square or round, 1 *prādeśa* high, 1 *aratni* broad XVI. 4.7; bricks (4) are put into it, and it is turned upside down over a pit, and fuel is added to burn the bricks XVI. 5.8-12. cf. Dumont L'Aśva 58.

ukhya mfn., m. fire preserved in an u° for a performer of *Cayana* Āp. Śr. XVI. 9.1.

उच्चैः *Uccaiḥ* ind. loudly, the manner of announcing the name of the human *Hotṛ* at the time of the *pravara* recital, as opposed to *upāṁśu*. The name of the *Hotṛ* is to be announced in a low tone (*upāṁśu*), but immediately after "human" (*mānuṣa*) is to be pronounced loudly Bh. Śr. II.15.13 (*Darśa*). At the time of choosing priests at *Soma* : "God Āditya is the divine *Adhvaryu*", is to be muttered inaudibly (*upāṁśu*), but "N.N. is the human" (*Adhvaryu* etc.) loudly X.1.4-7. see *upāṁśu*.

उच्छिष्ट *Ucchiṣṭa* n. remainder of the oblation, with which the unfinished portion of a sacrifice can be performed Bh. Śr. IX.17.7; it is consumed by the priests Āp. Śr. XVIII. 6.11; also in the sense of the leavings of food Bh. Śr. XI.12.19.

°*khara* m. a mound of sand raised to the north of the *śālā* where the sacrificial utensils smeared with the leavings of the oblation are cleansed Āp. Śr.XV.11.16. See plan 3.

°*pātra* n. utensils smeared with u°, cleansed on the *mārjālīya* Bh. Śr. XIII.8.6.

उच्छ्रयण *Ucchrayaṇa* n. See *yūpa°*

उत्कर *Utkara* m. rubble, a little mound, made up of the earth dug up for preparing the *vedi* (also of *mahāvedi*), situated to the north of the eastern portion of the *vedi* at a spot which is 32 *aṅgulas* from the eastern portion of the *vedi* ($\frac{1}{3}$ of its length) Āp. Śr. II.1.6-7 (*Darśa*); the *stambayajus* are dumped here Bh.Śr. II.1.10 and various other things. See plans 3, 4 & 6.

उत्तपनीय *Uttapanīya* m. name of a certain fire used for burning the dead body of women and men who are not *āhitāgni*, householder or *brahmacārin* B. Pi. III. 1. [Śr. K(S) I,818]. Cf. H. Dh. II(1), 232.

उत्तम *Uttama* mfn., high tone, the mode of recitation of the *mantras* taken from the RV; one of the tones (*sthāna*) K. Śr. III.1.5. All that follows the *sviṣṭakṛt* or *iḍā* till *śaṁyuvāka* are recited in this way Āśv. I.5.28 (*iṣṭi*); the whole of the third pressing (*Soma*) Āp. Śr. XXIV. 1.14.

उत्तरनाभि *Uttaranābhi* f. navel of the *uttaravedi*, a square hole measuring 1 *prādeśa* or as much as a cow's or a horse's hoof Āp. Śr. VII.5.1; it is sprinkled with *ājya* in *Paśu* 4; when the fire brought from the *āhavanīya* is laid on it the hearth becomes the new *āhavanīya* and the original ā° becomes the *gārhapatya* Āp. Śr. VII.7.3. See plans 3,5 & 6.

उत्तरवेदि *uttaravedi* f. the "upper" or "high" altar, erected in the east, situated within the sacrificial arena but outside the *śālā*; a square mound, measured with a yoke pin (*śamyā*), made from the earth dug up from the *cātvāla* Āp. Śr. VII. 3.13 (*Paśu*); but measurements differ XVI. 13.11, Bh. Śr. XII. 5.2. The u° is used also in the *Soma* C.H. 74-5; in the *Cayana* (on which the fire-altar is raised); in the *Varuṇapraghāsa* (where there are 2). Cf. Eggeling SBE XII, 392. See plans 3,5 & 6.

uttarā vedi-a *vedi* in the eastern side belonging to the *Adhvaryu* in *Varuṇapraghāsa*, situated to the north of the *dakṣiṇā vedi* (of the *Pratiprasthātṛ*) Āp. Śr. VIII. 5.5.

auttaravedika m. the hearth within the u° on which an offering is made in the *upasads* of *Soma* Āp. Śr. XI.6.10. It is used as the *āhavanīya*.

उत्तरेळा *Uttareḷā* f. See *iḍā*.

उत्पवन *Utpavana* n. purification of waters by moving the two upward-pointed *pavitras* forward and backward Āp. Śr. I.11.8.

उत्सर्ग *Utsarga* m. act of passing over certain days and rituals of a *sattra* Āp. Śr XXI.25.5; the rites consisting of such omissions are called *utsargiṇāmayanam*, variants of the *Gavāmayana* XXI. 24-25.

उत्सर्जन *Utsarjana* (*ud-√sṛj*, cl. 6 "to let loose") n. act of releasing the *barhis* held in a closed fist Āp. Śr. I.4.6; to let the fire extinguish V. 27.3; passing over (non-observance) certain acts of a rite VIII. 21.5.

उदकक्रिया *Udakakriyā* f. offering of water libation with joined palms (*añjali*) to the dead for a number of days Bh. Pi. I 8.7 (*Pitṛmedha*), Todten 77.

उदचन *Udacana* n. filling spoon or goblet (*camasa*, Āp. Śr. comm.), used for pouring *soma* juice (from the *ādhavanīya*) into other goblets Āp. Śr. XII. 13.2, B. Śr. VII. 6; also *udañcana*.

उदयनीया (इष्टि) *Udayanīyā* (*iṣṭi*) f. concluding rite of *Soma* at the end (*yajñapuccha*), opposite of the *prāyaṇīyā* but based on it, performed in the *prācīnavaṁśa* on the *śālāmukhīya* fire, with 4 oblations, the last of which is dedicated to Pathyā Svasti B. Śr. VIII.21, Āp. Śr. XIII. 23.1-5, C.H. 405.

उदवसानीया (इष्टि) *Udavasānīyā* (*iṣṭi*) (*ud-ava-√so*, cl. 4 "to leave off") f. rite of giving up the sacrificial ground, opposite of *adhyavasāna* (q. v.), consisting of an offering of a cake baked on 5 or 8 potsherds to Agni on the fire which is again produced by attrition Āp. Śr. XIII. 25.3-5, B. Śr. VIII. 22.

It marks the end of *Soma*, and is performed when the priests have "given up" the sacrificial ground C.H. 411.

उदायुवन *Udāyuvana* (*ud-ā-√yu*, cl.3 "to disjoin") n. head of a spoon (*darvī* : *darvy*°), used for scraping off the rice plate Āp. Śr. VIII. 11.16 (*Sākamedha*).

उदीचीनवंश *Udīcīnavaṁśa* m. a shed with beams directed to the north Āp. Śr. V.4.1. see *āhavanīyāgāra*.

उदूह *Udūha* (*ud-√ūh*, cl. 1 "to remove off") m. (1) a broom of plaited reeds for "pushing off" water (*Aśva*) Āp. Śr. XX. 3.19. cf *abhyūha*.

(2) name of a tone "pushed up high" in the sāmavedic recitation, L. Śr. I.5.1. comm, Puṣpa 518.

उद्गातृ *Udgātṛ* m. the "chanter" (chief of the choir) one of the 4 principal priests, who chants the hymn of the sāmaveda (*stotras*). The assistants of U° (*udgātṛs*) are : *Prastotṛ*, *Pratihartṛ* and *Subrahmaṇya* Āp. Śr.X.1.9.

He also participates in some minor acts. See also *ṛtvij*.

उद्गीथ *Udgītha* m. name of the 2nd portion, the principal part, preceded by *om*, of a *stotra* chanted by ths *Udgātṛ*s Āp. Śr. XXI. 10.4. see *sāman, stotra*.

उद्धि *Uddhi* m. superimposed layers or pieces which together make up the *mahāvīra*; they may be of 3 (*tryuddhi*), of 5 (*pañcoddhi*) or of unlimited layers (*aparimitoddhi*) Āp. Śr. XV.2.14, *tryu*° B. Śr. X.5.

उद्यतहोम *Udyatahoma* m. an oblation made in the "raised up" fire, when the burning faggot is held high (supported by sand in hand), and the oblation is made on the *āhavanīya* of the *uttaravedi* Āp. Śr. VII.6.5 (*Paśu*).

उद्यती *Udyatī* f. one of the varieties (*viṣṭuti* q. v.) of chanting the *trivṛt stoma* of the *bahiṣpavamāna stotra*; in which the verses are arranged in "ascending order" : in the 1st turn the first verses of the triplet, in the 2nd turn second verses, and in the 3rd turn the last verses : a a a, b b b, c c c. Cf Eggeling SBE XXVI, 310. See also *kulāyinī, parivartinī*.

उद्वपन *Udvapana* (*ud-√vap*, cl.1 "to pour out") n. act of pouring out the grains for oblation into the winnowing basket Bh. Śr. I.22.2; the relating formula °*mantra* XIII.18.10. see also *avahanana, āvapana, niṣpavana*.

उद्वासनीय *Udvāsanīya* See khara.

उन्नेतृ *Unnetṛ* (*ud-√nī*, cl. 1 "to draw out") m. name of a priest, one of the assistants of the *Adhvaryu*, who draws out *soma* juice. The U° alone can do this by virtue of his designation (*samākhyāna* K. Śr. IX.5.32) Āp. Śr. XII.14.11 (*camasonnayana* C.H 204). See also *ṛtvij*. Cf. *ud-√nī* "to decant" Āp. Śr. VI. 7. 6, B.Śr. VII. 13.

उपगातृ *Upagātṛ* m. a subordinate chanter, chorister; there are at least 4 u° who sing "*ho*" continuously in a low tone followed by "*om*" chanted by the sacrificer at intervals between the *prastāva* and other elements of the *bahiṣpavamānastotra* L. Śr. I.11.26, Āp. Śr. XII.17.11.

उपगीथ *Upagītha* n. the song of the *upagātṛs* Āp. Śr. XX.13.7.

उपग्रह *Upagraha* m. designation of an "e" used as *nidhana* (q.v.) at the end of a *sāman* L.Śr. I.6.3.

उपघात *Upaghāta* m. modification in the *prakṛti* B. Śr. XXVI.32.

उपचार *Upacāra* (*upa-√car*, cl.1 "to move about") m. performance of a sacrificial act : *uttarata upacāro vihāraḥ* all priestly performances take place on the northern side of the *vihāra* Āp. Śr. XXIV.2.10. cf. *uttarata upacāro yajñaḥ* K. Śr. I.8.26 (ŚBr.III.4.3.19).

उपतल्प *Upatalpa* m. benches, 36 in number, on which 36 *Adhvaryus* get up to offer oblation at night Āp. Śr. XX.10.5 (*Aśva*).

उपद्रव *Upadrava* m. the fourth part of a *stotra*, chanted by the *Udgātṛ*. See *sāman, stotra*.

उपद्रष्टृ *Upadraṣṭṛ* m. umpires engaged by a king for the dice game : *saṁgrahītṛ, bhāgadugha* (collector of taxes), *kṣattra* Āp. Śr. XVIII.19.6-8 (*Rāja*).

उपनहन *Upanahana* (*upa-√nah*, cl. 4 "to tie up") n. a cloth used for tying up *Soma* stalks. see *Soma*°.

उपबर्हण *Upabarhaṇa* n. pillow, used as a sacrificial material along with the *kaśipu, añjana* etc. at the *Mahāpitṛyajña* (*Cātur*) Bh. Śr. VIII. 18.7; sacrificial fee for the *Āgnīdhra* (*Ādheya*) V.12.15.

उपभृत् *Upabhṛt* f. one of the offering spoons, made of *aśvattha* wood K. Śr. I.3.35, Āp. Śr. I 15.7. see also *aupabhṛta*.

उपयमनी *Upayamanī* (*upa-√yam*, cl.1 "reach up") f. (1) name of clay or sand used for holding and carrying fire; it is held below a vessel in which the fire is carried K. Śr. V. 4.20, B. Śr. II.17 (the latter is called *agnyuddharaṇapātrī*).

(2) name of a long curved ladle (*sruc*) when used as a supporting ladle; made of *udumbara* wood Bh. Śr. XI.5.12 (*Soma*).

उपयाज *Upayāja* m. additional offerings at the end of *Paśu* during 11 *anuyāja*s Āp. Śr. VII. 26.9; there are 11 u° Vādh. Śr. (AO. VI.181); the offering consists of intestines of the animal, poured over the burning embers by *upayaṣṭṛ* Āp. Śr. VII.26.8.

उपयाम *Upayāma* m. name of an earthen vessel

for *soma* Āp. Śr. XII.10.7; for *surā*, 17 in number, XVIII.1.17 (*Vāja*).

उपर *Upara* m. (1) one of the lower crushing-stones on which *soma* stalks are laid for pressing (RV. I.79.3; X.94.5); the 5th one (largest) in the centre is called u° on which the crusher (*grāvan*) stone is struck Āp. Śr. XII.9.3

(2) the unchiselled, lower portion of a *yūpa* about a 5th portion of the whole log, which is dug into the pit VII.3.1.

उपरव *Uparava* m. name of the 4 "holes of resonance" (*rava*), dug in the ground in front of the southern cart (*havirdhāna*) Āp. Śr. XI.11.1 (*Soma*) by the *Adhvaryu*, each at the distance of 1 span from one another, 2 u° in 2 rows; each 1 arm in depth, 1 span in diameter, separated on the surface but connected by underground passages B. Śr. VI.25, K. Śr. VIII.4. 28 comm. When the pressing board (*adhiṣavaṇaphalaka*) and skin (°*carman*) are laid over the holes and *soma* stalks are pressed the sound of pressing is amplified through reverberation (whence the name). Details in Āp. Śr. XI.11.1-12.6. cf. C.H. 100-102. see plan 3. Measurements Āp. Śulb. II. 7.5-6. °*mantra* Mī XI.4.52.

उपला *Upalā* f. a small crushing-stone (the upper one) which rests on the *dṛṣad* Āp. Śr. I.20.3 (*Darśa*), and used for crushing grains.

उपवक्तृ *Upavaktṛ* m. See *Maitrāvaruṇa*.

उपवसथ *Upavasatha* (*upa*-√*vas*, cl.1 "to dwell near; secondarily, to fast" Pāṇ I.4.48) m. fasting or fasting day, before a main rite, on which the preliminary matters like preparation of an altar, fetching a *yūpa* etc. are done Āp. Śr. I.14.16 (*Agnihotra*), XX.8.15 (before the *sutyā* day). The sacrificer and others keep vigil near the sacred fire C.H. 77.

उप-वाजय *Upa*-√*vājaya*, cl. 1 (from *vāja*) "to fan up the fire" (*upavājayati*) Bh. Śr. II.12.3 (*Darśa*). Cf. Macdonell, Vedic grammar 569, d; 585,7.

(यज्ञ) उपवीत (*Yajña*) *Upavīta* (*upa*-√*vyā*/*vī*, cl 4 ? "to envelop over") n. sacred thread or a piece of cloth put on by a sacrificer or priest Āp. Śr. VIII.15.1 over his left shoulder and under the right arm, and the person wearing it in this fashion is called *yajñopavītin* mfn (sacrificially invested) I.8.10, as distinguished from a *prācīnāvītin* (q.v.). In all sacrificial operations for gods the priests as well as the sacrificer should wear the thread in *yajñopavītin* fashion XXIV.2.15 (also called simply *upavītin*, K. Śr. I.7.14 & comm). Cf. TS. II.5.11.1, ŚBr. II.4.2.1. The word is distinguished from *āvīta* (*prācīnāvīta*, °*āpavīta*, °*āvavīta*) which indicates wearing of u° in the reverse order for the funeral rites and the rites for the manes. *nivīta* stands for wearing the u° suspended from the neck (*Mahāpitṛyajña*) Āp. Śr. VIII.16.18. See also *Upanayana* (*Gṛhya*).

उपवेष *Upaveṣa* m. poker for stirring fire; made of *varaṇa* or *palāśa* wood, 1 span long, having 2 or 5 nails, hand shaped, used mainly for shoving the cinder and *kapāla*s away from the fire hearth Āp. Śr. I.6.7; size varies K. Śr. I.3.36 comm. Synonym *dhṛṣṭi*.

उपव्याहरण *Upavyāharaṇa* n. [?] an introductory rite which "announces" the main rite B. Śr. II.1, C.H. 1.

उपशय *Upaśaya* m. (1) name of the 12th *yūpa* which "lies near" the main *yūpa* to its south. Its entire length is chiselled and it is not planted into a pit Āp. Śr. XIV.5.8; used at the *Ekādaśinī* animal sacrifice as a post for tying an animal B. Śr. XVII. 14

(2) a female head dress B. Śr. XV.15 (*Aśva*).

(3) said of 10 priests who replace the *Adhvaryu* and the *Pratiprasthātṛ* for the oblations, offerered at night (*Aśva*) Vādh. Śr. (AO. IV.189).

उपसद् *Upasad* f. (siege or homage ŚBr. III.4. 4.4); an *iṣṭi* which comprises a group of rites taking place between the conclusion of the *dīkṣā*, and the *sutyā* but always after *pravargya* (q.v.) of the *Soma*. Like *pravargya* it is performed twice a day at least for 3 days. Oblation of clarified butter to Agni, Soma and Viṣṇu are offered into the *āhavanīya* with *juhū* (*iṣṭi*); and also *āhuti* called *upasad*° with *sruva* B. Śr. VI.20-21, Āp. Śr. XI.2.12-3.12. cf. C.H. 67-70, Eggeling SBE XXVI, 105-11. There are 11 days of u° (*Aśva*) 12 (*sattra*) Mī. III.3.15; 6 (*Cayana*) Āp. Śr. XVI.35.6.

aupasad mfn. relating to u°, specially said of a *vedi* B. Śr. VII.3; an *ekāha* XVIII.45.

उपसंतान *Upasaṁtāna* m. a mode of recitation, by joining a *nivid* or anything to the preceding syllable Āśv. Śr. V.9.14,18. cf *saṁtāna*.

उपसमास *Upasamāsa* m. recitation of a RV. stanza pronouncing the *praṇava* (*om*) at the end Āśv. Śr. VIII.8.7.

उपसर्ग *Upasarga* (*upa-√sṛj*, cl.1 "to pour on", RV.VI.36.4) m. (1) pouring of *nigrābhya* waters on the *soma* stalks Āp. Śr. XII.10.10; 12.4.

(2) liturgical interpolation of syllables, 3 at the end of the first 3 *pāda*s and 5 at the beginning of the last 2 *pāda*s Nid. II.12. cf. Caland on PBr. 306-07.

upasṛṣṭa mfn. said of a god to whom an adjective is attached, *i.e.* *Agnitapasvant* Ś. Śr. I.17.5.

upasarjanī f. water which is heated to be mixed with flour for preparing a dough K. Śr. II.5.1 (*Darśa*).

उपस्तम्भन *Upastambhana* n. a prop for the shaft of a (*Soma*) cart, made of 2 sticks held together by a rope, on which the front portion of the cart may rest Āp. Śr. X.28.1.

उपस्तरण *Upastaraṇa* n. act of spreading *ājya* below the *puroḍāśa* before *avadāna* Āp. Śr. I.8.3; opposite of *abhighāraṇa*. Similarly, "spreading" of *soma* juice drawn from the *droṇakalaśa* into 9 *camasa*s at the *camasonnayana* Bh. Śr. XIII.23.8. see *ubhayataḥśukra*.

upastīrṇa mfn. (the bowl) which has been spread with *ājya* K. Śr. II.8.14.

उपस्थान *Upasthāna* n. worship or homage of the fires, performed by the sacrificer in the evening after the oblations of *Agnihotra* with the *vātsapra mantra*s K. Śr. IV.12.1. *agnyu°* Āp. Śr. VI.16.1-6 prescribes various other *mantra*s. Similar rite performed at the end of the *avāntaradīkṣā* B. Śr. VI.31, Āp. Śr. XI.18. 1-2. cf. C.H. 116; at *Cayana* before the fire altar XVII.12.10; u° *mantra*s are to be murmured (*upāṁśu*) Āśv. Śr. I.1.20. cf. *agnyupasthāna*.

उपस्थावन् *Upasthāvan* mfn. name of the two *yūpa*s on both sides of the central y°, one on the north and the other on the south, used for tying the victims (*Aśva*) B. Śr. XV.14,22.

उपहव *Upahava* (*upa-√hvā*, cl.4 "to call near") m. rite of inviting the priests in the 1st, *upasad*, done by the sacrificer B. Śr. VI.19, or by the priests themselves to one another for drinking *soma* Āp. Śr. XII.24.16; the priests address one another by their official designation, and none can drink *soma* without this invitation XII.24.14-15. cf. C.H. 62. TS. II.4.12.1 : *tasminnindra upahavam aicchata* : Indra wished to get an invitation at that sacrifice.

upahavya m. name of an *ekāha* in which the names of the deities are pronounced cryptically L. Śr. VIII.9.1. cf. Caland PBr. 472.

upahvāna n. a *mantra* of invitation for drinking *soma* Āśv. Śr. V.6.3.

उपहोम *Upahoma* m. subsidiary (additional) oblation which takes place either after the *pradhāna* or before the *samiṣṭayajus* Āp. Śr. II.21.2 (*Darśa*).

उपांशु *Upāṁśu* ind., m. a mode of pronunciation of the *yajus* Āp. Śr. XXIV.1.9, also of *japa*, *anumantraṇa*, *āpyāyana* and *upasthāna mantra*s Āśv. Śr. I.1.20. This is explained as murmuring of a *mantra* in which a visible attempt is made to murmur the words but no sound can be heard, and the words are repeated without thought Āśv. Śr. I.1.21 comm; cf. Oldenberg SBE XXX, 318, Āp. Śr. III.8.8. comm. U° is explained as near (*upa*) the stalks (*aṁśu*) WR. see also *uccaiḥ*.

°graha (or simply *upāṁśu*) m. name of the first drawing of *soma* done before sunrise in the morning pressing; it takes place without recitation except some formulas are muttered in silence and without breathing Āp. Śr. XII.1.7. cf. Eggeling SBE XXVI, 244.

Some *soma* stalks, sufficient for one cup, are taken out of the heap and placed over the *upara* stone, and sprinkled with the *nigrābhya* water from the *Hotṛ*'s *camasa*. Then the stalks are pressed with the u° *savana* stones in 3 turns of 8, 11 and 12 beatings respectively. The extracted juice is poured directly into the u° cup or vessel without a strainer over it Āp. Śr. XII.9.1-11.10. This pressing is called *kṣullakābhiṣavaṇa* (little pressing), C.H. 149, to distinguish it from "the great one" (*mahābhiṣavaṇa*, C.H. 157) which follows immediately. See *graha*, *abhiṣavaṇa*.

°pātra n. vessel for the u° *graha* Āp. XII.1.7: into which *soma* juice is directly poured by the *Adhvaryu* from the pressing hide on which the stalks were pounded. cf. Eggeling ib.

°*yāja* m. oblation of clarified butter offered silently or with muttered prayers at the beginning of the *pradhānahoma (Darśa)* Āp. Śr. II.19.12, NVO 111; or only u° Āśv. Śr. I.3.12. This is a separate rite with change of deities Mī. II.2.9, VI.5.10.

°*śaṁsa*=*tūṣṇīṁśaṁsa* B. Śr. VII.17.

°*savana* m (fn) name of the 5 pressing-stones used at the °*graha* Āp. Śr. XII.1.9, K. Śr. IX.4.6 comm; description of the operation C.H. 150-154.

उपाकरण *Upākaraṇa (upa-ā-√kṛ*, cl.8 "to fetch, set about") n. "act of fetching"; rite of setting about the chanting of the *bahiṣpavamāna stotra* called *stotropākaraṇa*. The *Adhvaryu* gives signal to the *Prastotṛ* by handing him over a handful of *barhis* Āp. Śr. XII.17.6-8; XIII.15.3 (*Soma*); he also urges the *Hotṛ* to recite the *prātaranuvāka (upākaroti)* XII. 3.14. cf. C.H. 174, 369. A *stotra* is "yoked" to the face of a sacrifice : *vāçameva tad yajñamukhe yunaktīti brāhmaṇam* B. Śr. XIV.5. cf. C.H. 174 e. At the animal sacrifice : the *Adhvaryu* takes 2 *kuśa* blades and a branch of *plakṣa* tree and touches the victim with them, and recites 2 *mantras*. This is called *paśūpākaraṇa* by which the victim is dedicated to the deities Āp. Śr. VII.12.5-8 (*Paśu*).

उपाचार *Upācāra* m. Ś. Śr. I.1.12. See *upa*°.

उपावरोहण *Upāvarohaṇa* n. descent of fire by attrition of the 2 *araṇis* at the time of kindling a hearth; opposite of *samāropaṇa* (q.v.).

उपोषण *Upoṣaṇa* n. act of burning *barhis* at the end of the *Soma* sacrifice B. Śr. IV.11; cremation of a dead body Bh. Pi. II.1.10.

उभयत:शुक्र *Ubhayataḥśukra* mfn. "pure on both sides"; said of *soma* juice drawn by the *Unnetṛ*, first from the *droṇakalaśa*, and then from the *pūtabhṛt*, and finally again from the *droṇakalaśa* B. Śr. VII.13. The operation is called *upastaraṇa* and *abhighāraṇa* Āp. Śr. XII. 21.15 at the *camasonnayana* (*Soma*). Cf. C.H.204-6.

उलपराजी *Ulaparājī* f. litter of cut and dried grass, used for strewing between the *gārhapatya* and the *āhavanīya* Āp. Śr. I.15.4 (*Darśa*).

उलूखल *Ulūkhala* n. mortar, made of *palāśa* or *udumbara* wood K. Śr. I.3.36 comm, Āp. Śr. XVI.26.1; used for pounding corns at various sacrifices. Cf. Āp. Śr. I.7.5; VI. 29.15.

°*muṣale* (du) n. mortar and pestle Ś. Śr. IV.3.2.

उल्मुक *Ulmuka* n. burning firebrand used for kindling fire; it is carried by the *Āgnīdhra* who is called *prathama* since holding it he leads the procession to kindle the *śāmitra* fire B. Śr. IV.6, Āp. Śr. VII.16.2-3.

उष्णीष *Uṣṇīṣa* m. n. turban, twisted by an initiated sacrificer 3 times round his head Āp. Śr. X.9.9. (*Soma*); a piece of cloth with knots for tying up *soma* stalks X.24.14, and afterwards used as a turban at the *avabhṛtha* XIII. 22.3.

ऊ Ū

ऊर्णास्तुका *Ūrṇāstukā* f. ball of wool, used as a sacrificial implement for throwing at the face of the *soma* vendor Āp. Śr. X.26.14 (*Soma*).

ऊर्ध्वज्ञ *Ūrdhvajña* mfn. "with raised knees", the prescribed sitting posture of the priest at the *patnīsaṁyāja* offering Bh. Śr. III.7.7. (*Darśa*).

ऊर्ध्वपात्र *Ūrdhvapātra* n. vessels with raised brims, also called *vāyavya*, made of *vikaṅkata* wood, 1 *prādeśa* high, contracted in the middle, shaped like a mortar with a spout Āp. Śr. XII.1.4, K. Śr. IX 2.14 & comm; used as a bowl for *soma* juice from which offerings are made to the deities Āp. Śr. XII. 29.6: these are 12 *grahas* : *dadhigraha*, *upāṁśu*, *antaryāma*, *aindravāyavya*, *maitrāvaruṇa*, *āśvina*, *śukra*, *manthin*, 2 *ṛtu* and 2 *aupaśaya pātras* associated with the *ādityasthālī* and the *ukthyasthālī*; the number can be raised to 17 by adding the *aṁśu*, *adābhya* and 3 *atigrāhya* cups C.H. 108. cf. K. Śr. ib. comm.

ऊवध्यगोह *Ūvadhyagoha* m. pit (*goha*), dug up by a priest or a labourer, where the undigested grass or faeces (*ubadhya* or *uvadhya*, etymology unknown) of an immolated animal are buried (*Paśu*) Āp. Śr. VII.16.1; it is situated outside the *vedi*, to the west of the *śāmitra*. See plan 3.

ऊह *Ūha* (√*ūh*, cl. 1 "to remove") m. substitution of one word for another (its order, number etc.) in a *mantra* for adapting the *mantra* to the changed context, occasioned by the introduction of new objects like *śara* grass, *śyāmāka* grains, *sthālī* (cooking vessel) and porridge (*caru*) in the *vikṛti* in place of *barhis*, paddy, potsherds and rice cake respectively in the *prakṛti* Bh. Śr. VI.15.7-8. This modification of *mantra* can only occur in a *prakṛti* Āp. Śr. XXIV.3.49-50. As a modified *mantra* cannot be subjected to the rules of pronunciation prescribed for normal *mantras*, it is not classed strictly as a *mantra* 1.35. Also a versified *mantra* cannot be modified Āśv. Śr. V.4.8.

ऋ Ṛ

ऋगावानम् *Ṛgāvānam* (*āvānam* from √*ve*, cl.1 or 4 "to weave") ind. a mode of recitation in which the stanzas are "woven together" by reciting them one after another continuously without pausing for breath (une tenore) Āśv. Śr. IV.6.1; explained as: *ṛcamṛcam anavānam* (without breath) *uktvā praṇutyāvasyet* ib. 2.

ऋच् (क्) *Ṛc (k)* f. one of the 4 classes of *mantra*, having fixed syllable, *pāda* and pause K. Śr. I.3.1 & comm. as distinguished from the *yajus*, *sāman*, *nigada mantras*. cf. Mī. II.1.35.

When the *ṛks* are employed the *Hotṛ* is the dominant figure Bh. Śr. III.15.6.

ऋजीष *Ṛjīṣa* n. sediment, *i.e.* the dregs of *soma* Āp. Śr. XII.12.11 (=*kiṭṭila* B. Śr. VII.6 comm.); obtained at the 3rd pressing, and mixed with *dadhi* Āp. Śr. XIII.20.8; immersed at the *avabhṛtha* B. Śr. VIII.20.

°*kumbha* m. a vessel in which the sediment is kept K. Śr. X.9.1.

°*mukha* mfn the pressing stones on the surface of which the residue of *soma* juice is smeared, and the smeared faces are turned to one another while the sediment is collected· Bh. Śr. XIII. 12.10.

ऋतुग्रह *Ṛtugraha* m libation of 12 *ṛtus* (seasons), offered to various deities in the morning pressing by the *Adhvaryu* and the *Pratiprasthātṛ* alternately, and others singly Āp. Śr. XII. 26.8-27.8, B. Śr. VII.16. cf. C.H. 224, Eggeling SBE XXVI,319-20.

°*dīkṣā* f. *mantras* muttered on the sacrificer when he steps on the antelope skin Āp. Śr. XX.8.12 (*Rāja*).

°*pātra* n. a vessel used at the *ṛtugraha* XII. 27.13.

ऋत्विज् *Ṛtvij* m. a priest who performs a sacrifice on behalf of a sponsor: sacrificer (*yajamāna*). 16 such priests are enumerated in Āśv. Śr. IV.1.6: *Hotṛ*, *Maitrāvaruṇa*, *Acchāvāka*, *Grāvastut*; *Adhvaryu*, *Pratiprasthātṛ*, *Neṣṭṛ*, *Unnetṛ*; *Brahman*, *Brāhmaṇācchaṁsin*, *Āgnīdhra*, *Potṛ*; *Udgātṛ*, *Prastotṛ*, *Pratihartṛ*, *Subrahmaṇya*. Of these, *Hotṛ*, *Adhvaryu*, *Brahman* and *Udgātṛ* are the 4 principal priests called *mahartvij* or *madhyataḥkārin* (*ādyartvij also*) Āp. Śr. X.1.9; XIV.24.6; the other 3 mentioned after each are their assistants (*catvārastripuruṣāḥ* Āśv. Śr. IV.1.4). Only one priest: *Adhvaryu* is required for *Agnihotra*; for *Agnyādheya*, *Darśapūrṇamāsa* and all other *iṣṭis* four priests: *Adhvaryu*, *Āgnīdhra*, *Hotṛ* and *Brahman*; for *Cāturmāsya* the fifth priest is *Pratiprasthātṛ* besides the four of *Darśa*; *Maitrāvaruṇa* is the sixth priest in *Paśu*. But in *Soma* all the 16 priests are required B. Śr. II.3; and according to *Kauṣītakins* a 17 th called *Sadasya* is added Āp. Śr. X.1.10; and B. Śr. II.3 provides 3 more assistants to *Sadasya*. The functionaries like *śamitṛ*, *camasādhvaryus* are not recognized as *ṛ*° though they are engaged in the sacrificial work Mī. III.7.33. The priestly office belongs to the brahmins Āp. Śr. XXIV.1.21. The priests are chosen by the sacrificer in a solemn function B. Śr. II.4, C.H. 5. A priest is to follow a code of conduct; he is not to accept an office left by another, not to purchase the priesthood, nor to accept the office for a sacrificer who has scars etc. But in case of deprivation of the means of livelihood he is allowed to accept office if he gets lucrative remunerations; and Baudhāyana reminds the priest of a distressing situation described in RV.IV.18.13 : "In distress I cooked for myself the entrails of a dog. Among the gods I did not find any sympathizer. I saw my wife dishonoured. Then the falcon brought me sweet water" B. Śr. XXIV.13.

The priests are to get sacrificial fees according to their shares as laid down : the entire fee is divided into 4 shares to be distributed among the 4 groups of *Hotṛ, Adhvaryu, Brahman* and *Udgātṛ* so that the principal priests get each 12% of the whole amount; their first assistants (*Maitrāvaruṇa, Pratiprasthātṛ, Brāhmaṇācchaṁsin, Prastotṛ*) get half of the principal's share (6% each), whence they are called *ardhin* or *dvitīyin*; the 2nd assistants (*tṛtīyins*): *Acchāvāka, Neṣṭṛ, Āgnīdhra* and *Pratihartṛ* get similarly ⅓ (4% each); the 3rd assistants (*pādins*) : *Grāvastut, Unnetṛ, Potṛ* and *Subrahmaṇya* get ¼ (3% each) Āp. Śr. XIII.5.11-12, Chinna 76. See also *dakṣiṇā*.

In procedural matters of a sacrifice the *Brahman* is supreme; the priests function one by one Bh. Śr. III.15.6. Functions of the principal priests are mentioned in RV. X. 71.11.

ए E

एकधन *Ekadhana* n. an earthen jug in which the *ekadhanā* water is stored, 3 to 11 in number Āp. Śr. XII.2.13 (*Soma*). The *Ekadhanā* water is fetched from the running waters, early in the morning on the very day of pressing, mixed with *soma* juice in the *pūtabhṛt* XII. 16.11.

ekadhanin mfn. servants who are in the charge of e° water B. Śr. VII.3.

एकपातिनी *Ekapātinī* f. name of the 3 "isolated" stanzas recited in the *vaiśvadeva*° and *āgnimāruta śastra* Āśv. Śr. V.18.11. cf. C.H. 354,372.

एकपात्र *Ekapātra* n. synonym of the *ūrdhvapātra* Āśv. Śr. V.6.29 & comm.

एकश्रुति *Ekaśruti* f. monotone, i.e. the neutral tone in which the *mantras* are pronounced in ritual, except in cases like *subrahmaṇyā, japa, nyūṅkha,* and *sāman* recitations to be done by the sacrificer Āśv. Śr. I. 2.8, K. Śr. I.8.19. see *svara*.

aikaśrutya n. relating to e°, defined as *udāttānudāttasvaritānāṁ paraḥ saṁnikarṣaḥ aikaśrutyam :* the maximum close contraction of *udātta, anudātta* and *svarita* tones Āśv. Śr. i.b.9; derived from e°, explained as *svarāṇāmudāttādīnām avibhāgo bhedatirodhānam ekaśrutiḥ,* Kāśikā on Pāṇ. I. 2.33.

But there are three alternatives :

(1) it is an intermediate accent between *udātta* and *anudātta* ; (2) it takes the accent of the preceding vowel; (3) it is the seventh of seven accents Mbh on Pāṇ l.c.

एकादशिनी *Ekādaśinī* f. an animal sacrifice in which 11 victims are immolated; also called *Aikādaśinapaśu,* °*kratupaśu* or °*ijyā* Āp. Śr. XIV.5-7; a model of the *paśugaṇas* ib 1 comm. E° follows the pattern of *savanīyapaśu* Mī. VIII.1.14. There are 13 *yūpas* of which the 12th is called *upaśaya* and the 13th *pātnīvata*; or only 1 *yūpa* may serve the purpose K. Śr. VIII.8.27. The southernmost *yūpa* is the tallest of all ib. 19.

एकाष्टका *Ekāṣṭakā* f. See *aṣṭakā*.

एकाह *Ekāha* m. *Soma* sacrifice of one day duration; reckoned as a class of *Soma*, as distinguished from the *ahīna* and the *sattra*. *Agniṣṭoma* is an e° since the main rite relating to *soma* is performed in one day (*sutyā*). A large number e° are prescribed for fulfilment of certain desires B. Śr.XVIII, Āp. Śr.XXII. 1-3. see also *gosava, sadyaskrī*. cf. Keith RPV. 336.

ऐ Ai

ऐन्द्रवायवग्रह *Aindravāyavagraha* m. name of one of the *soma* drawings, dedicated to Indra and Vāyu, being a part of the offerings to the twin divinities (*dvidevatyagraha*) Āp. Śr. XII.20. 18-21.6, C.H. 199.

°*pātra* n. name of the cup used at the rite (one of the *ūrdhvapātras*) B. Śr. VII.12.

ऐन्द्राग्नग्रह *Aindrāgnagraha* m. name of a drawing of *soma* for Indra and Agni B. Śr. VII.16, Āp. Śr. XII.27.8, C.H. 229.

ओ O

ओदन *Odana* m. n. rice, cooked and served to the relatives of the sacrificer, and also consumed by all priests Bh. Śr. VIII.13. 1, 13-14 (*Sākamedha*), also at *Āgrayaṇa* VI. 18.13.

ओ श्रावय *o śrāvaya*=*āśrāvaya*, the call of the *Adhvaryu*. See *āśrāvaṇa*.

औ Au

औत्तरवेदिक *Auttaravedika*.See *uttaravedi*.

औदुम्बरी *Audumbarī* f. a post (*sthūṇā*), made of *udumbara* wood (Ficus religiosa), as high as the sacrificer, having a knot directed to the east (*prācīnakarṇa*), raised ceremonially by the *Adhvaryu* with the help of the *Udgātṛ* at a central point of the *sadas*, 6 *prakramas* to the east of the *antaḥpātya* and 1 *prakrama* to the south of the *pṛṣṭhyā*. It is the thickest of all posts of the *sadas*, and over which the *chadis* is laid. Raising and fixing it in a hole give rise to an *āhuti* of *ājya* K. Śr.VIII.5.31 & comm, Āp. Śr.XI.9.9-10.5, B. Śr. VI.26-27. See plan 3.

औद्ग्रहण *Audgrahaṇa* n. name of the 6 "elevatory" *ājya* oblations, also called *dīkṣāhuti* (q. v.), performed at the *dīkṣā* in which 12 ladling operations (*dvādaśagṛhīta*) take place : 4 *āhutis* with *ājya* taken from the *dhruvā* into the *sruva*, the 5th and the 6th (*pūrṇāhuti*) into the *sruc* Āp. Śr X.8.5-7=*audgrabhaṇa* K. Śr. VII. 3.16 (*Soma*).

There are 3 additional au° K. Śr. XX.4.3. (*Aśva*). Cf. Eggeling SBE XXVI.20; XLIV, 289.

औद्धव *Auddhava* m. left-over of the *barhis*, used for strewing Āp. Śr.VIII.14.4; it is a *prastara* 5

औपभृत *Aupabhṛta* mfn. limbs of an animal which are cut into the *upabhṛt* (cf. *avadāna*); enumerated as : the right forefoot (*sakthipūrvanaḍaka*), the left buttock (*śroṇi*), and the thinnest third part of the anus (*guda*); these 3 limbs (also called *tryaṅga*, q.v.) are meant for Agni *Sviṣṭakṛt* K. Śr. VI.7.7. (*Paśu*). Cf. H.Dh. II (2), 1126-27. See also *jauhava*.

औपवसथिक *Aupavasathika* or *Aupavasathya* mfn. See *upavasatha*.

औपशय (पात्र) *Aupasaya* (*pātra*) n. accessory cups (cf. *upasaya*) used for the *soma* drawing called *pratinirgrāhya* B. Śr. VII.12; included in the *ūrdhvapātra* group, associated with the *ādityasthālī* and the *ukthyasthālī* (Āp. Śr. XII.1.4).

औपासन *Aupāsana* (*upa*-√*ās*, cl.2 "to sit near") m. domestic fire on which au° oblation is offered Āp. Śr. I.10.8; from it fire is taken for cooking *brahmaudana* V.4.12 (*Ādheya*).

क Ka

कंस *Kaṁsa* m. n. a vessel, made of brass, used for holding clarified butter in the *Tānūnaptra* B. Śr. VI.19.

कटपरिवार *Kaṭaparivāra* (*pari-√vṛ*, cl. 5 "to cover, surround") m. enclosure of straw mat (*kaṭa*), used as ritual toilet, 2 in number, erected to the north of the *prācīnavaṁśa*; one on the eastern side for the sacrificer, and the other on the western side for his wife B. Śr. VI.1.

कण्डूयनी *Kaṇḍūyanī* f. a scratcher, made of the horn of a black antelope, used by an initiated sacrificer (*dīkṣita*) for scratching himself when necessary K. Śr. XV.6.8.

कपाल *Kapāla* n. a kind of burnt potsherd; they are broken pieces of a vessel K. Śr. II. 3.8 comm; recognized as sacrificial utensil (*pātra*). They are arranged in such a manner that the size and shape of a horseshoe is obtained; on these *puroḍāśa*s are baked, 7 to 12 k° are required for baking a cake for Agni, 11 for one for Indra, 12 for Savitṛ, 7 for the Maruts etc; 3 for roasting corns. They are 2 fingers in length and breadth Vai. Śr. XI.9. On the manner of arrangement of k° for baking cakes Āp. Śr. I.22.1-23.6 (*Darśa*). Cf. Eggeling SBE XII, 34. See plan 7-8.

°*yoga* m. "yoking", *i.e.* putting the k° on fire Āp. Śr. I. 23.2 (*Darśa*).

°*vimocana* n. "unyoking" of k°, *i.e.* removal of k°s from the fire with *mantra*s Āp. Śr. IV. 14.5; XII. 25.13 (*Soma*).

कमण्डलु *Kamaṇḍa(u)lu* m. n. a jug for carrying water, used for a rite performed by the sacrificer's wife Āp. Śr. III.8.1 (*Darśa*).

करम्भ *Karambha* m. barley or oats (the usual sacrificial food for Pūṣan who has no teeth to masticate hard food RV. III.52.7; VI.57.2); its grains are husked, slightly parched (*āma-bhṛṣṭa*) on the *dakṣiṇa* fire, pounded and mixed with curds K. Śr. V.3.2; °*pātrāṇi*, dishes made of k°, prepared by the sacrificer's wife Āp. Śr. VIII.6.3; the number of such dishes exceeds by one the number of children including grandchildren, unmarried daughters of the householder 5.41. With the rest of the ground and parched barley a figurine of a ram (*meṣa*) and a ewe (*meṣī*) are made by the *Adhvaryu* and the *Pratiprasthātṛ* respectively 5.42-43 (*Varuṇapraghāsa*).

The flour of k° is also used for preparing the *savanīyapuroḍāśa* at the pressings Bh. Śr. XIII. 18.1 (*Soma*).

कर्णातर्द *Karṇātarda* m. a hole on both sides of the *havirdhāna* cart in which poles are fixed Āp. Śr. XI.7.3 (*Soma*).

कर्मन् *Karman* n. a sacrificial act which must produce a result K. Śr. I.1.2 (as opposed to the speculative religion); indicated by injunction H. Śr. I.1.6. see also *mantra*.

कर्षण *Karṣaṇa* n. prolonging a syllable in a chant by inserting one or more tones; 5 types in all, of which the 2nd tone is the main Puṣpa 518, *e.g. bā 2 rhiṣo*. Cf. C.H. 466.

कर्षू *Karṣū* f. trench or furrow, 3 in number, dug out to the northern side of the rear of the cremation place; surrounded by stones and sand. The trenches are flooded with waters, and the relatives of the deceased have bath in the water Bh. Pi. I.7.11.

कशिपु *Kaśipu* m. n. a sort of mattress or cushion, embroidered in gold, on which the *Hotṛ* sits during the recitation (*ākhyāna*) K. Śr. XX.2.21 (*Aśva*); a kind of pillow laid on the *vedi* at the *Darśa* Āp. Śr. I.8.2; commented as *masūraka* or *phalaka* K. Śr. XV.6.4 comm. *śayanasyopari vistārikā* B. Śr. V.11. comm.

कस्तम्भी *Kastambhī* f. a wooden rod fixed below the pole of a cart either at the centre or at the rear serving as a prop of the stationary cart which carries ladles Āp. Śr. III.8.4 (*Darśa*). Cf. ŚBr. I.1.2.9.

कानिष्ठिनेय *Kāniṣṭhineya* m. son by the youngest wife, for whom 2 rear udders of the *agnihotra* cow is milked Bh. Śr. VI 9.1. see *jyaiṣṭhineya*.

कामन *K[illegible]na* n. formulation of a desire to perfor[illegible] sacrifice; this is the basis of a sacrifice, and one of the duties of a sacrificer Āp. Śr. IV.1.2.

काम्या *Kāmyā (iṣṭi)* f. rites for attainment of a specific desire (as distinguished from the regular or compulsory rites, *nitya*); the rites resulting from a particular desire and performed with a view to securing the desired object, *e.g. āyuṣkāmeṣṭi* (for long life), *putrakāmeṣṭi* (for having a son). *kārīrīṣṭi* (for rain) etc. Āśv. Śr. II.10, Āp. Śr. XIX. 18-27. These are performed on the new or fullmoon day 18.1, and are variations of *Darśa* which they follow.

कारोतर *Kārotara* m. a sieve of bamboo which is placed over the hide of a bull, and through which the wine (*surā*) is poured and purified Āp. Śr. XIX.6.1, K. Śr. XIX.2.7. (*Sautrāmaṇī*); RV. I.116.7.

कुम्ब *Kumba* m. n. thick end of a *śamyā* (yoke pin) Bh.Śr.VII.3.1.

कुम्बकुरीर *Kumbakurīra* (*kumba*, a kind of head-dress AV.VI.138.3) m. n. a headdress worn by the sacrificer's wife at the *dīkṣā* Āp. Śr. X. 9.5. B.Śr. VI.5 (*Soma*); apparently, a garland of thin pieces of bamboo and a net of black wool sewn together; explained as a net *jāla* ib. 7. But it occurs as 2 separate words: *kumbaṁ ca kurīraṁ ca* B. Śr. VI.1. *Kurīra* is interpreted as *jāla* (net) Bh.Śr. X.6.6, but headdress RV. X.85.8.

कुम्भ *Kumbha* m. an earthen jar in which *vasatīvarī* water is collected; it is placed on the southern and nothern *śroṇi* of the *uttaravedi* Bh. Śr. XII.20.6; 21.3. 3-4; charred bones of a dead body is collected into it Bh. Pi. I.9.6.

कुम्भी *Kumbhī* f. a large earthen urn for keeping the *āmikṣā* Āp. Śr. I.13.6; for cooking animal flesh (*paśu°*) VII.8.3. There are 2 k° for *sāṁnāyya* (*sāṁnāyya°*): one for keeping boiled milk, and the other for curdled milk I.6.13. In *Cayana*, *kumbha* and *kumbhī* are differentiated XVI.32.5; the first is probably a male urn (without any mark ?) and the other a female one with bulges like female breast.

कुरीर *Kurīra* n. See *kumbakurīra*.

कुलायिनी *Kulāyinī* f. one of the varieties of chanting the *trivṛtstoma* of the *bahiṣpavamāna* in the form of a "web" (*kulāya*). The 3 verses are arranged thus : a b c (1st turn), b c a (2nd turn), c a b (last turn). Cf Eggeling SBE XXVI,310. see also *udyatī*, *parivartinī*.

कुश *Kuśa* m. (1) grass (Poa cynosuroides). see *darbha*.

(2) small sticks, 21 in number, each 1 span long, cut from *udumbara* tree, used by the *Prastotṛ* in marking the several turns (*paryāya*), the number of verses and the order of a *stoma*, by placing them over a piece of cloth which is spread in the middle of the chanters. The k° are laid in the first *viṣṭuti* of the *pañcadaśastoma* (*mādhyandina pavamānastotra*) thus :

1st *viṣṭuti*	1st *paryāya*	2nd p°	3rd p°
3rd *ṛk*	—	—	≡
2nd *ṛk*	I	III	I
1st *ṛk*	≡	—	—
2nd *viṣṭuti*			
3rd *ṛk*	—	—	≡
2nd *ṛk*	I	I	I
1st *ṛk*	≡	—	—
3rd *viṣṭuti*			
3rd *ṛk*	—	—	≡
2nd *ṛk*	I	III	I
1st *ṛk*	—	—	≡

Chinna 92; for further varieties see 93-95; cf. PBr. II.4, C.H. 195, Eggeling SBE XXVI, 309. see also *pañcadaśastoma*, *pañcapañcinī*.

कूर्च *Kūrca* m. a bundle of grass used as a seat K. Śr. IV.13.14 (sort of a cushion, comm); it also means a seat with legs (embroidered in gold) on which the sacrificer and the *Adhvaryu* sit XX.2.19 comm (*Aśva*).

कृत्त्यधीवास *Kṛttyadhīvāsa* m. covering of skin, placed over the *āsandī* Āp. Śr. XVIII.18.6 (*Rāja*) (cf. *adhīvāsa*); laid on the spot where the horse is immolated XX. 17.8; also a sacrificial fee Bh. Śr. XIII.8.16 (*Soma*).

कृष्णाजिन *Kṛṣṇājina* n. skin of a black antelope which is spread by the *Adhvaryu* either on the sacrificer's seat or on the *vedi* at the *dīkṣā*; the sacrificer sits on it for the duration of the *dīkṣā*. Two pieces of hide, one over the other, are mentioned, the polished side being on the outside Āp. Śr. X.8.11. Also a sacred covering, spread on the ground I.7.5.

केशवपनीय *Keśavapanīya* m. hair-cutting ceremony (of the king), a *soma* ritual of the *Atirātra* type with the number of verses of the *stotras* decreasing at each *savana* : 21 at morning, 17 at the midday, 15 at the third and 9 at dawn (*Rāja*) B. Śr. XII.20, Āp. Śr. XVIII.22.9-11, Eggeling SBE XLI,126-7. cf. Heesterman 212-9.

keśavāpa m. hair-dresser Āp. Śr. XVIII.15.6.

केशश्मश्रु (वपन) *Keśaśmaśru* (*vapana*) n. rite of shaving hair on head and face of the sacrificer, and the wife pairs the nails, takes bath K. Śr. II.1.9 (*Darśa*), Āp. Śr. IV.1.4 K. Śr. IV.7. 11 (*Ādheya*), (=*apsu dīkṣā*) VII. 2.7. (*Soma*). Cf. C.H. 14.

क्रतुकरण *Kratukaraṇa* n. performance of a *Soma* (*kratu*, a sacrifice) rite Āp. Śr. XII.6.5; XIV. 1.5.

क्रतुपशु *Kratupaśu* m. another name of the *savanīyapaśu*, animal sacrifice, one of the 4 basic features of *Soma* Āp. Śr. XIV.1.5, with certain modifications XII.18.13. This is the 2nd and one of the three animal sacrifices associated with the *Soma* sacrifice apart from the *agnīṣomīya* and *anubandhyā* animal sacrifices. Cf. C.H. 125, 186, 283, 344; there can be 4 victims (called k° Āśv. Sr. V.3.4); also called *stomāyana* K. Śr. IX. 8.7.

क्रुष्ट *Kruṣṭa* mfn. name of the most raised tone (=*uttama*) in the series of the musical tones Puṣpa 523.

क्लोमन् *Kloman* m. n. gland in the right throat K. Śr. VI. 7.11 comm; right lung H. Dh. II (2), 1126; pancreas Kashikar Bh. Śr. II. 186 on VII. 19.11 (*Paśu*). See *jauhava*.

क्षीरहोतृ *Kṣīrahotṛ* m. a priest who offers milk oblation; at the *Agnihotra*, he takes up the *upaveṣa* and recites *mantra* over the *gārhapatya* Bh. Śr. VI.7.3, K. Śr. IV.14.31. Variously explained in Āp. Śr. VI.15.16 comm: one who gets the cow milked for the first *Agnihotra* or receives as remuneration a quantity of milk remaining after the offering, or gets any kind of wealth. He acts on the instructions of the sacrificer.

क्षुल्लकाभिषवण *Kṣullakābhiṣavaṇa* n. little pressing of *soma* stalks. See *upāṁśugraha*.

क्षौम *Kṣauma* n. linen garment, with two or three folds, spread over a skin, and *soma* is measured over it by the *Adhvaryu* with his hands at the time of purchasing it Bh. Śr. X.16.6.

ख Kha

खनि *Khani* f. a spot from where loose earth is brought and used for the preparation of a *vedi* at the preliminary measurements Āp. Śr. II.2.3, B. Śr. XXII.1.

खर *Khara* mfn., m. "rough"; a small square mound, made of earth, covered with sand, used as a table for keeping the (*soma*) cups Āp. Śr. XI.13.8, K. Śr. VIII.5.29; it is raised in front of the *havirdhāna* cart in the *havirdhāna maṇḍapa* with the earth drawn from the *uparavas* Āp. Śr. l.c. Two other kh° made of sand are raised within the *prācīnavaṁśa* for the *pravargya*; circular in shape, 1 span in size : one to the north of the *gārhapatya* called *pravṛñjanīya* on which the *mahāvīra* is placed, the other to the north of the *āhavanīya* called *udvāsanīya* B. Śr. IX. 5, Āp. Śr. XV. 6.20-21. *Ucchiṣṭakhara*, also called *adhinirṇejanīya*, having an outlet to the north is built in the north east; it is used as a storeroom for the "residues" where the utensils smeared with the sacrificial residues (*ucchiṣṭa*) are cleaned ib. 22. There are 2 kh° at the *Vāja* ŚBr. V.1.2.15, at the *Sautrāmaṇī* K. Śr. XIX. 2.3. By extension it designates the *dhiṣṇya*, and in general all the hearths. See plan 3.

खारीण्ड्व *Khārīṇḍva* n. basket with coverings (?) B.Pi. : Śr. K (S) I. 805. Cf. *mva*.‹ Gṛhya)

ग Ga

गण *Gaṇa* m. a group of *mantras*, *e.g.* the 7 groups accompanying the oblation of cakes to the Maruts Āp. Śr. XVII.16.16 (*Cayana*); other groups are: *araṇye 'nuvākya* and *grāme' nuvākya*.

गतश्री *Gataśrī* mfn. one (a sacrificer) who has acquired glory or wealth K. Śr. IV.13.5 comm; ŚBr. I.3.5.12. The following 3 are g° : a victorious kṣatriya king, a learned brahmin and a vaiśya who is a leading figure of his village K. Śr. ib comm. They are to perpetually maintain the three sacred fires Āp. Śr. VI. 2.12. Cf. H.Dh. II (2), 999.

गति *Gati* f. protraction of a syllable of the *stobha* by inserting *i* or *u*, *e.g. hoyi* or *ho-i* for *ho*; protraction of *i* or *u* in *āyi* and *āu* Puṣpa 520.

गधा *Gadhā* f. roof (*chadis*) of a cart (*anas*) Āp. Śr. XIX. 26. 2; the cart is called *trigadha*; *trigadham anasam* B. Śr. XIII. 37 (*Kārīriṣṭi*).

गर्दभेज्या *Gardabhejyā* f. ass sacrifice in which an ass is sacrificed on crossroads to Nirṛti, to be performed by an *avakīrṇin* (q v.) as an expiation K. Śr.I.1.13. It is also a domestic rite PGṛ III.12. Offerings are made on the common household fire (*laukikāgni*), *paśupuroḍāśa* is cooked on the ground and not on the *kapālas*, *avadāna* portions are offered into water. The *avakīrṇin* puts on the skin of the ass, goes about for alms proclaiming his deeds PGṛ. III.12. 2-9, K. Śr. I.1.13-17, TĀr. II. 18, H. Dh. IV, 112.

गर्हण *Garhaṇa* n. a rite in which the chief queen abuses the dead horse with whom she lies and dramatically attempts sexual copulation. All other queens and their retinues and the priests enter into an obscene dialogue Āp. Śr. XX.18.4, Āśv. Śr. X.8.10-13 (*Aśva*). Cf. ŚBr. XIII.5.2.2-9.

गवामयन *Gavāmayana* n. "going (course) of the cows (ray of the sun); a *sāṁvatsarika sattra* lasting 361 days (12 months of 30 days). It consists of 3 sections : the first and the third taking each 180 days and the central (*viṣuvat*) one day. The paradigm is as follows

A. The first section	**Total 180 days**
1 *Prāyaṇīya Atirātra* day (opening)	1
1 *Caturviṁśa* day, an *Ukthya*	1
5 months, each consisting of	
4 *Abhiplavaṣaḍaha* (6 days) 4×6= 24	
1 *Pṛṣṭhyaṣaḍaha* (6 days) 1×6= 6	
30×5	150
3 *Abhiplava* 3 x 6	18
1 *Pṛṣṭhya* 1 x 6	6
1 *Abhijit* (*Agniṣṭoma*) day	1
3 *Svarasāman* days	3

B. The central (*viṣuvat*) day	**1 day**

C. The third section	**Total 180 days**
The order of the A is reversed	
3 *Svarasāman* days	3
1 *Viśvajit* day	1
1 *Pṛṣṭhya* (6 days) 1×6	6
3 *Abhiplava* (6 days) 3×6	18
four months : 30×4, each consisting of	120
1 *Pṛṣṭhya* (6 days) 1×6=6 } 30	
4 *Abhiplava* (6 days) 4×6=24 }	
3 *Abhiplava* (6 days) 3×6=18	18
1 *Goṣṭoma* (*Agniṣṭoma*)	1
1 *Ayuṣṭoma* (*Ukthya*)	1
1 *Daśarātra* (10 days)	10
1 *Mahāvrata* (*Agniṣṭoma*)	1
1 *Udayanīya Atirātra*	1

Āp. Śr. XXI.15-22, B. Śr. XVI.13-23., Eggeling SBE XXVI, 427.

गवीधुक *Gavīdhuka* (*ā*) m. (f) wild grain grown in the rainy season (Coix barbata), resembling coarse barley, much liked by the cattle (whence the name); its flour is used as a soft polishing material for the *gharma* Āp. Śr. XV. 3.16. cf. V.S. Agrawala's observations Bh. Śr. II, 317.

गाथा *Gāthā* f. legends interspersed with the stanzas of RV. in the recital of the Śunaḥśepa legend (Keith RV.Br. 299-309) Āp. Śr. XVIII. 19.10 (*Rāja*); recited by the *Hotṛ*, and the *Adhvaryu*'s response (*pratigara*) after a g° is *tathā*, and *om* after a RV. stanza ib. 13.Cf. Heesterman 158, H.Dh. II (2), 1218.

nārāśaṁsī° f. epic songs, particularly heroic legends Eggeling SBE XLIV, 98.

गार्हपत्य *Gārhapatya* mfn., m. (belonging to the *gṛhapati*, the master of the house) one of the 3 sacred fires, the "domestic", used in the vedic sacrifice; it is kindled at first by the sacrificer by rubbing *araṇis* previously warmed over the household fire; situated in the shed (*śālā*) to the west of the arena, round in shape, 1 square *aratni* in area; used for warming the *havis* and the utensils, circumambulation, and also for (alternatively) cooking the *havis* K. Śr. I.8.34-35 & comm; logs are kindled in it to install fire in the other hearths; it is to be permanently preserved Āp. Śr. VI.2.13. This fire is also called *prājahita* (abandoned) Mī. XII.1.13. In *Paśu* the hearth of the *uttaravedi* is kindled with fire taken out from the *āhavanyīa*, and the hearth of the *uttaravedi* is now called the *āhavanīya*, the first *āhavanīya* functions as g° Āp. Śr. VII.7.3. Similarly, in the *Soma* after the transfer of fire to the *āhavanīya* of *uttaravedi*, the old *āhavanīya* is called g° or *śālāmukhīya*, *śālādvārya*, for the old *āhavanīya* replaces the old g° XI.5.10, C.H. 78; Eggeling SBE XLIII, 308 (*Cayana*). See plan 3-6. For measurements Āp Śulb. II.4.6-8.

गृहपति *Gṛhapati* m. "householder"; it stands for the *yajamāna* in the *praiṣa* of the *Adhvaryu* Āp. Śr. XII.27.6; at the *sattra* a sacrificer is called g° XXI.2.1; *mukhya* (Ś. Śr. XIII.14.4) or the chief participant.

गृहमेधीय *Gṛhamedhīya* mfn. an offering to the Maruts who are called *gṛhamedhin*; a caru boiled in milk is offered in the evening at the *Sākamedha* Āp. Śr. VIII.9.8-9.

गोसव *Gosava* m. name of an *ekāha* of *Ukthya* type in which the performers are required "to behave like cows" (*paśuvrata*) for one year Āp. Śr. XXII.12.19 (TBr II. 7.6, PBr. XIX. 13); this is of special interest as the rite involves incest with one's own mother, sister and a woman of one's own *gotra*; perhaps a record of primitive promiscuity. Cf Jaim. Br. II. 113, Āp. Śr. XXII. 13.1-3, Keith RPV 338. cf. ritual promiscuity among the Australian tribes SG NTCA 92-111.

ग्रह *Graha* m. drawing of liquid, specially of *soma* for libation; said also of the relating rite and the cups (*camasa*); also designates a libation Āp. Śr. XII.7.10. It is an elaborate ritual of pouring and decanting *soma* juice. In the *Agniṣṭoma*, which is the standard form of all Soma sacrifices, there are the following g° : in the morning (*prātaḥsavana*) *upāṁśu*° (which is of a special type), *antaryāma*°, *dvidevatya*° (and other similar to it), *aindravāyava*°, *maitrāvaruṇa*°, *āśvina*°, *śukra*°, *manthin*°, *āgrayaṇa*°, *ukthya*°, *dhruva*° 12 *ṛtu*°, *aindrāgna*°, *vaiśvadeva*°; at midday (*mādhyandina*) : *śukra*°, *manthin*°, *āgrayaṇa*°, 3 *marutvatīya*°, *ukthya*°; in the third (*tṛtīya*) : 2 *āditya*°, *mahāvaiśvadeva*°, *pātnīvata*°, *dhruva*°; finally at the end, *hāriyojana*. Apart from the *upāṁśu* the 8 main drawings are done in the following manner : the *Unnetṛ* draws *soma* juice with the *udacana* ladle or *camasa* from the *ādhavanīya* and decants it in a continuous flow (*dhārā*) into the *camasa* of the *Hotṛ* which already contains the *nigrābhya* water; then from the *Hotṛ*'s cup the sacrificer decants the liquid into the *droṇakalaśa* over which the *Udgātṛ* and his assistants hold a strainer (*pavitra*); finally, the *Adhvaryu* draws *soma* juice from the *droṇakalaśa* into his cup (*antaryāma*) covered with a *pavitra* Āp. Śr. XII.13.1-13, C.H. 160-8; similarly all other cups are filled. This is called *dhārāgraha*, in contradistinction to *adhārā*° which follows, and is drawn directly from the *droṇakalaśa* with the *pariplavā*. Every g° has its own cup C.H. 136. Some libations, *e.g. aindrāgna*, *vaiśvadeva* etc. are preceded by the recitation of a *śastra* (*saśastragraha*) K. Śr. IX.13.33-34. The *soma* juice remaining in the *droṇakalaśa* is called *śukra*, and juice remaining in the strainer is squeezed into it IX.5.15-25. In the *Vāja* there are 17 *soma* and *surāgrahas* I.3.36 comm. The drawing of curds is called *dadhi*° Āp. Śr. XII.7.5, C.H. 14.

ग्रावन् *Grāvan* m. pressing-stone for *soma* stalks, originally 2, RV. II. 39.1, later 4 Śāṅ Br. XXIX. I or 5 g° are mentioned ŚBr. III.5-4. 24 comm; actually, 4 g° and 1 *upāṁśusavana* K. Śr. VIII.5.28, Vai Śr. XI.9; according to some there are 5 g° in addition to the *upāṁśu* M. Śr. II.3.1.21. At the little pressing (*kṣullakābhiṣavaṇa*) the *Adhvaryu* strikes the *soma* stalks with the *upāṁśu* only Āp. Śr. XII. 10.2, B. Śr. VII.5. C.H. 153. At the great pressing (*mahābhiṣavaṇa*) 4 priests sitting round the *adhiṣavaṇacarman* beat the stalks with their stones, and sprinkle water over them K. Śr. IX.5.1, C.H. 158; they are sharp-edged, 1 *aratni* each K. Śr. I.3.36 comm.

ग्रावस्तुत् *Grāvastut* m. praiser of stone (*grāvan*); a priest who is an assistant to the *Hotṛ*. He recites the *grāvastotra* (Āśv. Śr. V. 12.9-25) or the *grāvastotrīyā* Āp. Śr. XIII. 1. 6, C.H. 269 during the midday pressing. He appears on the scene at that time, enters the *havirdhāna-maṇḍapa*, receives a turban from the *Adhvaryu*, puts it on his head, and starts the recitation without any summons (Āp. Śr. XIII. 1.6). This is a deviation from the general procedure of recitation. Cf. C.H. 268. He takes his share in *soma* drinks Mī. III. 5.27.

घ Gha

घर्म *Gharma* m. hot milk of a cow or a she-goat (mixed with boiling *ājya*), contained in the *mahāvīra*, used as offering to the Aśvins, Vāyu etc., and the remainder, consumed by the sacrificer and some of the priests : *Hotṛ*, *Adhvaryu*, *Brahman*, *Pratiprasthātṛ* and *Āgnīdhra* taken in the *upayamanī* Āp. Śr. XV. 11.10-13 at the *pravargya* (*Soma*). Cf C.H. XVI n. 2. *dadhi*° : The word is also used in the sense of *pravargya*. The container (*mahāvīra*) is also designated by it; see also *mahāvīra*.

°*duh* mfn. a cow whose milk is used as gh° Āp.Śr. XV.9.3 (=*dughā* B. Śr. IX.5).

घृत *Ghṛta* n. clarified butter. Cf. *ājya*.

च Ca

चण्डातक *Caṇḍātaka* n. a piece of cotton cloth with new and unwashed skirt, used for polishing the *gharma* vessel Āp. Sr. XV.3.16. Cf. comments of V.S. Agrawala. quoted in Bh. Śr. II, 317. See also *gharma*, *mahāvīra*.

चतुरवत्त *Caturavatta* n. "divided into four". The 4 parts (cf. *avadāna*) or operations involved in offering (specially) of a cake (*puroḍāśa*). The operations are : first, *upastaraṇa* of *ājya* on the *sruc*, cutting up of 2 slices of the *puroḍāśa*, finally *abhighāraṇa* over the cut up portions (whence the term). *Caturavattin* mfn. a follower of the above practice Āp. Śr. II.18. 9. Cf. ŚBr. I. 6.1.21. Also said of taking *ājya* 4 times by the *sruva* into the *juhū* Āp. Śr. ib.1 (*Darśa*).

The procedure differs in *pañcāvatta* which involves 5 operations : cutting up of 3 slices of the *puroḍāśa*, besides *upastaraṇa* and *abhighāraṇa*. The family of Jamadagnis follow this practice, and they are called *pañcāvattin*s Āp. Śr. II.18.2, K. Śr. I.9.3 & comm. In *Paśu* 5 simillar operations with the omentum of a victim take place even if one is a *caturavattin* Āp. Śr. VII. 20.10, Mī X. 7.72. Five drawings of milk and other liquid Āp. Śr. VI.8.2.

In *ṣaḍavatta* 6 operations are involved : *upastaraṇa* on the *Āgnīdhra*'s hand or in a bowl, cutting up of 2 slices, again *upastaraṇa* for one slice, finally 2 *abhighāraṇa*s on the second slice Āp. Śr. III.3.6; or alternatively 2 *upastaraṇa*s, 2 slices and 2 *abhighāraṇa*s ib 7. It is performed by the *Āgnīdhra* ib 5. But in the *Piṇḍapitṛyajña* a *pañcāvattin* follows the *ṣaḍavatta* and a *caturavattin* the *pañcāvatta* procedures Āp. Śr. VIII.15.5, Bh. Śr. VIII. 19.3 (*Cātur*). A *ṣaṭpātra* is a bowl, with 2 depressions, of *varaṇa* wood K. Śr. I.3.36 comm.

चतुरश्र *Caturaśra* mfn. four-cornered; a square mound, said of the *khara* K. Śr. VIII.5.29.

चतुर्होतृ *Caturhotṛ* m. name of a particular *mantra* mentioned in TĀr., recited in a rite Āp. Śr. IV.8.7 (*Darśa*); so called from the mention of four priests : *Āgnīdhra*, *Adhvaryu*, *Hotṛ* and *Upavaktṛ* in the *mantra*. Cf. Eggeling SBE XXVI, 452. Similar other *mantra*s are *pañca*°, *ṣaḍ*°, *sapta*°, *daśa*°. *Daśahotṛ*, the *mantra* of 10 *Hotṛ*s, a mystical *mantra* which identifies 10 objects connected with the human body with 10 objects of *homa*, used at the *Ādheya* Āp. V.10.8, at the *Agnihotra* VI.8.5; it is pronounced by the *Hotṛ* before the *sāmidhenī* IV.9.1. All these *mantra*s occur in TĀr.III. 1-10 quoted in Śr.K (S) I, 125.

चतुष्पथ *Catuṣpatha* m. n. a place where 4 roads meet; crossroads where an oblation is offered to Rudra Bh. Śr. VIII. 22.7 (*Mahāpitṛyajña*, *Cātur*). See also *sviṣṭakṛt*.

चनसित *Canasita* (√*can*, cl.ɔ "to be pleased") mfn. 'satisfied or gratified" (in vocative) the word is used by an initiated sacrificer in addressing a brahmin, after mentioning his name as: O *Devadatta, canasita* Āp. Śr. X. 12.8 (*Soma*). Similarly, a rājanya and a vaiśya are to be addressed with the word *vicakṣaṇa* (*vi*-√*cakṣ*, cl 2 "to see distinctly").

चमस *Camasa* m. a kind of cup (RV.IV.35.2. etc.) or ladle, with or without a handle (*tsarumat* or *atsaruka*), made of *nyagrodha* wood (Ficus Indica) Āp. Śr. XII.2.8; square in shape; the shape of the handle, which distinguishes one from the other, may be round or square or triangular depending on the owner of c° C.H. 108. Cf. K. Śr. I.3 36 comm. They are used as a dish for the meal of vow by the sacrificer in the *dīkṣā*; for containing *soma* for libation, and as a cup for drinking *soma* by the priests; also for containing the *praṇītāḥ* waters. There are 10 c° which belong to 10 *camasins*: *Hotṛ*, *Brahman*, *Udgātṛ*, *Maitrāvaruṇa*, *Brāhmaṇācchaṁsin*, *Potṛ*, *Neṣṭṛ*, *Acchāvāka*, *Āgnīdhra* and sacrificer who only are entitled to own a *camasa* B. Śr. II 3; optionally, a 11th is allotted to the *Sadasya* priest. These c° are carried and handled by 10 (or 11 B. II.3) assistants called *camasādhvaryus*, chosen and appointed by the *ṛtviks* Mī. III. 7.26-27, Āp. Śr. XII. 2.9 (or by the sacrificer himself Bh. Śr. X.2.1), but they are not priests. They perform the *prasthitahoma* C.H. 208. It is to be noted that the *Grāvastut* is not recognized as a *camasin* since he drinks *soma* from the c° of the *Hotṛ*.

°*camasīya* mfn. relating to the c° of the priests B. Śr. VII.5.

°*kampana* n. rite of shaking the cups (*camasa*) now called *nārāśaṁsa*, after the *śastra* has been recited and libation of *soma* offered, done by the *camasādhvaryus* K. Śr. IX.13.35 = *anukampana* (q.v.).

चमसोन्नयन *Camasonnayana* n. rite of filling in the *camasas* (*ud*-√*nī*, cl 1 "to lead up"). The filling in operation, performed by the *Unnetṛ*, involves 3 acts: first, *upastaraṇa*, pouring some *soma* into each c° from the *droṇakalaśa* (the content is called *śukra*, pure), then *soma* is poured from the *pūtabhṛt* bucket, finally *abhighāraṇa* again from the *droṇakalaśa*. In this way the c° are filled beginning with the *Hotṛ*'s, then of *Brahman*, *Udgātṛ*, sacrificer, *Maitrāvaruṇa*, *Brāhmaṇācchaṁsin*, *Potṛ*, *Neṣṭṛ*, *Āgnīdhra* B. Śr. VII.13, Āp. Śr. XII. 21.13-16, C.H. 204.

चयन *Cayana* n. See *Agni*°.

चरु *Caru* m. porridge prepared from unpounded rice or barley grains, cooked in water with butter or milk mixed with it, (and served in a *sthālī* called *carusthālī* Vai. Śr. XI.9) B. Śr. II.19; differentiated from a *puroḍāśa* (cake), and is substituted for a *puroḍāśa* in the modified rite (*vikṛti*) Bh. Śr. VI.15.7; used as oblation, and consumed by 4 priests B. Śr. l.c. (*Ādheya*). *Saumya*° at the *Soma* offered at the 3rd pressing to Soma, cooked by the *Pratiprasthātṛ*, and it is required to be looked at (*avekṣaṇa*) by the *Hotṛ* B. Śr. VIII. 14, C.H. 362-4. The *pañcabila*°, offered in a dish called *pañcabila* on account of 5 cavities in it K. Śr. XV.9.1 (*Rāja*), Eggeling SBE XLI, 120; Āp. Śr. XX. 25.2 (*Puruṣamedha*).

Pañcabila is also the name of oblations.

चषाल *Caṣāla* m. n. a wooden head-piece of the *yūpa*, made from the top portion of the same log of wood from which the latter is made. It is 8 cornered, contracted in the middle, made hollow, as long as one's hand from the wrist to the tip of the fingers. It is fitted on the top of the y° like a turban in such a manner that 2 or 3 *aṅgulas* of the y° protrudes above the c° K. Śr. VI.1.28-30 (*Paśu*).

चातुर्मास्य *Cāturmāsya* n. four-monthly sacrifices, of the *iṣṭi* type, consisting of 3 (or rather 4) *parvans* (part or joint), each taking place after 4 months (whence the name) K. Śr. V.I.1 comm. The *parvans*: *Vaiśvadeva*, *Varuṇapraghāsa*, *Sākamedha* (and *Śunāsīrīya*) are performed, each marking the advent of a particular season, on the fullmoon days of *phālguna* or *caitra* (*vasanta*: spring), of *āṣāḍha* (*varṣā*: rains), *kārttika* or *mārgaśīrṣa* (*hemanta*: autumn) and *Śunāsīrīya* on the 5th fullmoon from the day on which *Sākamedha* is performed (*phālguna*) respectively. Cf. K. Śr. V.11.1-2 & comm. There are five offerings common to all the *parvans*: a *puroḍāśa* on 8 *kapālas* to Agni, a *caru* to Soma, a *puroḍāśa* on 12 or 8 *kapālas* to Savitṛ, a *caru* to Sarasvatī, a *caru* of fine powdered rice to Pūṣan.

वैश्वदेव *Vaiśvadeva* n. the first *parvan*, "relating to all gods", consists of 2 days, and is the model of all other *parvans* Āp. Śr. XXIV. 3.37. On the *upavasatha* day (the first day), an oblation with the *pañcahotṛ* formula, a cake on 2 *kapālas* to *vaiśvānara* Agni, and *caru* to Parjanya are offered as an introductory rite.

The sacrificial grass is bundled. The *darbha* grass with flowers is used as *prastara*. The sacrificial fuel sticks are bundled up, and in the afternoon milk is warmed and curdled (*sāṁnāyya*).

Next morning, after the morning *Agnihotra*, the *Adhvaryu* makes 3 offerings, besides 5 usual offerings, a cake on 7 *kapālas* to Marut *svatavas* (self-strong), *āmikṣā* to the Viśve Devas, and a cake on one *kapāla* to Dyāvāpṛthivī. The *vājina* is decanted from the *āmikṣā*, and the two kept separately. A new fire is churned and mixed with the *āhavanīya*, fuel sticks are added into the fires. The offerings follow. There are 9 *prayājas* and *anuyājas*. An offering of the *vājina* is made to the deities called *Vājins*. The remainder of the *vājina* is treated like the *iḍā* : the vessel containing the *vājina* is held by the *Hotṛ* in his left hand, and on his right hand the *ājya* is sprinkled by the *Adhvaryu*, then 2 portions of v° are poured out on it and again some *ājya* is spread over it. The *upahava* is recited by the *Adhvaryu*, the *Brahman* and the *Āgnīdhra*, and the *vājina* is "consumed" by "smelling" by the *Hotṛ* and the other three. The sacrificer should actually consume it. On the conclusion of the rite the sacrificer may shave himself K. Śr. V.2.13. Āp. Śr. VIII. 1-4.

वरुणप्रघास *Varuṇapraghāsa* m. the word is used in masc. pl., fancifully derived as the rite in which Varuṇa eats (√*ghas*, cl 1 "to eat") *yavas* (barley grains) which belong to him (ŚBr. II. 5.2.1). There is an additional (5th) priest : *Pratiprasthātṛ*, besides the 4 others. The sacrificial procedure is almost similar to that of the Vaiśvadeva *parvan*. But there are two altars to the east of *āhavanīya* (*gārhapatya*) one to the north, assigned to the *Adhvaryu*, the other to the south assigned to the *Pratiprasthātṛ* Āp. Śr. VIII.5.4-5. See plan 6. Two *āhavanīyas* (new) are prepared on the two *uttaravedis*. The *Pratiprasthātṛ* performs the same tasks that the *Adhvaryu* does except certain functions K. Śr. V.4.33. A space of 2,3 or 4 *aṅgulas* or more separates the 2 *vedis* at the corner Āp. Śr. VIII.5.10. There is one *utkara*. Offering materials are mainly *yava* (barley), but rice is also used Āp. Śr. VIII. 5. 36-37. Figurines of a ram and a ewe are made (cf. *karambha*) by the *Adhvaryu* and the *Pratiprasthātṛ* respectively from barley flour. The milk for *sāṁnāyya* and *āmikṣā* for the Maruts and Varuṇa are arranged. Besides the 5 usual offerings, 4 more are offered : to Indra and Agni, the Maruts, Varuṇa and Ka (Prajāpati). The *Pratiprasthātṛ* puts the *āmikṣā* in a goblet, and places the figure of ewe upon it. He also places the leaves of *śamī*, flour of roasted *karīra* fruit and *āmikṣā* by the side of the figure. The *Adhvaryu* does the same with the figure of ram. Then the *Pratiprasthātṛ* brings the sacrificer's wife in the fire hall, asks her of her lovers (*jāra*). She should declare his name. The *Adhvaryu* and the *Pratiprasthātṛ* go through the rites : *prayājas*, *anuyājas*, *ājyabhāgas*, *sviṣṭakṛt* etc.

The *karambha* dishes are placed on a *śūrpa* and poured over the *dakṣiṇāgni* by the sacrificer and his wife Āp. Śr. VIII. 6.23. The *Pratiprasthātṛ* cuts off a portion of the *āmikṣā* together with the whole of the figure of the ewe and offers them into fire, the *Adhvaryu* does the same thing with the figure of the ram. The *viṣṇukrama* is done. The rite concludes with the bath (*avabhṛtha*) B. Śr. V. 5-6, Āp. Śr. VIII. 5-9, K. Śr. V.3-5, Āśv. Śr. II.17.

साकमेध (*Sākamedha*)m. the third *parvan* of the *Cātur*. The word is used in pl. and means, literally, kindling along at the same time. Two days are required. On the preliminary day three *iṣṭis* are performed at the 3 *savanas* : morning, midday and evening to the 3 deities respectively : to Agni *anīkavat* a cake on 8 *kapālas*, to *sāntapana* Maruts a *caru*, to *gṛhamedhin* Maruts a *caru* boiled in milk of all cows belonging to the sacrificer Āp. Śr. VIII. 9.8. The priests and sons and grandsons of the sacrificer may eat that *caru* Āp. Śr. VIII. 10.8; 11.8-10, K. Śr. V.6.29-30.

On the principal day a *homa* is performed with a *darvī*, scraping out the remainder of the cooked rice (of the previous day). A bull is brought and made to bellow. An *iṣṭi* to *krīḍin* Maruts is performed with a cake on 7 *kapālas* and a *caru* to Aditi.

The *mahāhavis* (great offerings) are 8 (including the common 5 offerings) : a cake on 12 *kapāla*s to Indra and Agni, *caru* to Mahendra, and a cake on 1 *kapāla* to Viśvakarman.

Then follows the *Mahāpitṛyajña* dedicated to *pitṛmat* Soma, *barhiṣad Pitṛ*s and *agniṣvātta Pitṛ*s. A *paitṛka* altar, square in shape, is traced out by the *Adhvaryu* towards the south or southeast, and the *dakṣiṇa* fire is set in its middle. The rice-cake for Soma, barley for the *Pitṛ*s and various other things: curtain, mattress, pillow etc. are arranged. The *Adhvaryu* makes the principal offerings. After the invocation of *iḍā*, the officiating priests should partake of the *mantha* by smelling it. The portions of paddy and the cake are mixed to make 3 *piṇḍa*s, and these balls are placed one each at the three corners of the *paitṛka* altar for the sacrificer's father, grandfather and great grandfather. The rite now follows the pattern of the *Piṇḍapitṛyajña*. The curtain with an opening to the north, which was hung round the altar, is now removed. The last part of the S° is the *traiyambakahoma*, Āp. Śr. VIII.17-19, B. Śr. V.16-17, K. Śr. V. 10, offered to Rudra. The *Pratiprasthātṛ* or the *Adhvaryu* bakes cakes on one *kapāla* each, the number of such cakes exceeding by one the number of the children of the sacrificer (his sons and grandsons together with their wives and unmarried daughters). All places where offerings are made must be to the north. The cakes which are not sprinkled with butter are cooked on the northern side of the *gārhapatya*. The sacrificer, his wife and the members of his family, taking along with them cakes, blue and red threads, a firebrand, a *palāśa* leaf, a pot of water, proceed towards the northeast and come to a place where four roads meet (*catuṣpatha*). A fire is kindled; portions cut out from the cakes are put on the *palāśa* leaf, and offered on the fire. The remainder of the cakes and the *palāśa* leaf is thrown into a rat hole. Returning from that place, the sacrificer, his children and the ladies go round the fire thrice from right to left with the *mantra*: "*tryambakaṁ yajāmahe*", striking their left thighs with their right hands. The unmarried daughter of the sacrificer, desirous of a husband, go round the fire from right to left and again left to right, thrice in each direction with the same *mantra* but with necessary alterations in her case. The sacrificer throws up the remaining cakes and tries to catch them. Then finally they are placed in two baskets and fastened on the two sides of a tree trunk in such a way that a cow or bull cannot reach them. B. Śr. V. 10-17, K. Śr. V.6-10, Āp. Śr. VIII. 9-19, Āśv. Śr. II.18-19.

शुनासीरीय *Śunāsīrīya* n. "belonging to Sunā-Sīra"; the *iṣṭi* rite belongs to the *Cāturmāsya*. Śunāsīrau, occurs in the RV. IV. 57.5, 8. According to WR. *sīra* means plough, and *śunā* growth making; therefore it means guide of plough; plough and furrow VR. I (¶ 123),125. Cf. VI. But Yāska, Nirukta IX. 40 : Vāyu and Āditya. Special offerings are a cake on 12 *kapāla*s to Śunāsīrau, to Vāyu and Āditya, according to K. Śr. V. 11.5 comm, and to Indra Śunāsīra, according to Āp. Śr. VIII. 20.5 comm, an oblation of fresh warm milk direct from the cow to Vāyu, a cake on one *kapāla* to Sūrya. There is no *uttaravedi* nor the fire is produced by churning. There are 5 *prayāja*s, 3 *anuyāja*s, or 9 each Āp. Śr. VIII. 20.6. B. Śr. V,18, K. Śr. V.11, Āp. VIII.20, Āśv. Śr. II. 20.

For details on the *Cāturmāsya* H. Dh. II, 2, 1091-1106, ŚrK (E) I (2), 646-769. B. Śr. V, K. Śr. V, Āp. Śr. VIII, Āśv. Śr. II. 15-20.

चात्वाल *Cātvāla* m. n. a pit, measuring one *śamyā* square, dug up outside the *vedi* near its north-eastern "shoulder" (*aṁsa*); the place from where loose earth (*purīṣa*) is drawn for constructing the *dhiṣṇya*s K. Śr. I.8.39, the *uttaravedi* at *Soma* and *Paśu* Āśv. Śr I.1.6 comm, Āp. Śr. VII.4.1-2, the sacrificial ground at *Cayana* XVI.15.1 Plan 3, 5 & 6.

चिति *Citi* f. piling of bricks, specially for the altar at *Cayana* Āp. Śr. XVI.35.8; made of 5 layers (*pañcacitīka* 15.3); the layers consist of a certain number of bricks (Eggeling SBE XLIII, 22) bearing special names: *svayamātṛṇṇā, lokampṛṇā, yajuṣmatī, aṣāḍhā* etc; each layer is separated by earth, set apart and taken from the *cātvāla*. The form of the altar varies: *droṇa* (bucket), wheel, *śyena* (falcon) etc. K. Śr. XVI.5.9; diagrams Eggeling ib. 17, 24, 48, 71, 98. Cf. *Agnicayana*.

punaś°, re-establishment of the altar Āp. Śr. XVII. 24.11. *loṣṭa*° or *śmaśāna*°, erection of the lumps of earth at the funeral rite (*Antyeṣṭi*).

चुबुक *Cubuka* n. front part of a cart (the *havirdhāna*) for *soma* (=*mukha*), while it is standing and stationary Āp. Śr. X. 24.4. B. Śr. VIII. 11 (*tuṇḍa* comm).

छ Cha

छदिस *Chadis* n. a covering for the *havirdhāna* cart (RV. X.85.10) Āp. Śr. X. 24.2; thatched roof on the *havirdhānamaṇḍapa*, in 3 sections : center, north & south B. Śr. VI.25, C.H. 88; of the *sadas*, in 9 sections as above Āp. Śr. XI 10.8-12; but 9 at *Agniṣṭoma*, 16 at *Ṣoḍaśin*, 17 at *Vājapeya*, 21 at *sattra* and *ahīna* ib. 13, or 9 at *Agniṣṭoma*, 15 at *Ukthya*, 17 at *Atirātra* and 9 or 15 at *Ṣoḍaśin* Bh. Śr. XII.10.3.

छन्दोम *Chandoma* m. name of the 7th, 8th and 9th days of the *Daśarātra*, and the 8th, 9th, 10th days in case of the *Dvādaśāha*, distinguished by special form of *stoma*s Āp. Śr. XXII.18.8.

(युग) छिद्र *(Yuga) chidra* n. 2 holes on the yoke of a cart; the gap between 2 holes=86 fingers (comm.), the length of the north-south line on the eastern side of the *Paśu* altar Āp. Śr. VII.3.8. See also *akṣa*, *īṣā*, *vedi*.

ज Ja

जन्यभयापनोदन *Janyabhayāpanodana* n. a rite, performed in order to "drive out the danger which emanates from men", consists of kicking out a ball of earth or dirt with leg outside the *vedi* (at the beginning of the *Soma*) Āp. Śr. XI.7.2, C.H. 85.

जप *Japa* m. a *mantra*, which is muttered (*upāṁśu*) Āśv. Śr. I.1.20; may consist of "*bhūrbhuvaḥ svar o3 m*" preceded by '*him*' I. 2.3 (*vyāhṛtis*; on some occasions it is the duty of the sacrificer to do j° Āp. Śr. XIV.15.4.

tūṣṇīm°, silent or inaudible recitation, done by the *Hotṛ* at the beginning of the *ājya*° and other *śastra*s (q.v.) in *Soma* Āśv. Śr. V.9.1. C.H. 231.

purastāj°, muttered recitation of *mantra* done by the *Udgātṛ*s while the *Adhvaryu* hands over 2 blades of grass to the *Prastotṛ* as a rite of introduction (*upākaraṇa*) of the *bahiṣpavamānastotra* K. Śr. IX.6.36 & comm, C.H. 174; also at the time of chanting the *ājyastotra*s Āp. Śr. XII.28.6, C.H. 236.

śastvā °=*ukthavīrya* (q.v.)

जाघनी *Jāghanī* f. flesh from a victim's tail, offered instead of *ājya* at the *patnīsaṁyāja* K. Śr. VI.9.14 (*Paśu*).

जार *Jāra* m. paramour of the sacrificer's wife whose name and identity are to be declared by her when asked by the *Pratiprasthātṛ* (how many paramours you have ?) so that a disaster can be averted; and her disclosure causes the paramour to be held in the snare (*pāśa*) of Varuṇa. It is an interesting episode of the *Varuṇapraghāsa* Āp. Śr. VIII.6.20-22.

जुहू *Juhū* (√*hu*, cl. 3 "to sacrifice") f. an offering spoon (RV. I.145.3), one of the *sruca*s, made of *palāśa* wood K. Śr. I.3.34; having a cup-shaped bowl; it is held in the right hand over the *upabhṛt* Āp. Śr. II.13.3; all *ājya* offerings are to be done with a j° XXIV.1.25, and when no other implement is mentioned for *homa* j° is to be used K. Śr. I.8.45.

जुहोति *Juhoti* m. "he sacrifices"; technical name of those rites (*homa*s) in which *ājya* (*sarpis*) is the oblatory material, the *juhū* is the implement and the *Adhvaryu* is the performer Āp. Śr. XXIV 1.23-25, or, as distinguished from the *yajati* class (q.v.), j° designates *homa* performed in a sitting position by pronouncing *svāhā* K. Śr. I.2.7. Cf. Mn. II.84.

जौहव *Jauhava* mfn. limbs (of an animal) which are cut into and offered with a *juhū*, 9 in number, enumerated as : heart (*hṛdayam*), tongue (*jihvā*), breast ? (*kroḍa*), left thigh (*savya sakthi*), upper joint of the left forefoot (*pūrvanaḍaka*), two flanks (*pārśve*), liver (*yakṛt*, *yakan*), kidneys (*vṛkya*, *vṛkka*), rectum with anus (*guda*), right buttock (*śroṇi*). The limbs are cooked and offered to the *devatā*s K. Śr. VI.7.6, Āp. Śr. VII.22.6, B. Śr. IV.8. The identification of the limbs is not certain. Cf. H. Dh. II (2), 1126-1127. see also *āupabhṛta*.

Apart from these, *kloman* (a gland in the throat, right lung ?), *plīhan* (spleen), *purītat* (pericardium ?), *adhyuddhi* or *adhyūdhnī* (a tubular vessel above the udder or testes with penis ?), *vaniṣṭhu* (large intestines), *medas* (fat), *jāghanī* (tail) may be cut up optionally K. Śr. VI. 7.10-11. The victim's heart, held on a pointed spit (*śūla*, q.v.), is roasted on the *śāmitra* fire; all other limbs are cooked in an *ukhā* (pot). Butter is sprinkled, the middle and the front portions are drawn in a *juhū*, and offered to Indra and Agni and another portion to Agni *sviṣṭakṛt*. H. Dh. II(2), 1127.

ज्यैष्ठिनेय *Jyaiṣṭhineya* m. a son by the eldest wife of a sacrificer; entitled to get milk of the 2 fore udders of the *agnihotra* cow Bh. Śr. VI. 9.1. See also *kāniṣṭhineya*.

ज्योतिष्टोम *Jyotiṣṭoma* m. "praise of light"; name of an *ekāha* (*Soma*); its standard form is *Agniṣṭoma* (J° is often a synonym of *Agniṣṭoma*) Āp. Śr. X.2.1-2; for other varieties of *Soma*, See *saṁsthā*.

The *stomas* of J° are *trivṛt*, *pañcadaśa*, *saptadaśa* and *ekaviṁśa* which are called four lights (whence the name); treated in Bh. Śr. X-XV.

त Ta

तक्षन् *Takṣan* m. carpenter, who takes up his cutting implement (*takṣaṇaśastra*) and goes with the *Adhvaryu*, the *Brahman* and the sacrificer to procure the *yūpa* Bh. Śr. VII.1.3-4 (*Paśu*).

तण्डुल *Taṇḍula* m. grains, winnowed, husked and crushed in a mortar and pestle; its flour is used as oblation Bh. Śr. I.23.4-9 (*Darśa*).

तन्त्र *Tantra* n. "web" RV. X.71.9; essential features (*aṅga*), *e.g.*, *prayājas* etc. of a sacrifice, which are performed once but help foster the whole sacrifice and thus become its framework Āp. Śr. XIV.5.3 & comm. They are performed only once along with the main (*pradhāna*) rite of a sacrifice and not with every main rite of the particular sacrifice. Like a lamp in a room, t° illuminates the entire sacrifice K. Śr. I.7.1 & comm. On account of this *Darśa* claims priority over all other *iṣṭīs* Āśv. Śr. I.1.3.

It also means the entire sacrifice Āp. Śr. XXIV.1.29. *bhinna*° offering performed by means of a different form of ritual K. Śr. XX.2.6.

तल्प्य *Talpya* mfn. one who deserves a bed or couch; said of those princes who protect the sacrificial horse in its wanderings and who deserve also a seat before the king Āp. Śr. XX.5.13 (*Aśva*).

तान *Tāna* m. tone which, on account of its "fixed" *(nitya)* character, is to be followed in pronouncing the *mantras* K. Śr. I.8.18= *ekaśruti* (q.v.). see *svara*.

तानूनप्त्र *Tānūnaptra* n. a ceremony to Tanūnapāt ("self-generated one") at the *upasads* of *Soma* : an oblation of *ājya* (also called t°) is touched by the sacrificer and 16 priests, and each priest is requested by him to invite him as a form of ritual alliance Āp. Śr. XI. 1.1. C.H. 61.

तार्प्य *Tārpya* n. name of a garment, made of a vegetable substance, worn by the sacrificer as an under-garment Āp. Śr. XVIII.5.7 (*Vāja*), 14.1 (*Rāja*); variously explained, a garment soaked in clarified butter or made from the materials of *tṛpā* plant ? B. Śr. XXV.34= *kṣaumam, tṛpānām va, ghṛtonnam* K. Śr. XV. 5.7-10; also a piece of cloth on which the sacrificial animals are laid Āp. Śr. XX. 17.8 (*Aśva*).

तिर्यक् *Tiryak*. See *paścāt*°.

तीर्थ *Tīrtha* (√*tṛ* , cl.1 "to pass") n. a ford; the passage for moving along within the sacrificial area; the path lies, in all *iṣṭis*, between the *utkara* and the spot where *praṇītā* water is kept (=*saṁcara* q.v) K. Śr. I.3.43; and between the *cātvāla* and the *utkara* for a rite which requires an *uttaravedi* 42, Āp. Śr. XII. 5.4. The t° for driving the cows which are sacrificial fees lies between the *śālā* and the *sadas* and from there to the south of the *āgnīdhra* K. Śr. X.2.13 (*Soma*); between the 2 *vedis* (*Cātur*) Āp. Śr. VIII.5.11. The *Adhvaryu* should always enter the *sadas* by its eastern gate and go out by the western gate, he should not go beyond the *dhiṣṇyas* XI.10. 16. Cf. *pitṛ*° and *mṛga*°.

तुरायण *Turāyaṇa* n. (*Tura*'s way) a *sattra* Āp. Śr. XXIII.14.1; also a *kāmyeṣṭi* in the paradigm of *Darśa* (of which it is a modification) Ś. Śr. III.11.15.

तुष *Tuṣa* m. husks of barley grain, used as *ṛjīṣa* at the *avabhṛtha* of the *Varuṇapraghāsa* Bh. Śr. VIII.11.7,9, winnowed at the *utkara*, and offered to the rakṣas in a potsherd I.22.5 (*Darśa*).

तूष्णींजप *Tūṣṇīṁjapa* m. See *japa*.

तूष्णींशंस *Tūṣṇīṁśaṁsa* m. silent recitation, being the 2nd part of the *ājyaśastra*, consists of *bhūragnirjyotirjyotiragno3m*, Āśv. Śr. V.9.11, recited by the *Hotṛ* in a low voice after the *pratigara* of the *Adhvaryu* C.H. 232.

तूष्णीकम् *Tūṣṇīkam* ind. "silent"; performance of a sacrificial act without *mantra*, as opposed to *mantravat* (with *mantra*) Āp. Śr. III.18.7.

तृच *Tṛca* m. n. a triplet, group of 3 *ṛks*, Ś. Śr. I.4.8, which is the basis of a *stotra*. By repeating the 3 stanzas of a hymn a *stoma* of certain number (*trivṛt* 9, *pañcadaśa* 15 etc.) is obtained.

°*bhāga* m. the first part of the *paryāya* (turn) of a *viṣṭuti* which consists of the thrice chanted verse. Cf Caland PBr. 19 & 33.

तृतीयिन् *Tṛtīyin* mfn. priests who are entitled to a third part of the sacrificial fees Āp. Śr. XXI.2.18. see *ṛtvij*.

त्याग *Tyāga*(√*tyaj*, cl.1 "to forsake") m.forsaking, i.e., offering of an object (*dravya*), one of the 3 basic elements which constitutes a sacrifice K. Śr. I.2.2.; one must, it is explained, offer an object (possessed by him) : *puroḍāśa*, *caru* etc. to a presiding deity (*devatā*) by saying "this is not for me, but for the deity" ib. comm.

त्रिवृत् *Trivṛt* ("three fold") m. a type *stoma* in which by a form of chanting the 9 (*trivṛt*) verses are obtained. The first 3 stanzas of each *tṛca*(in the *gāyatrī* metre) are chanted without repetition, then the 2nd stanzas, and finally the 3rd (3×3). This is specially the method of chanting the *bahiṣpavamānastotra*. This is called *udyatī* variety and the other 2 are *parivartinī*, *kulāyinī*. Cf. Eggeling SBE XXVI,308-10. See *stoma*.

त्रैधातवी *Traidhātavī* f. "three fold", said of an oblation of cake, first rice, then barley and again rice; offered at *Rāja* K. Śr. XV.7.29 to Indra and Viṣṇu. Cf. Āp. Śr. XIX.27.15.

त्र्यङ्ग *Tryaṅga* n. three limbs of a victim, offered to *Sviṣṭakṛt* (Agni) Āp. Śr. XX. 18.13 (*Aśva*). Cf. VII.22.6. Also called *aupabhṛta* (q.v.).

त्र्यम्बक (होम) *Tryambaka* m.(*homa*) "three-eyed or three-mothered", identified with Rudra or Śiva (RV. VII.59.12) to whom an offering of cakes is made in a *palāśa* leaf at the cross road (*catuṣpatha*) with the *mantra* : *tryambakaṁ yajāmahe* (VS. III.6); it is the last rite of *Sākamedha* (*Cātur*) K. Śr. V.10, Āp. Śr. VIII. 17-19, B. Śr. V.16-17. Also called *traiyambaka*° K. Śr. V.10.1.

त्सरु *Tsaru* m. a handle; a *camasa* may be with (*tsarumant*) or without a handle (*atsaruka*) Āp. Śr. XII.2.8.

द Da

दक्षिणा *Dakṣiṇā* f. sacrificial fees, consisting of cow or other animals and other things; but number varies. In simpler sacrifices it consists of *anvāhārya* (q.v.). But fabulous d° is demanded in complex rites, see H. Dh.II (2), 1221 for *Rāja* (also Heesterman 162-6), for *Aśva* 1236 (also Dumont L' Aśva 117) for *Vāja* 1210. Even a non-brahmin may get fees if he is learned Bh. Śr. XIV.5.17; on the other hand, a learned brahmin but not belonging to a *ṛṣi gotra* or though belonging to it but not learned is not entitled to get it ib.14. A sacrifice becomes singed (*prakṣāma*) if no fees are paid, and the sacrificer becomes short-lived Āp. Śr. IX.15.20, Bh. Śr. IX.18.9-10. For rules of distribution of d° Āp. Śr. XIII.5.11-12. see also *ṛtvij*. In *Agniṣṭoma* the payment of fees is preceded by 3 libations of *ājya* on the *śālāmukhīya* C.H. 289 (called *dakṣiṇa* (*ā*) *homa* or *dākṣiṇa* K. Śr. X.2.4; there is also a solemn ceremony for giving away and receiving the fees C.H. 293.

°*patha* m. literally, path of fees and southern path; the path, south of the *mahāvedi*, by which the fees in cow (*dakṣiṇā*=cow) are led to the north K. Śr. XV.6.16.

दक्षिणाग्नि *Dakṣiṇāgni* m. the southern fire, one of the 3 sacred fires; situated within the *śālā*, near the *gārhapatya*, to the south east; the method of measurement Āp. Śulb. II.4. 6-8. It is semi-circular or bow-shaped. The fire in it is laid by various methods : brought from the *gārhapatya* B, Śr. II.17, from the house of a *Vaiśya* or and rich man or produced by attrition Āśv. Śr. II.2.1. It protects the sacrifice from the evil forces coming from the south; to be preserved permanently (*nitya*) K. Śr. IV.13.4. to be established, optionally, on *upavasatha* ib.7, or *nitya* only if produced by attrition Āp. Śr. VI.2.14. It is established in an elaborate rite, *Ādheya* (*q.v.*). Cf. Dumont L'Agni 3,36. It is also called *anvāhāryapacana*.

°*homa* m. an oblation on d° K. Śr. VIII.9. 14.

दण्डप्रदान *Daṇḍapradāna* n. a rite in which the *Hotṛ* gives a staff to the *Maitrāvaruṇa*, who holds it in *Paśu*; called *maitrāvaruṇadaṇḍa*, made of *udumbara* wood, as long as one's height from the toe to the jaw (*cubuka*) or mouth (*āsya*) Āp. Śr. VII.8.3. Similarly, a staff of the same specification is given to the sacrificer at his *dīkṣā* (*Soma*) by the *Adhvaryu*; it is called *dīkṣitadaṇḍa* X.10. 4-5, K. Śr. VII. 4.1.

दधि *Dadhi* n. curds (cf. *ātañcanam*), used for curdling fresh, hot milk Bh. Śr. I.14.4, and offered as oblation II.18.11, cf. Āp Śr. II. 20.4, and consumed by the sacrificer at *Darśa* Bh. Śr. IV.22.4; used as an oblation at *Āgrayaṇa* VI.14.14. At *Paśu* it is an ingredient of the *pṛṣadājya* (q.v.) and also at *Cātur* VIII. 8.2. At the *dīkṣā* it is consumed by the sacrificer along with other food X.4.6 (*Soma*).

°*graha* m. a drawing of curds offered to Prajāpati just before the morning pressing Āp. Śr. XII.7.5-7, C.H. 148; and the vessel used is called *dadhigrahapātra*, made of *udumbara* wood, 4 cornered (*catuḥsrakti*) 2.1.

°*gharma* m. a beverage of hot milk and curdled milk, poured into a warm pot (*gharma* or *mahāvīra*) by the *Adhvaryu*, and used as a libation at the midday pressing B. Śr. XIV.9, Āp. Śr. XIII. 3.2 (*Soma*)=*sṛta*° Bh. Śr. XI. 10.13.

°*mantha* m. a beverage of grains (*saktu*) mixed with curds Āp. Śr. VI.31.5.

दर्भ *Darbha* m. sacrificial grass, (=*kuśa*) used at various rites for strewing over the hearth Āp. Śr. V.27.9, for carrying fire from the *āhavanīya* to another hearth 11, for purifying the *ājya* (*utpavana*). The *barhis*, *upaveṣa*, *veda* are made of it; the sacrificer is symbolically "purified" with 21 clusters (*puñjīla*) 3 times, each time with 7 clusters at the *apsudīkṣā* Bh. Śr. X.5.1 (*Soma*), C.H.13(d).

दर्भण *Darbhaṇa* n. a mat of grass, sewn with a needle and cord to the post of the *havirdhāna* B. Śr. VI.25, Āp. Śr. XI.8.5 comm.

दर्वी *Darvī* f. a drawing ladle Āp. Śr. VIII.19. 19.

darvīhoma m. a sort of simplified oblation in which a d° full of *ājya* is offered in *Agnihotra* K. Śr. V.6.36; also at *pravargya* Āp. Śr XV. 6.7; of curds at the curd offering, *dadhigraha* (*Soma*). General rules and description Āp. Śr. XXIV.3.2. A rite of *juhoti* class. An independent rite Mī VIII.4.1-28. see *udāyuvana*.

दर्शपूर्णमास *Darśapūrṇamāsa* (*darśa*, literally means the time when the moon is "seen" only by the sun=*amāvāsyā*; *pūrṇamāsa* the moment when the moon is full) m. a rite of *iṣṭi* type, performed with the help of the 4 principal priests on *amāvāsyā* (new moon day) and *pūrṇamāsa* (fullmoon day), and the principal offerings on the next day, the conjunction between the *parvan* and the *pratipad*. D° is an archetype (*prakṛti*) of all other *iṣṭis*.

The preliminaries are performed on the day called *upavasatha* : bathing, shaving etc. done by the sacrificer, the *anvādhāna* rite is performed by putting logs into the fires, *veda* and *prastara* are arranged; in the afternoon of the new moon day *Piṇḍapitṛyajña* follows, in which the *piṇḍas* of cooked rice are offered to the father, the grandfather and the great grandfather. After the *Agnihotra* rite in the evening, cows are milked (*sāyaṁ doha*); milk is purified, heated, curdled and preserved to be used later.

On the next *pratipad* day paddy grains are pounded, winnowed; the flour is mixed in *madantī* water, stirred by *mekṣaṇa* and thus a dough is prepared. Thereafter the altar is prepared (see plan 4), and the utensils are placed on it.

Now begins the recitation of the *sāmidhenī* verses, and the fuel sticks are put into the fire, and after it the *pravaras* of the sacrificer are announced by the *Hotṛ*, followed by an *āghāra* libation of the *Adhvaryu*. The *prayājas* (5) and *ājyabhāgas* (2) follow. Then the principal offerings are offered with the accompaniment of the *puro'nuvākyās* and the *yājyās* : for *Darśa*, a cake to Agni, an *upāṁśu* oblation of clarified butter to Prajāpati, a cake each to Agni-Soma and to *vaimṛdha* Indra; for *Pūrṇamāsa*, one cake each to Agni and Indra-Agni; then an oblation called *pārvaṇahoma* and the *sviṣṭakṛt* offering are performed. The *iḍā* is offered and consumed by the priests. The *Adhvaryu* offers 3 *anuyāja* oblations into the *āhavanīya* and 5 or 8 *patnīsaṁyāja* oblations into the *gārhapatya*. Now the *yoktra* is removed from the waist of the sacrificer's wife and the rite is concluded with the 3 *viṣṇukramas* of the sacrificer. Āp. Śr. I-IV, B. Śr.I, H.Dh.II(2), 1009-90, Śr.K(E). I(1), 211-528.

दशपेय *Daśapeya* m. rite of 10 drinks in which 10 *camasin* priests and 90 other eligible brahmins join in the drinking festival. These *Soma* drinking (*somapā*) 90 brahmins are called *anuprasarpaka*. The rite is of *Agniṣṭoma* type, and *Soma* drinking is a modification of *prasthitabhakṣaṇa*, Āp.Śr.XVIII.20.11-21.7 (*Rāja*). Cf. Heesterman 179-95.

दशरात्र *Daśarātra* m. ten principal days of a 12 day *sattra* Āp. Śr.XXI.15.19. *Sarvamedha* is a d° XX.25.3; =*daśāha* Ś. Śr. XIII.21.13.

दशहोतृ *Daśahotṛ* m. *mantras* of ten *Hotṛs*. See *caturhotṛ*.

दशापवित्र *Daśāpavitra* n. a fringed woollen filter ŚBr. IV.2.2.11, held over the *droṇakalaśa* for purifying soma Āp. Śr. X.26.11; its navel (*nābhi*) is made of the white wool of a living ram K. Śr. IX.2.16; said to be 1 *aratni* in length ib. comm. It has fringes whence the name, *daśā*.

दशाह *Daśāha* m. See *daśarātra*.

दहन (कल्प) *Dahana* (*kalpa* m.) rite of cremation. See *Antyeṣṭi*.

°*deśa* m. cremation ground, selected by the *Adhvaryu* for a dying person (*āhitāgni*), inclining towards the south west, not arid, without cleavings, with waters going towards the southwest and meandering to the north to flow into a great river, thus becoming an eastward flowing river. Bh. Pi. I.1.2-3. All the sacred fires are established here ib.8.

दाक्षायण *Dākṣāyaṇa* m. a modified *Darśa* practised by the *Dākṣāyaṇas* Āp. Śr. III.17.4; included in the *kāmyeṣṭi* Āśv. Śr. II.14.7, Mī.II.3.5.

दाक्षिणहोम *Dākṣiṇahoma* m. See *dakṣiṇā*°

दारुचिति *Dāruciti* f. a pile of wood, a funeral pyre, arranged on the cremation ground Bh. Pi. 1.1.8; the sacred fires : *āhavanīya*, *sabhya*, *āvasathya* and *aupāsana* on the east, *gārhapatya* on the west and *anvāhāryapacana* (*dakṣiṇa*) on the south are laid 3.8.

दार्षद्वत *Dārṣadvata* n. name of a *sattra* in which some rites are performed on the bank of the river *Dṛṣadvatī* Āp. Śr. XXIII.13.11, K. Śr. XXIV.6.32.

दीक्षणीया *Dīkṣaṇīyā* (*iṣṭi*) f. oblation of *puroḍāśa* on 11 *kapālas* to Agni and Viṣṇu taking place before the *dīkṣā* of the sacrificer in *Soma* Āp. Śr. X.4.1 : *dīkṣā prayojana* Āśv. Śr. IV.2.1 comm; many of the rites belonging to an ordinary *iṣṭi* are lacking in it Mī. X.1.4. Cf. C.H 15. There are 17 d° in the *Aśva* K. Śr. XX. 4.7.

दीक्षा *Dīkṣā* f. consecration of the sacrificer at the beginning of a *Soma* sacrifice. It takes place after the preliminary *iṣṭi* and *āhuti*. The proper d° consists of a series of attitudes and manipulations, adopted and made by the sacrificer, who is provided with a garment, a girdle of *muñja* grass to be used as a belt, a piece of cloth for his headdress, a staff, and skin of an antelope to sit on. His wife also gets a *yoktra*, a headgear of net etc. He contracts the fingers of both hands one after another, finally clinches his fists, touches the forehead, scratches his body with the horn of an antelope. He stammers (*parihvāla*). The consecration is proclaimed (*āvedana*) by the *Adhvaryu* who mentions his *ṛṣi* ancestor, names of the father and the grandfather. It is to be noted that whatever may be the caste of the sacrificer he should be declared as a brahmin (Bh. Śr. X.7.9) B. Śr. VI.5, Āp. Śr. X.8.11-15; 9-10; 11.1-4. Cf. C.H. 17-20. The word may also mean the day of d° Āp. Śr. X.15.1. In *Vāja* 17 d° are performed Āśv. Śr. IX.9.2. Various theories have been put forward for explaining the nature of d°. Cf. Keith RPV

300-03, Keith TS. cxiii-cxv. The description of it given in ABr. I.3 and the statement in ŚBr. III.3.3.12 that the consecrated person becomes an embryo make the d° closely resemble the initiation rites as practised in ancient and modern times by the primitive people. Cf. Thomson : SAGS 45-49. Cf. the cutting off of the hair of the Semites Smith Semites 328; initiation of the Australian tribes SG NTCA 212-386; birth of Zeus and the initiation rites Themis 13-19.

apsu° (*apo°* Āp. Śr. XVIII.20.14), the first part of the d° in which the sacrificer and his wife perform ritual bathing, anointing each other, and hair cutting is done by a barber B. Śr. VI.2-3, C.H.11.

avāntara°, an intermediary consecration which takes place in the 1st *upasad* and in which the sacrificer tightens his girdle and clinches his fists more firmly B. Śr. VI.19, Āp. Śr. XI.1.13-2.4, C.H 66.

°āhuti f. 6 oblations of consecration performed after the *dīkṣaṇīyeṣṭi* and before the d° Āp. Śr. X.8.4-6, C.H.16. For observances after d° C.H.20-25.

दीक्षितदण्ड *Dīkṣitadaṇḍa* m. a staff for the consecrated sacrificer. See *daṇḍapradāna*.

°vimita n. a shed for the consecrated sacrificer, who should stay within it Bh. Śr. X.8.7 (*Soma*)=*prācīnavaṁśaśālā* ABr.I.3.

दुन्दुभि *Dundubhi* m.f. sort of a large kettle-drum used at the *Vāja* Āp. Śr. XVIII.4.4, *Mahāvrata* XXI.18.1. At *Mahāvrata* a ground drum (*bhūmi°*), a piece of damp leather placed over a hole, half inside half outside the *vedi* (to the west of the *āgnīdhra* shed), and a piece of strap is used instead of a drum-stick Āp. Śr. XXI.18.2-3; 19.8.

दूरोहण *Dūrohaṇa* n. a mode of recitation in ascending and descending form in which the stanza is recited, first by *pāda*, then by half verse, thereafter by 3 *pādas* at a stretch followed by a pause. This is the ascent. The descent is in the reverse order by 3 *pādas*, half verse, *pāda*, the 4 *pādas* without a pause Āśv. Śr. VIII.2.12-13 comm.

दृषद् *Dṛṣad* f. large (lower) millstone over which the *upalā* is placed; used for crushing grains Āp. Śr. I.20.3-4 (*Darśa*).

देवयजन *Devayajana* n. sacrificial arena; its characteristics are mentioned : the ground must be free from salinity, of holes, be inclined towards the northeast or east or north B. Śr. II.2, Āp. Śr. X.20.1, C.H.7. The *prācīnavaṁśa* and altar are built here.

°yācana n. a rite by which the sacrificer asks for a d° from a king Āp. Śr. X.2.9, C.H.6. Cf. H.Dh.II.(2), 988, 1134-5.

देवयोनि *Devayoni* m. f. See *araṇi*.

देवसु (हविस्) *Devasu* (*havis*) or *devas* (*u*) *vāṁ havis* n. oblation of rice and various types of corn to the eight deities : "divine inciters" Āp. Śr. XVIII.12.4 (*Rāja*), XVII.22.9 (*Cayana*). Immediately after the principal offerings the *Brahman* takes the royal sacrificer by the hand, and prays to the deities to hasten him to the dominion. The sacrificer is proclaimed to the *ratnins* : This is your king, O Bhārata (or as the case may be) or simply *O janatā* Āp. Śr. XVIII.12.7. Then the *Brahman* hastens to add : Soma is the king of us, the brahmins. Cf. *Sīmantonnayana*. Heesterman considers the rite D°as the procreation of the king, 69-78. (√*sū*, cl 2 or 6 "to generate, impel" or again √*su*, cl 5 to "press out"; the forms and meanings of both of them are irretrievably mixed up. Cf. Whitney Roots 188).

देविकाहविस् *Devikāhavis* (pl) n. oblations to the minor female deities Āp. Śr. XIII.24.1 (at the end of *Soma*). Cf. C.H. 408; also at *Rāja*, consist of 5 offerings : a cake on 12 *kapālas* to Dhātṛ, and 4 *carus* to Anumati, Rākā, Sinīvālī, Kuhū XVIII.10.1-11. Cf. Heesterman 41-45.

दोग्ध्र *Dogdhra* n. milk pail, 2 in number, made out of the same earth as the *mahāvīra*; it resembles the lip of an elephant, has a beak and looks like a ladle without handle. It contains milk of a she-goat and a cow Bh. Śr. XI.3.5, Āp. Śr. XV.3.10 (*Pravargya*).

दोह *Doha* m. (1) milk (du) : sweet, boiled milk and curdled milk for the *sāṁnāyya* Āp.Śr. II. 11.8.

(2) "milking", i.e. performance of a *stotra* or *śastra* in order to attain the desired result B. Śr.XIV.9.

(3) milking of cows, twice in the morning (*prātar*) and twice in the evening Āp. Śr. III.16.12,13; an elaborate rite in *Darśa* : the calves are tied with rope, cows are milked

into the pails (*kumbhī*) while the *Adhvaryu* recites *mantra*, and later purifies the milk through a strainer (*śākhāpavitra*) Bh. Śr. I.12-15.3. Cf. H.Dh.II(2), 1015-19. see *sāyaṁ*°.

दोहन *Dohana* n. (1) a milk pail with wooden or metal lid Āp. Śr.VI.3.15; (2) a rite of "milking", i.e. receiving *soma* juice in the pots Āśv. Śr. V.12.18; (3) milking of a cow, not passed through a strainer, and therefore a Śūdra is forbidden to milk Bh. VI.8.18 (*Agnihotra*). *dohunī* f. a milk pail with the capacity of 1 *prastha* Vai. Śr. XI.8.

द्रव्य *Dravya* n. any sacrificial material : cake, *ājya*, milk, *soma* etc; an offering; one of the basic elements of a sacrifice K. Śr. I.2.2 & comm. see *tyāga*. The procurement (*prakalpana*) of d°, used in a rite, is the duty of a sacrificer Āp. Śr. IV.1.2.

द्रोणकलश *Droṇakalaśa* m. a bucket of *vikaṅkata* (*droṇākṛtiḥ* comm). Āp. Śr. XII.2.10; it is placed on 4 pressing stones (*ṛjīṣamukha*), and is covered with a filter (*daśāpavitra*) K. Śr. IX.5.14-15; it contains *soma* called *śukra* ib. 19.see *graha*. It may also hold barley 1.3.36 comm. It is installed behind the *havirdhāna* cart. Cf. C.H.159. in abbrev. *kalaśa*.

द्वादशाह *Dvādaśāha* m. a *soma* sacrifice lasting 12 days, comprising a *Daśāha* (10) : *Pṛṣṭhya-ṣaḍaha* (6) (of which the 1st and the 4th days are *Ṣoḍaśin*s, the rest *Ukthyas*), 3 *Chandomas* (*ukthyas*) days, 1 *Atyagniṣṭoma* day; the *Daśāha* is preceded and followed by 1 *Atirātra* day (2 days). D° is both an *ahīna* and a *sattra*. Āp. Śr. XXI.

द्वारबाहु *Dvārbāhu* m. door post, B. Śr. VI.25, of the *havirdhāna* (*dvārasthūṇā* Āp. Śr. XI.8.5 comm). C.H.90.

द्विदेवत्य (ग्रह) *Dvidevatya* (*graha*) mfn., m. offering of *soma* from the cups belonging to the twin divinities : Indra and Vāyu, Mitra and Varuṇa and the two Aśvins Āp. Śr. XII.20. 18-21.6, (*dvidevatyacaraḥ*) K. Śr. IX.9.13-21, C.H. 199.

ध Dha

धरुण *Dharuṇa* n. the spot where *ājya* drawing is done Vādh. Śr (AO.II.162).

धवित्र *Dhavitra* (√*dhū*, cl.5 "to shake") n. fan (3 in number), made of the skin of a black antelope with black and white hair for fanning the *gharma* Āp. Śr. XV.5.12 (*Pravargya*).

धातु *Dhātu* (√*dhā*, cl.3 "to put") m. layer or row (3 or 5, *tri*°, *pañca*°) of strewn grass on the altar Bh. Śr. II.8.13. (*Darśa*).

धाना *Dhānā* f. grains of barley, parched and pounded, for *savanīyapuroḍāśa* Āp. Śr. XII.4.10 (*Soma*); mixed with *soma*, and a rite is performed at *hāriyojana* with the *Adhvaryu* holding a pot full of d° on his head; grains are chewed without breaking them, and swallowed with a sound (*ciṣciṣākāraṁ*) by the priests XIII.17.3-8. C H. 386.

धाय्या *Dhāyyā* (√*dhā*, cl.3 "to put") f. technical name of the additional stanza interpolated in a *śastra*, e.g., *marutvatīya*° C.H. 300; particularly, 2 stanzas in the *sāmidhenī* for increasing it from 15 to 17 Āp. Śr. VI.31.18 (*Darśa*). Cf. Eggeling SBE XII,112.

धारा *Dhārā* f. flow of *soma* from the *camasa* in a continuous stream through a filter Āp. Śr. XII.13.1. This operation is called *dhārāgraha* in contradistinction to the *upāṁśu*°. Also said of the sprinkling of water from the *gārhapatya* to the *āhavanīya* Āśv. Śr. II.2.14 (*udaka*°).

°*graha* m. act of filling up of the cups (*camasa*) from the *antaryāma* to the *dhruva* with *soma* juice flowing in stream from the *Hotṛ's camasa* through the strainer K. Śr. IX.6.26 comm. see *graha*.

धिष्ण्य *Dhiṣṇ(i)ya* m. small seat, 8 in number, raised for the Soma priests : *hotrīya* (for *Hotṛ*), *āgnīdhrīya* (*Āgnīdhra*). *praśāstrīya* (*Maitrāvaruṇa*) and for *Brāhmaṇācchaṁsin*, *Potṛ*, *Neṣṭṛ*, *Acchāvāka* (the 7 priests TBr. II. 3.6), and lastly *mārjālīya*. Of these, 6 are situated within the *sadas* (see plan 3); 4 to the north of the *pṛṣṭhyā*, the *hotrīya* on the *pṛṣṭhyā* in front of the eastern door of the *sadas* and the *praśāstrīya* to the south of the *pṛṣṭhyā* Āp. Śr. XI.14.4-6. The *āgnīdhrīya* and the *mārjālīya* are situated to the north and the south of the *havirdhāna* respectively. Within the *sadas* they are separated from one another by the distance of 18 *aṅgulas*; they are square (18 *aṅgulas*) or round (18 *aṅgulas* in diameter), made of the earth taken from the *cātvāla* or of sand (*pāṁsu*° XII.18.3). Fire is installed on them, and oblation can be offered on the *āgnīdhrīya* (XI.14.1) K. Śr. VIII.6.16-22. Cf C.H. 104-6, Eggeling SBE XXVI, 148. The word also designates other mounds : *cātvāla*, *utkara* etc Āp. Śr. XI.14.9. At *Cayana* they are made of bricks and hemmed by gravels XVII.21.6.

धुर् *Dhur* (du) f. the two ends of a yoke of a cart which carries *havis* or *soma*, and explained as the space between the 2 holes of the yoke Āp. Śr. I.17.6 comm. (*Darśa*) ; X.28.1-2 (*Soma*). C.H.49.

धुर्य *Dhurya* n. "to be yoked"; name of those *stotras* which, in addition to the principal *stotras* (*pavamāna*), are chanted in *Soma*, e.g. the *ājyastotras* of the morning pressing and the *pṛṣṭhastotras* of the midday pressing of the *Agniṣṭoma* Eggeling SBE XXVI, 307.

धुवन *Dhuvana* (√*dhu*, cl.5 "to shake") n. literally, shaking (whence sexual intercourse); rite of fanning the charred bones of the dead. The relatives, women and 4 *brahmacārins* go round a pitcher and a peg below which the bones are placed. While doing so for 3 times they strike the pitcher with a piece of leather and fan it with the end of their garments. Dancing and playing on instruments follow Bh Pi.II.3.15. But before this a curious dialogue takes place between the first wife of the deceased and a Śūdra or a *brahmabandhu*, who seeks sexual intercourse with her. She refuses for 2 days, but on the 3rd day she gives her consent to it for only one night ib. 4-8.

धूपन *Dhūpana* n. act of fumigating the *gharma* by setting fire to the dried dung of a horse Āp. Śr. XV.3.17 (*Pravargya*).

धृति *Dhṛti* f. 4 oblations on the *āhavanīya* for "holding back" the horse K. Śr. XX.3.4 (*Aśva*).

धृष्टि *Dhṛṣṭi* m. stirring stick, 2 in number, held by the *Adhvaryu* and the *Pratiprasthātṛ* for removing burning embers (*aṅgāra*) from the *gārhapatya* (=*upaveṣa* q.v.) Bh. Śr. XI. 8.1; used in the preparation of *gharma* Āp. Śr. XV.5.11. Any stick as long as 2 *tālas* Vai. Śr. XI.9.

ध्रुवगोप *Dhruvagopa* m. one of the three assistants of the *sadasya* B. Śr. II.3; he is the protector (*gopa*) of the *dhruvagraha* (or *dhruva*), a drawing of *soma* designated as "firm" K. Śr. IX.8.1. The protector remains in the charge of the *graha* till the third pressing; he is a *rājaputra* (son of a king) B. Śr. VII.7, Bh. Śr. XIII. 16.3, 6. The offering is made with the vessel called °*sthālī* B. Śr. VIII.15, K. Śr. IX. 6.22. Cf. C.H. 167.

°*graha* m. a drawing of *Soma* by the *Pratiprasthātṛ* K. Śr. X.7.7, C.H. 379.

ध्रुवा *Dhruvā* f. an offering spoon, made of *vikaṅkata* wood, belonging to the *sruc* class (q.v.) Āp. Śr. I.15.10.

Usually it remains constant on the *vedi* (whence the name). The clarified butter drawn with it for libation is called *dhrauva* Ś. Śr. V.8.2 comm. It is specially used in the offering of *ājyabhāga*. Cf. Āp. Śr. VIII. 10.4.

ध्वान *Dhvāna* m. a mode of pronunciation in which consonants and vowels can be distinguished but as a whole letters cannot be distinguished, *i.e.* murmur; a little louder than *upāṁśu*, used at the *patnīsaṁyāja* B. Śr. XX.15, Āp. Śr. III.8.8 & comm (*Darśa*).

न Na

नग्नहु *Nagnahu* m. coarse portion of the parched barley grains, used for preparing wine Āp. Śr. XIX.5.10; or explained as, ginger, nutmeg, myrobalan etc. K. Śr. XIX.1.20. *Soma* juice is sprinkled on it. Cf. *māsara*.

नम् *Nam* (cl.1 "to bend") to modify the content of a *mantra* so as to adapt it to another context Āp. Śr. XVIII.7.6 (*namati*).

नलद *Nalada* m. n. Indian spikenard (H. Dh. IV, 202); a garland of n° is hung on the corpse Bh. Pi. I.1.21. see *preta*.

नाभि *Nābhi* f. "navel", a hole in a *pavitra*

(q.v.) Āp. Śr. XII.13.1. see also *uttara°*, *daśā-pavitra*.

नामव्यतिषञ्जनीय (होम) *Nāma-vyatiṣañjanīya (homa)* m. rite of "interchange of names" between the royal sacrificer and his son (heir apparent) after the unction ceremony during the disposal of *abhiṣeka* waters; 2 libations with the remainder of water into the *aupāsana* fire are made in which, the heirapparent is mentioned wrongly as the father of his own father (*i.e.* Rāma is the father of Daśaratha) and then in the right order (*i.e.* R° is the son of D°). Āp. Śr. XVIII.16.14-16, K. Śr. XV. 6.10-12; cf. Heesterman, 123-6 for interpretation etc.

नाराशंस *Nārāśaṁsa* m. name given to the *camasas* after *soma* has been drunk from them and they have been caused to "swell" (*āpyāyana*) Āp. Śr. XII.25.24. Cf. C.H. 220.

निकायिन् *Nikāyin* m. a group of sacrifices : 4 *Sāhasras*, 4 *Sādyaskras* 4 *Dvirātras* Āp. Śr. XXII.1.2, Mī. VIII.1.19.

निगद *Nigada* (*ni-√gad*, cl.1 "to declare") m. commands (*praiṣa*) of the *Adhvaryu* to another priest for doing certain things; it is composed of the *yajus* formulas but distinguished from them, for n° is pronounced loudly K. Śr. I.3. 11 & comm; it is classed as a *mantra* ib.1 & comm, Āp. Śr. VIII.5.18. For the difference between a n° and *yajus* Mī II.1.38-45. *Adhrigu* is a n°.

निगम *Nigama* m. a type of *mantra* in which the names of deities are changed for the name abandoned in consonance with the offerings Āp. Śr. I 2.7 & comm.

devatā° address of the deity (in appropriate context) in the *mantras* XXIV.4.18.

निग्राभ *Nigrābha* m. name of a *mantra* (TS. I. 4.1 f.) recited over the *vasatīvarī* waters contained in the *Hotṛcamasa* for turning it into the *nigrābhya* waters (*ni-√grabh*, cl 9 "to seize") Āp. Śr. XII.9.1, B. Śr. VII.5.

nigrābhya mfn. waters so invoked and contained in the *Hotṛcamasa*, into which *soma* stalks are poured and thrice stirred for *upāṁśugraha* Āp. Śr. XII.9.8. This act is called *nigrābhopāyana* 10.10 or *upayana* and *āpyāyana* b. Śr. VII.6; used for sprinkling the stalks of *soma* during the pressing K. Śr. IX. 4.16-17.

नित्य *Nitya* mfn. constant or obligatory, said of the *gārhapatya* in the sense that its maintenance is for life (as opposed to *kāmya*, *naimittika*) Āp. Śr. VI.2.12; also said of a rite which is obligatory VI.4.3, 9.

निदान *Nidāna* n. 2 ropes for tying the hind feet of a cow near her hooves Āp. Śr. I.11.5 (*Darśa*), XV.5.20 (*Pravargya*). See also *abhidhānī*.

निधन *Nidhana* n. (1) finale, the 5th and the last part of a *sāman* Āp. Śr. XIII.20.4 & comm., chanted in chorus by the 3 *sāman* chanters : *Prasotṛ*, *Udgātṛ* and *Pratihartṛ*. It consists of interjections, *e.g.* *sāt*, *sām*, *suvāḥ*, *iḍā*, *vāk* and *ā* for 9 *bahiṣpavamāna* verses. See *sāman*.

(2) bundle of grass comprising of a certain number of *muṣṭis* Āp. Śr. I.4.3 (*muṣṭīnāṁ rāśayaḥ* comm.).

निधान *Nidhāna* n. laying of a jar containing the charred bones in a mound (*śmaśāna*) K. Śr. XXV.8.8.

निनर्द *Ninarda* (*ni-√nard*, cl.1 "to bellow") m. a mode of pronouncing the second syllable of the third *pāda* of a verse in *udātta*, the first syllable in *anudātta*. The sound O is repeated 4 times in such a way that in the beginning it is in prolation and *udātta*, then in *anudātta*, and *anudāttatara* and finally in prolation and *udātta* Āśv. Śr. VII.11.11. Similar phenomenon is *nyūṅkha* (q.v.).

निनाह्य *Nināhya* m. earthen water jar, dug into the ground for keeping water cool K. Śr. VIII.9.8.

नि-मृद् *Ni-mṛd* (cl.9) to crush the fire brand (*ulmuka*) for setting up the *śāmitra* fire Bh. Śr. VII.12.13 (*nimṛdnāti*).

नियोजन *Niyojana* n. fastening an animal to the sacrificial post, accompanied with a *mantra* Āp. Śr. VII. 12.9 (*Paśu*).

निरूढपशुबन्ध *Nirūḍhapaśubandha* or *Paśubandha* (*nir-√ūh*, cl.1 "to remove off") m. sacrifice of a disembowelled animal, reconstructed by the *sūtrakāras* as an independent rite from the animal sacrifice prescribed in the Brāhmaṇas (cf. *agnīṣomīya*, *kratupaśu*) which is a model for animal sacrifice. But N° is held as a model for all optional animal sacrifices. Cf. Mī. VIII.1.13. N° is performed every six months or once a year K. Śr. VI.1.1 and takes one or two days Āp. Śr. VII. 6.3. Six priests are engaged, 4 of the *iṣṭi* and 2 additional : *Pratiprasthātṛ* and *Maitrāvaruṇa* (=*Praśāstṛ*). The altar is prepared as in the *Varuṇapraghāsa*; on the *nābhi* of the *uttaravedi* a new *āhavanīya* is installed Āp. Śr. VII.3.7-9; 8.3. See plan 5.

The preliminary rites constitute of an oblation of a cake or of *ājya* to Agni-Viṣṇu, preparation of the *yūpa*, *caṣāla* and *svaru* with the help of a carpenter (*takṣan*) and the *vedi* on which various implements are laid. The *yūpa* wound thrice with a cord (*raśanā*), with the *svaru* thrust into the cord, raised into the pit ceremoniously (*yūpocchrayaṇa*). The victim remains tied to the *yūpa*.

The principal part of the rite begins with the putting of logs into the fire with the accompaniment of *sāmidhenī* recitations. The sacrificial animal, a goat, is bathed, anointed with *ājya*, touched with a twig and *darbha* blades (*upākaraṇa*). The victim is led to the *śāmitra* shed by the *Āgnīdhra* while the *Hotṛ* recites the *adhrigu*. The victim is immolated there (cf. *saṁjñapana*) and all the priests return to the sacrificial shed. After the immolation the sacrificer's wife is led to the *śāmitra* shed and she pours water on its limbs, and she is sent back.

The victim's belly is cut open by the *Adhvaryu* to draw out the omentum (*vapā*), which is roasted on the *āhavanīya* by the *Pratiprasthātṛ*, and sprinkled and offered as oblation to Indra and Agni. The animal is dissected, limbs (*paśupuroḍāśa*) are cooked over the *śāmitra* fire followed by an invocation to and partaking of the *iḍā*.

When the *śamitṛ* replies in the affirmative to the question : "Have the limbs been properly cooked" ? (asked thrice), *pṛṣadājya* is poured over its heart, *ājya* over other limbs, and all are taken to the altar where the *avadāna*s of various limbs are cut into the *juhū*, *upabhṛt* and *iḍāpātrī* (cf. *aupabhṛta* and *tryaṅga*, *jauhava*), and offered with the utterance of *vaṣaṭ*. Then the invocation to and partaking of *iḍā* are repeated;preceded by the *sviṣṭakṛt* oblation. The *patnīsaṁyāja* offerings are made with the flesh of the victim's tail (*jāghanī*), which is also offered to the *Hotṛ* and the *Āgnīdhra* (K. Śr. VI.9.14-18).

The sacrificer, his wife and all the priests go from the *cātvāla* and to the *utkara* with the spit for the heart (*hṛdayaśūla*) to a place outside the *vedi* and stick it into the ground. All sprinkle themselves with water, return to the sacrificial shed without looking back and pray to the *āhavanīya*. B. Śr. VI, Āp. Śr. VII, K. Śr. VI, Āśv. Śr. III.1-8. Cf. H. Dh. II (2), 1109-1132, Śr. K(E). I(2), 770-876.

निर्-मन्थ् *Nir-manth* (cl.9 or √*math* cl.1) "to produce fire by rubbing the *araṇi*s Āp. Śr. V.4.14.

°*manthana* n. Vt. Śr. VIII.12. *nirmathya* mfn. the place where the fire is produced, the fire thus produced and the related rite Āp. Śr. VIII.6.18, Mī. I.4.12 (as distinguished from *āhārya* Āp. Śr. XIV.21.11).

निर्लेहन *Nirlehana* (*nir*-√*lih*, cl.2 "to lick") n. act of licking the sacrificial residues (*lepa*) sticking to the two ladles (*sruc*), done twice by the *Adhvaryu* Āp. Śr. VI.11.5; 12.2, B. Śr. III6 (*Agnihotra*).

निर्-वप् *Nir-vap* (cl. 1 "to strew, pour out"). *nirvapana*, a typical act in the *iṣṭi*s, an act of bringing grains in a dish from a cart, pouring them (as in sowing) into another bowl, done by the *Adhvaryu* Āp. Śr. I.7.7 (*Darśa*), also of clarified butter II.6.1, of *vapā* and milk VII.8.7: performance of an *iṣṭi* Mī. III.1.7.

nirvāpa m. putting apart a portion of grains from a large vessel into a smaller one (later to be winnowed, parched, pounded and cooked by mixing *ājya* for preparing a cake) Āp. Śr. I.17.10 (*Ādheya*; *devatārthatvena pṛthakkaraṇam* comm), H.Dh.II(2), 1023 (*Darśa*); cake offering at *soma* pressing (*savanīyapuroḍāśa*) Āp. Śr. XII.4.4 (*Soma*). C.H.135.

निवपन *Nivapana* (*ni*-√*vap*,cl. 1 'to scatter, pour out") n. act of pouring out *soma* stalks on the skin of a red bull placed over the ground selected for the *uttaravedi* or the *uparava* at the time of purchase of *soma* Āp. Śr. X.20.13 (*nivapati*); at the *prāyaṇīya* (*nivapana*) Bh. Śr. X.14.17. Also the rite of digging the bones of a dead person into a hole Bh. Pi I.10.1-2.

निवर्तन *Nivartana* (*ni*-√*vṛt*, cl.1 "to turn back") n. act of returning after the conclusion of a rite by the sacrificer Bh. Śr. VIII.11.18.

निविद् *Nivid* (*ni*-√*vid*, cl.2 "to proclaim") f. short *mantra*s, consisting of 12 clauses (ABr. X.2), in the middle or at the end of a *śastra* (of which it is a part), recited at the midday and the third pressings; they declare the names of the deities concerned, and are repeated loudly after the *tūṣṇīṁśaṁsa* Āśv. Śr. V. 9.12; also called *puroruc* Cf. H.Dh.II(2), 1180, C.H. 300.

°*dhānīya* mfn. a hymn in which a n° is inserted or appended Ś. Śr. XII.8.6, 9.

निवीत *Nivīta* n. See *upavīta*.

निश्रयणी *Niśrayaṇī* f. a ladder for climbing up the sacrificial post (*Vāja*) K. Śr. XIV.5.5 =*niśreṇī* Āp. Śr. XVIII.5.13.

निषादस्थपति *Niṣādasthapati* m. a chieftain (*sthapati*) who is himself a *niṣāda* (a tribal community). Though a *niṣāda* like a *rathakāra* does not belong to the three eligible *varṇas*: brāhmaṇa, kṣatriya and vaiśya who are entitled to perform a sacrifice, he is here allowed to offer a *caru* of *gav(ī)edhukā* corn to Rudra. The offering is to be made on the household fire (*laukikāgni*), and he cannot perform the *Ādhāna* K. Śr. I. 1.12, 14, H.Dh. II(1), 45-46. See also *rathakāra*, *varṇa*.

There is a controversy whether the word means a *niṣāda* who himself is the chieftain of his community or a person belonging to a higher eligible *varṇa* who has become a chieftain of the *niṣāda* community. The first meaning is accepted Mī. VI.1.51, K. Śr. I.1.12 comm.

निष्क *Niṣka* m. n. golden ornament for the neck RV.II.33.10; the ornament of gold or 4 *suvarṇa* or *karṣa* which the *Adhvaryu* puts on the sacrificer's neck K. Śr. XX.1.9 (*Aśva*); silver ornament XXII.4.16 (*Vrātyastoma*).

निष्कास *Niṣkāsa* m scrapings of *ājya* from a pan, mixed with chaff (*tuṣa*), offered to Varuṇa Āp. VIII.7.14 (*Cātur*), XIII.20.7 (*Soma*).

aniṣkāsin mfn. a spoon to which no residue of the previous drawing sticks II.7.2 (=*śeṣa*, comm).

निष्केवल्य *Niṣkevalya* (*śastra*) n. a *śastra* consisting of RV. stanzas, recited by the *Hotṛ* (the 2nd *śastra* at the midday pressing Āśv. Śr. V.15.1. Cf. C.H. 310; the 3rd n° by the *Maitrāvaruṇa*, the 4th by the *Brāhmaṇācchaṁsin*, the 5th by the *Acchāvāka* 16.1-2, Ś. Śr. VII.22.1-5. C.H. 315, 319, 325.

निष्क्रयण *Niṣkrayaṇa* n. rite of redemption in which the sacrificer "gives away" his mind, life, eyes etc. to the priests, and "buys" them back at a price which he intends to give away as fees (*dakṣiṇā*) Āp. Śr. XIII.6.4-5 (*niṣkrīṇīte*).

निष्पवण *Niṣpavaṇa* (*nis-√pū*, cl.9 "to purify by winnowing") n. act of winnowing the sacrificial grains with a winnowing basket Bh. Śr. XIII.18.10; relating formula °*mantra* ib.

निह्नव(न) *Nihnava(na)* (*ni-√hnu*, cl 2 "to hide, beg pardon for") m. n. act of begging pardon, done by the priests at the *āpyāyana* of *soma* stalks; they place their hands, right hand palms turned up, left hand palms turned down, on the *prastara* Āp. Śr. XI.1.12. C.H. 63, 72. But *nihnava* is a salutation according to Āśv. Śr. IV.5.7 comm.

नीड *Nīḍa* m. n. rear portion of the cart (*śakaṭa*) on which *soma* stalks are loaded B. Śr. VI.28, Bh. Śr. X.19.3.

नेष्टृ *Neṣṭṛ* m. "one who leads"; a priest who is an assistant to the *Hotṛ*. He leads the wife of the sacrificer, and prepares wine (*surā*) Āp. Śr. XII.5.2 (*Soma*). He owns a *dhiṣṇya* (q.v.), takes part in the great pressing XII.12.2.

न्यूङ्ख *Nyūṅkha* m. alteration of the 2nd syllable of each half-verse of the *prātaranuvāka* (to be recited by the *Hotṛ*) by an O sound as a substitute for that vowel, e g. *āpo3 00000 03 00000 03 000* Āp. Śr. XXI.7.2; for details Āśv. Śr. VII.11.1-8; *ninarda* is a similar phenomenon.

These *O* sounds are 16 in number, and are not to be recited in monotone (*ekaśruti*, q.v.) Kāśikā on Pāṇ .I.2.34.

प Pa

पक्ष *Pakṣa* m. wings (aisles) on 2 sides, north and south, of the altar, each being a rectangle; 1 *puruṣa* on 2 sides, the other 2 sides increased by one *aratni* to the south for the southern p° and to the north for the northern p° K. Śr. XVI.8.18, Āp. Śr. XVI.17.10. 12 (*Cayana*). See plan Eggeling SBE XLI, 419.

पच्छः *Pacchaḥ* (*pad-śas*) ind. by *pādas* the

gāyatrī verse is to be recited while the *Adhvaryu* purifies the flour for dough with the strainers Bh. Śr. I.25.1 (*Darśa*).

पञ्चदश *Pañcadaśa* (*stoma*) m. a variety of *stoma* in which 3 verses are so chanted as to produce 15 verses in 3 turns by repeating them in various patterns (*viṣṭuti*) as in the case of the 4 *ājya* and the *mādhyandinapavamāna stotras* (*Soma*). C.H. 237, 243, 247, 261, 279. Cf. Chinna 92. see *stotra*.

पञ्चपञ्चिनी *Pañcapañcinī* f. one of the varieties (*viṣṭuti*) of chanting a *pañcadaśa stoma* in which the *tṛcas* are so repeated that in each turn (*paryāya*) 5 verses are obtained (finally 5×3=15) : aaa b c, a bbb c, a b ccc C.H. 237, Eggeling SBE XXVI,308. see *kuśa*, *stoma*.

पञ्चबिल *Pañcabila* mfn. See *caru*.

पञ्चशारदीय *Pañcaśāradīya* m. a *soma* sacrifice comprising 5 days (*pañcāha*), 1 *Agniṣṭoma*, 3 different *Ukthyas*, 1 *Atirātra*; each day represents 5 years Āp. Śr. XXII.5.9.

पञ्चहोतृ *Pañcahotṛ* m. a mystical *mantra* in which 5 priests are mentioned, recited specially at the *Vaiśvadeva* Āp. Śr. VIII.1.3. see *catur°*.

पञ्चाङ्गी *Pañcāṅgī* f. rope halter in 5 parts, made of triple stranded *muñja* grass K. Śr. XVI.2.4 (*Cayana*).

पञ्चावदान *Pañcāvadāna* n. See *caturavatta*.

पञ्चाह *Pañcāha* m. a rite lasting 5 days within a *sattra*, consisting of *Jyoti(ṣṭoma)*, *Go°* *Āyus°* Āp. Śr. XXIII.2.14.

पञ्चेध्मीय *Pañcedhmīya* n. (?) offering of 5 *ājya* libations on the "5 kindling sticks", performed at night in the *Rāja*. The *āhavanīya* fire is poked to 4 directions, the middle portion remaining undisturbed, 5 kindling sticks are placed, followed by 5 *ājya* libations Āp. Śr. XVIII.9.10-11; =°*vātīya* (5 vital forces or winds) K. Śr. XV. 1.20; it corresponds with *pañcāvattīya* TBr.I.7.1.5. Cf. Eggeling SBE XLI, 48, Heesterman 31, 37 (for annotations).

पतन्तक *Patantaka* m. a modification of the *Rāja*, with 12 *dīkṣā* and 12 *upasad* B. Śr. XXVI.3.

A variety of *Aśva*, a three-day *ahīna* L. Śr. IX.11.6, Nid.VIII.8.

पतित्थ *Patittha* m. one standing near the husband, *i.e.* one representing the husband Bh. Pi.I.5.7 =*patihita* B.Pi. I.8.1-2 (see *patnī*), who makes the wife of the deceased to lie down by the side of her husband's body (on the pyre) and again he raises her up holding her left hand with a *mantra* (RV.X.18.8).

पत्नी *Patnī* f. wife of a sacrificer, who participates in the *śrauta* rites in a very limited way, *e.g.* sweeping the shed, smearing and decorating the sacrificial ground Āp. Śr. I.6.12, grounding grains for *puroḍāśa* 7.5; she has a slightly more important role at the *dīkṣā* along with her husband X.15.13 (*Soma*), at the procession with *soma* stalks XI.16.4, later she performs *pannejanī* rite XII.5.3, C.H.140. At the *Varuṇapraghāsa* she has to declare the name of her paramours (*jāra*). The royal wives : *mahiṣī* (principal queen), *vāvātā* (the favourite), *parivṛktī* (discarded) and *pālāgalī* (of low origin) along with their maids and retinue take part in an obscene dialogue with the priests K. Śr. XX.5.15; 6.18 (*Aśva*), and the principal queen simulates sexual copulation with the dead horse Āp. Śr. XXII.18.3-4. But the wife of a sacrificer has been actually relegated to the unenviable position of a silent spectator of the tedious details that had to be gone through by her husband and the priests. The *paddhati* on K. Śr. IV.13 states : *upaveśanavyatiriktaṁ patnī kimapi na karotīti sampradāyaḥ. tacca sādhutaram.* Cf. H.Dh.II(2), 1000 n. She can perform her portions only but not any other rites which are to be performed by her husband because, as Jaimini says, she does not possess the same religious status as her husband (*atulyatvāt*) Mī. VI.1.24. See also *pretapatnī*. Cf. K. Śr. I.1.8. and comm.

°*śālā* f. a hut or tent for the wife within the *prācīnavaṁśa* B. Śr.VI.1, which is screened off during the *pravargya* Āp. Śr. XV.5.2 so that she cannot see the rite.

°*saṁyāja* m. literally, offering made to the wives (of the gods). Four offerings of *ājya* made in a series to Soma, Tvaṣṭṛ, the wives and Agni *gṛhapati*, made with a *sruc* or *sruva* on the *gārhapatya*, by uttering *mantras* in a *dhvāna* tone at the end of *Darśa* Āp. Śr. III. 8.1-8. Cf. H.Dh.II(2),1076-7; in place of *ājya* the tail of the victim is offered at *Paśu* Āp. Śr. VII.27.9 (also occuring at *Darśa* III.8.10); at *Soma* K. Śr. X.8.10. Additional offerings to Rākā, Kuhū, Sinīvālī Bh. Śr. III.7.16 (*Darśa*).

°*saṁnahana* n. rite of tying up a yoke halter (*yoktra*) round the waist of the sacrificer's wife; done by the *Āgnīdhra* either over her garment or inside Āp. Śr. II.4.1; 5.2-5, B. Śr. I.12 (*Darśa*). In this way she is made fit to participate in the rite. The girdle is removed either by herself Āp. Śr. III.10.6 or by the *Āgnīdhra* Bh. Śr. III.12.7 (*patnīṁ vimuñcati*). Cf. H.Dh.II(2), 1040-41. She is also girdled up with a *yoktra* at the *dīkṣā*, done by the *Pratiprasthātṛ* Āp. Śr. X.9.13 (*Soma*). Cf. H. Dh.II(2), 1136, C.H.18.

पद *Pada* n. a foot length, one tenth part of the *puruṣa* (sacrificer's height); each p° is divided into 12 *aṅgula*s, 3p° make a *prakrama* K. Śr. XVI.8.21; but cf. B. Śulb. I.1.

पदसंलोपन *Padasaṁlopana* n. act of obliterating the footprints, when, after cremation, the relatives walk towards the east, done by the last man in the line with a reed of cane (*vetasa*) and *avakā* Bh. Pi. I.11.10.

पदाहुति *Padāhuti* f. libation of *ājya* on the (7th) footprint of the *somakrayaṇī* cow whom the *Adhvaryu* follows (the first *upasad* of *Soma*) B. Śr. VI. 13, Āp. Śr. X.23.2. CH. 38.

पद्धरणी *Paddharaṇī* f. a bowl (*sthālī*) for dust collected from the 7th footprint of the cow (see *padāhuti*) B. Śr. VI.10,12,13, C.H.38.

पन्नेजनी *Pannejanī* (√*nij*, cl.3 "to wash") f. waters for washing feet Āp. Śr. XII.5.12, B. Śr. VII.3. The rite in which the sacrificer's wife exposes her right thigh and pours p° waters over it from the knee joint Āp. Śr. XIII.15. 8-11, C.H.371.

pānnejana(ī) m.f. a vessel in which p° is preserved Āp. Śr. XII.5.3, K. Śr. IX.3.11.

पयस्या *Payasyā* f. a synonym of *āmikṣā*; cf. *āmikṣāpayasyam*=*āmikṣā* Āp. Śr. VIII.5.33, K. Sr. IV. 3.10 comm.

परापावम् *Parāpāvam* ind. shaking grains repeatedly in a winnowing basket Āp. Śr. I.7.5.

परिकर्मिन् *Parikarmin* mfn. servants of the *Adhvaryu* Āśv. Śr. II.4 16 (*paricāraka*, comm), also those who take away the animals (*Aśva*); B. Śr. XV.28.

परिक्रय *Parikraya* m. redemption of a cow (with which *soma* was bought) by means of a fee Āp. Śr XXIV.2.8.

परिग्राह *Parigrāha* m. (1) line traced on the ground to mark the extent of a *vedi* (altar) on its northern, southern and western sides, by the *Adhvaryu* with a *sphya*. He begins first from the south (south-western *śroṇi*) and goes to the east upto the southern *aṁsa*, then from the south-western *śroṇi* to the north-western *śroṇi*, and finally from the north-western *śroṇi*, to the east upto the northern *aṁsa*. This is the first rough outline called *pūrva*°. The drawing is completed by a repetition of the same process, and is called *uttara*° B. Śr. I.11. These are the preliminary operations in raising the altar, and *mantra*s are used during the operations; =°*graha* K. Śr. II.6.25.

(2) fork for lifting up the *gharma* M. IV.2.2 (*pravargya*)=*śapha* Āp. Śr. XV.5.11=*pariśāsa* K. Śr. XXVI.5.12.

parigrahaṇa n. act of tracing the outlines of an altar as above after which levelling is done. See *yoyupana*.

परिघर्म्य *Parigharmya* m. materials which are associated with the *gharma*, *e.g.* the *mahāvīra*, *āsandī*, *sruc* etc. Āp. Śr. XV.5.6, B. Śr. IX.5.

(अग्नि) परिचर (*Agni*) *Paricara* m.=*parikarmin* B. Śr. XXVI.5.

परिचरा *Paricarā* f. the third part of a *paryāya* of the *viṣṭuti*; a circulating *viṣṭāva* L. Śr. VI. 5.3. cf. Caland PBr. 33.

परिधानीया *Paridhānīyā* (*pari*-√*dhā*, cl. 3 "to surround, to conclude") f. the concluding verse, finale, of a *śastra* Āśv. Śr. II.16.8, as in the *sāmidhenī* verses Āp. Śr II.12.6; always repeated thrice. Also said of RV. V.75.9 which is a concluding verse of the *prātaranuvāka*.

परिधि *Paridhi* (*pari*-√*dhā*, cl.3) m. technical name of the 3 encircling sticks of wood called *madhyama*, *dakṣiṇa* and *uttara* marking the boundary of the *āhavanīya* on the west, south and north. They are placed before the oblation commences. They are made of any one of the sacrificial trees : *palāśa*, *kārśmarya*, *khadira*, *udumbara* etc.; dried or undried but having bark on them. Each p° is one arm long; the middle one (on the west) is the thickest, the one on the south is the longest, and the one on the north is the shortest and thinnest Āp. Śr. I.5.7—10, K. Śr. II.8.1. There are 2 p° (*madhyama* and *uttara*) at the *Pitṛyajña* Āp. Śr. VIII.14.9; and

13 at the *pravargya* XV.5.11 used for encircling the *gharma*.

°*saṁdhi* m. the joint of p° formed when 2 p° meet at one point, *i.e.* the angles, north-west and south-west, of the *āhavanīya* VII.5.7; and the angle formed by the northern stick and southern stick 13.6.

परिपशव्य *Paripaśavya* mfn. name of 2 libations : *svāhā devebhyaḥ* and *devebhyaḥ svāhā*, offered before and after the immolation of the sacrificial horse K. Śr. XX.6.11 (*Aśva*); VI.5.24 (*Paśu*).

परिप्लवा *Pariplavā* f. name of a spoon without a handle, like a *sruc*, for drawing out *soma* Āp. Śr. XII.2.7; used for drawing *soma* without stream (*adhārā*) from the *droṇakalaśa* XII.18.11. B. Śr. VII.7 mentions *pariplu* (*pātra*) "floating spoon" (*pariplavamāna*, comm.).

परिभोजनीय *Paribhojanīya* mfn., n. one of the small bunches of grass (*barhis*), used as seat by the priests, sacrificer and his wife B. Śr. I.2. Cf. Eggeling SBE XII, 84.

परियज्ञ *Pariyajña* m. secondary rites ("round about") of the *Vājapeya*, consisting of an *ekāha* of different type K. Śr. XIV.1.9.

परिलेखन *Parilekhana* n. act of tracing a circle round the (7th) footprint of a cow with a *sphya* or a horn of a black antelope B. Śr. VI.13. cf. *paddharaṇī*. C.H. 39; also with a spade around the spot where the *audumbarī* post is to be fixed within the *sadas* VI.25. cf. C.H. 92.

परिवर्तिनी *Parivartinī* f. a reverting mode of chanting a *viṣṭuti* (variety) of the *trivṛtstoma* of the *bahiṣpavamānastotra* in which the 3 verses are arranged in a recurring order (natural), *e.g.* a b c (1st turn), a b c (2nd turn), a b c (3rd turn) cf. Eggeling SBE XXVI, 310. The other varieties are *udvatī*, *kulāyinī*.

परिवाद *Parivāda* m. a *mantra* of censure to Prajāpati in the *Dvādaśāha* Āp. Śr. XXI.12.1.

परिवाप *Parivāpa* (*pari-√vap*, cl. 1 "to scatter around") m. (1) fried grains of rice, husked but not pounded, put in a bowl containing *ājya* and boiled for making a cake (*savanīya-puroḍāśa*) Āp. Śr. XII.4.13; commonly known as *lāja* ib. 14 (*Soma*). C.H.134.

(2)=curds, *dadhi* K. Śr. VIII.9.27. comm; °*vāpyā* the cow which gives milk for curds to be offered to Sarasvatī K. Śr. ib.

परिवासन *Parivāsana* (*pari-√vas*, cl. 1 "to dwell around, to cut off ?" cf. Whitney Roots) n. cut off portion of the bundles of *darbha* (grass), called *veda*, which is to remain on the altar Āp. Śr. I.6.8 (*Darśa*). Cf. Eggeling SBE XII,84.

परिवृक्ती *Parivṛktī* f. the discarded queen (*anapacitā* L. Śr. IX.10.2) Āp. Śr. XX.10.2. see *Aśvamedha*, *patnī*.

परिवृत *Parivṛta* n. covered enclosures (2), one used by the sacrificer, and the other by his wife as their sacrificial toilet; situated to the north of the *śālā* (for *apsu dīkṣā*) K. Śr. VII. 2.7. A similar hut, to the south of the *mārjālīya*, where sexual copulation takes place XIII.3.9 (*Mahāvrata*) ; see also *kaṭaparivāra*.

परिव्ययण *Parivyayaṇa* (*pari-√vyā*, cl. 4 ? "to tie round") n. rite of putting a rope (*raśanā*) round the *yūpa* to which the animal is tied; done thrice at the height of one's navel (*Paśu*) Bh. Śr. VII.9.2, K. Śr. VI.3.5; the accompanying verse (RV. III.8.4) is called *parivyayaṇīyā* Āśv. Śr. V.3.5-6.

परिश्रयण *Pariśrayaṇa* (*pari-√śri*, cl.1 "to cover around") n. act of covering the altar with a mat at the time of pounding grains Āp. Śr. VIII.13.15 (*Pitṛyajña*, *Cāturmāsya*); similar cover 15.1. *soma*°, a piece of cloth for tying up *soma* stalks XIII.22.3, later worn by the sacrificer's wife at the *avabhṛtha*.

pariśrit f. stone "enclosures", 261 or 394 in number, used as support for the bricks of the *agnikṣetra* K. Śr. XVI.8.22(*Cayana*).

pariśrita n. an enclosure of mat around the *śālā* at the *dīkṣā* (cf. *parivṛta*) X.5.1 (*Soma*); a sort of screen in front of the *gārhapatya* III.9.3 (*Darśa*), in front of the *patnīśālā* so that the wife cannot see the *mahāvīra* XV.5.2 (*pravargya*), around the spot where *soma* stalks are weeded out by the vendor Bh. Śr. X.13.10-11 (*Soma*).

परिसमूहन *Parisamūhana* (*pari-sam-√ūh*, cl.1 "to sweep round together") n. act of sweeping round the three fires before and after the offering of *Agnihotra* Bh. Śr. VI 8.11-12 (*parisamūhati*).

परिस्तरण *Paristaraṇa* n. See *agni*°

परिस्रुत् *Parisrut* (*śrut*) f. wine (*surā*) or, according to some, undistilled wine or made from immature grains Āp. Śr. XVIII.1.10; XIX.1.8 (*Vāja* & *Sautrāmaṇī*). For preparation of wine, see H.Dh. II(2), 1225-6;

परिहरण *Pariharaṇa* n. procession (carrying forward) with the *vasatīvarī* waters (kept overnight) B. Śr. XV.21; act of carrying an object round the sacred fire Āp. Śr. III 1.5, the burning log (*ulmuka*) round the offering Āśv. Śr. II.3.7:

परिहोम *Parihoma* m. the offering on both sides, *i.e.* before and after B. Śr. XX.19.

परिह्वालम् *Parihvālam* ind. faltering manner of speaking "human" (*mānuṣī*) words, to be practised by the sacrificer at the *dīkṣā* Bh. Śr. X.7.14 (*Soma*).

परीशास *Parīśāsa* (du.) m. a pair of tongs for raising up the *gharma* from fire K. Śr. XXVI.2.10 (*Pravargya*)

पर्यग्निकरण *Paryagnikaraṇa* n. rite of going three times round an object with a firebrand (*ulmuka*) drawn from the *āhavanīya*, performed by the *Āgnīdhra* who holds the *ulmuka* in his hands and moves round keeping the object always on his right (*pradakṣiṇa*). The objects are *yūpa*, *āhavanīya*, *cātvāla*, *śāmitra* and offering materials Āp. Śr. VII.15.2; I.25.8. In *Paśu*, 6 times round the animal, according to comm. K. Śr. VI.5.2-4.

The object thus circled with fire is called *paryagni* m. Āp. Śr. VII.15.1 & comm.

पर्यङ्ग्य *Paryaṅgya* mfn. technical name of 12 animals whose limbs are tied to the limbs of the sacrificial horse with a branch of *plakṣa* tree Āp. Śr. XX.13.12 (*Aśva*). The list of animals, Dumont L'Aśva 327.

पर्याणहन *Paryāṇahana* n. See *soma*°

पर्याय *Paryāya* m. (1) a turn or round of beating of *soma* stalks with stones, done by the priests during the pressing of *soma*; there are three such rounds Āp. Śr. XII.12.8-9 (*Soma*).

(2) a turn of chanting a triplet in the *stoma*; there are always 3 turns which together make up a *viṣṭuti* (variety). Each p° contains each stanza in different or equal number depending on the *viṣṭuti* and *stoma*; each p° is composed of 3 repetitions (subdivisions), called *viṣṭāva*: *ṛcabhāga*, *āvāpa* (*sthāna*) and *paricarā* (*ṛc*). See also *sāman*, *stotra*, *stoma*. Cf. Eggeling SBE XXVI, 308-9; Caland PBr.19.

rātri° rounds of *Soma* sacrifice performed at night, consisting of 4 *stotras*, 4 *śastras*, 4 libations. Three r° make the noctural portion of the *Atirātra* Āp. Śr. XIV.3.9.

पर्यास *Paryāsa* m. concluding portion of a hymn immediately preceding the *paridhānīyā*, *e.g.* the 4th part of the 2nd *ājyaśastra* C.H. 244, the 5th of the *niṣkevalya* C.H.315, 319, 325.

पर्वन् *Parvan* n. periods (parts) of the *Cāturmāsya* rite : *Vaiśvadeva*, *Varuṇapraghāsa*, *Sākamedha*, *Śunāsīrīya*, each comprising a "joint" of the whole year Āp. Śr. VIII.4.4.

पर्शु *Parśu* m. the rib of either a horse or a bull, used by the *Adhvaryu* as a sickle (*dātra*) for cutting *darbha* grass Bh. Śr. I.3.5-6 (*Darśa*); see *prastara*.

पल्व *Palva* m. n. winnowing basket containing sacrificial grains B. Śr. XX.6.

पवन *Pavana* (√*pū*, cl.9 "to cleanse, purify") n. rite of purification of the body of a sacrificer at the *dīkṣā* by means of 21 tufts of *darbha* Āp. Śr. X.7.5 (*Soma*), C.H.13.

पवमानग्रह *Pavamāna* (*graha*) m. name of the drawings of "purified" *soma* at the morning pressing just before the *bahiṣpavamāna stotra* commences Āp. Śr. XII.16.12 : this drawing is done directly with the *pariplavā* from the *ādhavanīya* into the *droṇakalaśa* or the *pūtabhṛt* B. Śr. VIII.7. Cf C.H.169.

पवमानस्तोत्र *Pavamānastotra* n. literally, the *stotra* during the chanting of which *soma* is "purified"; name of the first *stotras* of each pressing Āp. Śr. XII.17.8 (*Soma*). At the three *savanas* (pressings) they are called *bahiṣpavamāna* in the morning C.H.177, *mādhyandina*° in the midday C.H.277 and *tṛtīya*° or *ārbhava*° at the third C.H. 337.

पवित्र *Pavitra* (√*pū*, cl.9 "to cleanse, purify") n. (1) a filter for *soma*, made of white wool Āp. Śr. X.26.12=*daśāpavitra* (q v.)

(2) a "filter", made of 2 blades of *darbha*; both of them of equal breadth, 1 *prādeśa* (12 *aṅgulas*, 1 span) in length, with unbroken ends; used for purifying waters called *prokṣaṇī* (to be used for sprinkling all the sacrificial vessels and implements Āp. Śr. I.11.9) in the

following manner : water fetched in the *agnihotrahavaṇī* covered with p° and poured again in a bowl containing p° whose blades are turned towards the north; waters now called *prokṣaṇī*; this process called *utpavana* is repeated thrice Āp. Śr. I.11.7-8 *(Darśa)*. Cf. Mī. III.8.32.

(3) a "filter" consisting of 3 stranded *darbha* blades, 1 *prādeśa* in length, bound to that branch of *palāśa* out of which the *upaveṣa* is prepared. This is called *śākhāpavitra* Āp. Śr. I.6.9, Bh. Śr. I.6.11 with which warm milk in a *kumbhī* is stirred and purified Bh. Śr. I.12.14 *(Darśa)*. A filter or *muñja* grass is used at the *pravargya* Āp. Śr. XV.5.20.

(4) name of a rite which is a Soma sacrifice of the ordinary *Agniṣṭoma* type, and constiutes the opening days of the *Rāja* Ap. Śr. XVIII. 8.3-4, K. Śr. XV1.4-7; also called *prāyaṇīya* B. Śr. XII.1. Cf. Heesterman 12-14.

पशु *Paśu* (pl) m. animal sacrifices, 29 or 30 in number, if *agnīṣomīya* p° is reckoned (Āśv. Śr. III.8.2). The animal sacrifice, one of the *haviryajña*, is differentiated as *iṣṭavidha* and *somavidha*; the former differing from the latter in respect of certain acts and offerings : preparation of (*praṇītā*) waters and carrying it, making viṣṇu steps, offering certain limbs of the victim etc. Āp. Śr. VII.28.1, K.Śr.VI.2.4 *(haviryajñavidha)* comm. There are however 2 types : the independent animal sacrifice generally known as *Nirūḍhapaśubandha*, which is called *nirmita* (made) and explained as *svatantra* (Āśv. Śr. III.8.3 & comm.), and the animal sacrifices belonging to Soma sacrifice (*saumya* Āśv. Śr. ib. 2) : *Agnīṣomīya*, *Savanīya* and *Anubandhyā* (and therefore *aṅgas* of *Soma*).

But *Nirūḍha* is considered as a modification of the *Agnīṣomīya* Mī.VIII.1.13. Many *sūtras* however put forward the paradigms of both. The *Nirūḍha* is the model of all other animal sacrifices.

°*puroḍāśa* m. an oblation of cake on 11 or 12 *kapālas* offered to the principal deities of the *Paśu* before the immolation of a victim Āp. Śr. VII.22.1, 11; offered after the limbs of the animal have been cooked or after the offering of the omentum Bh. Śr. VII.17.10. At the *Savanīyapaśu* the p° is offered at the midday pressing Āp. Śr. XIII.1.12.

°*śrapaṇa* n. See *śrapaṇa*.

पश्चात्तिरश्ची *Paścāttiraścī* f. the rear transversal line connecting the 2 *śroṇis* (north-south) on the west of the *vedi* Āp. Śr. VII.3.8 (°*tiryak*). Cf. *prācī*, *purastāt (tiraścī)*.

पष्ठौही *Paṣṭhauhī* f. a heifer, four years old, given as sacrificial fee to the priest Bh. Śr. XIII.8.16 (*Soma*).

पाजक *Pājaka* m. a basket, made of bamboo, in which the *brahmaudana* is kept before cooking Bh. Śr. V.3.2. (*Ādheya*).

पाण्डार *Pāṇḍāra* m. n. a kind of turban, worn by the sacrificer, said to be white Āp. XVIII. 14.1-2 (*Rāja*).

पाण्ड्व *Pāṇḍva* n. a blanket (*kambala*, comm.). worn by the royal sacrificer over his *tārpya* dress at the unction ceremony K. Śr. XV.5.12 (*Rāja*).

पात्नीवत *Pātnīvata* mfn. name of the 13th *yūpa*, not higher than the navel height when imbedded into the pit, to which the animal belonging to Tvaṣṭṛ and the divine wives is tied Āp. Śr. XIV.5.9 (*Ekādaśinī*). Cf. H.Dh.II(2), 1132.

°*graha* m. drawing of *soma* for Agni and the divine wives K. Śr. X.6.16. Cf. C.H. 366.

पात्र *Pātra* n. name of various cups, goblets which are *upāṃśu*°, *ūrdhva*°, *ṛtu*°, *śukra*°, *manthi*° etc. P° are made of *vikaṅkata* wood K. Śr.I.3.31. The word p° (or *yajña*°) includes all the sacrificial utensils Āp. Śr. I.7 5; 11.10. *Karambha*° see *karambha*.

°*caya* (*na*) m., n. stacking of the sacrificial utensils on the funeral pyre near the corpse Bh. Pi.II.1.9.

pātrī f. an earthen vessel on which the dough for a cake is prepared Āp. Śr. I.24.1 (*Darśa*); *pātrīnirṇejana* water for cleansing a vessel 25.14.

पाद *Pāda* m. a quarter of a stanza, i.e. a line. In technical usage in the *sūtras* a whole verse is to be understood when its first line is mentioned (*ṛcaṁ pādagrahaṇe*) Āśv. Śr. I.1.17. Similarly, the entire hymn by a part of the first line ib. 18.

पादिन् *Pādin* m. priests who are entitled to get a quarter of what their principals get as sacrificial fees Āp. Śr. XXI.2.19. see *ṛtvij*.

पान्नेजन *Pānnejana*(*ī*) mf. See *Pannejanī*.

पारिघर्म्य *Pārigharmya* m. See *pari.°*

पारिप्लव *Pāriplava* (*ākhyāna*) (*pari-√plu*, cl. 1 "to float around") mfn., n. "recitals moving in a cycle", containing popular legends recited by the *Hotṛ* at *Aśva*; so called because it is renewed every 10 days throughout a year K.Śr. XX.3.1. It is composed of the legend of *Śunaḥśepa* in which more than a hundred or more than a thousand *ṛks* and *gāthās* are collected Āp. Śr. XVIII.19.10 (*Rāja*). cf. Heesterman 158-61. The list of legends (*ākhyāna*) Āśv. Śr. X.7.

पार्वण *Pārvaṇa* (*homa*) mfn., m. libation of *ājya* with a *sruva* on the "joint" (*parvan*) day of 2 periods of the *pūrṇamāsa* and the *darśeṣṭi* Āp. Śr. II.20.5. This is immediately followed by the principal oblations of *Darśa*. Cf. H. Dh. II(2), 1081.

पार्श्व *Pārśva* m.n. implement used for stirring up the *vasā* in a spoon at the *vasāhoma* Āp. Śr. VII.25.4 (*Paśu*).

pārśva (du), 2 flanks or 2 thoracic walls Bh. Śr. VII.18.12. See *jauhava*.

पालागली *Pālāgalī* f. a queen of low origin = *pālākalī* Āp. Śr. XX.10.2. See *Aśvamedha*, *patnī*.

पावन *Pāvana* n. stalks of *soma* used as purifier of the *upāṁśugraha* Āp. Śr. XII.12.1.

पाश *Pāśa* m. noose (*raśanā*) used for strangling an animal; thereafter loosened, pierced with a one-pronged fork, then cast away on the *utkara* or *cātvāla* Āp. Śr. VII.17.4-6, Bh. Śr. VII.13.6-7.

पिच्छोला *Picchlolā* f. a flute, played at the chanting Āp. Śr. XXI.17.16 (*Mahāvrata*).

पिण्ड *Piṇḍa* m.n. a lump, the ball of boiled rice; 3 p° offered by the sacrificer to his 3 immediate paternal ancestors, partly consumed, partly thrown away Āp Śr. I.9.1. (*Piṇḍapitṛyajña*); VIII.16.6 (*Mahāpitṛyajña*, *Sākamedha*) prepared from the remnants of oblatory materials.

piṇḍī f. 3 balls made of flour of *kharjūra*, *karīra* offered in the *Kāmyeṣṭi* Āp. Śr. XIX.26.1, B. Śr. XIII.38.

There is also a rite in which the portions of the *savanīyapuroḍāśa* are offered to the *Pitṛs* B. Śr. VIII.12. C.H.350.

पिण्डपितृयज्ञ *Piṇḍapitṛyajña* m. sacrifice of lump offering to the manes (*pitṛ*), recognized as a part (*aṅga*) of the *Darśa* K. Śr. IV.1.30, also performed at the *Sākamedha* and called *Mahāpitṛyajña* Āp. Śr. VIII.13-16. Also considered an independent rite Mī IV.4.19-21.

As a part of *Darśa* it is performed on the *amāvāsyā* day. The paddy stored on the *śakaṭa* is taken into the *carusthālī*; the paddy is beaten, husks removed with a winnowing basket by the sacrificer's wife. The rice is cooked on *dakṣiṇāgni*, sprinkled with *ājya*, and a portion of the cooked rice is stirred with a *mekṣaṇa*, cut off into 2 portions, again sprinkled with *ājya* and offered into d° agni. A line is drawn on the ground with the *sphya*, 3 balls of rice (*piṇḍa*) are prepared, and the sacrificer, wearing the sacred cord in the *prācīnāvītin* fashion, drops the *piṇḍas* from his palm on the line one after another for the father, the grandfather and the great-grandfather. The higher the generation, the bigger is the size of the *piṇḍa*. It is a matter of great controversy whether only the dead ancestors should get *piṇḍas* and the living one be only honoured. No *piṇḍa* is to be offered to any ancestor beyond the great grandfather and none to anybody alive Āśv. Śr. II.6.20-23, the living father is honoured with a *homa* Āp. Śr. I.9.8. If the sacrificer has two fathers (owing to adoption) in each higher generation, two names are to be mentioned for each *piṇḍa* offered.

Then the *piṇḍas* are covered with the hem (*daśā*) of a garment. The Fathers are made to depart by pouring water over the *piṇḍas*. The wife is made to eat the middle *piṇḍa* so that she may conceive. The two other *piṇḍas* are either cast off into water or collected in a pot, smelt by the sacrificer. B. Śr. III.10-11, K. Śr. IV.1, Āp. Śr. I.7-10, Āśv. Śr. II.6-7. cf. H.Dh. II(2), 1085-1090.

पितृतीर्थ *Pitṛtīrtha* n. way of the manes; part of the hand between the thumb and the fore-finger through which water is offered for the *pitṛs* H.Dh. IV, 435n & also II(1), 316n.

पितृमेध *Pitṛmedha* m. funeral rites for *pitṛs*, consisting of cremation of the corpse, gathering of bones, piling of the lumps of earth etc. B.Pi. [Sr. K(S)I, 802-23].

पितृयज्ञ *Pitṛyajña* m. = *piṇḍapitṛ°* Āp. Śr. III.16.7, *Mahā°* VIII.13.1. Kauśikasūtra describes the rite very succinctly : the rite is performed, unlike a sacrifice to the gods, by the sacrificer wearing the sacred cord in the *prācīnāvītin* fashion; facing the south (north or east for the gods) he begins, and ends facing the south west; circumambulation is done in anti-clockwise direction (*prasavya*) as opposed to the *pradakṣiṇa* movement.

All offerings are made by uttering *svadhā* as opposed to the use of *svāhā* and *vaṣaṭ* in the services to gods Kauś. S. I.9-23. cf. B. Śr. II.2.

पिन्वन *Pinvana* n. milk pail, 2 in number K. Śr. XXVI.1.20 (*Pravargya*).

पिष्टपात्री *Piṣṭapātrī* f. a vessel for holding flour (*piṣṭa*), of very big size K. Śr. I.3.36 comm; cf. *piṣṭasaṁyavani*° Vai Śr. XI.9, *piṣṭodvapanī* B. Śr. I 4.

पिष्टलेपहोम *Piṣṭalepahoma* (or *āhuti*) m. offering made from the sacrificial residue sticking to a vessel, scraped off by means of a spoon, mixed with *ājya* (Bh. Śr.III.9.6), on the *dakṣiṇāgni* Āp. Śr.III.9.12 (*Darśa*). cf. *ājyalepa* 8.1.

पुंश्चली *Puṁścalī* f. a prostitute, who abuses a *brahmacārī* Āp Śr. XXI.19.5 (*Mahāvrata*)= *puṁścalū* K. Śr. XIII.3.6.

पुच्छ *Puccha* m. n. "tail" of the fire-altar, forming a rectangle of which the 2 sides are 1 *puruṣa* each, and the other 2 extended by 1 *prādeśa*=12 *aṅgula*s or 1 *vitasti* (13 a°) each, to the west K.Śr. XVI.8.20, Āp. Śr. XVI.17.10, 14 (*Cayana*). Cf. *yajña*°. Plan Eggeling SBE XLI, 419.

पुनराधेय *Punarādheya* n. reinstallation of fires which takes place under certain contingencies, *e.g.* illness, loss of wealth or desire for prosperity, and is performed in the same paradigm as in the *Ādheya* with a few deviations Āp. Śr. V.26-29. It is a *prāyaścitta* if the *gārhapatya* and *āhavanīya* have been extinguished or discontinued Mī. VI.4.26-27.

पुनर्दहन *Punardahana* n. rite of recremation of charred bones. The fire is churned, the jar containing the bones is taken out, and the bones are crushed into powder with the mortar and pestle placed over the skin. The powdered bone mixed with butter is offered into the fire with the *juhū*. The other utensils are thrown away B. Pi. II.3-4, Bh. Pi.1.10.4.

पुनश्चिति *Punaściti* f. See *citi*.

पुरस्ताज्जप *Purastājjapa* m. See *japa*.

पुरस्तात्तिरश्ची *Purastāttiraścī* f. the front transversal line joining the 2 *aṁsa*s of the *vedi* on the east Āp. Śr. VII.3.8. Cf. *paścāt*° *aṁsa*, *śroṇi*. See plans.

पुरीतत् *Purītat* n. pericardium (?) of an animal Bh. Śr. VII.19.11. See *jauhava*.

पुरीष *Purīṣa* n. rubbish, obtained at the time of digging the ground for a *vedi* (=*khanana*° Bh. Śr. II.3.1) as distinguished from *āhārya*, earth "fetched" from outside for preparing a *vedi* Āp. Śr. II.3.4-5, Bh. Śr. l.c.; p° is dumped on the *utkara* Āp. Śr. l.c., and it can also be brought for the construction of *dhiṣṇya*s etc. from the *cātvāla* K. Śr. I.8.39. The altar is called *purīṣavatī* Āp. Śr. II.2.7. Also used for filling up the gaps between the bricks XVII.24.14; *sāma*° for the same purpose XVII. 25.4 (*Cayana*). The *uttaravedi*, 2 *khara*s are constructed with p° brought from the *cātvāla* XIX.1.15. (*Sautrāmaṇī*).

पुरुष *Puruṣa* m. length of a "man", *i.e.* the height of a sacrificer, a standard of measurement, used for constructing the *agnikṣetra* K. Śr. XVI.8.21 (*Cayana*); the length is measured from the finger to the foot when the sacrificer stands raising his hand Āp. Śr. XVI.17.8.= 120 *aṅgula*s B. Śulb. I.1.

पुरुषमेध *Puruṣamedha* m. human sacrifice, lasting 5 days, a type of *Soma* sacrifice Āp. Śr. XX. 24-25, B. Śr. XXIV.11. But cf. Eggeling SBE XLIV, xi—xiv.

पुरोडाश *Puroḍāśa* m. cake, made of pounded rice or barley flour etc. baked on the *gārhapatya* on the *kapāla*s (potsherds) of variable number (8,11 etc.) Āp. Śr. I.24.6; shaped like a tortoise, back of the cake being neither too high nor too low like an *apūpa*, as large as the hoof of a horse 25.4. *Avadāna*s are taken from it III.1.2. For preparation of a p° H. Dh.II(2), 1032-3. This is a typical offering material at *Darśa*, *Soma*, *Paśu* (VII.22.11, cf. *paśu*°). *Savanīya*° a series of 5 cakes at the pressing : a p° of rice on 11 *kapāla*s to Indra, of *dhāna* (parched barley) for Indra *harivat*, of *karambha* (flour mixed with curds for Pūṣan, of *parivāpa* (parched grains) for Sarasvatī, *āmikṣā* for Mitra and Varuṇa B. Śr. VII.12, C.H. 134, and oblations offered with them at *Soma* C.H. 196. cf. Eggeling SBE XXVI, 315-6. See also *paśu*°.

Rauhiṇau puroḍāśau, 2 cakes, made of ground rice but not husked (*aphalīkṛta*) Āp. Śr. XV. 5.20; 9.1 (*pravargya*). *Puroḍāśīya* grains for a cake Bh. Śr. I.19. 4. °*pātrī* f. a vessel for p° K. Śr. I.3.36 comm.

पुरोऽनुवाक्या *Puro'nuvākyā* f. an invitatory verse recited by the *Hotṛ* on the instructions of the *Adhvaryu* before the latter pours out oblation Āp. Śr. II.18.4. P° is recited by the *Hotṛ* while sitting, and employed in *ājyabhāga*, *āvāpa*, *sviṣṭakṛt*, *patnīsaṁyāja*.; it is also called *anuvākyā* (q.v.).

पुरोरुच् *Puroruc* f. "shining in front"; name of some *nivid mantra*s (recited loudly ABr. X.7) recited at the morning pressing at the beginning of the *śastra*s Ś. Śr. VII.9.2, as in the first *ājyaśastra* C.H. 232, in which they are recited with a pause; in the *praügaśastra* there are 7 p° interpolated into each triplet of the principal hymn C.H.239. cf. H.Dh.II(2), 1180. See *nivid*.

पुरोहविस् *Purohavis* mfn. "*havis* in front", said of the sacrificial arena (*devayajana*); "the place where the sacrifice faces the east" Keith TS(VI.2.6), 507. cf. Bh. Śr. X.13.6.

पुरोहित *Purohita* m(fn). "placed in front", a domestic or, later, royal chaplain whose *pravara* is taken into consideration by a royal sacrificer in selecting a priest for the *śrauta* sacrifice Āp. Śr. II.16.10; some *ekāha*s are performed by them XXII.10.19; 13.10.

पूतभृत् *Pūtabhṛt* m. name of a *sthālī* for *soma* (literally, a container of the purified *soma*); a clay trough with a large opening, kept for some time on the yoke of a cart which carries *soma*; during the drawing it is covered with a filter (*daśāpavitra*) and *soma* is poured into it Āp. Śr. XII.2.12; 16.11. See also *abhiṣavaṇu*, *graha*.

पूतीक *Pūtīka* m. a plant used as a substitute for *soma* plant; p° itself is replaced by *ādāra*, *phālguna* Āp. Śr. XIV.24.12. or *arjuna* PBr. IX 3.3. cf. Mī. VI.3.31.

पूतुद्रु *Pūtudru* m. stick of p° (Pinus deodara), 3 in number, used as enclosing sticks of the *uttaravedī* (*Paśu*) Bh. Śr. VII.5.1 (*pautudrava*).

पूर्णपात्र *Pūrṇapātra* m. n. a vessel filled with water; water is sprinkled in all directions Āp. Śr. III.10.7 (*Darśa*)=*udakamaṇḍalu* Bh. Śr. III.7.1; also a measure for paddy given as sacrificial fee to the *Āgnīdhra* (*Ādheya*), said to be 4 *puṣkala*s (=32 handfuls)=128 handfuls Āp. Śr. V.20.7 & comm.

पूर्णाहुति *Pūrṇāhuti* f. "full oblation"; an oblation of *ājya* made by means of a *juhū* (*sruc*) which is filled with 4 or 12 (*sruva*) spoonfuls of *ājya*; this generally marks the end of *Ādheya* Bh. Śr. V.11.1. The entire procedure of *āhuti* is followed K. Śr. IV.10.5 comm. This is also done at *dīkṣā* Āp. Śr. X.8.6 (*Soma*). See also *āhuti*.

पूर्वाग्नि *Pūrvāgni* m. original fire of the householder (*āvasathya*) K. Śr. XV.6.14; but the term is obscure. B. Śr. XVIII.16 mentions p° together with the other fires. cf. Heesterman 148.

°*vahana* n. a cart for carrying the fire; °*vāh* n. a bull drawing the cart with p° K. Śr. XV.7.21 (*Rāja*).

पृषदाज्य *Pṛṣadājya* n. "speckled butter", clarified butter with which curdled milk is mixed, used specially for sprinkling the heart of a sacrificed animal by the *śamitṛ* (*Paśu*) Āp. Śr. VII. 23.7; *ājya* is drawn in *juhū* and *upabhṛt* and poured twice into the mixing vessel called °*grahaṇī* as *upastaraṇa*, then curds are poured (*upastaraṇa*) into the vessel over which 2 *darbha* blades are placed; *darbha* blades are removed and again *ājya* is poured twice over the curds (*abhighāraṇa*) B. Śr. IV.3; p° used optionally at *Soma* Āp. Śr. XII.19.5.

°*dhānī* f. a vessel for p°, a substitute for the *upabhṛt* VII.26.12 (*Paśu*).

पृष्ठ (स्तोत्र) *Pṛṣṭha* (*stotra*) n. "backed up", a particular form of chanting a *stotra* L. Śr. II.9.7, in which two verses (RV. VII.32.22-23). one in *bṛhatī*, the other in *satobṛhatī*, are so manipulated by repeating the last *pāda* of the first and the 2nd of the 2nd verse as to produce a three-versed chant; these chants are used as "*pṛṣṭha*s", *i.e.* chanted twice with another *sāman* sandwiched between them, symbolically serving as a womb for an embryo. There are 4 p° *stotra*s at the midday libation of *Soma* : the first, in the *rathantara* and *bṛhatsāman* C.H.306; the second, called *vāmadevya* (RV.IV.31.1-3) in the same manner as the first C.H. 314; the third, *naudhasa* (R.V. VIII.88.1-2) C.H.318, and finally the fourth, *kāleya* (RV. VIII.66.1-2) C.H.323. cf. Eggeling SBE XXVI, 339; XLI, xx, H.Dh. II(2),1191.

पृष्ठ्य (षडह) *Pṛṣṭhya* (*ṣaḍaha*) m. a period of six *soma* days; the other of its type is *Abhiplava*°; so called because the *pṛṣṭha* *stotra*s in it, unlike in *Abhiplava*°, are chanted in ordinary *Agniṣṭoma* way (see p° *stotra*) Āp. Śr. XXI.8.8. The six days of p° consist of 1 *Agniṣṭoma* day, 2 *Ukthyas*, 1 *Ṣoḍaśin* and again 2 *Ukthyas* at the end. Cf. Eggeling SBE XXVI, 403. In total there are 6 *pṛṣṭhasāmans* in it : *rathantara, bṛhat, vairūpa, vairāja, śākvara, raivata* ib. 406. cf. Mī. X.6.4.

पृष्ठ्या *Pṛṣṭhyā* f. a ridge, the "spinal" line running along the back of the *vedi* between the *gārhapatya* and the *āhavanīya* B. Śr. I.4, Āp. Śr. XI.4.16; marked by a peg (*śaṅku*) driven into the ground at a distance of 3 or 6 *prakramas* towards the east from the original *āhavanīya* (called *antaḥpātya* or *pṛṣṭhyāśaṅku*), then from this place another peg at 36 *prakramas*, towards the east at the *yūpāvaṭīya*, finally a rope connects the two points B. Śr. VI.22, K. Śr. VIII.3.11 comm. cf. C.H.74 (*mahāvedi*). See also *spandyā*. See plan 3. For the method of drawing the pṛ° Āp. Śulb. I.1.4.

पेषणी *Peṣaṇī* f. two crusher stones, the *dṛṣad* and the *upalā* Vai. Śr. XI.9.

पोतृ *Potṛ* m. "one who purifies", one of the 16 officiating priests, an assistant to the *Brahman*, but actually to the *Hotṛ* (cf. RV. I.76.4 : Agni is a p° priest), Āp. Śr. X.1.9, and recites a *yājyā* at the morning pressing XII.24.1.

पौर्णमास *Paurṇamāsa* m. n. sacrifice of the full moon Āp. Śr. III.16.5; see *Darśa*; also called *paurṇamāsī* f. I.14.17, which actually means the *tithi* (day) on which the sun and moon are at the greatest distance from each other, whence the sacrifice takes place at the night of full moon ib. P° is the opposite of *amāvāsyā* (q.v.).

प्रउग *Praüga* (probably from *pra-yuga*) n. forepart of the shaft of a cart carrying *soma* on which the *pūtabhṛt* trough is kept Bh. Śr. XIII.2.14; and the other utensils (also called *pradhura*) Āp. Śr. XII.2.12.

°*śastra* n. the second *śastra* or litany recited by the *Hotṛ* at the morning pressing (Āśv. Śr. V.10.6) C.H. 239. The litany is composed of RV. I.2 and 3 containing 21 verses, divided into 7 triplets; each triplet is preceded by a *puroruc* in recitation.

प्रकृति *Prakṛti* f. a natural order; a model (archetype) of all other rites (*vikṛti*). All *iṣṭis* are based on the *Darśapūrṇamāsa* which is a p° for them Āp. Śr. XXIV.3.32. *Agniṣṭoma* is a model for all other *Soma* sacrifices.

प्रक्रम *Prakrama* m. step, a measurement of length; equal to 2 or 3 *padas* (a *pada*=15 *aṅgulas* Āp. Śr. V.4.3. comm) or ⅓ *pada* K. Śr. VIII.3.14 comm; used for preparing the altar etc. The measuring rope is called °*sthānīyā* Āp. Śr. XIV.5.11. cf. H.Dh. II(2), 989n & 1152n. B. Śulb. I.1.

प्रगाथ *Pragātha* m. stanzas which constitute the parts of the *marutvatīyaśastra* : *Indranih(n) ava*° (RV. VIII.53.5-6), *Brāhmaṇaspatya*° (RV. I.40.5-6) and *Marutvatīya*° (RV. VIII.89.3-4); each composed of 2 stanzas, one in *bṛhatī* and the other in *kakubh* metres (*bārhata*) or *kakubh* and *satobṛhatī* (*kākubha*). By repetition and combination of *pādas*, out of the 2 stanzas, a triplet is produced Ś. Śr. VI.9.7, Āśv. Śr. V.14 (midday pressing, *Soma*). cf. H.Dh. II(2), 1190, C.H. 300.

प्रग्रथन *Pragrathana* n. (*dharma*) a procedure of combining the verses by repeating the last *pāda* and joining it to the first *pāda* of the next Ś. Śr. VII.25.3.

प्र-चर् *Pra-√car* (cl.1) to proceed; specially, to perform rites, as in *savanīyaiḥ pracarati* (performs with the *savanīyapuroḍāśa*) Bh. Śr. XIV.3.10.

प्रचरणी *Pracaraṇī* f. a ladle of *vikaṅkata* wood (the 7th *sruc* in addition to the *juhū*), used for *vaisarajana* offerings Āp. Śr. XI.16.6, 15.

प्रजनन *Prajanana* n. hole in the lower *araṇi* from which fire is churned=*yoni* B. Śr. II.6, L. Śr. II.5.5.

प्रणयन *Praṇayana* (*pra-√nī*, cl.1 "to lead forward") n. conveyance, bringing forward; the word is specially used for the processional transport of Agni and Soma at the *Soma* sacrifice; see *Agni*° and *Agnīṣoma*°.

praṇayanīya mfn. the fire brand (*idhma*) placed on the *gārhapatya* for "bringing forward" the fire for the *āhavanīya* Āp. Śr. V.13.3 (*Ādheya*), also at *Paśu* VII.6.4 etc.

प्रणव *Praṇava* m. the mystical interjection *om*, considered highly sacred, but not occuring in RV, only alluded to once in TS. Keith TS, 252n; it begins with a prolated (*trimātra*) or non-prolated *O* and ends with a *ma(ṁ)* Ś. Śr. I.1.19 (*O* is prolated Āśv. Śr. I.2.10); pronounced by the *Hotṛ* at the end of *sāmidhenī* verse the moment the *samidh* is thrown into the *āhavanīya* Āp. Śr. II.12.4 (*Darśa*), H.Dh. II(2),

1049; at the end of an *anuvākyā* VIII.15.14, at the end of a *śastra* XII.27.14. cf. *Om*: A.B. Keith ERE IX, 490-92.

प्रणीता: *Praṇītāḥ* f. (pl.) "fetched" waters, purified with *pavitras* (*utpavana*) in a *camasa* which is filled almost to its brim, carried in a vessel called *praṇītāpraṇayana*, by the *Adhvaryu* from the north of the *gārhapatya* to the north of the *āhavanīya*; accompanied with *mantras* this rite of fetching waters is known as *Praṇītāpraṇayana* Āp. Śr. I.15.7; 16.3-5 (*Darśa*). The p° waters is used for making a dough of the pounded grains for the *puroḍāśa* (see also *nirvāpa*). Cf. H.Dh.II(2), 1022-3.

प्रतिगर *Pratigara* (*prati-√gṛ*, cl.9 "to respond") m. formula of response, uttered loudly by the *Adhvaryu* as a return call to the *āhāva* (q.v.) of the *Hotṛ*. There are several *āhāvas* and *pratigaras* in the course of recitation of a *śastra*, and like the *āhāva* the *pratigara* assumes a mystical significance, and therefore by various permutations and combinations bizarre liturgical contortions are produced : *othāmo daiva* (pronounced *daivā*), the most common one Āśv. Śr. V.9.5, *śoṁsāmo* (*śaṁsā*) *daiva*; *othā moda iva* (at the end of a half-verse), *omothā moda iva* (at the end of a verse), or as an alternative *othā moda ivaṁ* (end of a half-verse), *hotarmoda ivam* (end of a verse), *othā moda ivam* (end of a *śastra*) Āp. Śr. XII.27.14-15; it varies in the *vaiśvadeva-śastra* XIII.13.8-10, *ṣoḍaśiśastra* XIV.3.4; *havai hotar* K. Śr. XX.3.2 (*Aśva*); *hoyi hotar* Ś. Śr. XV.1.23; or, simply, *om* Āp. Śr. XVIII. 19.13 (*Rāja*).

प्रतिनिग्राह्य *Pratinigrāhya* mfn. name of a drawing of *soma*, "to be taken out with a ladle", offered to the twin divinities (*dvidevatyagraha*) at the morning pressing (*Soma*) Āp. Śr XII.20. 19=*pratinirgrāhya* B. Śr. VII.12. Cf. C.H.199.

प्रतिनिधि *Pratinidhi* m. representative; a substitute for a missing thing; the substitute must be similar to and take the nature of the thing replaced, as *nīvāra* may be substituted for *vrīhi* Āp. Śr. XXIV.3.52-53; but if the quantity of a thing like *puroḍāśa* is reduced, it cannot be replaced ib. 54. Moreover, the substitution is not allowed for a sacrificer, the fire altar (*Cayana*), the deity, the word (of *mantras*), the act (of a sacrifice), and a prohibition 4.1. Cf. Oldenberg SBE. XXX, 352-53. A sacrificer of a *sattra*, where there are many, can be replaced Mī. VI.3.22. cf. H.Dh.II.(1), 684.

प्रति-पद् *Pratipad* (*prati-√pad*, cl. 4 "to set foot upon") f. an introductory verse, before *sāmidhenī* Āp. Śr. IV.9.2; specially, the first triplet which begins the *marutvatīya*-and *mahāvaiśvadeva-śastra* at the midday and third pressings Āśv. Śr. V.9.22. C.H. 300, 354. See *śastra*.

प्रतिप्रस्थातृ *Pratiprasthātṛ* m. priest who serves as the first assistant of the *Adhvaryu*; his special function is to lead the sacrificer's wife, and to cut off the entrails of a victim into 11 parts and offer with them the *upayāja* (*Paśu*) Āp. Śr. VII.18.1; 21.8; to prepare the *savanīya-puroḍāśa* XII.3.15 (*Soma*). He carries out the sacrificial duties without uttering *mantras*; *mantras* are recited by the *Adhvaryu* only VIII.5.17. His cup for drinking *soma* is called *pratiprasthāna* XII.21.21 which is smaller than that of the *Adhvaryu* XV.3.11.

प्रतिलोम *Pratiloma* mfn. against the hair, *i.e.* in the reverse direction (as opposed to *anuloma*), said of a ladle which is held with its beak turned towards the offerer of an oblation (*Pitṛmedha*) Bh. Pi. I.11.3.

प्रतिवेश *Prativeśa* mfn. "neighbouring"; auxiliary rice (*odana*), cooked on the *gārhapatya* or *dakṣiṇa* fire and consumed by the sacrificer's wife Bh. Śr. VIII.12.16; 13.16 (*Sākamedha*).

प्रतिसमेधनीय *Pratisamedhanīya* mfn. fire which is to be kindled by means of another fire, said of the *āhavanīya* B. Śr. X.21; also of the fire brand (*samidh*) XXII.3.

प्रतिहर्तृ *Pratihartṛ* m. one of the 16 priests; he is an assistant to the *Udgātṛ*, and is the third chanter who chants the *pratihāra* Āp. Śr. X.1.9. The *pratihāra* is a part of a *sāman*, and is preceded by the *prastāva* L. Śr. VII.10.22, and is a sort of a response to the latter; see *sāman*. cf. Simon Pañcavi 7.

प्रतिहित *Pratihita* m. (n.) a substitute for a king, his near relations ("one who is the nearest to someone") B. Sr. XII.11 (*Rāja*), Āp. Śr. XVIII.16.14.

प्रत्यवरोहणीय *Pratyavarohaṇīya* m. rite of descent to the earth; a concluding rite annexed to the *Vāja*, consisting of an *Agniṣṭoma* L. Śr. VIII.11.14. It is the counterpart of the *abhyārohaṇīya*. Cf. Heesterman 13.

प्रत्याम्नान Pratyāmnāna (*prati-ā-√mnā*, cl.1 "to note against") n. a corollary rule of altered purpose which debars the operation of a rule in the *prakṛti*, when it is said, for instance, instead of *kuśa* grass let him make a *barhis* of reeds Āp. Śr. XXIV.4.2.

Pratyāmnāya m. verse used as a substitute VI.30.9 For use of p° in the domestic rites H.Dh. II(1), 200.

प्रत्यायन *Pratyāyana* (*prati-√i*, cl.2 "to go towards") n. rite of sending off the *Pitṛs* at the *Piṇḍapitṛyajña* with the relevant *mantra* Bh. Śr. XIV.12.2 (third pressing of *Soma*).

प्रत्याश्रावण *Pratyāśrāvaṇa* n. call of the *Āgnīdhra* (also called °*āśruta* Āp. Śr. II.15.6) consisting of *astu śrau3ṣaṭ* (yes, let him hear), in response to the *āśrāvaṇa* of the *Adhvaryu* 16.2. It is pronounced loudly XXIV.1.10, by the *Āgnīdhra* standing behind the *utkara*, facing the south, holding a *sphya* and a rope for the faggot (*idhmasaṁnahana*) in his hand II.15.4 (*Darśa*), and standing in the *āgnīdhrāgāra* (*Soma*) ib.5. cf. H.Dh.II(2), 1054.

प्रथमस्थान *Prathamasthāna n.* "the first position"; a tone, which is slightly higher than the *upāṁśu*, for the *mantras* used in the performances prior to the *sviṣṭakṛt* K. Śr. III.1.3 & comm.

प्रदान *Pradāna* n. offerings which are made always on the *āhavanīya* fire unless countermanded Āp. Śr. XXIV.1.27.

प्रधान (होम) *Pradhāna* mfn. (*homa* m.) principal acts of a sacrifice, enumerated as : offerings of a cake baked on 8 *kapālas* to Agni in *Darśa*, a cake on 11 k° to Agni and Soma in *Soma*, *upāṁśuyāja* at *Paurṇamāsī*; the other acts are considered as *aṅga* (auxiliaries) : *pra-* and *anu-yājas*, Āp.Śr. XXIV.2.30-31. The *aṅgas* along with the p° make up a complete sacrifice ib.39. The p° acts which yield result are to be performed by the sacrificer himself K. Śr. I.7.20 & comm; considered equivalent of *āvāpa*, hence take place between the *ājyabhāga* and *sviṣṭakṛt* Ś. Śr. I.16.3.

प्रधि *Pradhi* m. rim of the wheel of a cart; the shape of the pressing boards (*adhiṣavaṇaphalaka* in the front (°*mukha*) Āp. Śr. XI.13.1; also the shape of the *citi* called *rathacakraciti* B. Śr. XXX.16.

प्रयाज *Prayāja* m. "fore-offering"; 5 preliminary oblations of *ājya* introduced before the principal offerings at *Darśa* Āp. Śr. II.17.1 and at all *iṣṭis* Āśv. Śr. I.5.2. After the principal offerings the *anuyāja* follows. The p° offerings are addressed to five deities : Samidh, Tanūnapāt (or Narāśaṁsa), Iḍ, Barhis, Svāhākāra, Āp. Śr. ib. 2, to be performed in the strict order mentioned Mī V.1.4. There are 11 p° at *Paśu* Āp. Śr. VII.14.6; 9 at *Cāturmāsya* VIII.2.14; five when the *soma* stalks are placed on the *āsandī* X.31.13 (*Soma*), C.H. 30. see *anuyāja*.

प्रवर *Pravara* (*pra-√vṛ*, cl. 9 "to choose") m. "choosing" of the *Hotṛ* by the *Adhvaryu* in a sacrifice. This rite of choosing is expressed technically as *ārṣeyam (pra) vṛṇīte* ŚBr. I. 4.2.3, *ārṣeyān pravṛṇīte* Āśv. Śr. I.3.1, simply, *pravṛṇīte* K. Śr. III.2.7, *hotāraṁ vṛṇīte yathārṣeyo yajamānaḥ* Āp. Śr. II.16.5, giving rise to a serious dispute as to the exact meaning of the word *ārṣeya*, relating to the *ṛṣi* (adjective qualifying Agni) or the *pravara* list relating to the *ṛṣis*, and the meaning of the verb *pravṛṇīte*, chooses or recites; cf. Brough Gotra 15, Eggeling SBE XII,115. The *pravara* is mainly connected with the *Darśa*, and takes place immediately after the first *āghāra* and recitation of the *sāmidhenī* verse. The *Hotṛ* invokes Agni as one who had formerly served as the *Hotṛ* in the sacrifice of the *ṛṣi*-ancestors of the present sacrificer by reciting a *mantra* : *agne mahānasi brāhmaṇa bhārata* Āśv. Śr. I.2.27, and by mentioning the names of the *ṛṣi*-ancestors of the sacrificer. This is the choosing of the divine *Hotṛ*. Later, after the second *āghāra* the *Adhvaryu* chooses the human *Hotṛ* by addressing a *mantra* to Agni mentioning the *ṛṣi*-ancestors of the sacrificer. Generally 3 names of such "*mantra* maker" *ṛṣis* are to be recited, and never more than 5 Āp. Śr. II.16.6, 8. In choosing Agni, the divine *Hotṛ*, the recital of *pravara* should begin with the oldest ancestor and end with the youngest; but at the time of choosing the human *Hotṛ* the recital is in the reverse order, beginning with the youngest and ending with the oldest ib. 9.

In case of a royal sacrificer the *pravara* of his *purohita* is to be used, ib.10, or there is an option K. Śr. III.2.10, but obligatory in case of a *kṣatriya* and a *vaiśya* sacrificer K. Śr. ib.11. After choosing the human *Hotṛ* the *Adhvaryu* announces his names Āp. Śr. ib. 14. In all *iṣṭis*, and even in other rites *pravara* is followed. At the *dīkṣā*, the *Adhvaryu* after making the *āśrāvaṇa* (*aśrāvya*) simply says *sīda hotar* (take your seat, O Hotar), and this is a *pravara* but not according to the *ṛṣi*-ancestor list Āp. Śr. XI.3.8, also at *Sākamedha* VIII.14.21-22. At the *savanīyapaśu* the *Adhvaryu* does the *pravara* of the other priests, and after each *pravara* 2 *pravṛtahomas*, libation of *ājya*, on the *āhavanīya* are performed, one by the *Adhvaryu* and the other by the sacrificer Āp. Śr. XI.20.1, C.H. 187, 166, 170. Also called *pravṛtāhuti* B. Śr. VII.9, Āśv. Śr. III.1.13. cf. Brough Gotra 8-10. See also Gotra : R. Fick ERE VI, 353-58.

प्रवर्ग्य *Pravargya* (*pra-√vṛj*, cl.7 "to twist; to perform the P° rite" Āp. Śr. XI.2.6) m. an independent rite (*apūrva*) but actually incorporated in the *Soma* sacrifice. Āp. Śr. XIII.4.3-5 does not consider it as an essential part of the *Agniṣṭoma*; dealt separately in Āp. Śr. XV.5-12, K. Śr. XXVI. The P° takes place generally before the *upasad*, but the *upasad* may precede it. Both of them are performed twice a day, morning and evening, for 3 days—the 2nd, the 3rd and the 4th days. There are 3 vessels called *mahāvīra* (1 principal, 2 supplementary), 2 milking bowls. The main *mahāvīra* is placed on a mound to the north of the *gārhapatya* and heated, and *ājya* is poured into it. The 2 supplementary vessels are used in the same way (*apracaraṇīya* Āp.Śr. XV.6.11), K. Śr. XXVI.2.17. The *mahāvīra*, which is sprinkled with *prokṣaṇī* waters, is lifted up with a pair of tongs (*parīśāsa* or *śapha*), and placed over the stool called *samrāḍāsandī*. Milk of a cow and a she-goat are added to the boiling ghee which is called *gharma*, and with it offerings are made to the Aśvins, Vāyu, Indra, Savitṛ, Bṛhaspati and Yama. The sacrificer drinks the remainder by the *upayamanī*; the priests only smell it. During the performance of the rite all the doors of the *prācīnavaṁśa* are kept closed. The wife's shed is also screened off, but she sits in it. Two *kharas* are built to the north of the *gārhapatya*. Cf. Eggeling SBE XLIV, xlvi.

pravṛñjana n. act of placing on the fire, performance of the rite Āp. Śr. XV.18.11; *pravṛñjanīya* see *khara*.

°*udvāsana/utsādana* n. rite of banishment of P° in which all sacrificial utensils, *kharas*, *methī*, *mayūkhas* are cleared away by the attendants from the *śālā*, and disposed of; other rites are performed Āp. Śr.XV.13-16, B. Śr. IX.11-16, K. Śr. XXVI.7.

प्रशास्तृ *Praśāstṛ* m. "director", another name of the *Maitrāvaruṇa*, the first assistant to the *Hotṛ*; he belongs to Mitra and Varuṇa, who are considered as the divine P° (as mentioned in a *mantra*) Āp. Śr. VII.14.5; *praśāstrīya* the *khara* belonging to the *Maitrāvaruṇa* XI.14.4.

प्रष्टि *Praṣṭi* m. (1) libation of 2 oblations on the same spot B. Śr. XX.13; (2) a leader horse of the sacrificer's chariot, harnessed by the side of the other yoked horses or in front of them (*Vāja*) Āp. Śr. XVIII.3.3.

प्रसर्पक *Prasarpaka* m. See *prasarpaṇa*.

प्रसर्पण *Prasarpaṇa* (*pra-√sṛp*, cl.1 "to creep up to") (also *sam*°, or only *sarpaṇa*) n. a ritual procession taken out by the priests to the *āstāva* for chanting the *bahiṣpavamānastotra*. Five or six priests and the sacrificer take part in the procession led by the *Adhvaryu*; getting hold of one another's garment, "stealthily they proceed, bending their heads, licking lips, manoeuvring like a hunter in pursuit of a deer, since the sacrifice is a deer" Āp. Śr. XII.17.3-4, B. Śr. VII.7. During this march, specially called *sarpaṇa*, the chanters throw the blades of grass held in their left hands to the south C.H.171.

At the *prātaḥsavana* the p°, in the same manner as the *sarpaṇa*, takes place in which the priests move out to the *sadas* for paying homage to various things B. Śr. VII.10-11, C.H. 188; also at the midday pressing for paying homage to the *dhiṣṇyas* B. Śr. VIII.1. They follow the same path when they return Āp. Śr. XII.29.16.

prasṛpta mfn. those who have marched to the *sadas* Āp. Śr. XIII.15.6=*sam*° B. Śr. VII.12.

prasarpaka m. spectators who are allowed to enter the *sadas* (*sadasyāsīna*) and to see the rite Āp. Śr. XI.9.8; they are entitled to get fees XIII.6.6; 7.1;=*anu* .

niḥ-√sṛp, to leave the *sadas* by the way used at *sarpaṇa* XII.29.16.

प्रसव *Prasava* (*pra-√su* or *√sū*,cl.5, 2, 6 "to generate; press out, impel") m. consent given by the *Brahman* to the *Adhvaryu* for performing any particular function Āp. Śr. I.16.6 (comm: *anujñā*), it contains those words relating to actions with and for which the *Adhvaryu* sought his permission : *brahman, apaḥ praṇeṣyāmi*, and p° will be : *om praṇaya* etc. (***prasauti***) **III.19.1-2** (***Darśa***). **Consent given by the** ***Brahman*** **and (*Maitrāvaruṇa*) to the** ***Prastotṛ*** **to begin the** ***bahiṣpavamāna stotra*** **when the latter says :** ***brahman, toṣyāmaḥ*** XIV. 9.7; the same procedure is followed for all *stotras* 10.1-2.

प्रसुत *Prasuta* mfn. =*sutyā* Āp. Śr. X.15.1.

प्रसृत *Prasṛta* m. hollow of a hand; one handful, a measure used for cooking the *brahmaudana* K. Śr. XX.1.4 (*Aśva*).

°*ākṛti* mfn. shaped like a hand, said of the *agnihotrasthālī* Āp. Śr. VI.3.7.

प्रसेक *Praseka* m. a decanting bowl, made of *udumbara* wood B. Śr. X.50; its front portion is shaped like a ladle (*sruc*) and the middle portion like a cup (*camasa*) XV.35 (*prasicyate ...anena,* comm).

prasecana n. bowl of a ladle for decanting liquid more conveniently Āp. Śr. XV.3.10 (*ānayanārthaṁ mukham,* comm).

प्रस्तर *Prastara* (*pra-√stṛ,* cl.9 "to strew") m. the first handful of *darbha* blades, held in a closed fist (*muṣṭi* q.v.) and cut with a sickle Āp. Śr. I.3.17, when grass is cut for making the *barhis* 4.4; tied in a bundle, placed over the *vedi,* and on this are placed the offering ladles (*sruc, juhū*) filled with clarified butter II.9.15 (*Darśa*). Similar handful of grass, *barhirmuṣṭi* held in the hand by the *Adhvaryu* and other chanters of *stotra* are, thrown away later as a rite of "fetching" (*upākaraṇa*) of all *pavamāna stotras* Āp. Śr. XII.17.7. cf. C.H. 171, PBr. VI.7.16.

प्रस्ताव *Prastāva* (*pra-√stu,* cl.2 "to praise before") m. the first part, prelude of *sāman* (q.v.), chanted by the *Prastotṛ* Āp. Śr. XXI. 10.4, C.H.178; *prastuta* chant of the *prastāva* XVIII.5.7. On the nature of p° cf. Simon, Pañcavi 6, L. Śr. VI.10.1; VII.5.21 comm.

प्रस्तोतृ *Prastotṛ* (*pra-√stu*) m. "the eulogist", the first assistant to the *Udgātṛ*; the second chanter who is specially responsible for chanting the *prastāva* Āp. Śr. X.1 9; he participates in the *prasarpaṇa* XII.17.1. He performs solo the laud to Yama after the sacrificial killing XX. 17.11. (*Aśva*).

प्रस्थित *Prasthita* mfn. "placed in front or standing before the altar", said of the limbs of a victim K. Śr. VI.6.26 (*Paśu*).

Also said of the *soma* juice "brought forward" for a libation called °*homa,* consisting of libations of *soma* with *camasas* filled by the *Unnetṛ*, offered by the *camasādhvaryus* on the fire at the morning service (*Soma*) B. Śr. VII.14, Āp. Śr. XII.23.4-10, C.H. 208; a second libation by pronouncing the second *vaṣaṭkāra* by the *camasādhvaryus* and the 4 principal priests, by the *hotrakas* at the midday service B. Śr. VIII.4, Āp. Śr. XIII. 4.15-16, C.H. 286, and at the third B. Śr. VIII.12, Āp, Śr. XIII.12.1-8, C.H. 346.

°*bhakṣaṇa* n. drinking of *soma*; See *somabhakṣaṇa*.

प्राग्वंश *Prāgvaṁśa* m.(fn.) Āp. Śr. X.3.4. See *prācīna*°.

प्राची *Prācī* f. the "eastern line", drawn between the 2 posts of the *pāśukī vedi*; running from the west through the centre of the altar upto the *āhavanīya*; 1 *īṣā* or 3 *aratnis* in length K. Śr. II.6.4 (*Darśa*); equivalent of the *pṛṣṭhyā* (q.v.). See plan 4. cf. Eggeling SBE XII, 63; XXVI, 112.

प्राचीनकर्ण *Prācīnakarṇa* mf(*ā*)n. knot at the top of the *audumbarī* post, facing the east B. Śr. VI.27.

प्राचीनवंश *Prācīnavaṁśa* (or *Prāg*°)m.(fn.) literally, the "east-oriented" bamboos; these are the upper beams (*uparivaṁśa*), and specially the supporting beams (*pṛṣṭhyavaṁśa* or *madhyavala*), the end portions of which protrude over the door lintels B. Śr. VI.1, Āp. Śr. X. 3.4; 5.1. Since these beams are used for the construction of the *śālā* (shed), the shed itself is commonly referred to as p°. cf. C.H.7.

प्राचीनावीतिन् *Prācīnāvītin* mfn. one who wears the sacred cord over the right shoulder and under the left arm at all rites to the manes (in contradistinction to the *yajñopavītin* fashion) Āp. Śr. I.8.9.

प्राजहित *Prājahita* m (fn.) "abandoned fire", *i.e.* the original *gārhapatya* installed in the *śālā* Āp. Śr. XI.15.1, replaced and its functions taken over by the original *āhavanīya* after the transport of fire (*praṇayana*). Thereafter the *āhavanīya* is variously called : *gārhapatya* (for taking up the original one's function, though with certain reservations Mī.XII.1.13), *śālāmukhīya* or *dvārya* (for its position at the entrance of the *śālā*). The newly transported fire on the *uttaranābhi,* now called *āhavanīya,* replaces the original *āhavanīya* C.H. 78.

प्राण *Prāṇa* m. breath=nose Bh. Śr. I.18.6; the vital limbs of an animal which are caused to swell (cf. *āpyāyana*) VII.14.2 (*Paśu*), B. Śr. XV.29 (*Aśva*).

°*dāna* n. rite of bestowing life to the utensils by anointing them with *ājya* before placing them on the *vedi* or anointing the cakes contained in the utensils K. Śr. II.8.14, Eggeling SBE XII, 438-9. Similar operation performed on the limbs of a victim (cf. *jauhava*) H. Dh. II(2), 1127; on the utensils H.Dh ib. 1128.

°*bhakṣa* m. "eating" by breath, *i.e.* smelling, in contradistinction to the direct, *i.e.* actual (*pratyakṣa*) eating (*bhakṣa*) L. Śr. IV.12.15. cf. *prāṇān bhakṣayanti* Vt. Śr. VIII.15. The priests eat the sacrificial food by smelling it, while the sacrificer actually eats it, as in eating the *vājina* H.Dh. II(2), 1064 (*Cātur*).

°*śodhana* n. rite of purifying the vital limbs of a victim : ear, nose, eye, mouth, navel etc. with the *pannejanī* waters by the sacrificer's wife K. Śr. VI.6.2-3 (*Paśu*).

°*āpyāyana* n. See *āpyāyana*.

प्रातरनुवाक *Prātaranuvāka* (*anu-√vac*, cl.2 "to recite *mantra*") m. morning litany, but actually recited by the *Hotṛ* in the last part of the night preceding the *sutyā* day Āp. Śr. XII.3.14. After offering an *ājya* libation the *Hotṛ* sits between the yokes of the 2 *havirdhāna* carts and starts the recitation which is followed shortly by the *prātaḥsavana* C.H. 130. The litany consists of 3 sections called *kratu* : *āgneya*°, *uṣas*°, *and āśvina*°. There are 100 *ṛks* according to the *Aitareyins*, 360 according to the *Kauṣītakins* (Keith RV. Br 146, 411) arranged in seven metres. But the number of verses has been exaggerated in Āśv. Śr. IV.13; about 2000 verses in 3 *kratus* which make up nearly 1/5th of the RV. Cf. H.Dh.II(2), 1163; through a gradual modulation of voice the recitation passes upwards through 7 tones (*yama*) of the deep scale (*mandrasvara*). Cf. Eggeling SBE XXVI, 229-30.

प्रातरवनेक *Prātaravaneka* (*ava-√nij*, cl.3 "to wash") m. morning ablution, a rite of the *Agnihotra*, consisting of an *upasthāna* to the fire by reciting a group of *mantras* called "ablution of hands in the morning" and washing hands Āp. Śr. VI.20.1.

प्रातर्दोह *Prātardoha* m. morning milking of cows, performed early in the morning; the procedure is the same as in the evening milking (*sāyam*°). With a portion of it *sāṁnāyya* is prepared Āp. Śr. II.10.5 (*Darśa*).

प्रातःसवन *Prātaḥsavana* n. pressing of *soma* stalks in the morning service and other rituals; see *savana*.

प्रायणीया *Prāyaṇīyā* (*iṣṭi*) (*pra-√i*, cl.2 "to go forth") f. an introductory (opening) rite of the first day of the *Soma* sacrifice, after the *dīkṣā* day, by which one "goes forth" to buy *soma* stalks; it consists of an offering of *caru*, cooked in milk, for Aditi, 4 libations of *ājya* for Pathyā Svasti, Agni, Soma and Savitṛ B. Śr. VI.10, Āp. Śr.X.21-22, C.H. 28; it corresponds to the *prayāja* of the *Darśa*. With this rite the initiated persons begin the *soma* sacrifice Āp. Śr. X.21.1 comm. The opposite of p° is the *udayanīyā* (concluding) *iṣṭi* of the *Soma* corresponding to the *anuyāja* of *Darśa*. Cf. Eggeling SBE XXVI, 48.

प्रायश्चित्त *Prāyaścitta*(*i*) n (f.) expiation or atonement, occasioned by a violation of the sacrificial rule (*vidhyaparādhe* Āśv. Śr. III. 10.1); and the rite of atonement is also to be performed for not doing what is enjoined or doing otherwise, with a view to making good (*sandhāna*, literally, joining together) the loss thus incurred, Nārāyaṇa comm on Āśv. Śr. l.c. No distinction is drawn between the neglect of ceremonial duties, intentional or unintentional, natural defects, accidents and real offence against moral law. Cf. Sin : A.B. Keith ERE XI, 560-62. The vedic ritual is complicated beyond any measure, and therefore the possibility of making faults is endless and so is the list of such possible faults. There are provisions of p° for such occasions when a wild boar or a ram or a dog runs between the sacrificial fires or if the *agnihotra* milk is spilled or if the cow lies down while being milked etc. ŚBr. XII.4.

The performance of a p° is a prerogative of the *Brahman* who uses the three vedas KBr. VI.12; but the *Adhvaryu* can also perform it. It is performed immediately after the fault occurs Āp. Śr. IX.1.5, and consists of *japa*, *homa*, *ijyā* ib. 3. P° relating to the *iṣṭis* and *Paśu* Āp. Śr. IX, to the *Soma* XIV.16-34, Āśv.Śr.III.10-14; for various occasions Kauś. S. XLVI, 14-55. For p° in the smṛti and later literature H.Dh.IV, Ch.1-6.

प्राशन *Prāśana* (*pra-√aś*, cl.9 "to eat") n. consumption of the residues of cakes (*havis*) by the priests and the sacrificer at the *āgnīdhra* shed Āśv. Śr.V.7.10 (end of the first pressing). cf. C H. 223;=*bhakṣaṇa* Āp. Śr. XII.25.12; eating of *piṇḍas* (q.v.) at *Darśa* Bh. Śr. I.10.10.

प्राशित्र *Prāśitra* n. food; the cut off portion of the *havis* left over after offering, eaten by the *Brahman* either after or before the *iḍā* ceremony Āp. Śr. III.1.1; from the centre of the *puroḍāśa* a portion of the size of a barley grain or of a berry of *pippala* is taken out by inserting the thumb and the ring-finger ib. 2. The dish for the p° is generally called °*haraṇa* Āp. Śr. I.15.7, made of *khàdira* wood, shaped like a mirror (an elongated circle) or a *camasa* (rectangular) K.Śr. I.3.40; less frequently called °*pātra*, and its size Vai. Śr. XI.8.

प्रेङ्ख *Preṅkha* (*pra-√iṅkh*, cl.1 "to swing") m. n. a sort of hammock or swing, made of *udumbara* wood, having a cord of *muñja*, used by the *Hotṛ* (*pleṅkha*) Āp. Śr. XXI.17.13 (*Mahāvrata*).

प्रेत *Preta* (*pra-√i*, cl.2 "to go") m. the departed, a deceased Bh.Pi.I.1.15. For the last rite of a deceased see *antyeṣṭi*.

°*patnī* f. wife of the deceased, taken to the cremation place, made to lie on her dead husband's funeral pyre, then raised from it; see *patittha* 1.5.6-7; not debarred from studying, she may not continue fasting after her husband's death, but must take food only once a day throughout her life, and observe sexual abstinence I.8.13.

प्रैष *Praiṣa* (*pra-√iṣ*, cl.9 "to send forth, impel") m. directions of the *Maitrāvaruṇa* to the *Hotṛ* for reciting *mantras* for the deities Āśv. Śr. III. 2.2, 4. The directions are issued on a supplementary direction called *upa*° of the *Adhvaryu*. Thereafter the *Hotṛ* recites the *adhrigu*° ib. 10=*ati*° B. Śr. XVI.3. Sometimes p° is pro nounced by the *Pratiprasthātṛ*.

atipreṣay,—to make the p cf. Pāṇ II. 3.61; VIII. 2.91,Vt Śr. XX. 2 The *Hotṛ* recites the *yājyā* after p° of the *Maitrāvaruṇa* Āśv. Śr. V.4.3.

प्रोक्षण *Prokṣaṇa* n. consecration by sprinkling *ājya* over a sacrificial animal Āp. Śr. VII. 12.9.

प्रोक्षणी *Prokṣaṇī* f. water for sprinkling, purified through the *pavitras* (q.v.), and used for sprinkling the sacrificial utensils and implements or offerings Āp. Śr. I.11.6, Mī.I.4.11.

°*dhānī* f. (1) a container for such waters Āp. Śr. XV.5.10 (*pravargya*); (2) one of the 2 curved (the shorter) ladles (*sruc*) Bh.Śr. XI.5. 12.

प्रौहेण *Prauheṇa* ind. by indicating the place where a *mantra* is to be inserted B.Śr.XXVI.6.

प्लीहन् *Plīhan* m. spleen of a sacrificed animal, cooked and used as an offering (*Paśu*) Āp. Śr. VII.22.6; see *jauhava*.

फ Pha

फलक *Phalaka* n. (1) two press boards; see *adhiṣavana*°. (2) rails of a cart for *soma* Āp. Śr. X.24.2 (*uddhṛtapūrva*°) cf. C.H.28.(3) said also of the seats, having no legs, used by the *Adhvaryu* and the sacrificer K. Sr. XX.2.20 and comm (*Aśva*).

फलीकरण *Phalīkaraṇa* n. act of separating grains from the husks; the husks are called *phalīkaraṇas* (pl.) Bh. Śr. I.22.12. It is done on the directions of the *Adhvaryu* who declares: *triṣphalīkartavai* (to be done thrice), first by the sacrificer's wife, then by the *Āgnīdhra* and finally by the wife again Āp. Śr. I.20.11; 21.2.

°*homa* m. oblations of the husks offered on the *anvāhāryapacana* along with the scrapings of a dough (*piṣṭalepa*) Bh. Śr. III.9.4 (*Darśa*).

ब Ba

बन्धु *Bandhu* m. relatives, particularly ancestors to whom the *piṇḍa*s are offered (*Darśa*) Bh. Śr. I.9.1.

बर्हिस *Barhis* (√*bṛh* or √*vṛh*, cl.6 "to tear") n. "that which is plucked up"; sacrificial grass, *kuśa*, strewn over the sacrificial ground, specially over the *vedi*, in layers, to serve as a sacred surface for keeping the sacrificial vessels and the oblations, and as a seat for the deities and the performers; method of cutting the grass Āp. Śr. I.3.1, of tying them in rope (śulba) in 3 or 5 strands (*tridhātu* or *pañca*° I.4.14), of strewing around the fires I.7.5, of scattering them in sheaves of 3 or 5 strands (*tridhātu* or *pañca*°) on the *vedi* II.9.2. The scattering of b° takes place on various occasions throughout *Darśa* and *Soma*. In du. the word means two blades of *darbha* used for symbolically pushing (*upākaraṇa*) the sacrificial animal VII.12.5,8 (*Paśu*). B° is distinguished from the *prastara* (q.v.). It is commonly known as *kuśa* Mī.I.4.10, K.Śr. I.3.12.

बहिष्पवमान *Bahiṣpavamāna* n.(*stotra* n.)"outside *pavamāna*", name of a *stotra* chanted during the morning pressing of *Soma* L. Śr. I.12.7. Cf. C.H.177-81. This is the first among the *stotra*s chanted in *Soma*, and consists of 9 verses (3 *tṛca*s) : RV.IX.11.1-3; 64.28-30; 66.10-12=SV.II.1.1.1-3; chanted in the *trivṛt* style (*stoma*) Eggeling SBE XXVI, 310. So called because the *stotra* in which *soma* is praised is chanted outside the *sadas* or the *vedi* in a place called *āstāva* (q.v.). See also *sāman*.

बृहस्पतिसव *Bṛhaspatisava* m. a *soma* ceremony of one day duration (supposed to confer the rank of *purohita* on the performers; considered as an *aṅga* of the *Vāja*) which it follows Mī.IV. 3.29, Āp. Śr. XXII.7, B.Śr. XVIII.1.

ब्रह्मन् *Brahman* (from √*bṛh*, cl.1 "to make big") n. "growth"; m. one of the 4 principal priests. He is the most learned of all, and is required to know the 3 vedas for his professional duties ŚBr.XI.5.8.7. He acts as a presiding officer of a sacrifice, remains silent most of the time, does not participate in the *stotra* or *śastra* Bh. Śr. III.15.4,6. He gives various instructions (*prasava*) to the *Adhvaryu* when the latter asks him for it III.16.1-4; he recites the *anumantraṇa* in an ātharvaṇic rite; but only at a later period he is associated with the *Atharvaveda*. It is he who decides the question of *prāyaścitta* Āśv. Śr. I.1.16. His assistants are called the *brahman*s; see *ṛtvij*.

brahmabhāga m. portion of sacrificial food for B°, given to him by the *Adhvaryu* Bh. Śr. III.18.5.

°*medha* m. cremation rite of a *brahman* (=*brahmavid*); said to be the higher form of the *pitṛmedha* Bh.Pi.II.1, Āp. Śr. XXXI.4.

°*vādya* n. a theological dialogue on the *brahman* consisting of riddles in question and answer form Āp. Śr. XXI.10.12 (*Dvādaśāha*) =*brahmodya*, between the *Brahman* and the *Hotṛ* in the *sadas* XX.19.6 (*Aśva*); cf. Dumont L' Aśva 154, H.Dh.II(2), 1235=*brahmavadya* Ś. Śr. XIV.4.7, Āśv. Śr. VIII.13.14 (*Daśarātra*).

°*saman* n. name of the third *pṛṣṭhastotra* Āp. Śr. XIV.19.6 (*Soma*).

ब्रह्मौदन *Brahmaudana* m. mess of rice, cooked for the brahmins (=priests) or the *brahman* (comm), 4 plates of rice cooked in 4 measures of water Āp. Śr. V.5.4,6 (*Agnihotra*); also for the priests, the king, and his 4 wives and their 400 maidens, rice (or barley according to the scholiast) measuring 4 bowls, 4 double palmfuls (*añjali*) and 4 fistfuls (*prasṛta*) K.Śr. XX. 1.4. (*Aśva*).

brahmaudanika mfn. the fire for cooking the b° Āp. Śr. V.5.1.

ब्राह्मण *Brāhmaṇa* n. class of works being a part of the vedas, as distinguished from the *saṁhitā* and *upaniṣad* portions. The *brāhmaṇa*s contain rules for the use of the hymns at particular rites, for performance of rites with detailed explanations of their origin and meaning. Very often, these explanations are obscure and fanciful. According to Sāyaṇa there are 2 categories in a *brāhmaṇa* : (1) *vidhi*—rules and directions for the sacrifices, and (2) *arthavāda*—explanatory remarks. Cf Āp. Śr. XXIV.1.30-33. Each veda has its own *brāhmaṇa*s. For details see Winternitz I, 187-225.

ब्राह्मणाच्छंसिन् *Brāhmaṇācchaṁsin* (from *brāhmaṇāt*-√*śaṁs*, cl.1) m. reciting after the *Brāhmaṇa* or the *Brahman*, a priest who assists the *Brahman* (actually he is an assistant of the *Hotṛ*); he recites a number of verses, *e.g.* the 3rd *ājyaśastra* to Indra B. Śr. VII.19, Āp. Śr. XII.29.2, C.H. 248.

brāhmaṇācchaṁsīya n. the *dhiṣṇya* of the B° Āp. Śr. XXVII.21.3.

भ Bha

भक्ति *Bhakti* f. division; one of the 5 parts of a *sāman* (q.v.) L.Śr. VI.1.14, Hoogt 59, Puṣpa 521.Also called *vibhakti*, *vidhā*.

भस्मन् *Bhasman* n. ashes of the cremated body, gathered by the *Adhvaryu*, piled up in the shape of a human figure Bh.Pi.I.9.12.

भाषिकस्वर *Bhāṣikasvara* m. accent of the *brāhmaṇa* texts K.Śr.I.8.17; see *svara*.

भिन्नतन्त्र *Bhinnatantra* n. See *tantra*.

भूमिदुन्दुभि *Bhūmidundubhi* m. f. See *dundubhi*.

भौवन्यव *Bhauvanyava* mfn. a recitation mentioning the "sovereigns" : Manu, Yama, done by the *Hotṛ* (*Aśva*) Āp. Śr. XX.6.7. See also *pāriplava*.

भ्रातृव्य *Bhrātṛvya* m. hostile cousin, from whom the sacrificer desires to get something, and names them Bh. Śr.IV.19.2 (*Darśa*). It is laid down that the sacrificer should remain outside the *mahāvedi* until the *āditya* cup is drawn if his hostile cousin is performing a *Soma* sacrifice Bh. Śr. XIV.8.3 (during the 3rd pressing); cf. Āp. Śr. XIII.9.4.

म Ma

मदन्ती *Madantī* (√*mad*, cl.4. "to revel") f. boiling (bubbling RV. X.17.8) waters B. Śr. VI.19, used for mixing with flour Āp. Śr. I.23.6, or for other purposes at the *Pravargya*. All sacrificial acts in which water is to be used by the sacrificer and his wife from the *avāntaradīkṣā* till the time of relaxing the fist (*dīkṣā*) are to be performed with m° waters K.Śr. VIII.1.10-11. Also called *piṣṭa-saṁyavanīya* B.Śr.I.8. A rite is performed in which the *Adhavaryu* asks the *Āgnīdhra* to bring m° waters Āp.Śr. XI.1.8-10 (*Soma*). C.H.62.

मधुपर्क *Madhuparka* (√*pṛc*, cl.7 "to mix") m. a honey-mixture, mixed with curdled milk or butter Āp. Śr. VI.31.5. A similar beverage is *madhumantha* m. a mixture of flour and stirred honey, also *madhugluntha* m. a lump-of solid honey ib. See *mantha*; see also Gṛhya section.

मध्य *Madhya* m. n. middle tone, consisting of 7 degrees (*yama*), in which the *prātaranuvāka* is recited;=*madhyama* in which the *mantras* before the *sviṣṭakṛt* (*Darśa*) and after the *ājyabhāgas* are recited Āśv. Śr. I.5.27, Āp. Śr. XXIV.1.13, and all recitations at the midday pressing (*Soma*) ib,

मध्यतःकारिन् *Madhyataḥkārin* m. 4 principal priests Āp. Śr. XII.23.4; see *ṛtvij*.

मन्त्र *Mantra* (√*man*, cl. 4/8 "to think") m. "instrument of thought"; sacred text of speech RV I.147.4 etc. The portion of the vedas which contain the *ṛc*, *yajus*, *sāman* and *nigada* K. Śr. I.3.1, as distinguished from the *brāhmaṇa* and *upaniṣad* portions; it constitutes a part of the veda Āp. Śr. XXIV.1.31. The sacrificial formula which is employed in the rituals H. Śr. I.1.15; the *mantras* are indicated by their beginnings (*ādipradiṣṭa*) Bh. Śr.I.1.21, the end of a previous *mantra* is known by the beginning of the next I.2.1; if a *mantra* is short and the rite lengthy, it is to be murmured at the beginning of the rite I.2.3; they follow one another without a break, and with the end of a *mantra* the beginning of a ritual should coincide K. Śr. I.3.5, H. Śr. I.1.30, Bh. Śr. I.2.2. M° are said to be instrumental in the accomplishment of a sacrificial act (*karmakaraṇa*) Āśv. Śr. I.1.21; cf. *karaṇamantra* Mī. III.8.21. The nature of a *mantra* II.1.32; XII.3.22-25. But the *mantras* generally do not bear on the actions and occasions of the ritual. Cf. Keith RPV. 310-12.

मन्थ् √*Manth* or *math* (cl. 9 "to shake") to produce fire through friction or by churning the *araṇis* Āp. Śr. V.10.7; to churn the *āśir* (with the *mekṣaṇa*) XIII.10.8 (*Soma*).

मन्थ *Mantha* m. porridge, prepared by mixing milk taken from a cow which has no calf of its own (*abhivānyā*) with half-ground barley, and stirred with a sugar-cane stick Āp. Śr. VIII.14.14-15 (*Mahāpitṛyajña*). Cf. RV. X.86. 15. Also porridge of barley, stirred in water or butter XII.4.13 (*Soma*); similarly, *madhu*°, *dadhi*° and various other *manthas*, "stirred" porridge, are mentioned for the *savas* XXII. 26.1; see also *madhuparka*.

मन्द्र *Mandra* mfn. m. soft voice, composed of 7 degrees (*yamas*) Āśv. Śr. I.5.25; one of the three basic tones (*sthāna*); the other 2 are *madhyama* and *uttama*; the recitation upto *śaṁyu* (q.v.) is done in m° ib. 26; so also the recitations before the *ājyabhāga* (*Darśa*) and at the morning pressing (*Soma*) Āp. Śr. XXIV. 1.12. Cf. Oldenberg SBE XXX, 319-20.

मयूख *Mayūkha* m. a kind of peg, made of *udumabra* wood, 3 in number, Bh. Śr. XI.5.13 (*Pravargya*).

मरुत्वतीय *Marutvatīya* mfn(*graha*) m name of 3 drawings of *soma*, dedicated to Indra *Marutvat* at the midday pressing. First 2 cups are offered to the deity by the *Adhvaryu* and the *Pratiprasthātṛ*, who also drink the remnants. Then a third m° cup is filled while the *marutvatīyaśastra* [text Śr.K(S).II(1), 383, C.H. 299-304] is being recited by the *Hotṛ* Āp. Śr. XIII.2.3-4; 8.1-2, K. Śr. X.3.3, C.H. 276, 297-8.

महदुक्थ *Mahaduktha* n. great litany; see *uktha*.

महर्त्विज् *Mahartvij* m. four principal officiating priests : *Adhvaryu*, *Brahman*, *Hotṛ* and *Udgātṛ* Āp. Śr. XIV.24.6; also called *ādyartvij*; see *ṛtvij*.

महानाम्नी *Mahānāmnī* f. name of a group of 3 *tṛcas* (9 verses) of the SV. beginning with the words *vidā maghavan*; also called *śakvarī* verses; chanted on various occasions (*ahīna*) L. Śr. VII.5.9. It is composed of 2 elements, one is called *śākvara*, and the other *aśākvara* (considered to be composed of *stobha*); cf. Caland PBr. 317.

महापितृयज्ञ *Mahāpitṛyajña* m. = *piṇḍapitṛyajña*, called variously as *mahāpiṇḍa*° or *mahāyajña* B. Śr. XVII.61, *pitṛyajña* Mī. IV.4.19; included in the *Sākamedha parvan* of *Cātur* (q.v.).

महाभिषव (ण) *Mahābhiṣava(ṇa)* m(n). the great pressing of *soma* stalks for extraction of its juice in order to fill various cups (*graha*) for libation. The pressing is done by the *Adhvaryu* and his assistants, *Pratiprasthātṛ*, *Neṣṭṛ* and *Unnetṛ*, in 3 rounds of 3 turns; and the number of strokes with the pressing stones, unlike the little pressing (*upāṁśugraha* q.v.), is unlimited. The pressing takes place thrice in a day of *Soma* sacrifice : *prātaḥsavana* (morning pressing), *mādhyandina*° (midday) and *tṛtīya*° (the third) Āp. Śr. XII.9.7.

The *Adhvaryu* places the *upara* stone on the *adhiṣavaṇa* hide, and the stalks over the stone. The stalks are sprinkled with *nigrābhya* waters, and the priests holding the other stones in their right hand start beating the stalks. This is the first turn (*paryāya*). The scattered stalks are collected. The process is repeated thrice XII.10.4-9; 12.8-9.

The wet and battered stalks are collected into the *sambharaṇī*, and transferred from there into the *ādhavanīya* which contains water. The stalks in the *ādhavanīya* are stirred, washed, pressed by the *Unnetṛ*, and again taken out and placed over the skin for collecting *ṛjīṣa*. This goes on till the third round. Then the *droṇakalaśa* having been covered with a wollen strainer is brought by the *Udgātṛs* and placed on the 4 pressing-stones covered with pressed out *soma* stalks. The *Hotṛ*'s *camasa* containing *nigrābhya* waters is held by the sacrificer and filled with *soma* juice drawn from the *ādhavanīya* by *Unnetṛ*. The sacrificer pours it out in one continuous stream from the *Hotṛ*'s *camasa* into the *droṇakalaśa* through the *pavitra*. The *soma* juice contained in the *droṇakalaśa* is called *śukra*, "pure" K. Śr. IX.5.15. Various cups are filled with the juice : *antaryāma*, *aindravāyava*, *maitrāvaruṇa*, *śukra*, *manthin*, *āgrayaṇa*, *ukthya*, *dhruva*; cf. C.H. 157, Eggeling SBE XXVI, 256, H.Dh. II(2), 1164-65.

महाभिषेक *Mahābhiṣeka* m. or *aindrābhiṣeka*. See *abhiṣeka*.

महावीर *Mahāvīra* m. name of an earthen pot in which milk for *pravargya* is boiled; also called *ukhā*, *gharma* Āp. Śr. XV.2.14; earth is crushed, lumped into balls, mixed with the *madantī* waters, and moulded by the *Adhvaryu* with 2 thumbs : 1 span in height having 3 or 5 elevations (*uddhi*); it resembles a wooden cup (*vāyavya*) Āp. Śr. l.c., Bh. Śr. XI.2.22-24. In *pravargya* there is one main m° and 2 secondary pots, kept as reserve, called *apracaraṇīya* Āp. Śr. XV.6.11. M° is made hollow, polished with new garments of a bride and *gavīdhuka* grains etc., held with a pair of tongs, fumed with horses' dung over the *gārhapatya* fire Bh. Śr. XI.3.1, 9-10, 13-14. cf. Dumont L'Aśva 72, 80, H.Dh. II(2), 1148-50.

महावेदि *Mahāvedi* f. the "great altar" for *Soma* sacrifice, also called *saumikā*, prepared by the *Adhvaryu* on the 2nd *upasad* day after having performed the morning *pravargya* and *upasad*. The m° is a trapezium, measuring 36 steps (*prakrama*) east to west, 30(or 33) steps north to south on the west (facing the *śālā*) and 24 steps north to south on the east. The area is marked out by driving a peg (*śaṅku*) called *antaḥpātya* or *śālāmukhīya* on the ground at the distance of 6 (or 3) steps to the east in front of the *āhavanīya* fire, then another peg called *yūpāvaṭīya* at the distance of 36 steps from there to the east, and both are connected with a cord (*spandyā*) to make the *pṛṣṭhyā* line. On both the north and south sides of the *antaḥpātya* 2 pegs are driven at the distance of 15 (or 16½) steps to mark the *śroṇis*; similarly, on the north and the south sides of the *yūpāvaṭīya* 2 pegs are driven at a distance of 12 steps each to make the *aṁsas*. A rope (*spandyā*) marks the boundary of the m° B. Śr. VI.22, Āp. Śr. XI. 4.11-16, K. Śr. VIII.3.7-12. Within the m° the *sadas*, the *havirdhānamaṇḍapa* and the *uttaravedi* are constructed in such a way that the visibility is not obstructed (*sāṁkāśina* q.v.). cf. C.H. 74, H.Dh. II(2), 1152-53. See plan 3. Construction of m°=*saumikī vedi* Āp. Śulb.II.5.

महाव्रत *Mahāvrata* n. "great observance", the name of a rite which takes place on the last but one day of the *Gavāmayana sattra*. Among other usual offerings of *soma* cups, a *mahāvratīya* cup is offered accompanied with a *sāman* called *mahāvrata* (whence the name of the rite) followed by the *mahaduktha* (great laudation) *śastra* of the *Hotṛ*. An animal is offered for Prajāpati. The manner of performance of the rite is very interesting. At the time of the chanting of the *pṛṣṭhastotra* a brahmin plays on a harp (*vāṇa*). The *Udgātṛ* sits on a chair (*āsandī*) of *udumbara*, the *Hotṛ* on a swing (*preṅkha*), the *Adhvaryu* on a board (*phalaka*), the other priests, singers and the wives of the performers sit on grass Āp. Śr. XXI.17.10, 12-15. A brahmin in the front of the *sadas* and a *śūdra* at the back alternately praise and abuse the performers; a mimetic fight takes place between an *ārya* and a *śūdra* to the west of the *āgnīdhra* shed; a prostitute and a *brahmacārī* revile each other (K. Śr. XIII.3.6); a *kṣatriya* occupies a chariot and goes round the *vedi* thrice, and shoots 3 arrows at a hide which has been hung up. A man and a woman (both are strangers) actually perform sexual intercourse in a screened shed to the south of *mārjālīya* (K. Śr. XIII.3.9). The drums (*dundubhi*) are beaten on all corners of the *vedi*; the *bhūmidundubhi*, a skin placed over a hole, is also beaten. The wives join in the chant and play some instruments Āp. Śr. XXI.17.15-16.

Servants and maids and slave girls with water jars on their heads dance round th *mārjālīya*, and sing popular songs Āp. Śr. XXI.19.17-20; XXI.20.

The entire procedure has been succinctly stated in T Ār. V.1.5. Āp. Śr. XXI.17-20. cf. Eggeling SBE XLIII, xxv, 282. For the dramatic elements Keith Drama 29.

महाहविस् *Mahāhavis* n. great offering, which is the main offering of the *Sākamedha*, consisting of 8 oblations to 8 deities : 5 common to all *Cāturmāsya* rites, the 6th, a cake on 12 *kapālas* to Indra and Agni, the 7th, a *caru* to Mahendra or Indra, the 8th, a cake on 1 *kapāla* to Viśvakarman Āp. Śr. VIII.12.1, Āśv. Śr. II.18.18.

महिम (ग्रह) *Mahima* (*graha*) m. name of the 2nd *soma* drawing called "strength" (*Aśva*) Āp. Śr. XX.12.6.

महिषी *Mahiṣī* f. crowned (principal) queen K. Śr. XX.5 15. See *Aśvamedha*, *patnī*.

महेन्द्र (ग्रह) *Mahendra* (*graha*) m. a *soma* drawing dedicated to Mahendra at the midday pressing and the libation Āp. Śr. XIII.8.4, 6 (*Soma*). C.H 305, 313.

माध्यन्दिनपवमानस्तोत्र *Mādhyandinapavamāna stotra* n. "purifying" litany, consisting of 8 verses, increased to 15 verses by repetition, chanted at the midday pressing B. Śr. VIII.2. C.H.279, Eggeling SBE XXVI, 333; text Śr. K(S).II(1), 357.

मार्जनी *Mārjanī* (√*mṛj*, cl.2 "to wipe") f. act of "wiping" by sprinkling water on the head; done by the priests themselves after they have eaten the *iḍā* (*Darśa*) Bh. Śr. III.2.6; IV.16.1 =*mārjana* n. Āśv. Śr. I.8.1-2.

मार्जालीय *Mârjālīya* (√*mṛj*, cl.2 "to wipe") m. a mound of earth, one of the *dhiṣṇyas*, where the sacrificial utensils are cleansed ("purified"); it is situated outside the *sadas*, opposite the *āgnīdhra*, to the south of the *mahāvedi*. It is half inside and half outside the *vedi*. It has a shed, and a door facing the north, and a seat facing the south B.Śr. VI.27, Āp. Śr. XI.14.6; see plan 3.

मासर *Māsara* n. beverage, obtained from a mixture of the hot watery scum of boiled rice, powdered barley and the extract of certain vegetables like myrobalans, ginger, nutmeg. The beverage is kept in a pot for 3 days to allow fermentation and milk is added to it. The wine thus obtained is purified and offered at the *Sautrāmaṇī* K.Śr. XIX.1.20; cf. H.Dh. II(2), 1225. According to Āp. Śr. XIX.4.7 m° is prepared like *ṛjīṣa* and is explained as *balkasa* (dregs of wine).

मिथुन *Mithuna* n. sexual copulation between a man and woman, performed in a screened hut, south of the *mārjālīya* K.Śr. XIII.3.9 at the *Mahāvrata* rite (*Gavāmayana*).

मुष्टि *Muṣṭi* (from?√*muṣ*, cl.9 "to steal") m.f. handful (*i.e.* the position when the fist is closed the nails of the thumb and the forefinger should meet) of *darbha* grass for scattering as *prastara* around and inside the *vedi*. The m° must be of odd number Āp. Śr; I.4.2, tied in sheaves (*nidhana*) ib. 3; but the *prastaras* may or may not be of odd number ib. 4, Bh. Śr. I.3.13,22. Also handful of grains Āp. Śr. I.18.2 (*Darśa*).

°*karaṇa* or *karman* n. act of closing two fists, as a part of the manipulations prescribed for *dīkṣā*, done by the sacrificer Āp. Śr. XVI.11.10; cf. *muṣṭīkṛ* B.Śr. VI.5;

°*karṣaṇa* n. closing the fist more tightly at the *avāntaradīkṣā* Bh.Śr.XII.2.4, and °*visarjana* n. opening of the closed fists at the end of *dīkṣā* XII.18.10 (*Soma*).

मुसल *Musala* (often spelt as *muṣala* or *muśala*) m.n. pestle, generally made of *khadira* wood (Acacia catechu) K. Śr. I.3.36 comm, used for pounding grains(*Darśa*)Āp. Śr. I.19.8; 4 hands in length (or the size may vary) Vai. Śr. XI.9.

मूत *Mūta* (from?√*mīv* or √*mū*, cl.1 "to push") m.(n.) a kind of woven basket K.Śr. V.10.21 in which paddy or cooked dough is kept Bh.Śr. VIII.22.3(*Cātur*). °*kārya* wicker work K. Śr.I. 3.23.

मृगतीर्थ *Mṛgatīrtha* n. "deer track", the path used by the *Hotṛ* and others for *sarpaṇa* at the end of *savana*; the *Hotṛ* starts from the south of *audumbarī* post, and others from the western gate to the north by skirting the north *śroṇi* of the *mahāvedi* Āśv. Śr. V.11.2; see also *tīrtha* and *prasarpaṇa*.

मृगारेष्टि *Mṛgāreṣṭi* f. offering comprising 10 oblations to Agni after the animal sacrifice at the end of *Aśva* Āp. Śr. XX.23.2. Cf. B.Śr. XV.37.

मृताग्निहोत्र *Mṛtāgnihotra* n. See *preta*°.

मृत्खन *Mṛtkhana* m. a clay pit from which clay is collected for making the utensils of the *pravargya* Āp. Śr. XV.1.9. See *khani*.

मेक्षण *Mekṣaṇa* n. a mixing rod, made of *aśvattha* wood (Ficus religiosa), one *aratni* long, having at one end a small square board of 4 fingers for stirring and mixing the flour in boiling water to prepare a *puroḍāśa* Vai. Śr. XI.8, used at the *Darśa* Āp. Śr. I.7.5; also used for dividing (*avadāna*) the *caru* (*Soma*) XIII. 13.17.

मेखला *Mekhalā* f. a large girdle, woven in 3 strands, made of *muñja* grass, tied round the waist of the sacrificer above his garment at the *dīkṣā* Āp. Śr. X.9.13. see also *yoktra*.

मेथी *Methī* f. a wooden post used as a prop for the shaft of the *havirdhāna* cart, fixed into a hole (*karṇātarda*) Āp. Śr. XI.7.3 or close to the axle B.Śr. VI.25, C.H. 87. Also a post fixed to the ground outside the southern gate of the *prācīnavaṃśa* at the *pravargya* (*Soma*) Bh.Śr. XI.6.10.

मेषप्रतिकृति *Meṣapratikṛti* f. figurine of sheep, made of *karambha* flour; a ram prepared by the *Adhvaryu*, and a *ewe* (*meṣī*) by the *Pratiprasthātṛ*; they are provided with the appropriate sex signs; later placed into the *āmikṣā* (*Varuṇapraghāsa*) Bh. Śr. VIII.7.3-5; 8.7.

मैत्रावरुण *Maitrāvaruṇa* m. "belonging to Mitra and Varuṇa", the first assistant of the *Hotṛ*; he recites hymns to Mitra and Varuṇa, as in the *ājyaśastra* at the morning pressing (*Soma*) B.Śr VII.18, Āp. Śr. XII.28.14-16, C.H.244. He is also called *Praśāstṛ* and *Upavaktṛ* ("instructor") as he gives instructions called *praiṣa* to other priests. He joins in the *Paśubandha* sacrifice as the 6th priest.

°*graha* m. one of the drawings of *soma* at the morning pressing dedicated to Mitra and Varuṇa, being reckoned as a part of the twin divinity drawing (*dvidevatyagraha*) B. Śr. VII. 6, K.Śr. IX.6.8-9, C.H.163.

य Ya

यकन् *Yakan* n. the liver=*yakṛt* (n.) of a victim (*Paśu*) Bh. Śr. VII.18.12. See *aupabhṛta*, *jauhava*.

यज् √*Yaj* (cl.1, "to worship")

(1) to invite to the sacrifice with the *yājyā* formula, done by the *Hotṛ* Āp.Śr. VIII.3.9. (2) to perform an *iṣṭi*; defined as *yāga*, a ceremony in which offerings or oblations are dedicated to a deity by relinquishing one's right over it by saying, this is for the deity and not for me Mī IV.2.27.

anuyaj, to utter the *anuvaṣaṭkāra* formula Āp. Śr. VIII.3.10 (*Cātur*). See also *vaṣaṭ*.

यजति *Yajati* m. technical name of those rites in which *homa* (q.v.) is performed in a standing position with the utterance of *vaṣat* followed by *yājyā* and *puro'nuvākyā* K.Śr. I.2.6, in contradistinction to the *juhoti* class of rites; cf. Kullūka and Medhātithi on Mn.II.84.

यजमान *Yajamāna* (√*yaj*, cl.1. *ātmanepada*, "to worship for one's own benefit") m. "he who sacrifices for himself"; originally, as the word indicates, the y° must have been the person who performed his own rituals without the help of any priest. But in the recorded period he has a very minor role to play in the performance of a rite.

He is the institutor, sponsor of a sacrifice; he engages priest or priests to get a ritual performed on his behalf. He bears the cost of a sacrifice. He is called a "master", *svāmin* who can dedicate an offering to a deity K.Śr. I.7.20. He has been relegated to the position of a mere donor (*dadātīti yajamānam*) Āśv. Śr. I.1.15. His functions in a sacrifice and the extent of his participation have been described succinctly as follows : *dāna* (gives fees to a priest), *vācana* (utters some *mantras*), *anvārambhaṇa* (touches some object, being offered, or some implement, with which some work is done), *varavaraṇa* (chooses boon or priests), *vrata* (observes vow connected with the sacrifice) and *pramāṇa* (measurements of the *vedi*, *śālā* etc. are done according to the size of a sacrificer) K.Śr. I.10.12. He has to undergo the *dīkṣā* along with his wife, and participates in a sacrifice only in a limited way. His duties are called *yājamāna* Āp. Śr. IV. See also *patnī*.

यजुस *Yajus* n. a sacrificial *mantra*, RV.VIII.41.8 etc., a technical name of the *mantras*, as distinguished from the *ṛc*, *sāman* and *nigada* K.Śr. I,3.1, Mī.II.1.37; defined as the *mantras*, the syllables and *pādas* of which are pronounced without a pause K.Śr. ib. comm; they are full sentences and not dependent on other words for their meaning (*nirākāṅkṣa*) ib.2, pronounced in *upāṁśu* ib.10, while others are pronounced loudly.

yajuryukta mfn. name of a cart, harnessed at the *Vājapeya* Āp. Śr. XVIII.3.10.

यज्ञ *Yajña* m. a sacrifice, composed of 3 elements : *dravya* (oblatory materials), *devatā* (a deity) and *tyāga* (giving away the materials) K.Śr. I.2.2; equivalent of *yāga*, *iṣṭi* and *yajana* ib. comm. cf. Mī. IV.2.27. See also *yajati*.

°*patra* n. utensil and implements of a sacrifice, also called °*āyudha*, the 10 principal ones are enumerated : *sphya*, *kapālas* (whatever the number they should be considered as one unit), *agnihotrahavaṇī*, *śūrpa*, *kṛṣṇājina*, *śamyā*, *ulūkhala*, *musala*, *dṛṣad*, *upalā* TS. I.6.8. 2-3, B.Śr. I.4, K.Śr. II.3.8. Besides these, there are *juhū*, *upabhṛt*, *sruc*, *dhruvā*, *prāśitraharaṇa*, *iḍāpātra*, *mekṣaṇa*, *piṣṭodvapanī*, *praṇītāpraṇayana*, *ājyasthālī*, *veda*, *dārupātrī*, *yoktra*, *vedaparivāsana*, *dhṛṣṭi*, *idhmapravraścana*, *anvāhāryasthālī*, *madantī*, *phalīkaraṇapātra*, *antardhānakaṭa* B.Śr.I.4, K.Śr.l.c. comm. The *pātras* are to be got ready according to necessity K.Śr. l.c. An *āhitāgni* is cremated alongwith his sacrificial vessels. This is called the *pratipattikarma* (disposal) Mī.XI.3.34.

°*puccha* n. tail of a sacrifice *i.e.* the concluding part of the *Soma* B.Śr. XXV.26, C.H. 383-92.

°*sampradāya* m. the rites of a sacrifice Bh.Śr. III.15.6.

यज्ञायज्ञीय *Yajñāyajñīya* n. name of a *stotra*, the last and the principal one chanted at the third pressing of *Agniṣṭoma*; also called *agniṣṭomasāman* or *stotra*. It derives its name from the opening words : *yajñā*, *yajñā* of the *stotra* Āp. Śr. XIII.15.3. The *Udgātṛ* begins the chant; all the chanters and choristers cover their heads and ears during the chant; even the sight seers join in the chant ib.6. The sacrificer's wife is brought into the *sadas*, and she pours water (*pannejanī*) over her thigh during the chant. The text Śr.K(S).II(1), 453. C.H.369-70.

यज्ञायुध *Yajñāyudha* n. sacrificial "weapons", *i.e.* the implements, with which a sacrifice is performed B. Śr.I.4; 10 in number TS.I.6.8. 2-3, Mī.III.1.11; see *yajñapātra*.

यज्ञोपवीतिन् *Yajñopavītin* mfn. See *upavīta*.

याज्या *Yājyā* f. "that which is to be sacrificed"; the technical name of a formula of consecration, composed of a verse recited by the *Hotṛ*, which accompanies a libation of *ājya* offered by the *Adhvaryu*. Before the recital begins the *Adhvaryu* gives directions (*praiṣa*) to the *Hotṛ*, *e.g. samiddho yaja* or *agnim* (*amum*) *yaja* etc. K.Śr. I.9.15. The *Hotṛ* begins the appropriate *yājyā* formula preceded by the invocation "*ye3yajāmahe*" (*āguḥ*) and followed by "*vauṣaṭ*" Āśv. Śr. I.5.15. The y° occurs in *prayāja*s and *anuyāja*s, *ājyabhāga*, *āvāpa*, in *sviṣṭakṛt* and in *patnīsaṁyāja*s, pronounced very loudly, and the last syllable is prolated. cf. Āśv.Śr. I.5.9-14. H.Dh.II(2), 1058-60.

°*anuvākyā* f. formula which is associated with the y°, and recited in the above cases except in *prayāja*s and *anuyāja*s. See *anuvākyā* and *puro'nuvākyā*.

युज √*Yuj* (cl.7 "to join") to yoke the sacrifice, *i.e.* to introduce it with the *mantra* : *kastvā yunakti* Āp. Śr. IV.4.8; to put the fire altar in use (*Cayana*) XVII.23.1 (*agniyojana*).

यून *Yūna* n. cord for tying up *idhma* and *barhis* K. Śr. I.3.14; contains odd number of grass ib. *tri*° 3 pieces of cord ib. 21.

यूप *Yūpa* m. a stake to which a sacrificial animal is tied, made of *palāśa*, *khadira*, *bilva* or *rauhītaka* wood depending on the reward one wishes to obtain Āp. Śr.VII.1.16.

The size of y° varies from 1 to 33 *aratnis* depending on the type of sacrifice : usually for *Paśu* 3 to 4 a° Bh.Śr. VII.2.7, for *Soma* 5 to 15 K.Śr. VI.1.31. According to Āp. Śr. VII.2.13-15 it is as high as the sacrificer standing with or without raised hands, or standing on a chariot. It is 8 cornered (*aṣṭāśri*), tapering at the top, and the unchiselled (1/5th) part called *upara* planted inside a pit. Cf. *svaru*, *audumbarī*, *caṣāla*, *upaśaya*, *pātnīvata*. There are 13 y° at *Ekādaśinī*, 21 at *Aśva* H.Dh.II(2), 1110-12.

yūpya mfn. the tree from which y° can be made Āp. Śr. VII.1.15.

viśāla° m. a great stake to which 3 goats are tied Āp. Śr. XX.22.14 (*Aśva*).

°*veṣṭana* n. wrapping the y° with cloth (*vāsas*) K. Śr.XIV.1.20 (*Vāja*).

यूपावट *Yūpāvaṭa* m. the pit in which the *yūpa* 's planted; it is situated in front of the *āhavanīya* half within, half outside the *vedi* Āp. Śr. VII.9.6 (*Paśu*); in abbrev. *avaṭa* ib.9.

yūpāvaṭīya m. name of a *śaṅku* (peg) which is fixed at the eastern side of the *mahāvedi* (q.v.) to mark the *pṛṣṭhyā* line (*Soma*) B. Śr. VI.22. The other peg is called *antaḥpātya* or *śālāmukhīya*. See plan 3.

यूपावरोहण *Yūpāvarohaṇa* n. rite of climbing up a post, which is the principal feature of *Vājapeya*; done by the sacrificer Āp. Śr. XVIII.5.13.

यूपाहुति *Yūpāhuti* f. oblation to the sacrificial post in the *āhavanīya* at the beginning of *Soma*, offered by the *Adhvaryu* B. Śr. VI.1; of *Paśu* K. Śr. VI.1.4.

यूपोच्छ्रयण *Yūpocchrayaṇa* (*ud*-√*śri*, cl. 1 "to raise") n. rite of raising the *yūpa* by putting it into the pit (*avaṭa*) K. Śr. VI.3.7. The y° is strewn with *kuśa*, sprinkled and anointed with *ājya*; into the pit a *śakala* is thrown and a libation poured; and after fixing the y° earth is poured into the pit 2.11-3.10.

येयजामह *Yeyajāmaha* m. name of the invocation : *ye3yajāmahe* Āp. Śr. V.28.9. See *āguḥ* and *yājyā*.

योक्त्र *Yoktra* n. cord of *muñja* grass (Saccharum sara), having 3 strands, with which the *Āgnīdhra* or *Adhvaryu* at the *patnīsaṁnahana* rite girds round the waist of the sacrificer's wife over or under her garment Āp. Śr. II.5.5-6 (*Darśa*). This makes her fit for the sacrifice. Also at the *dīkṣā* the *Pratiprasthātṛ* girds up the cord round her upper garment B. Śr. VI.5 (*Soma*). She also wears a girdle called °*pāśa* and removes it Āp. Śr. III.10.6 (*Varuṇapraghāsa*); °*pāśa* is also used for tying round the neck of a bullock which draws the *soma* cart Bh. Śr. X.19.11.

योनि *Yoni* m.f.(1) see *araṇi*. (2) verses, specially of the *ārcika* of the SV. which are considered as "womb" from which a melody originates; a verse to which a melody (*sāman*) is set Āśv. Śr. V.15.16, Winternitz I, 165. cf...*tadetat etasyām ṛci adhyūḍham, tasmād ṛci adhyūḍhaṁ sāma gīyate* Chāndogya Upaniṣad I.6.1.

योयुपन *Yoyupana* (√*yup*, cl.4 "to obstruct") n. act of levelling the *vedi* with a *sphya*, (*yoyupyate* B. Śr. I.11) B. Śr. XX.9=*anumārṣṭi* (√*mṛj*, cl 2 "to wipe") K. Śr. II.6.32 (*samīkaroti*).

र Ra

रत्निन् *Ratnin* m. officials of a king; possessor of "jewels"; 12 offerings called *ratninām haviṁṣi* are performed for 12 days one after another in their houses at *Rāja*. 12 persons, according to K. Śr. XV.3, are : sacrificer, commander of the army, *purohita, sūta, grāmaṇī, kṣattṛ, saṁgrahītṛ, akṣāvāpa* (dice thrower), *govikarta, dūta* or *pālāgala, parivṛkt*. (discarded queen) *mahiṣī* (chief queen); also Āp. Śr. XVIII.10. cf. Heesterman 49—57.

रथकार *Rathakāra* m. chariot maker, mentioned as a separate caste, who can set up the sacred fire Bh. Śr. V.2.4. Cf. Oldenberg SBE XXX,316. See also *niṣādasthapati, varṇa.*

रराटी *Rarāṭī* (or *rarāṭyā*) f. a pediment, made of a garland of twisted *iṣīka* grass, suspended in front of the *havirdhānamaṇḍapa* on 2 posts, having a bar connecting them; r° is sewed to it Āp. Śr. XI.8,1, 4. C.H.89.

रशना *Raśanā* f. rope of woven *darbha* grass, one having 2 strands (*guṇa*), measuring 2 *vyāyāmas* (v°=4 *aratnis*) in length, used for tying an animal; and the other, 3 strands, 3 *vyāyāmas*, used for twining round the *yūpa* Āp. Śr. VII.11.2 (*Paśu*).

राजगवी *Rājagavī* f.=*anustaraṇī* (q.v.).

राजसूय *Rājasūya* (√*su* or √*sū*, cl.5/2 "to press out or generate") m. "birth of king"; the rite of royal consecration, performed by a *kṣatriya* only (*rājan*) L. Śr. IX.1.1. It lasts more than 2 years beginning with a *dīkṣā* on the 1st day of the bright half of *phālguna* (February-March). The preliminary part is opened with a *Soma* rite : *Pavitra* (of *Agniṣṭoma* type) lasting 5 days and followed by a series of *iṣṭis* one after another : *Anumati, Cātur* (taking one year), *Indraturīya, Pañcavātīya* (or *Pañcedhmīya*), *Apāmārgahoma, Ratninām haviṁṣi* (lasting 12 days), *iṣṭi* for Mitra and Bṛhaspati.

The *Abhiṣecanīya* (unction) rite is the core of the *Rāja*; then the *abhiṣeka* water, prepared elaborately is poured over the royal sacrificer. At the time of disposal of waters, the rite of *nāmavyatiṣañjanīya* is performed. Then a chariot race, as in the *Vāja*, and a mimetic raid on a group of cows, 100 or more, belonging to his kinsmen take place. He seizes the cattle, but restores them to the relatives.

After he has alighted from the chariot he is enthroned; the king sits on a throne, placed in front of the *āgnīdhra*, surrounded by the *ratnins*. In a place, marked out by the *akṣāvāpa*, the ritual gambling of dice takes place in which the king always wins. Thereafter the legend of Śunaḥśepa (dog's tail) is recited. For the next 10 days after the *Abhiṣecanīya*, one on each day, 10 *iṣṭis* called *saṁsṛpāṁ haviṁṣi* are performed which make him a *dīkṣita* for the next *Daśapeya*, a *Soma* rite. After the *avabhṛtha* in the *Daśapeya* the king has to observe certain vows (*devavratas*) for one year, at the end of which the *Keśavapanīya* (of *Atirātra* type) is performed.

A fantastic amount of sacrificial fee for the rites within the *Rāja* has been recommended, 32,000 cows for each of the 4 principal priests, 16,000 to each of the *dvitīyins*, 8,000 to each of the *tṛtīyins* and 4,000 to each of the *pādins* in the *Abhiṣecanīya* Āśv. Śr. IX.4.3-5. cf. Heesterman 162. Treated in B.Śr. XII, Āp.Śr. XVIII.8-22, K. Śr. XV.1-9, Āśv. Śr. IX.3-4. For annotation and interpretation Heesterman.

राजा *Rājā*•(nom sg.) m. a king in the proper sense Āp. Śr. II.16.10 etc But *soma* stalks are almost always referred to as king Āp. Śr. X.3.7 etc.

°*āsandī* f. See *āsandī*.Cf. *soma.*

रात्रिकर्मिन् *Rātrikarmin* m. servants, 4 in number, who help the priests in sacrificial work at night B. Śr. XV.22 (*Aśva*).

रात्रिपर्याय *Rātriparyāya* m. See *paryāya*.

रास्ना *Rāsnā* f. a border of clay, resembling a rope, round the *mahāvīra* vessel Āp. Śr. XV. 3.3 (*Pravargya*). Cf. *raśanā*.

रुक्म *Rukma* m. two plates, one made of gold and the other of silver Bh. Śr. XI.5.19. The silver plate is laid below and the golden plate over the *mahāvīra* vessel 7.7; 8.6 (*Pravargya*). An ornament of gold K.Śr. XV. 8.24.

रौहिण *Rauhiṇa* m. name of 2 *puroḍāśas*, prepared on 2 round, horse-shaped pieces of potsherd called °*kapāla* (Āp. Śr. XV.3.12), and offered into fire to Day in the morning and to Night in the evening XV.5.20 (*Pravargya*).

ल La

ललाटिक *Lalāṭika* mfn. frontal line ("forehead") of the *prācīnavaṁśa* Āp. Śr. XI.4.12.

लाज *Lāja* m. fried or parched rice grains, not pounded previously Āp. Śr. XII.4.10.

लेखा *Lekhā* f. lines (3), drawn with a *sphya* inside the altar Āp. Śr. I.25.14 (*Darśa*); on the bricks XVI.34.1 (*Cayana*). See also Gṛhya section.

लेप *Lepa* (√*lip*/*limp*, cl.6 "to smear") m. smearings of flour or clarified butter, sticking to a *puroḍāśa* Āp. Śr: III.2.7; to a spoon B. Śr. III.6, wiped on the *barhis* Bh. Śr. VI.13.9. cf. *piṣṭa*°.

लोकंपृणा *Lokaṁpṛṇā* (√*pṛ*, cl.3 "to fill") f. "filling up the space"; a kind of brick, used for constructing the altar; the bricks are set up with the *mantra* : *lokaṁ pṛṇa, chidraṁ pṛṇa*, "fill the space (empty), fill in the holes" Āp. Śr. XVI.14.9. Actually, they are used for filling the gap between the other bricks. The bricks are also set up with the *mantra* called *yajuṣmatī* (*Cayana*).

लोष्टचिति *Loṣṭaciti* f. =*śmaśānakaraṇa* n. Bh. Pi.II.2-5; rite of piling up of the clods of earth or unburnt (*āma*) bricks into a mound over the bones of a deceased. As high as one's neck in front and as high as navel in the rear B. Pi. I.14—16. Bones are deposited after an odd number of days Bh. Pi II.2.1, 4. A shed is built in between the village and the cremation ground, and there 3 pegs are fixed to the ground, the jar containing the bones is placed on the ground. A pitcher having a hundred holes (*śatātṛṇṇa*) 3.11, containing *vājina* "the scum" and curds, is hung up over it. The liquid is made to stream over the bones. The bones are fanned with a piece of leather called *dhuvana*; *dhuvana* (q.v.) is also a rite which is associated with sexual intercourse.

The cremation spot is sprinkled with water, swept clean, measured with a cord. Kauś. S. prescribes various other rites (LXXXIII-LXXXVI). The ground is ploughed. The bones are mixed with butter and arranged according to the human anatomy Bh. Pi. II. 4.26-27. The jar is placed within the furrowed plough, and 5 pots of cooked rice and *apūpa*s are also laid down. The jar containing the bones is fixed with pebbles (*śarkarā*) and sand. 1000 bricks are laid in various directions B.Pi.I.19. 4-7. RV. X.18.12 & 13 mention pillars and posts (*sthūṇā*) as shelter and support of the manes represented by bones.

लौकिक *Laukika* mfn. said of ordinary fire, originating from the *brahmaudanika* or *gārhapatya* Āp. Śr. V.13.8; used for setting up the *dakṣiṇāgni* ib.

व Va

वंश *Vaṁśa* m. bamboo beams or lintels, used for constructing a sacrificial shed; there is a central beam, *madhyama*°, in front of which the *gārhapatya* hearth is prepared Bh. Śr. V. 2.13; a lintel on which the *rarāṭī* is hung up XII.8.7. cf. *prācīna*°.

वनिष्ठु *Vaniṣṭhu* m. large intestine of an animal Bh. Śr. VII.19.10. (*Paśu*). See *jauhava*.

वनीवाहन *Vanīvāhana* n. coming and going of the vessel containing fire on a cart, used for *agnipraṇayana* K. Śr. XVI.6.22 (*Cayana*) Cf. Eggeling SBE XLIII, 297.

वपा *Vapā* f. omentum, about 4 fingers below the navel of a victim, shorn of flesh, cut off the immolated animal by the *Adhvaryu*; the narrowest part is pricked with an one-pronged spit for roasting, by the *Pratiprasthātṛ* on the *āhavanīya* fire, held out by the *śamitṛ* till the offering of v° (*vapāhoma*) Āp. Śr. VII.19.2, Bh. Śr. VII.14.11-12, 14-16.

°*śrapaṇī* f. two spits, made of *kārṣmarya* wood, used for roasting the v°, one having 1 point (*ekaśūla*) and the other having 2 points (*dvi°*) Āp. Śr. VII.19.1, with which the victim is touched by the *Pratiprasthātṛ* K. Śr. VI.5.7 (*Paśu*).

°*utkhedana* n. act of drawing out the v° Bh. Śr. VII.14.11.

°*uddharaṇa* n. the part (hole) of the body from which the *vapā* is taken out Āp. Śr. VII. 19.3; it is filled with a handful of grass by the *śamitṛ*.

वर *Vara* m. a gift that is wished for, said of a cow, the gift par excellence Āp. Śr. V.II.5, given by a sacrificer to the priests VII.21.5.

ati° m. a gift which by-passes the choicest gift, *i.e.* a gift of lesser value V.11.5.

वरण *Varaṇa* (√*vṛ*, cl.9 "to choose") n. ceremonial selection of the officiating priests by a sacrificer Āp. Śr. XI.19.10; also the relevant *mantras* X.1.13; see *pravara*.

ati° n. act of ignoring somebody at the time of the selection of priests B. Śr. XXIV.12.

वरुणप्रघास *Varuṇapraghāsa* m. See *Cāturmāsya*.

वर्ण *Varṇa* m. caste (literally, colour) Bh. Śr. IV.4.1. A sacrifice is meant for the three castes: *brāhmaṇa*, *rājanya* (*kṣatriya*), *vaiśya* Āp. Śr. XXIV.1.2, Oldenberg SBE XXX, 315, though certain acts are specially prescribed for a brahmin sacrificer Bh. Śr. ib. See also *rathakāra*, *niṣādasthapati*.

वशा *Vaśā* f. (1) barren cow, 1 or 3, offered to Mitra and Varuṇa at the *udayanīyā* Bh. Śr. XIV.24.11-12 (*Soma*). (2) name of bricks used at *Cayana* Āp. Śr. XVI.32.4.

वषट् *Vaṣaṭ* ind. a mystical exclamation, uttered loudly by the *Hotṛ* at the end of all *yājyās*, and in *anuyāja*s Āśv. Śr. I.5.5, after which the *Adhvaryu* pours out oblation into fire; it is to be pronounced by the day ib. 18. For other variants Āp. Śr. XXIV.14.11; it qualifies one to drink *soma* Mī. III.5.31.

°*kartṛ* (synonym, *dhiṣṇyavat*) m. name of priests who utter the v°, and are provided with *dhiṣṇyas*: these are the *camasins* (q.v.) who are asked by the *Adhvaryu* to utter v°; they are also called *hotrakas* (q.v.).

°*kāra* m. the exclamation v°, uttered by the *Hotṛ* after being requested to recite the *yājyā* (*yajetyukte*) Āp. Śr. II.16.2; at the rite to the manes the *vaṣaṭkāra* is replaced by *svadhā namaḥ* VIII.15.11.

anuvaṣaṭkāra m. the formula, pronounced by the *Hotṛ*, at the *anuyāja*, for the *sviṣṭakṛt* libation; this *mantra* is *vājinasyāgne vīhi* VIII. 3.8, 10. See *yaj*.

vauṣaṭ ind. probably a lengthened form of *vaṣaṭ* of which it is a variant XXIV.14.11.

वसतीवरी *Vasatīvarī* f. probably, "desirable for abode or dwellers"; technical name of waters, kept overnight; fetched from a stream coming out of a hill by dipping a pitcher against the current before the sunset on the day before the *sutyā* Āp. Śr. XI.20.5, C.H.119; v° is carried round the fire and the altar by the *Adhvaryu* XI.21.3-5, C.H. 120, later mixed with the *ekadhanā* waters C.H. 143. The v° is transformed into *nigrābhya* (q.v.). V° is used in the extraction of *soma* juice, *somopasargārthāḥ* Āp. Śr. XI.20.5. The pitcher is called °*kalaśa* B. Śr. VIII.8.

वसा *Vasā* f. fat, which comes from animal flesh and floats on the surface when the flesh is cooked. An oblation of fat called *vasāhoma* is offered Āp. Śr. VII.25.1 (*Paśu*).

°*homahavanī* f. name of the second *juhū* for the *homa* 8.3 (*Paśu*).

वसोर्धारा *Vasordhārā* f. "flow of wealth", name of an oblation of clarified butter poured in a continuous stream on the altar Āp. Śr. XVII. 17.8 (*Cayana*).

वाग्यमन *Vāgyamana* n. restraint of speech (silence), maintained by the *Adhvaryu*, the *Brahman* or the sacrificer at various services of sacrifices, *e.g.* at *Darśa* the *Adhvaryu* and the sacrificer remain silent from the *praṇītāpraṇayana* till the call to the *haviṣkṛt* Āp. Śr. I.16.7-19.8; at the *Agnihotra* by the *Adhvaryu* from the milking of cow till the *homa* K. Śr. IV.14.31. According to Āp. Śr. I.12.5 comm. *vācaṁ yacchati* means not uttering any word other than *mantras*. The *Brahman* withholds his speech in all services of a ritual Āp. Śr. III.18.6, or in those services in which *mantras* are being used (by the other priests) ib. 7, Bh. III.15.6 (*vācaṁ yamaḥ*), K. Śr. II.2.2,

B. Śr. III.24. As a part of his *dīkṣā* the sacrificer restrains his speech VI.5, and the opposite of this is *vācaḥ visargaḥ*, releasing voice at the *dīkṣā* VI.7 (*vācaṁ visṛjate*). C.H. 20,23.

वाचन *Vācana* n. act of causing recitation of *mantras*, one of the functions of a sacrificer K. Śr. I.10.12; XIV.3.19 (*Vāja*).

वाजपेय *Vājapeya* ("drink of strength or of food") m. n. the 6th *saṁsthā* of *Soma*. Although it follows the pattern of the *Ukthya*, it has many features which distinguish it from all other rites of the class. The V° incorporates many popular rites. The number 17 is very much emphasized in the rite : there are 17 *stotras* and *śastras* (of which the 17th is the V° *stotra* and *śastra*), the same number of animals are sacrificed. It takes 17 days : 13 *dīkṣā* days, 3 *upasad* days and 1 pressing day.

17 cups of wine and of *soma* are prepared; wine is purchased readymade. Its special feature begins with the midday pressing. 17 chariots (yoked with 4 horses except that of the sacrificer) are made ready; one of which belongs to the sacrificer (yoked with 3 horses). An archer shoots an arrow, and from the spot it hits the archer again shoots the arrow. This goes on for the 17th time, and the spot of the 17th shooting is the limit of the chariot race. The *Brahman* fixes a wheel upon a pole, and sits on it. When the sacrificer and other competitors (*vājasṛt*) Āp. Śr. XVIII. 4.13, start the race 17 drummers beat 17 drums, placed on the northern *śroṇi* of the *vedi*. After the *soma* cups have been offered, 16 wine cups are given to 16 competitors who drink the wine. A ladder is placed against the *yūpa*, which is quadrangular (elsewhere octagonal). The sacrificer and his wife climb up the ladder onto the top of the *yūpa*. 17 bags of salt tied to a long pole are raised to them to the top of the *yūpa*. Āp. Śr. XVIII.1-7, K. Śr. XIV.

वाजप्रसवीय *Vājaprasavīya* m.n. name of 14 oblations divided into 2 groups of 7, the first group begins with "*vājasyemaṁ prasavaḥ*" (VS.IX.23—29) and the second with "*vājasya nu prasave*" (VS.XVIII.30-36) *mantras*, and offered with an *udumbara sruva*, which is finally thrown into the fire Āp. Śr. XVII.19.1-3, B.Śr. X.54 (*Cayana*). cf. Eggeling SBE XLIII, 223.

वाजसृत *Vājasṛt* mfn. running in a race (RV.IX. 43.5); 16 competitors who participate in a chariot race in the *Vāja* ceremony. Their chariots are yoked with 4 horses. A piece of gold (*kṛṣṇala*) is given to and retrieved from them after the race. They drink wine from their cups. Āp. Śr. XVIII.4.13; 5.4-5; 6.17.

वाजिन *Vājina* n. scum (watery part) of curdled milk, obtained by pouring out the solid portion called *āmikṣā* (q.v.); prepared by adding sour milk of the previous day to fresh warm milk drawn in the morning Āp. Śr. VIII.2.6; it tastes bitter Śab on Mī.II.2.23; IV.1. 22. V° is offered to the deities called *Vājins* (Vaiśvadeva: *Cātur*), and the remainder is consumed by the *Hotṛ*, the *Adhvaryu*, the *Brahman*, the *Agnīdhra* and the sacrificer (by smelling Āśv. Śr. II.16.19) by inviting each other (*upahava*) Āśv. Śr. ib.17; VIII.4.4, 6.

Its bowl (*pātra*) is made of *palāśa* Āp. Śr. VIII.2.1.

वाण *Vāṇa* m. a harp with a hundred strings, made of *muñja* grass Āp. Śr. XXI.17.10, played at the chanting of a *stotra* at the *Mahāvrata*.

वातहोम *Vātahoma* m. oblation of air, name of 3 libations offered with the hollow of joined palms (*añjali*) in the northern, the southern and the western parts of the chariot K.Śr. XVIII.6.1. (*Cayana*)

वात्सप्र *Vātsapra* (√*prī*, cl.9 "to please") n. rite of adoration of fire, performed by reciting 11 stanzas of Vatsaprī (RV.X.45=VS.XII.18-28) at the *dīkṣā* (*Cayana*) K. Śr. XVI.5.21.

वायव्य *Vāyavya* n. name of a bowl used in *soma* libation for various deities Āp. Śr. XI.17.1= *ūrdhvapātra*; it is shaped like a mortar with raised corners and having a beaker lip, 1 span in length XII.1.4.

वाल *Vāla* m. filter made of cow's hair for filtering *surā* B. Śr. XI.3; °*srāva* hair-sieve for *surā* Āp. Śr. XIX.1.17 (*Sautrāmaṇī*).

वावाता *Vāvātā* f. favoured queen K.Śr. XX.5 15. See *Aśvamedha*, *patnī*.

विकृति *Vikṛti* (*vi*-√*kṛ*, cl. 8 "to modify"; *vikriyate* Āp. Śr. VII.27.6) f. modification of a model rite (*prakṛti*); a derived rite, e.g. all *iṣṭis* are v° of *Darśa*.

The *mantras* used in such rites are adapted according to sense XXIV.3.50.

vikāra m. the modified form of a rite VII. 27.2.

vaikṛtī f. deities and offerings belonging to a modified rite IV.10.1.

विग्रह *Vigraha* (*vi-√grah*, cl.9 "to take out") m. separation of *soma* juice out of the stock, i.e. distribution of a portion of juice K.Śr. IX.14.13. Cf *acchāvāka*° XXII.10.3. Also a break in recitation between *pādas* of a *ṛc* or between the syllables of a *pāda* Āśv.Śr. VIII.1.10.

विघन *Vighana* (√*han*, cl. 2 "to smite") m. mallet for breaking up the lumps of earth on the *mahāvedi* Āp. Śr. XI.5.2, in pl. B.Śr. VII.9 (*Soma*).

वितष्टि *Vitaṣṭi* (from √*takṣ*, cl.1 "to chisel") f. ladle, made of *udumbara* wood, having a round rim and without a pointed head B.Śr. X.50 comm.

वितस्ति *Vitasti* f. a measurement, 12 fingers Bh. Pi.II.5.8.

वितान *Vitāna* (√*tan*, cl.8 "to stretch") m.n. extension, i.e. establishment of fires at the appropriate place K.Śr. XXV.7.15 comm.

vaitānika (mf) n. rites like *Agnyādheya* etc Āśv. Śr. I.1.2, ĀśvGṛ.I.1.1.

वितृतीयदेश *Vitṛtīyadeśa* m. a third part of the altar or of the *mahāvedi*, which is considered to be divided in 3 parts both in the eastern and western half. Cf. Kashikar on Bh. Śr. II.1.5; the *utkara* is situated 2 steps north of the eastern one third part of the altar Āp. Śr. II.1.6-7; on the western side the *janyabhayāpanodana* rite is performed XI.7.2.

विधा *Vidhā* f. a portion; a part of the *sāman*, obtained by separating it from a verse, and is assigned to a particular singer. Cf. Simon Pañcavi 12; synonym (*pāda*) *gīti* and *vacana*; more precisely (as opposed to *gīti*), it designates a part or the whole of a *pāda*; with or without *stobha*, consisting of one or more *parvans*, and set to one and the same melody Hoogt 53; elsewhere, v° signifies simply one of the (5) parts of the *sāman*, synonym (*vi*) *bhakti* Hoogt 58.

विधृती *Vidhṛtī* (du.) (*vi-√dhṛ*, cl. 1 "to keep apart") f. partition; technical name of 2 blades of grass (*darbha* at *Darśa* or 2 large sugar-cane sticks at *Paśu*), of the same size, laid on the *barhis* to symbolically separate the latter from the *prastara* on the *vedi* where both are placed Āp. Śr. II.9.12; VII.7.7.

विपथ *Vipatha* m.n. a cart in bad condition, belonging to the people of east, used by the *vrātyas* Āp. Śr. XXII.5.5, K.Śr. XXII.4.14 (which is difficult to drive).

विपरिक्रमण *Viparikramaṇa* n. act of walking by the priests inside the sacrificial arena in a changed order : the *Brahman* walks to the north, the *Hotṛ*, the *Āgnīdhra* and the *Adhvaryu* to the south Āp. Śr VIII.15.1. (*Pitṛyajña*) This is explained as change of places ib. comm.

विप्रतिषेध *Vipratiṣedha* (√*sidh*, cl.1. "to hinder") m. conflict arising out of 2 contradictory injunctions Āp. Śr. XXIV.1.20.

विप्रुड्ढोम *Vipruḍḍhoma* (*vi-√pruṣ*, cl.5 "to sprinkle") m. *vipruṣ* f. a drop or spray; also called *vipruṣāṁ homaḥ* or *vaipruṣāḥ* (*homāḥ*), 4 expiatory oblations of clarified butter performed by the *Adhvaryu*, the *Prastotṛ*, the *Pratihartṛ*, the *Udgātṛ* and the *Brahman* with the *pracaraṇī* so that the drops of *soma* which are scattered during the pressing of *soma* stalks may go to the gods Āp. Śr. XII.7.11; 16.15 comm, K.Śr. IX.6.30. Cf. C.H.169. Also said of the drops of milk (called *stoka* and *drapsa* in *mantras*) for which a *mantra* is uttered Āp. Śr. I.13.7 (*Darśa*).

विभक्ति *Vibhakti* (*vi-√bhaj*, cl.1 "to divide") f. (1) division of a *sāman*, also called *bhakti* (q.v.). (2) declensional forms (divisions) of the names of the invoked deity (of Agni, e.g. *agne*, *agnau*, *agnim*, *agninā* as necessary in 4 *prayāja* formulas Āp Śr. V.28.6, Nid III.9; *v°√vac* to say the v° Āp. Śr. ib.8, *v°√dhā* to insert the v° B.Śr. III.2, Bh. Śr. V.19.20 (*Ādheya*).

विभागमन्त्र *Vibhāgamantra* m. *mantra* used at the time of dividing the pounded grains for the oblatory material Bh.Śr. V.14.6 (*Ādheya*) Āp.Śr. XVIII.11.13 (*Vāja*).

विभाग्यसामन् *Vibhāgyasāman* n. *sāmans* of which the *bhaktis* are obtained by dividing the verse in equal parts, thus there may be *padavibhāgya*, *stobha*°, *padastobha*°; in *avibhāgyasāman* the division is in unequal parts Simon Pañcavi 12.

विमित *Vimita* (*vi-√mi*, cl.5 "to fix, erect") n. shed for the sacrificer at the *dīkṣā*. Cf. *dīkṣita*° Āp. Śr. X.15.5 (*śālā*). Another shed resting on 4 posts XVIII.18.5 (*Rāja*); "construction" of the *prācīnavaṁśa* Bh. Śr. X.3.1.

विमुख *Vimukha* m. name of a *mantra* VS. XXXIX.7 which one recites with one's "head turned away" after the immolation of the horse K.Śr. XX.8.5 (*Aśva*).

विमोचन *Vimocana* (*vi-√muc*, cl.6 "to release") n. act of unfastening the girdle from the waist of the sacrificer's wife Bh.Śr. III.9.11 (*Darśa*); act of "releasing" the *praṇītā* waters from its sacrificial use (*vimuñcati*) with the *mantra* : *ko vo'yokṣīt sa vo vimuñcatu* Āp. Śr. III.13.5; also said of the detachment of *kapālas* from one another 14.4 (*Darśa*).

vimocanīya homa m. name of a libation for "detaching" the drums (*dundubhi*) XVIII.5.2 (end of *Vāja*).

विवेचना *Vivecanā* (*vi-√vic*, cl.7 "to sift grain by tossing") f. sifting of grain with a winnowing basket (*śūrpa*) Bh. Śr. VI.16.26 (*Āgrayaṇa*).

avivekam ind. without sifting chaff from grains Āp. Śr. I.7.5.

विशय *Viśaya* m. space between the *vedi* and the *gārhapatya* B. Śr. V.2 (the middle part); bricks placed at the joint between the *ātman* and *pakṣa* of the fire altar Āp. Śr. XVII.8.5 (*Cayana*).

विशस् *Vi-√śas* (cl 2) "to cut up" Āp. Śr. VII. 14.13; *viśasana* a *mantra* with which the victim is cut up B. Śr. XXIV.7.

विशाख *Viśākha* m. n. bifurcation of *darbha* blade Āp. Śr. I.3.11; also at the top of the *audumbarī* post where a piece of gold is tied, and a libation of *ājya* is offered XI.10.4 (the 3rd *upasad*, *Soma*), C.H.96= *karṇa* (q.v.).

°*dāman* n. two-pronged (*dviśiraska* XV.5.20 comm) cord, 3 in number, made of *muñja* grass with which a calf, a she-goat and a lamb are tied to a peg Bh. Śr. XI.5.22; 6.14 (*Pravargya*).

वि-शास् *Vi-√śās* (cl.2) to give directions, specially concerning the manner of cutting up an animal Āp. Śr. VII.22.5 (*viśāsana* giving of different directions B. Śr. XXVI.12);

विश्वजित् *Viśvajit* m. "all conquering"; name of a *soma* festival, an *ekāha* of the *Agniṣṭoma* type, performed on the 4th day after the *viṣuvat* in the *Gavāmayana* Āp. Śr. XXII.1.6. The *dakṣiṇā* is very large : 100 horses, 1000 cattle or the entire property L. Śr. VIII.1.28. cf. Raghuvaṁśa V.1.

(कृष्ण) विषाण (*Kṛṣṇa*) *Viṣāṇa* n. horn of a black antelope, 1 span in length, having 3 or 5 folds (*trivali, pañca°, pañcāvṛt*), which is fastened to the sacrificer's body either by the *Adhvaryu* or by himself Āp. Śr. X.9.17-18. (*dīkṣā, Soma*). With it he takes out a lump of earth from the *vedi*, touches his forehead, and if he wants he scratches his body 10.1-3 (*Soma*); ties a knot in the garment XVIII.16.9 (*Rāja*).

विषुवत् *Viṣuvat* mfn, m. "having both sides in equal parts", the central day which divides the *Gavāmayana sattra*, lasting one year, equally in 2 parts. The *sāman* chanted is *ekaviṁśatistoma* Āp. Śr. XXI.15.16.

विष्टाव *Viṣṭāva* m. one of the sub-divisions of a *paryāya* containing 3 repetions : *ṛcabhāga, āvāpa* (*sthāna*) and *paricarā* (*ṛc*). See *paryāya, viṣṭuti*. Cf. Eggeling SBE XXVI, 309, Caland PBr. 19.

विष्टुति *Viṣṭuti* f. technical name of the variety in repetition of the verses of a *stoma* at the time of chanting. There are different varieties differing from one another in number and order of verses to be chanted in each *paryāya*. Thus the *ājyastotra* which is a *pañcadaśastoma* (see *stoma*) has 3 different varieties for repeating the triplets :

(a) *pañcapañcinī* f. "consisting of 5 in each row" : *aaa b c, a bbb c, a b ccc*;

(b) *aparā* f. "other or second" : *aaa b c, a b c, a bbb ccc*.

(c) *udyatī* f. "ascending" : *abc, a bbb c, aaa b ccc*. Cf. C.H. 237, Eggeling SBE XXVI, 308. See also *paryāya, sāman*.

विष्णुक्रम *Viṣṇukrama* m. three "*viṣṇu* steps", actually 4, taken by the sacrificer with 4 matching *mantras*, each of which begins with *Viṣṇoḥ kramo'si* (whence the name). He begins from the southern *śroṇi* towards the east along the southern side of the *vedi* putting his right foot always first, and he increases his steps a little longer with each step, and does not go beyond the *āhavanīya* Āp. Śr. IV.14.6-7 (*Darśa*). At the end of *Soma* the 4th step has been mentioned XIII .18.9. At the *pravargya* of *Aśva* the sacrificer proceeds, turning towards the northeast, holding the *ukhā* in his hand which he raises a little higher with every step K. Śr. XVI.5.11. There is also another *mantra* called *viṣṇvatikrama* Āp. Śr. IV.14.9.

विसंस्थितसंचर *Visaṁsthitasaṁcara* m. a path (*saṁcara*) which lies to the north of every *dhiṣṇya*; provided for egress and ingress of the priests as long as the ceremony remains unifinished (*visaṁsthita*) B. Śr. VII.11.

विसर्ग *Visarga* m. See *vāg°*.

विसर्जनी *Visarjanī* f.=*madantī* (q.v.).

विसूर्मिका *Visūrmikā* **f. handful of *darbha* grass, 3 in number, used instead of fuel logs (*idhma*) for carrying fire B. Śr. III.1 (*Punarādheya*)=** *kapāla* Renou Vocabulaire.

विहार *Vihāra* (*vi-√hṛ*, cl. 1 "to keep separate") m. literally, "separation" of the sacrificial fires; generally, the 3 sacrificial fires and the place between them Āśv. Śr. I.1.4 comm, Mī. XII.2.1; v° may even mean a *vedi* Āp. Śr. VIII.5.5; v° is the sacrificial sanctuary Bh. Śr. I.1.14.

°*yoga* m. appliance, e.g. cord (*rajju*), used for measurement of a v° Āp. Śulb I.1.1.

vi-√hṛ to take and carry fire from the *āhavanīya* to other hearths, as used in the *praiṣa* to the *Āgnīdhra* : *agnīn vihara* K. Śr. IX.7.5.

वृक्कौ *Vṛk(k)au* (du) m. kidneys of a victim, cut off, cooked and offered as oblation Āp. Śr. VII.22.6 (*Paśu*). See *aupabhṛta, jauhava*.

वृत्तिप्रेक्ष *Vṛttiprekṣa* m. "search for livelihood"; in case of deprivation of the means of subsistence priests may ignore the professional rules B.Śr. XXIV.13. See *ṛtvij*.

वृषारव *Vṛṣārava* m. "roar of a bull"; name of the striking-stone (=*aśman* Āp. Śr. I.20.2), used for striking on the *dṛṣad* and *upalā* B.Śr. I.6 (*Darśa*).

वेद *Veda* m. name of a bunch of *darbha* grass, tied with a rope, shaped like a calf's knee or a woven basket or a head with 3 strands (*trivṛt śirasam*) Āp. Śr. I.6 5, K.Śr. I.3.23 comm. It is used for sweeping the *vedi*. At the *pravargya* 2 v° are used Āp. Śr. XV 5.18.

°*parivāsana* n. cut up top portions of *darbha* blades of the *veda*; it is cut at about 1 span above the tying cord I.6.6, and ladles are cleansed with it II.4.2.

वेदि *Vedi* f. altar, an elevated or excavated plot of ground, strewn with *darbha* grass where sacrificial materials, utensils and implements are placed. It is situated within the shed (*śālā*) between the *āhavanīya* and the *gārhapatya*. A *vedi* is a rectangle, and it is supposed to have the shape of a young woman with broad hips (2 *śroṇis*), shoulders)2 *aṁsas* (and a slender waist (2 sides : north and south are concave, *madhyamasaṁgṛhīta* K.Śr. II.6.7) Āp. Śr. II.3.1.

The altar of *Darśa* is called *yoṣā*, a girl Āp. Śulb. II.4.15.

All works on the *vedi* are done with a *sphya* Bh. Śr. II.2.5 (*dārśikī*). Measurements and shape of a v° vary according to the type of rite and the texts. For *Darśa*, in length as much as the height of the sacrificer, 3 finger breadths in depth, 1 *vyā* (*yā*)*ma*=4 *aratnis* on the western side, 3 *aratnis* on the east and sloping either towards the east or the north K.Śr. II.6.1-22, Āp.Śr. II.1, H.Dh.II(2),1034-37. For *Paśu*, 6 *aratnis* in length, 3 on the east and 4 on the west Āp. Śr. VII.3.7-9. For *Varuṇapraghāsa* there are 2 v° : one, northern (*uttarā*), for the *Adhvaryu* and the other, southern for the *Pratiprasthātṛ* VIII.5.5, K.Śr. V. 3.9-33, also for *Sautrāmaṇī* XIX.2.1; for *Soma* see *mahāvedi, uttaravedi*; see also *parigrāha, yoyupana*. For details about the construction of the v° ŚBr.I.2.5.7-20. See plans.

°*karaṇāni* n. (pl) tools used for preparing the v° Āp. Śr. XII.19.6.

वैश्वदेव *Vaiśavadeva* (1) n. the first *parvan* of the *Cāturmāsya* (q.v.) (2) m. name of a *graha*, occuring twice, at the first pressing B.Śr. VII. 17, Āp. Śr. XII 28.4 and at the third B.Śr. VIII.13, Āp. Śr XIII.13.4-5. The former is called *kṣullaka°* and the latter, *mahā°* C.H. 235, 354. The *stotra* following the first is the first *ājyastotra* Śr.K(S).II(1), 328, the *śastra* following the second is called *vaiśvadevaśastra* Śr.K(S).II(1), 440. Cf. C.H.236, 354.

वैसर्जन *Vaisarjana* n. name of the *ājya* libations with the *pracaraṇī* ladle into the *śālāmukhīya* at the 3rd *upasad* (*Soma*) Āp. Śr. XI.16.15. The relatives are called out; the sacrificer touches the *Adhvaryu*, the wife touches the sacrificer and sons and brothers of the sacrificer touch the wife while the oblations are poured; done with a view to setting them free ŚBr. III 6.3.2. C.H.110.

व्यतिषक्त *Vyatiṣakta* (*vi-ati-√sañj*, cl.1 "to intertwine") mfn. (1) a mixed way of pouring *āghāra* libation into the fire both on the east and the west Āp. Śr. II.12.8 (*Darśa*); (2) mixed up offerings: *caru* and *puroḍāśa* XXIV.3.23; (3) *vyatisaj* said of the handful of grass alternately pointed to the east and the south B Śr. VI.27

of alternate drawing of *soma* and *surā* Āp.Śr. XVIII.2.7 (*Vāja*); (4) "interwoven" *pratigara* of the *Hotṛ* recited in the *ṣoḍaśiśastra*, e.g. "*othā moda iva made*" after every half verse and "*madā moda ivomatha*" at the end of a verse XIV.3.4; (5) *vyatisañjanīyau homau*. See *nāma*°

व्यापात *Vyāpāta* m. (meaning unknown) Āp.Śr. XIV.22.13; probably, separation of fires, in contradistinction to *saṁnivāpa* Renou Vocabulaire.

व्या(या)म *Vyā(yā)ma* m. a fathom=4 *aratnis* Āp. Śr. XVI.1.7, B. Śulb.I.1.

व्याहाव *Vyāhāva* m. mystical call of the *Hotṛ* in a *śastra* : *śoṁsāvom* Āp. Śr. XII.27.17. The *pratigara* of the *Adhvaryu* to this is : *śoṁsā moda iva* and *othā moda iva*.

व्याहृति *Vyāhṛti* (pl) (*vi-ā-√hṛ*, cl.1 "to utter") f. three mystical utterances : *bhūḥ, bhuvaḥ* and *svaḥ*, (*suvaḥ*), sometimes called *mahā*°; pronounced separately or, generally, together on various occasions Āp. Śr. V.12.1; murmured by the *Adhvaryu* and by the *Brahman* in the rite of atonement. ŚBr.I.5.2.16 refers to 5 utterances : *ā śrāvaya*, Bid him hear (*Adhvaryu*'s call), *astu śrauṣaṭ* (*Āgnīdhra*'s response) Yes, may he hear, (*samidho*) *yaja*, Pronounce the prayer (to the kindling sticks) (*Adhvaryu's* summons to *Hotṛ*), *ye yajāmahe*, We who pronounce the prayer (*yājyā* of *Hotṛ*), *vauṣaṭ*, May he bear the sacrifice to gods (conclusion of a *yājyā*). Cf. Eggeling SBE XII, 142-3. See also *vyāhṛtihoma* and *sāvitrī* (Gṛhya).

व्युष्टि (द्विरात्र) *Vyuṣṭi(dvirātra)* (*vi-√vas*, cl. 2 "to shine") m. 2 day *Soma* rite called "dawn" comprising an *Agniṣṭoma* and an *Atirātra*, performed at the end of *Rāja* Āp. Śr. XVIII.22. 12-22. Heesterman 220.

व्रत *Vrata* (√*vṛ*, cl. 5 or 9 "to choose", SW) n. command or religious duty, whence a religious observance, a vow or a pattern of conduct. For the controversy over the etymology and the meaning of the word H.Dh.V(1), 1-21. In the sense of religious observance Āp. Śr. IV.2.6 (*vratam upaiti*), K. Śr. II.1.11, *vratopeta* B. Śr. I.1, which includes abstinence from certain food : beans (*māṣa*) and flesh (*māṁsa*) Āp. Śr. IV.2.5, and from sexual intercourse K.Śr. II.1.8. Cf. Nirukta II.14. Therefore v° means hot milk which is consumed as a food of vow in consequence of religious observance Āp. Śr. X.12.4, B.Śr. VI.7. *Vratana* n. preparation of the *vrata* Āp. Śr. XVI.12.10, B.Śr. l.c.; *vrataya* (Pāṇ III.1.21 & Kāśikā) to consume milk, food at v° Āp.Śr. X.16.7, B.Śr. l.c: or any other prescribed food Āp. Śr. X.16.10. *Vratya* n. a rite T Br. III. 7.1.9 (also m. I.7.4.3.) Āp. Śr. IX.2.1 (*vratye' han*); rules suitable for a *vrata* K.Śr. XII.2.12, whence also food of vow VIII.7.23. *Avratya* n. offence against *vrata* rules VII.5.2.

°*caryā* f. observance of vow Bh. Śr. VIII. 11.18.

°*cārin* mfn. observer of vow IV.4.12.

°*dughā* f. cow which gives milk for v° K.Śr. VII.4 19.

°*prada* mfn. one who serves v° milk to the sacrificer Bh.Śr. X.10.15.

°*śrapaṇa* m fire on which v° milk is warmed, *dakṣiṇāgni* B.Śr. VI.6 or *gārhapatya* Bh.Śr. X. 10.1 (*śrapayati*).

vratopāyana n. entering into a religious observance (by the sacrificer), which is different from consuming food (*aśana*) Āp. Śr. IV. 2.8.

vratopāyanīya mfn. relating *mantra* IX.1.13; appropriate food mixed with clarified butter to be consumed during the period of vow K. Śr. II.1.10, B.Śr. II.12.

व्रात्यस्तोम *Vrātyastoma* m. "praise of *Vrātya*"; name of *stomas*, 4 in number; a rite of adoption consisting of 4 *ekāhas*, performed by the *vrātyas* so that they can renounce the vrātyahood and thus become socially eligible (*vyavahāryā bhavanti*) K.Śr. XXII. 4.28. A remarkable rite, and it is the only instance of proselytization in the vedic ritual. In contrast to the later notion of the *vrātyas* being *patitasāvitrīkas* (q.v.), they are considered divine (*daiva*) Caland PBr.454, and glorified in AV.XV.1.1 to the discomfiture of Sāyaṇa, who finds it difficult to explain the apparent contradiction. The word *vrātya* is probably derived from *vrāta* meaning group. Cf.RV.III.26.6; V.53.11; VI. 75.9; IX.14.2; X.34.12, also *vrātacphañyorastriyām* Pāṇ V.3.113 and on it Kāśikā supplies names of the *vrātas* which are evidently totemic, e.g. *kāpotapākyaḥ* etc. A fairly good idea can be formed from PBr.XVII.1-4 on the vrātyahood. Those who led the *vrātya* life (*vrātyām pravasanti*) were neither cultivators nor traders; they ate food meant for *brahman* So they are called *garagirā*, swallower of poison. They did not practise *brahmacarya* nor were initiated, yet they spoke the speech of an initiate PBr.XVII.1.1-2, 9, K.Śr. XXII.4.

1-28, Āp. Śr. XXII.5.4-14, B.Śr. XVIII.24-26. For the details on the problem of the *vrātyas* I.W.Hauer: Der Vrātya, Vol. I. Stuttgart, 1927, Hara Prasad Sastri : Absorption of the *vrātyas*, London, Oxford univ, 1926, Chitrabhanu Sen, Journal of the Oriental Institute XII, 3(1963).

श Śa

शंयुवाक *Śaṁyuvāka* m. "utterance of *śaṁyu*"; *śaṁyu*=beneficient, RV.I.43.4; X.143.6. A formula of benediction which contains the word *tat śaṁ yor āvṛṇīmahe* we long for that *śaṁ yoḥ* (TBr. III.5.11), uttered by the *Hotṛ* who is requested by the *Adhvaryu* to do so while the *prastara* and the *paridhi* are being thrown into the fire (*Darśa*) Āp. Śr. III.7.10. *Śaṁyvanta* or *śaṁyuvanta* an *iṣṭi* which is concluded with the ś°, introductory *iṣṭi* of *Soma* X.21.13, at *Cātur* Bh. Śr. VIII.21.17 (optionally).

शकट *Śakaṭa* n. a cart, yoked and used for carrying the *soma* stalks in its *nīḍa* Āp.Śr. X.27. 10 (*Soma*); for containing rice grains at *Darśa* I.7.6; for carrying the *gārhapatya* in the *nīḍa* and the *āhavanīya* in the *praüga* B.Śr. VI.9.

शकल *Śakala* m.n. chips of a tree obtained at the time of cutting it for *yūpa*; the first ś° is offered as oblation Āp. Śr. VII.9.10 (*Paśu*). See also *adhimanthana, svaru*. At *pravargya* ś° are offered as oblation XV.11.6-7; also means a slice of *puroḍāśa* B. Śr. VII.15.

शक्वरी *Śakvarī* f.=*mahānāmnī* (q.v.).

शङ्कु *Śaṅku* m. (1) wooden splinter, tied to the clothes of the sacrificer's wife; she can use it during the *dīkṣā* as a scratcher, if needed B. Śr. VI.5; (2) wooden pegs driven into the ground for marking the area of *mahāvedi*, *sadas* etc. Āp. Śr. XI.4.12, K.Śr. VIII.3.7-11; also pegs, fixed towards the south of the eastern post of the southern door of the *prācīnavaṁśa* to which a calf (*vatsa*) is tied, on the opposite side of this another ś° for *ajā*, inside the shed for a lamb (*barkara* or *ajāvatsa*) Bh. Śr. XI.6. 11-12.

शतरुद्रिय *Śatarudriya* mfn. (*homa* m.) oblation of wild sesamum, with the flour of *gavīdhuka*, offered with a leaf of *arka* (instead of *juhū*) on the western corner of the northern side of the fire altar; 425 oblations are offered to Rudra as a rite of appeasement Āp. Śr. XVII.11.3. K.Śr. XVIII.1.1 (*Cayana*).

शफ *Śapha* m. a pair of wooden (*udumbara*) tongs, 2 in number, used for raising the *ukhā* from fire Āp.Śr. XV.5.11, B.Śr. IX.5 (*Pravargya*).

शमितृ *Śamitṛ* m. butcher, who in the animal sacrifice slaughters a victim by suffocation or strangulation (*saṁjñapana*) Āp. Śr. VII.16.5 and cuts its limbs with a sharp knife 14.14. Identification of ś° is a matter of controversy; he is generally considered a person other than the 16 priests. Cf. K.Śr. VI.7.1-3 & comm. Ś° is the *Adhvaryu* himself Mī. III.7.28-29. He may be a brahmin or a non-brahmin Āśv. Śr. XII.9.11. See also *śāmitra*.

शमीगर्भ *Śamīgarbha* m. See *araṇi*.

शम्या *Śamyā* f. wooden yoke pin of *khadira* wood (RV. X.31.10); length variously given as 32 *aṅgulas* Āp. Śr. I.15.13, 1 span (*prādeśa*) K.Śr. I.3.36 comm, 1 arm Bhardvāja cited in Āp. Śr. l.c, of the same length as a *juhū*, and its thicker portion is called *kumba* Vai. Śr. XI.8. It is used for measuring the *uttaravedi* Āp. Śr. VII.3.12 (*Paśu*). It serves as a prop for the cart carrying *soma* stalks B. Śr. VI.15, Āp. Śr. X.28.1. Cf. texts quoted C.H. 49n. With a ś° the *Āgnīdhra* strikes the *dṛṣad* and *upalā* stones Āp. Śr. I.20.4 (*Darśa*). Ś° is thrown like a projectile for measuring the sacrificial ground IX.1.17; the spot where the ś° thus hits is called *śamyāpravyādha* B.Śr. XI.7.

शय *Śaya* (√*śī*, cl. 2 "to lie") m. two days, called reserved days, which are added after the *prāyaṇīya* (*Gavāmayana*) Āp. Śr. XXI. 15.9.

शरण *Śaraṇa* (√*śṛ* or √*śri*, cl. 1 "to resort") n. a shelter (shed) having bamboo beams turned towards the north; below its central beam (*madhyamavaṁśa*) the *gārhapatya* is situated; it is used by the *Adhvaryu* at *Ādheya* Āp. Śr. V.4.1-2.

शरेषीका Śareṣīkā f. a brush, made of *śara* and having cotton (*tūlā*) B.Śr. VI.1 (*Soma*). See *iṣīkā*.

शर्करा Śarkarā f. pebbles or stones with which the place of cremation Bh.Pi.I.10.9, and the jar containing charred bones of the deceased are enclosed II.4.15.

शलली Śalalī f. porcupine's quill, having 3 stripes (*treṇī*), with which the hair of a sacrificer is parted (*Vaiśvadeva*) Bh. Śr. VIII.4.12. See Gṛhya section.

शल्क Śalka m.n. chips of wood with which the fire is kept burning by the sacrificer throughout the night before the installation of fire Bh. Śr. V.4.3. (*Ādheya*)

शस्त्र Śastra (√*śaṁs*, cl.1 "to praise") n. a laud which is to be recited, as distinguished from a *stotra* which is chanted. A ś° complements and follows a *stotra* Āśv. Śr.V.10.1. The ś° is composed of verses which are recited by the *Hotṛ* and his associates called *hotrakas* as an accompaniment of *soma* libation 10-12. With the recitation of a ś° several other elements are involved : *āhāva*, *pratigara*, *tūṣṇīṁjapa* and °*śaṁsa*, *nivid* or *puroruc*, (*japa* of) "*ukthaṁ vāci*" and *yājyā* V.9.2-11, and terminated with *om* pronounced by the *Adhvaryu* ib.10. A ś° has several parts as in the *ājya*° and *praüga*° : (1) *stotrīya*, a triplet which has been chanted in the corresponding *stotra* (whence the name), (2) *anurūpa*, a triplet which agrees in metre, deity with the *stotra* triplet 10.26-27, (3) *ukthamukha*, the principal part of the ś° Ś Śr. VII.11.3; or the parts are *pratipad*, *anucara* etc. as in the *marutvatīya*° C.H.300.

In consonance with the 12 *stotras* in the *Agniṣṭoma* there are also 12 *śastras* distributed in the three *savanas*. In the morning pressing : *ājya*° and *praüga*° (both recited by the *Hotṛ*), 3 *ājya*° (by the *hotrakas* : *Maitrāvaruṇa, Brāhmaṇācchaṁsin* and *Acchāvāka*) C.H.230. 239, 244, 248, 262; text Śr.K(S).II(1), 323, 332, 338, 343, 348; in the midday : *marutvatīya*° and *niṣkevalya*° (both by the *Hotṛ*), 3 more *niṣkevalyas* (by the *hotrakas*) C.H. 299, 310, 315, 319, 325; text Śr.K(S) II(1), 383, 392, 401, 406, 413, in the third : *vaiśvadeva*° and *āgnimāruta*° (both by the *Hotṛ*) C.H. 354, 372; text Śr.K(S).II(1), 440, 457.

Immediately after the ś°, the *Hotṛ* pronounces *vaṣaṭ* and the *Adhvaryu* pours the *soma* libation (*graha*) into the *āhavanīya*. This is followed by the *anuvaṣaṭkāra* and drinking of the remnant of *soma* libation.

शस्त्रिन् Śastrin m. one who (among the *hotṛakas* is entitled to recite a ś°, i.e. *Maitrāvaruṇa*, *Brāhamaṇācchaṁsin* and *Acchāvāka* Āśv. Śr V.10.10.

शाकल होम Śākala homa m. offering of chips (*śakala*) of the tree from which the *yūpa* was made, into the *āhavanīya*; a rite of atonement (Āp. Śr. XIII.17.9) B. Śr. VIII.17. C.H. 388 (*Soma*).

शाखा Śākhā f. a twig of *palāśa* or *śamī* tree, fetched and cut by the *Adhvaryu* and used for driving away the calves from their mothers Bh. Śr. I.2.8, 12 (*Darśa*). This rite called °*haraṇa* is performed both for morning and evening milking (*doha*) Mī. III.6.28-29.

°*pavitra* n. a purifying instrument, made from the branch out of which the *upaveṣa* was prepared, and to its top is tied *darbha* blades rolled up in 3 plaits (*Darśa*) Āp. Śr. I.6.9; 11.5. cf. *pavitra*.

शान्तिकर्मन् Śāntikarman n. act of "appeasement" of the *madantī* waters by pronouncing *mantras* Bh. Śr. XI.5.4 (*Soma*).

शामित्र Śāmitra m. name of the fire belonging to *śamitṛ*; on this fire the limbs of an animal are roasted. The fire brand (*ulmuka*) is drawn out of the *āhavanīya*, and carried round the victim (*paryagni*) by the *Āgnīdhra*, who crushes (*nimṛdnāti*) it at a previously arranged spot; this spot becomes the ś°. Optionally, the fire can be produced by attrition Bh. Śr. VII.12.10,13, 15 K. Śr. VI.5.14 (*Paśu*). cf. Mī. XII.1.12. See also *saṁjñapana*.

शाला Śālā f. the sacrificial shed, situated to the west of the *mahāvedi*, having east oriented beams whence the name *prācīnavaṁśa* B. Śr. VI.1, Āp. Śr. X.5.1, *prāgvaṁśa* 3.4; also called *vimita*. It is a quadrangular shed measuring 20 x 10 *aratnis* K. Śr. VII.1.24 comm, 16 x12 *prakramas*, having 4 doors or openings (*atīkāśa*) corresponeing to the 4 cardinal regions, also windows at the corners (Āp. Śr. X.5.4) and covered and enclosed with mat. To the south there is a room for cooking *vrata* milk (*vrataśrapaṇāgāra*) and on the west a hut for the sacrificer's wife (*patnīśālā*); to the north 2 lavatories, enclosed by mat (*kaṭaparivāra*), are provided, the eastern one for the sacrificer and the western one for his wife if the *tīrtha* is in the distance. Inside the ś° three fires are installed (cf. *vihāra*). B. Śr. VI.1, Āp. Śr. X.5.1-5. cf C.H. 7. The word also means *agniśālā* Āp. Śr. III.4.8 comm=*agnyāgāra* (q.v.). See plan 3.

°*dvārya* K. Śr. IX.1.2 or °*mukhīya* Āp. Śr. XI.7.10 m name of the original *āhavanīya* after its transfer to the *uttaravedi*; then it functions as a new *gārhapatya* at the *Soma*. See *agnipraṇayana*, *āhavanīya*. So called because it is situated at the entrance of the *śālā*. Cf. Āp. Śr. XI.5.10.

शिक्य *Śikya* n. a rope with loop, suspended from the wall of the shed (*śālā*) for holding the pot containing curdled milk B. Śr. VI.6 (*Soma*), or the *ukhā* Āp. Śr. XVI.10.8 (*Cayana*).

शुक्र *Śukra* (√*śuc*, cl.1 "to shine") m. "purified" *soma* juice which remains in the *droṇakalaśa* K. Śr. IX.5.19. The cup used at °*graha* is called °*pātra* B. Śr. VII.6 together with the *manthigraha* C.H. 164. *Śukrāmanthinau* (du) m. ś° and *soma* mixed with meal Āp. Śr. XII.1.12.

ubhayataḥ° said of a drawing of *soma* juice in which ś° remains on "both sides" (*ubhayataḥ*) in the *hotṛcamasa*, first drawn from the *droṇakalaśa*, then from the *pūtabhṛt*, finally again from the *droṇakalaśa* at the *camasonnayana* B. Śr. VII.13 (*Soma*).

शुनासीरीय *Śunāsīrīya (rya)* n. a *parvan* of the *Cāturmāsya* (q.v.).

शुल्ब *Śulb(v)a* n. rope made of *darbha* grass, woven in 3 or 5 strands, used specially for tying the *prastara* Āp. Śr. I.4.10. At *Darśa* ś° is stretched out from the southern *śroṇi* to the northern *aṁsa* of the altar Bh. Śr. II.8.12. The word in pl. designates the *śulbasūtras* Āp. Śr. XVII.26.2.

शूद्र *Śūdra* m. a person belonging to the fourth ś° caste, debarred from milking the *agnihotra* cow K. Śr. IV.14.1, but allowed to do so optionally by Āp. Śr. VI.3.11-14. See *Agnihotra*, *āryakṛtā*, *varṇa*.

शूर्प *Śūrpa* n. a winnowing basket, made of bamboo or reed K. Śr. II.3.8 comm, used for winnowing grains Āp. Śr. I. 7.5 (*Darśa*).

शूल *Śūla* m.n. a wooden spit having sharpened point, used for roasting the heart of an animal (*hṛdaya*) Āp. Śr. VII.8.3; the *vapā* of the animal is placed on a two-pronged spit (*dviśūla*) and pierced with an one-pronged (*ekaśūla*) spit VII.19.1 (*Paśu*). Cf. *vapāśrapaṇī*.

शृतातङ्क्य *Śṛtātaṅkya* (√*śṛ*, *śrā* or *śrī*, cl. 4 or 9 "to boil" & √*tac*, *tañc*, cl. 7 "to coagulate") n. curds obtained by curdling the hot milk, used at the *ādityagraha*, the 3rd *upasad*, and at the third pressing B. Śr. VI.31, Āp. Śr. XI. 21.8; XIII. 9.6. cf. C.H. 122, 330. See also *ātañcana*.

शृतावदान *Śṛtāvadāna* n. name of a wooden implement, 1 *prādeśa* in length, having a bowl in the front (K. Śr. I.3.36 comm), with which the cooked *puroḍāśa* (*śṛta*) is cut up into slices (*avadāna*) II.6.49.

शेष *Śeṣa* m.n. remnant of *soma* drunk by the *Adhvaryu* in the *sadas* after the libation (the first pressing) Bh. Śr. XIII.8.3 (*Soma*).

शोंसावोम् *Śoṁsāvom*. See *āhāva*.

श्मशान *Śmaśāna* n. (etymology doubtful). cf. *śmaśā* f. elevated ridge or edge of a trench for water, or of a vessel RV. X.105.1; for other derivations, Eggeling SBE XLIV, 421. An elevated place used for cremation, measured by means of pegs, outside the village, not close to dwelling houses. The plot must have sufficient light (sun-ray), surrounded by trees, be distant from the road. A pole having a bundle of grass tied to its top is brought in the ground, held by a person during cremation and taken back to the house of the deceased for hoisting there K. Śr. XXI.3.15-34. See also *dahanadeśa*, *antyeṣṭi loṣṭaciti*.

°*āyatana* n. a place of cremation Bh. Pi. I.3.7.

श्रपण *Śrapaṇa* (√*śṛ*, *śrā* or *śri* cl.4 or 9 "to boil") n. a cooking vessel Āp. Śr. XIX.1.17 (*Sautrāmaṇī*); in pl. logs for cooking sacrificial food (*havis*) B. Śr. I.8. See *vrataśrapaṇāgāra*.

श्रोणि *Śroṇi* f. two "hips" of the *uttaravedi*, i.e. the south western and the north western corners Āp. Śr. VII.5.5; of the *vedi* of *Darśa* II. 3.1; also of the *mahāvedi* XI.4.13. The parts of a *vedi* are compard to a female body. Cf *aṁsa*, *nābhi*, *vedi*. See plans 3-6.

श्रौषट् *Śrauṣaṭ* ind. See *pratyāśrāvaṇa*.

ष Ṣa

षडवत्त *Ṣaḍavatta* n. See *caturavatta*.

षडह *Ṣaḍaha* m. a period of six *soma* days, specially the 2nd to the 7th day of the *Dvādaśāha*. Ṣ° is a principal feature of the *sattra* in which it occurs in 2 forms *abhiplava*° and *pṛṣṭhya*° (q.v.).

षड्ढोतृ *Ṣaḍḍhotṛ* m. name of the *mantra*s of the six *hotṛ*s (4 principal priests and *Āgnīdhra* and *Prastotṛ*), occuring in TĀr. III.4, Śr.K(S).I, 125, recited at the beginning of *Paśu* Āp. VII. 1.2; also on different occasions of *Soma*; also recited by the sacrificer XIII.12.11. Cf *caturhotṛ*.

षोडशिन् *Ṣoḍaśin* m. name of a *soma* sacrifice, the 3rd *soma saṁsthā*, dedicated to Indra, consisting of 15 *stotra*s and 15 *śastra*s belonging to the *Ukthya*, and the additional 16th *stotra* and *śastra* (both being called *ṣoḍaśin*) in the 3rd *savana* Āp. Śr. XIV.2-3, Eggeling SBE XLI, xvi-xvii.

°*graha* m. name of a drawing at the *Agniṣṭoma* Āp. Śr. XII.18.20; of an additional drawing of Ṣ° XIV.2.3. cf Eggeling SBE XXVI, 397.

°*camasa* m. Āp. Śr. XIV.3.8, °*pātra*, n. an additional cup, made of *khadira* wood, quadrangular in shape XII.2.6 (*Agniṣṭoma*), used in the morning or in all the *savana*s (*Ṣoḍaśin*) XIV.2.3-5.

°*śastra* n. the recitation and °*stotra*, the chant of the Ṣ°. Cf. XIV.3.1.

स Sa

संयवन *Saṁyavana* (*sam-√yu*, cl.2 "to unite") n. act of mixing water with the flour paste B. Śr. XX.8; and water used for s° is called *saṁyavanīya* I.8=*madantī* water.

संयाज्या *Saṁyājyā* f. "combined" *yājyā*, i.e. *yājyā* and *anuvākyā mantras* accompanying the oblation to Agni *Sviṣṭakṛt* Āp. Śr. III.15.5 (*Darśa*).

संवरण *Saṁvaraṇa* n. act of closing all doors of the *prācīnavaṁśa* in the *pravargya* rite Bh. Śr. XI.5.1.

संवाद *Saṁvāda* m. conversation (obscene dialogue) between the priests and the queens etc. K. Śr. XX.6.18 (*Aśva*); a dialogue between 2 priests, e.g. asking permission for some ritual acts Āp. Śr. XXIV.1.10.

संश्राव *Saṁśrāva* (or *srāva*) m. helpers of the *sadasya*, who, at the morning pressing, remind the *Adhvaryu* when to pronounce *vaṣaṭ* B. Śr. II.3 comm.

संसर्जनीय *Saṁsarjanīya* (*sam-√sṛj*, cl.6 "to send forth together") mfn various materials to be mixed with clay for making the *ukhā* Āp. Śr. XVI.4.2 (*Cayana*); *saṁsarjana* n. in the same sense XV.2.7 (*Pravargya*).

संसव *Saṁsava* (*sam-√su*, cl.5 "to press out together") m. confusion arising out of libations performed by priests at the same time and on the same arena Āp. Śr. XIV.20.4. It is considered sinful.

संसादन *Saṁsādana* n. act of putting the sacrificial utensils (*pātra*°) on the *darbha* grass Āp. Śr. III.16.15. Cf. *pātrayoga* VII.22.2.

संसृपां हवींषि *Saṁsṛpāṁ havīṁṣi* n. "offerings of creeping together"; a series of 10 *iṣṭi*s taking place between the *Abhiṣecanīya* and the *Daśapeya* in the *Rāja*, replacing the ordinary *upasad*. The offerings are *caru* or *puroḍāśa* to Agni, Sarasvatī, Savitṛ, Pūṣan, Bṛhaspati, Indra, Varuṇa, Soma, Tvaṣṭṛ, Viṣṇu. For various views on the rite Eggeling SBE XLI, 116-17. It derives its name probably from the curious provision of shifting the place of sacrifice at each *iṣṭi* further to the east in such a manner that the *āhavanīya* of the previous day accommodates the *gārhapatya* on the next day until the 8th *iṣṭi* is performed on the site of the *Daśapeya* Āp. Śr. XVIII.20.8-10, Heesterman 173-8. *saṁsṛpeṣṭi* Āśv. Śr. IX.3.17.

संस्कार *Saṁskāra* (*saṁ(s)-√kṛ*, cl.5 or 8 "to embellish") m. an act in a sacrifice Āp. Śr. I.10.21, e.g. strewing round the fires, bringing logs for the hearths etc. VIII.5.19, which are called ordinary functions; purification of *ājya* XV.6.8, of utensils XXIV.1.29; *ātma*° m.

performance of *dīkṣā*, by the sacrificer XXI. 3.8.

संस्था *Saṁsthā* (*sam-√sthā*, cl.1 "to stand together") f. (1) termination, conclusion of a rite B.Śr. XII.1 (*saṁsthāṁ karoti*); *saṁtiṣṭhate* Bh. Śr. VIII.1.4; *ā saṁsthātoḥ* ind. till the completion of the rite Āp. Śr. I.16.11 whence *saṁsthāpya* to be completed X.21.13. cf. *siddham* (q.v.) *iṣṭiḥ saṁtiṣṭhate* V.20.19, Bh. Śr. V.13.3.

(2) basic form of a sacrifice Āp.Śr. XIV.2.1. It is said there are 7 fundamental forms of *Soma* sacrifice : *Agniṣṭoma, Atyagniṣṭoma, Ukthya, Ṣoḍaśin, Vājapeya, Atirātra, Aptoryāma* (the last six being modifications of *Agniṣṭoma*) K. Ś:. X 9.28. Cf. Eggeling SBE. XXVI, 397-8.

°*japa* m. prayer, muttered on completion of a rite, done by the *Hotṛ* after performing his final rite Āśv. Śr. I.11.14-15 (*Darśa*).

संस्राव *Saṁsrāva* m. (1)See *saṁśrāva*.(2) remnants of *ājya*, the drops of which are poured from the *juhū* and the *upabhṛt* on the *paridhi* (a part of p° *homa*) Āp. Śr. III.7.14 (*Darśa*); *saṁsrava* K. Śr. III.6.18. Also the residue of *soma* of a previous drawing Āp. Śr. XII. 23.11.

सकृदाच्छिन्न *Sakṛdācchinna* mfn. cut at one stroke (of a scythe), said of *barhis* which is strewn on the altar Bh. Śr. I.7.8 (*Darśa*).

सक्तु *Saktu* (√*sañj*, cl.1 "to cling") m. powder of parched barley, consumed as a *vrata* food by the sacrificer Bh. Śr. X.10.8 (*Soma*); offered at a *homa* B. Śr. IV.11 (at the end of *Soma*) C.H.410; also at *Cayana* Āp. Śr. XVII. 23.11.

सख्यविसर्जन *Sakhyavisarjana* n. rite of "dissolution of alliance" between the priests and the sacrificer, entered into at the *Tānūnaptra* rite (q.v.), which takes place at the end of *Soma* Āp. Śr. XIII.18.2 (*tānūnaptriṇaḥ sakhyāni visṛjante*); the relevant *mantra* is called *sakhyavaisarjana* B. Śr. VIII.18. cf. C.H. 391.

संक्राम *Saṁkrāma* m. transgression (non-performance) of a prescribed rite Āp. Śr. III.16 8.

संक्षालन *Saṁkṣālana* n. cleansing water for the milk pail (*kumbhī*) B. Śr. VIII 4. Āp. Śr. I 13.10.

संगव *Saṁgava* (*sam* and *go*) m. milking time, morning or forenoon, when cows return from the pasture to which they were taken at dawn RV. V.76.3. The time for *prātarhoma* is from dawn till the milking time Āśv. Śr. III. 12.2. One may enter into *vrata* at s° B. Śr. XX.1. The time for performing *pravargya* Āp. Śr. XV.18.13. It is reckoned as one of the 5 divisions of the day (12 hours): *prātaḥ* or *udaya* (sunrise), *saṁgava, mādhyandina* or *madhyāhna* (midday), *aparāhṇa* (afternoon) and *sāyāhna* (evening).

संग्रहीतृ *Saṁgrahītṛ* m. collector (of taxes ?), who being asked by the king acts as one of the umpires (*upadraṣṭṛ*) of the game of dice Āp. Śr. XVIII.19.6-8 (*Rāja*); also sprinkles the horse XX.4.4 (*Aśva*).

संचर *Saṁcara* (*sam*-√*car*, cl.1 "to go together") m. (1) a path, assigned to the priests for their movement within the sacrificial arena during the performance of a sacrifice, lying between the *cātvāla* and the *utkara* in those rites which require an *uttaravedi* (*Varuṇapraghāsa, Paśu, Soma*), and between *praṇītā* and *utkara* in all *iṣṭis* K. Śr. I.3.42-43; used by the priests for offering *homa* III.1.17=*tīrtha* (q.v.). Also the path between the *cātvāla* and the *utkara* or between the *āgnīdhra* and the *cātvāla* for movement of the *Adhvaryu* and the observers at *Soma* Āp. Śr. XI.13.10.

(2) adj. (moving from one place to another) said of the 5 common oblations which recur in all the 4 *parvans* of the *Cātur* VIII. 2.3. For (1) plan 3-6.

संज्ञपन *Saṁjñapana* (*sam*-√*jñā*, cl. 9 caus. "to cause to give consent") n. act of killing a sacrificial animal by choking or strangling it to death by using a halter round its throat without allowing it to give out a cry. The killing is done by the *śamitṛ* (*saṁjñapayanti*). Āp. Śr. VII.16.5 (*Paśu*) & comm on it : *akṣatasya māraṇaṃ saṁjñapanam* it is a killing without causing a wound, i.e. bloodless killing. Also at *Aśva* XX.17.9. This is a euphemistic technical term which literally means that the victim is caused to give consent to its own killing.

It is interesting to note that Kālidāsa compares a merciless beating to this cruel manner of animal slaughter. Vidūṣaka : *aham jena iṭṭipaśūmāraṁ māridaḥ* (*aham yena iṣṭipaśumāraṁ māritaḥ*). Abhijñānaśakuntalam Act VI.

saṁjñaptahoma m., °*āhuti* f. oblation offered by the *Adhvaryu* on the *āhavanīya* for the immolated (*saṁjñpata*) animal B. Śr. XI.4, Āp. Śr. VII.17.3.

संज्ञानी (इष्टि) *Saṁjñānī (iṣṭi)* f. an *iṣṭi* for obtaining "agreement" of the relatives of the sacrificer for recognizing him as a chief B. Śr. XIII.20, Āp. Śr. XIX.20.3 (*Kāmyeṣṭi*).

सत *Sata* m. n. large vessel, 2 in number, for carrying burning embers B. Śr. II.13, or for carrying fire II.17 (*Ādheya*); made of *palāśa* wood, contains clarified *surā* Āp. Śr. XIX.1.17 (*Sautrāmaṇī*).

सत्त्र *Sattra* n. sacrificial session, a type of *soma* sacrifice; its duration varies from 12 days to a year or more, theoretically, upto 100 years. The model (*prakṛti*) of s° is *Dvādaśāha*; the essential feature is *Ṣaḍaha*. The *Gavāmayana* is a model of the one-year (*sāṁvatsarika*) s°. There is also another type of s° called *rātri°* (Āp. Śr. XIX.15.7). There is no sacrificer in it, only the brahmins can perform it, and consequently there is no fee either Āp. Śr. XXIII, K. Śr. XXIV.1-7.

सदन *Sadana* n. seat of the priests in the sacrificial area : *Hotṛ°*, *Brahma°* Bh. Śr. III.12.5; 14.2.

सदस् *Sadas* n. "assembly"; an oblong shed within the *mahāvedi*, measuring 9 (width) × 27 (length, north-south) *aratni*s or as much would be necessary to accommodate the priests, their *dhiṣṇya*s and the *prasarpaka*s; erected at the distance of 3 *prakrama*s to the east of the *prācīnavaṁśa*. It is constructed on bamboo posts which are as high as the navel of the sacrificer on the sides and as high as the *audumbarī* post in the middle, with the beams running from the south to the north and the west to the east. It is covered with 9 mat roofs (*chadis*) (15 in *Ukthya*, 16 in *Ṣoḍaśin*, 17 in *Vājapeya* etc. Āp. Śr. XI.10.13). The *audumbarī* post at the distance of 1 *prakrama* from the *pṛṣṭhyā* is raised in its centre. Within the s° the *dhiṣṇya*s face the *havirdhānamaṇḍapa*. Like the *havirdhānamaṇḍapa* the 2 doors, on the east and the west, are so fixed in the s° that the view along the entire length of the *pṛṣṭhyā* is not obstructed B. Śr. VI.26, Āp. Śr. XI.9.5-10; 10.6-14. C.H. 92. Plan 3.

सदस्य *Sadasya* m. "one who remains in the *sadas*". The 17th priest who appears to be a 5th *mahartvij* according to B. Śr. II.3, and confirmed as such by the *Kauṣītakin*s Bh. Śr. X.1.8. His function is called *sādasya*, and he has 3 assistants : *Abhigara*, *Dhruvagopa* and *Saṁsrāva* B. Śr. l.c. But according to Vt. Śr. XI.3, S° is an assistant of the *Brahman*. He supervises the sacrificial acts Āp. Śr. X.1.11, ĀśvGṛ I.23.5.

सद्यस्काल *Sadyaskāla* mfn. sacrifice in which the preliminary rites (*upavasatha* etc.) and the main rite are performed on the same day. The *iṣṭi* and *Paśu* may be a s°, or can be performed on the next day of the preliminary rite (*asadyaskāla*) Āp. Śr. VII.6.3: *sadyaskālā vā varuṇapraghāsāḥ* VIII.5. 31.

सद्यस्क्री *Sadyaskrī* m. a *soma* rite, an *ekāha*, in which the *soma* is purchased on the day the actual rite is performed, unlike the *Agniṣṭoma* etc. in which the *soma* is purchased on the previous day B. Śr. XVIII.20 = *sādyaskra* Āp. Śr. XXII.2.6.

सनीहार *Sanīhāra* mfn. agents whom the sacrificer engages after his *dīkṣā* to collect money and materials for the sacrifice B. Śr. VI.7, Āp. Śr. X.18.5 (*Soma*). cf. C.H. 25.

संतत *Saṁtata* n. "stretched and continuous" mode of recitation of the *sāmidhenī* verses in which the vowel at the end of the verse is rendered into *O* of 3 *mātrā*s and '*m*' is added to it, *e.g.* *sumnayu* = *sumnayo3m* and then it is continuously joined to the next verse Āśv. Śr. I.2.10. For illustration H.Dh. II(2), 1049.

saṁtati f. continuity of a rite (*ahīna*) B. Śr. XVI.3.

संतृप्त *Saṁtṛpta* mfn. "satiated", said of *soma* stalks which have been swollen with water B. Śr. VII.5.

(वाक्) संद्राव (*Vāk*) *Saṁdrāva* m. movement of voice in a recitation Āp. Śr. XXIV.1.15.

संधि *Saṁdhi* m. See *paridhi°*

संनमन *Saṁnamana* n. (1) causing curvature on the 2 sides of the altar of the *Darśa* Bh. Śr. XII.5.1. See *vedi* and plan 4.

(2) modification of a *mantra* according to the need of a rite Bh. Par. 68; °*virodha* m. case of disharmony in the modified *mantra*; it is to be dropped ib.

संनहन *Saṁnahana* (√*nah*, cl.4 "to tie") n. act of tying up the *darbha* blades intended for strewing Āp. Śr. I.5.5; the relevant *mantra* *saṁnahanī* ib. Also a cord (śulba, comm) for tying up the *muṣṭi*s and the *prastara*s together II.9.1 (*Darśa*)

संनिपातन *Saṁnipātana* (*sam-ni-*√*pat*, cl. 1 caus) n. act of causing the beginnings of a sacrificial act to coincide with the end of a *mantra.* A sacrificial act should immediately follow the *mantra* which indicates the nature and purpose of the act Āp. Śr. XXIV.2.1 (*sāṁnipātya* K. Śr. I.3.5); act of pouring *āhuti* should follow *vaṣaṭkāra* Āp. Śr. XXIV.3.14.

संनिवाप *Saṁnivāpa* (*sam-ni-√vap*, cl.1 "to mingle or throw together") m. rite of reunification of the fire of the *ukhā* and of the *pratisamedhanīya* B. Śr. XV.17 (*Aśva*).

सप्त पदानि *Sapta padāni* n. seven steps taken by the *somakrayaṇī* cow; on the seventh footprint an oblation is offered and various other rites are performed B. Śr. VI.13, Bh. Śr. X.15.7-21. (*Soma*) C.H. 38. cf. *padāhuti, paddharaṇī.*

सप्तसप्तिनी *Saptasaptinī* f. "each (*paryāya*) containing seven (verses)"; name of a *viṣṭuti*, specially applied to the *yajñāyajñīya* (*agniṣṭoma*) *stotra* (PBr. II.15) in which 3 *stotrīya* verses are made up 21 verses (*ekaviṁśatistoma*) by repetition, each *paryāya* containing 7 verses; the 1st *paryāya*: *a a a, b b b, c*; the 2nd p°: *a, b b b, c c c*; the 3rd p°: *a a a, b, c c c* C.H. 369. For laying *kuśa* during the chant Chinna 93.

सप्तहोतृ *Saptahotṛ* m. *mantra* of the "seven *hotṛs*", an inaudible *japa* of the sacrificer Āp. Śr. IV.11.7 (*Darśa*); at the morning pressing accompanied with an oblation before the *bahiṣpavamāna stotra* XII.16.17. see also *catur*°. Text Śr.K(S).I, 125.

सभा *Sabhā* f. a hall in which the gambling place (*adhidevana*) is situated Āp. Śr. V.19.2= *dyūtaśālā* V.4.7 comm (*Ādheya*). cf. RV. X. 34.6.

°*sad* m. those who sit in the gambling-hall, i.e. gamblers. They get the stake which is a cow Bh. Śr. V.12.9, or rice is purchased with the cow, and cooked and offered to them Āp. Śr. V.20.2-3 (*Ādheya*).

sabhya m. the fire established in the gambling-hall, to the east of the *āhavanīya* by attrition or by fetching it from the *ā*° or from the domestic fire 17.1. Some are against its establishment, while others accept it optionally, but it is obligatory according to Āp. Śr. l.c. comm. It is a square hearth, each side being 12 fingers in length Vai. Śr. I.3. cf. *āvasathya.*

समवत्त *Samavatta* (*sam-ava-√dā/do*, cl. 6 ? "to cut off together") mfn. cuttings of the *iḍā* Āp. Śr. XIII.11.4.

°*dhānī* f. vessel, used for holding the cut up pieces of the limb of a victim VII.23.11= *iḍāpātrī* (*Paśu*).

समस्तहोम *Samastahoma* m. a condensed offering of milk, a form of *Agnihotra* which is performed on road as was done by the *ṛṣis* called *yāyāvaras* B. Śr. XXIV.31. cf. Bh. Par. 211.

समाख्यान *Samākhyāna* (*sam-ā-√khyā*, cl. 2 "to designate") n. designation, specially of a *camasa* (e.g. *Brahmacamasa, Hotṛ*° etc.), by virtue of which some priests who own such *camasas* (including the sacificer) are entitled to drink *soma* juice Āp. Śr. XII.25.18. This is also called *samākhyābhakṣaṇa* n. K. Śr. IX.12.3 comm. cf. C.H. 218. See *somabhakṣaṇa.*

By virtue of his designation only the *Unnetṛ* can draw and fill up the cups K. Śr. IX.5.32.

समारोपण *Samāropaṇa* (*sam-ā-√ruh*, cl.1 caus. "to cause to ascend") n. rite of causing the fire to mount the *araṇis* (or into the body of the priest himself) by warming them over the fire for carrying them to establish the fire (once established) elsewhere Āp. Śr. VI. 28.8, K. Śr. XXI.1.17. The reverse operation is *upāvarohaṇa* n.

°*rūḍha* mfn. fire set up on the *araṇis* Āp. Śr. VI 29.12.

समिध् *Samidh* (*sam-√indh*, cl. 1 "to set fire to") f. logs of wood, part of 21 *idhmas*, with which *agni* is fed at the time of recitation of the *sāmidhenī* Āp. Śr. II.12.4. There are 3 s° of which 2 are required for the *āghāra* and 1 for the *anuyāja* I.5.11. The 3 sticks with which the *brahmaudana* is stirred is also called s°, dry sticks having leaves, 1 span long V 5.10 (*Ādheya*).

समिष्टयजुस् *Samiṣṭayajus* n. literally, a *yajus* formula indicating completion of a sacrifice or sacrificing together; an oblation to the wind god Āp. Sr. III.13.2; B. Śr. I.21. (*Darśa*) There are 9 s° XIII.18.4 (*Soma*), 11 at *Cayana* XVII.23.9.

संपत्नीय (होम) *Saṁpatnīya* (*homa*) m. a libation poured with a *sruva* while the wife touches the *Adhvaryu*; the *mantra* is *saṁpatnī patyā sukṛtena gacchatam* TBr. III.7.5.11 (whence the name) Āp. Śr. III.9.10 (at the end of *Darśa*).

संपात *Saṁpāta* m. (1) residue of *soma* juice Āp. Śr. XII.11.5.

(2) remnants of the clarified butter, which is poured into a vessel after each oblation at the funeral rite Bh. Pi. I.11.5, and women who are not widows wash their faces with it ib. 13.

संप्रसर्पण *Saṁprasarpaṇa* n. See *pra°*.

°prasṛpta mfn. B. Śr. VII.12=*prasṛpta*.

संप्रैष *Saṁpraiṣa* (*sam-pra-√iṣ*, cl. 9 "to send forth") m. a call, summons pronounced by the *Adhvaryu* to another priest asking him to carry out some work connected with a sacrifice, e.g. *prokṣaṇīrāsādaya, idhmābarhirupasādaya* : Do you (*Āgnīdhra*) place the *prokṣaṇī* waters (within the altar), place the faggot and grass etc. Āp. Śr. II.3.11 (*Darśa*). It is pronounced in a high tone K. Śr. I.3.11 & comm. S° is differentiated from *praiṣa* (q.v.).

संभरणी *Sambharaṇī* f. "container"; a vessel of *varaṇa* wood in which the wet and pounded *soma* stalks containing juice are gathered before putting them into the *ādhavanīya* B. Śr. VII.6, K. Śr. IX.5.6 & comm.

संभार *Sambhāra* (*sam-√bhṛ*, cl. 1/3 "to gather together") m. pl. materials required in a sacrifice, consisting of 5 or 7 types of substances derived from earth (*pārthiva*) : sand, saline soil (*ūṣā*), earth dug out by rats (*ākhūtkara, ākhukarīṣa*), earth from ant-hill (*valmīkavapā*) etc., and of 5 kinds of objects derived from tree (*vānaspatya*) : *aśvattha, udumbara, vikaṅkata* etc. Āp. Śr. V.1.4, 7; 2.5. Also said of other sacrificial materials, e.g. *kṛṣṇājina*, a pot of goat's milk etc. For the list of materials in *Soma* B. Śr. VI.1, C.H. 8. see also *yajñapātra*.

संभेद *Sambheda* m. point of contact between the 2 sliced up (*avadāna*) portions of a cake= the middle portion of the cake Āp. Śr. III. 1.8; the spot where 2 *āghāra* libations cross each other 5.1.

संमार्ग *Saṁmārga* (pl) m. binding cords for *idhma* Āp. Śr. II.15.4 =*idhmasaṁnahana* (q.v.); also a wisp of grass used for cleansing the hearth Vt. Śr. I.9.

संमार्जन *Saṁmārjana* (*sam-√mṛj*, cl.2 "to wipe together") n. cleaner; the *darbha* grass called *veda* with which the sacrificial utensils are cleansed Bh. Śr. II.5.1.

सम्राडासन्दी *Samrāḍāsandī* f. See *āsandī*.

सम्राड्दुह् *Samrāḍduh* f. the (king) cow from which milk for *gharma* is milked B. Śr. VI.34.

सर्पण *Sarpaṇa* n. See *pra°*.

सर्पिस् *Sarpis* mfn., n. "running"; (common) clarified butter Bh. Śr. I.7.7 (used for cooking rice) (*Darśa*).

sarpirdhāna n. a bowl for butter Āp. Śr. II.6.1 (*Darśa*).

सव *Sava* (may be derived from any one of the three : *√su* cl 6, *√sū*. cl.2 "to give birth to or to generate", and *√su*, cl. 5 "to press out") m. a rite in which the pressing of *soma* stalks takes place. cf. Āp. Śr. XVII.19.11. But generally, a class of *ekāha* sacrifices in which an unction (*abhiṣeka*) occurs, and it is performed for fulfilment of some desire, e.g. *Bṛhaspati°*, *Soma°* (actually an animal sacrifice), *Odana°* etc. Āp. Śr. XXII.25-28. 7 *savas* are mentioned TBr. II.7c. See *Savayajñas* Kauś. S. LX-LXVIII and discussions on them Gonda *Sava*.

सवन *Savana* (*√su*, cl.5 "to press out") n. rite of pressing of the *soma* stalks on the *sutyā* day, which constitutes the *soma* rite proper. Actually, the word designates the time divisions of the *sutyā* day on which, besides the actual pressing, various other rites are performed Āp. Śr. XII.18.2 : *prātaḥsavana* (morning pressing and service), *mādhyandina°* (midday) and *tṛtīya°* (the third). The last two follow the pattern of the *prātaḥ* Āp. Śr. XIII.1.2. The climax is reached at the midday service.

Actual pressing of stalks is called *abhiṣavaṇa*, *mahābhiṣavaṇa*.

savanīya mfn. offerings belonging to the *soma* libation, an *ājya* oblation Āp. Śr. XII.3.3, a *puroḍāśa* 4.4, an animal 18.12, offerings in general XIII.10.7. For *°paśu* see *Paśu*.

साकमेध *Sākamedha* m. (pl) literally, with (*sākam*) fuel (*edha*); the third *parvan* of *Cātur*.

साकंप्रस्थायीय *Sākaṁprasthāyīya* m. ancillary rite of *Darśa* in which the *Adhvaryu* "proceeds" taking with (*sākam*) him many milkpails (*doha* or *kumbhī* comm.) for offering oblation with the desire of obtaining cattle (*paśukāma*) Āp. Śr. III.16.10. cf. 17.1.

सांकाशिन *Sāṁkāśina* (*sam-√kāś*, cl.1 "to appear together") n. overall visibility along the *pṛṣṭhyā* line, ensured by placing the doors of the *prācīnavaṁśa*, the *sadas* and the *havirdhānamaṇḍapa* in such a way that a person sitting in any one of these sheds can see through in easterly or westerly directions Āp. Śr. XI.7.10. Hence the path along the *pṛṣṭhyā* is called °*patha* B. Śr. VII.8 (*Soma*). See plan 3.

सांग्रहणी *Sāṁgrahaṇī* f. one of the *kāmyeṣṭis* by which the sacrificer obtains power to acquire ("collect") a village Āp. Śr. XIX.23.6.

साद्यस्क्र *Sādyaskra* m.=*sadyaśkrī*.

सांनाय्य *Sāṁnāyya* (*sam-√nī*, cl. 1 "to put together") n. a mixture of fresh boiled milk and sour milk or curds of the preceding night's milking, offered as oblation to Indra or Mahendra by one who has (or has not) performed a *Soma* Āp. Śr. I.11.4 (*Darśa*). S° is sprinkled with *ājya* Bh. Śr. II.10.6. cf. Haug's note quoted in Eggeling SBE. XII, 178-9 for its preparation as practised in western India.

°*kumbhī* f. jar, 2 in number, for s° Bh. Śr. I.6.15; also °*pātra* n. 2 utensils Āp. Śr. I.11.4.

°*vikāra* m. modification of the offerings of s° Bh. Par. 162.

सामन् *Sāman* (etymology doubtful) n. a melody set to a verse (*ṛc*), and it is considered as a *mantra* K. Śr. I.3.1. Mentioned in RV. X.90.9. It is a melody mostly set to the verses of RV., hence the word sometimes designates the chanted verse (*gīti*) Mī.II.1.36, but actually s° is simply a melody (Mī. IX.2.1-2) independent of the verses. A *sāman* is primarily associated with certain verses, which are, therefore, called *svakīya*. But a *sāman* can be set to the verses other than its own. Thus by *rathantara* (a *sāman*) its own verses (*svakīya*) RV. VII.32.22-23 are meant. But the same melody can be set to different verses, the *kavatī* verses (RV. IV.31.1-3) PBr. XV.10.1. cf. *tasmāt ṛcyadhyūḍhaṁ sāma gīyate*, Chāndogya upaniṣad I.6.1. A chant is executed by resorting to certain changes in the verse itself such as, distortion of vowels, repetition of syllables, addition of musical interjections (*stobha*). Śab comments : *sā* (*gīti*) *niyataparimāṇā ṛci ca gīyate. tatsaṁpādanārthā ṛgakṣaravikāro viśleṣo vikarṣaṇamabhyāso virāmaḥ stobha ityevamādayaḥ sarve samadhigatāḥ samāmnāyante* Mī. IX.2.29. S° is chanted by the *Udgātṛs* in 5 parts (*bhaktis*) : (1) *prastāva* (prelude) preceded by *hum* (by *Prastotṛ*), (2) *udgītha* (the principal part of s°) preceded by *om* (by *Udgātṛ*), (3) *pratihāra* introduced by *hum* (by *Pratihartṛ*), (4) *upadrava* (by *Udgātṛ* again), (5) *nidhana* (finale) (by the trio) L. Śr. VI.10.1 comm, Simon Pañcavi I.1. The first verse of the *bahiṣpavamānastotra* runs : *upāsmai gāyatā naraḥ pavamānāyendave. abhi devān iyakṣate*, which transformed into a chant will be :

prastāva : *hum upāsmai gāyatānarom*

udgītha : *om pā 2 vā 2 mānāyendāvā 2 abhi devam iyā 1212.*

pratihāra : *hum ā 2.*

upadrava : *kṣāto*

nidhana : *sā 345t*. cf. C.H. 178-80; for problems on chants H.Dh. II (2), 1169-71, C.H. 461-7.

A s° is chanted in *Soma*; also optionally in *Ādheya* by the *Brahman* Bh. Śr. V.10.6-7.

sāmapatha m. path of the chanters, the spot behind the *dhiṣṇya* of the *Neṣṭṛ* where none can go, and which can be seen by the *Udgātṛ*. This is the spot where the *pannejanī* is placed B. Śr. VII.15 (*Soma*).

सामिधेनी *Sāmidhenī* (from *samidh*) f. "kindling verses", recited by the *Hotṛ* in monotone (*ekaśruti*) at the time when Agni is being kindled (whence the name), consist of 11 verses (RV. III.27.1; VI.16.10-12; III.27.13-15; I.21.1; III.27.4; V.28.5-6) Āśv. Śr. I.2.7; the number is increased to 15 by repeating the 1st verse : *prá vo vā́jā* (RV. III.27.1) and the last one *ā́ juhota* (RV. V.28.6) thrice The last one is called *paridhānīya*. A fuel log is put into the *āhavanīya* as soon as *om* is pronounced at the end of each verse Āp. Śr. II.12.4, and the recitation is done continuously. cf. *saṁtata*. Rules of recitation Āśv. Śr. I.2.8-22, example cited H.Dh. II(2), 1049. There are 15 s° at *Darśa* Āp. Śr. II.12.2, and the 15 *idhma* (logs) are called *sāmidhenīdāru* Bh. Śr. I.5.4; 17 verses at *Ādheya* Āp. Śr. V.22.2, at *Paśu* VII.13.12, at *Vaiśvadeva* (*Cātur*) VIII. 2.13, at *Soma* X.4.5, but 3 at *Pitryeṣṭi* VIII. 14.18. cf. Eggeling SBE XII, 102, 112.

सायंदोह *Sāyaṁdoha* m. rite of milking of cows (3 or 6) in the evening for preparing *sāṁnāyya* Āp. Śr. I.11.3 (*Darśa*). The milker, who may be anybody other than a *śūdra* 12.15, draws milk into a milkpail, and the *Adhvaryu* decants the milk through a *pavitra* into a *kumbhī*. See *doha*.

सावित्र *Sāvitra* m. name of a *mantra* : *devásya tvā savitúḥ* (TS. II.6.8.6), pronounced by the *Brahman* while holding the *prāśitra* Āp. Śr III.19.7.

°*graha* m. name of a *soma* drawing to Savitṛ at the third pressing and the *homa* XIII.13. 1-3. C.H. 352.

सिद्धम् *Siddham* ind. "in the prescribed manner", said of an *iṣṭi* when performed according to the scheme laid down in the *prakṛti* (*siddhamiṣṭiḥ saṁtiṣṭhate* Bh. Śr. V.13.3 see *saṁsthā*.

सीता *Sītā* f. furrows, 6 in number, ploughed on the cremation spot (in the *Loṣṭaciti*) Bh. Pi. II.4.9.

सुत्या *Sutyā* (√*su*, cl.5 "to press out") f. day of pressing of the *soma* stalks which constitutes the principal part of a *Soma* in contradistinction to the preliminaries, e.g. *dīkṣā, upasad* etc. Āp. Śr. XV.18.I; also *sutyam ahaḥ* the day of fullmoon or a sacrificial (*yajanīya*) day X.15.2 (*Soma*).

सुन्वत् *Sunvat* m. sacrificer who extracts *soma* juice Āp. Śr. XI.19.9, K. Śr. XIV.4.6.

सुब्रह्मण्य *Subrahmaṇya* mfn., m. "belonging or relating to good *brahman*"; name of the 4th chanter, an assistant of the *Udgātṛ* Āp. Śr. X.1.9. He drives the cart loaded with *soma* stalks holding 2 *palāśa* twigs in his hands as whips Āp. Śr. X.28.3, B. Śr. VI.16, C.H. 50. His special duty is to recite a litany called *subrahmaṇyā*, which is an *āhvāna* (call) to Indra (while, according to Āp. Śr, *soma* stalks are being taken to the *prācīnavaṁśa*), repeated thrice. To this the sacrificer mutters prayers: "Here art thou, O *Subrahmaṇyā*" etc. Āp. Śr. X.28.4-6. This litany, which is required on the 2nd and the subsequent days of *Agniṣṭoma* and almost on all days of other *Soma*, is an invitation to Indra beginning with *subrahmaṇyo3m* (repeated thrice) and then "Come, O Indra" etc. Āp. Śr. l.c. C.H. 64 (the 1st *upasad*), and necessary changes occur in the *mantra*, mentioning the day of recitation. cf. H.Dh. II(2), 1144-5. Its feminine gender explained in ABr. XXVI.3. It gets an *udātta* accent instead of a *svarita*, unlike the other *mantra*s which are almost all recited in *ekaśruti* (monotone), Pāṇ I.2.37-38. For variants at the 3rd *upasad* C.H.118.

It is interesting to note that in this litany Indra is mentioned as a lover (*jāra*) of Ahalyā (Maitreyī, wife of the sage, Gautama). Cf. Eggeling SBE XXVI, 81. The word *subrahmaṇyā* also designates the priest Āśv. Śr. IX.4.11, K. Śr. VIII.2.14.

°*pitāputrīyā* f. name of the s° litany, recited by the priest when the omentum of the animal (*agnīṣomīyapaśu*) is offered in which the sacrificer is described as the son, grandson and great grandson of so and so, and as the father, grandfather of so and so. In this form s° is to be recited thereafter Āp. Śr. XI.20.3-4 (=*paitāputrīyā* K. Śr. VIII.9.12).

सुरा *Surā* f. a sacrificial beverage prepared from germinated rice grain (*śaṣpa*), germinated barley grain (*tokma*), parched rice grain (*lāja*) and vegetable substance serving as yeast (*nagnahu*) K. Śr. XIX.1.20-21. All the substances are powdered. The rice grains are boiled in sufficient water, and the powdered barley is also boiled separately. The watery scum is strained from these two pots and kept separately. Then the powdered yeast is poured into them to prepare the *māsara*. The yeast is also mixed with the boiled rice and barley, and the mixture is preserved in a jar along with the *māsara*. The jar is allowed to remain in a pit for 3 nights. During this period cow's milk and powdered *lāja* are poured into the pot. The liquor is strained through a sieve (*parisrut*). Preparation of wine K. Śr. XV.9.28-30; XIX. 1-2 & comm. The method of distillation differs in Āp. Śr. XIX.5.7-11, The wine is used at *Sautrāmaṇī* VS. XIX.1 & comm, Eggeling SBE. XLIV, 225, Dumont L' Aśva 233, at *Vāja* Āp. Śr. XVIII.1.9.

सूक्त *Sūkta* n. "well said"; a hymn of RV., as distinguished from a *ṛc* (verse). In the śrauta sūtras an entire s° is indicated by mentioning its beginning Āśv. Śr. I.1.18. Particularly, s° designates the main body of a *śastra*. cf. ABr. X.1.

°*vāka* m. "speech of adoration", a *mantra* recited by the *Hotṛ* being urged (*praiṣa*) by the *Adhvaryu* who says: *sūktavākāya sūktā brūhi* Āp. Śr. III.6.6; and it also means a deity ib. 5 (*Darśa*). Cf. Sāyaṇa on TBr. III. 6.15, Āśv. Śr. I.9. There are some variations at *Cātur* Āp. Śr. VIII.3.4. The *praiṣa* for s° is called *sūktavākapraiṣa* which is altered (*vikriyate*) at *Paśu*, for now *Maitrāvaruṇa* recites it VII.27.6. cf. H.Dh. II(2), 1072-3.

सूदवत् *Sūdavat* mfn. "containing sweetened drink" (*sūda*, drink RV. VII.36.3); said of the *antaryāma* cup containing *soma* juice Āp. Śr. XII.23.11.

sūda m. a puddle, mud V.1.7 comm.

सूना *Sūnā* f. sort of basket for sacrificial utensils B. Śr. III.4.

सोम *Soma* m. (1) the *soma* plant, said to be a creeper, used in the *Soma* sacrifices for the preparation of libation. The entire ninth maṇḍala of the RV. is devoted to it. Various parts of it are named V.I. II, 474. cf. *aṁśu*; said to grow on the *Mūjavat* RV. X.34.1 and in *Ārjīkīya* country VIII.64.11. But exact identification is difficult cf. Eggeling SBE XXVI, xxiv-xxvii, George Watts Dictionary of economic products of India III, 247-51, Delhi 1972 [rpt]. The plant became certainly rare and its substitutes are mentioned ŚBr. IV.5.10. see *pūtīka*. *Soma* plant is often referred to as *rājan*.

(2) extracted juice, for the process see *aṁśu*, *adhiṣavaṇa*, *mahābhiṣavaṇa*, *grāvan* etc. C.H. 29,40,43,48.

(3) sacrifice based on *soma* Āp. Śr. IV.16.15, which has 7 *saṁsthās* (q.v.).

°*krayaṇa* (pl) mfn. things with which *soma* stalks are bought B. Śr. VI.15; a piece of gold, a goat, clothes etc.

°*krayaṇī* f. the cow with which *soma* is bought, but ultimately redeemed by another cow Āp. Śr. X.22.2; 27.5; its characteristics X.22.3-6, H.Dh. II(2), 1142.

°*krayāhuti* f. oblation before buying *soma* B. Śr. VI.2. C.H. 35.

°*pa* m. the *soma* drinker, i.e. 100 brahmins who are entitled to drink s° juice Āp. Śr. XVIII.21.5 (*Rāja*). See also *camasa*.

°*pariśrayaṇa* or *paryāṇahana* n. a piece of cloth for tying the bundle of *soma* K. Śr. VII. 7.4, and after the *avabhṛtha* it is worn by the sacrificer's wife Āp. Śr. XIII.22.3.

°*pravacana* n. "proclamation" of *soma*, i.e. invitation extended to the priests to officiate at *Soma* by *soma* heralds called *somapravākas* (4 in number) (*tebhyaḥ somaṁ prāha* Āp. Śr. X.1.2), C.H. 4; at the *ekāhas* Āp. Śr. XXII. 2.18. cf. PBr. XVI.13.10.

°*bhakṣa* (*ṇa*) n. "eating", i.e. rite of drinking of the *soma* juice contained in the *camasa*, taking place at each *savana* after a series of *soma* libations and shaking of the *camasas*, by the persons who are entitled to do so. They are of 3 categories: (1) the *vaṣaṭkartṛs* who own *camasas* from which the *Adhvaryu* offers libation, and those who are asked to pronounce *vaṣaṭ*: *Hotṛ*, *Maitrāvaruṇa*, *Brāhmaṇācchaṁsin*, *Potṛ*, *Neṣṭṛ*, *Acchāvāka*, (2) those who take part at pressing and libation: *Adhvaryu* and *Pratiprasthātṛ*, (3) those who possess *camasas* bearing reciprocal names (*samākhyāna*), e.g. *hotṛcamasa* etc.: *Brahman*, the (3) *Udgātṛs*, and the sacrificer. It appears that only the *Unnetṛ*, the *Grāvastut* and the *Subrahmaṇya* are excluded from the list of *soma* drinkers. The priests invite one another (*upahava*) and proceed to drink *soma* in a rather complicated way. The *Hotṛ* drinks once from all the *camasas* and twice from his own, while the *Maitrāvaruṇa* and other priests drink twice from their own Āp. Śr. XII.24.6-7; 25.16-23, K. Śr. IX.12.3-4 & comm, C.H. 216.

°*lipta* mfn. smeared with *soma*, said of all utensils used at *Soma* Āp. Śr. XIII.19.6.

°*vikrayin* m. seller of *soma* for the ritual; he belongs to the *Kutsa gotra* or any other *gotra* of the brahmin caste or even a *śūdra*. The *Adhvaryu* asks him, "Is the *soma* for sale?" He sells *soma* for a cow (cf. *somakrayaṇī*) Āp. Śr. X.20.12-16, Bh. Śr. X.13.7-8; 16. 15. He bargains over the price of *soma* with the *Adhvaryu*, and the dialogue, which follows, is one of the earliest evidences of drama (Bh. Śr. X.17). Cf Keith Drama 23. Earlier, the *soma* v° weeds out the *soma* stalks remaining out of sight behind a screen. It is interesting to note that the *soma* v°, after the transaction is closed, is driven away by the *Adhvaryu* with a leather whip (*varatrākāṇḍa*) or a clod of earth or clubs (*lakuṭa*) Bh. Śr. X.18.13-14.

सोमातिपवित *Somātipavita* mfn. a sacrificer who is excessively "purified" by excessive drinking of *soma* B. Śr. XIII.25; °*pūta* K. Śr. XV.10.21.

सोमोपनहन *Somopanahana* n. a piece of cloth used for bundling up *soma*; later, after the *avabhṛtha*, worn by the sacrificer's wife Āp. Śr. XIII.22.3; or she wears the °*pariśrayaṇa*.

सौत्रामणी *Sautrāmaṇī* f. a rite for Indra *Sutrāman* ("a good protector;" an epithet of Indra RV. VI.47.12-13; X.63.10; 131.6-7); one of the 7 *haviryajñas*; 2 varieties recognized: *Caraka*° and *Kaukilī*° Āp. Śr. XIX.5.1, and both are of the *Nirūḍhapaśubandha* type 1.2; 5.2. While *Kaukilī*° is an independent rite, the *Caraka*° is a part (*aṅga*) of the *Rājasūya* and *Agnicayana*. There is an additional *khara* for keeping wine-cups (*surāgraha*) 1.15. The principal characteristic of S° is wine offering; the wine is not drunk by the officiating priests but by a hired brahmin 3.3. Out of the 4 days required by the rite 3 days are allotted for the preparation of *surā* which is redesignated as *parisrut* after purification (Āp. Śr. XIX.1.8, 18). The purified wine is filled in the cups by the *Pratiprasthātṛ* for offering to the Aśvins, Sarasvatī and Indra. The animals slaughtered are : a goat for the Aśvins, an ewe for Sarasvatī, a bull for Indra *Sutrāman*. K. Śr. XIX.1-7, Āp. Śr. XIX.1-10.

स्कन्न *Skanna* (√*skand*, cl.1 "to leap") mfn. "jumped off"; said of spilled milk Bh. Śr. IX. 5.23; spilling of *gharma* requires muttering of a *mantra* XI. 17.1. Similarly, *mantra* is muttered when the *soma* stalks are scattered during the pressing Āp. Śr. XII.7.11, C.H. 153.

स्तन *Stana* m. female breast-like mark, protruding from the border (*rāsnā*), 2 to 8 in number, of the *ukhā* Āp. Śr. XVI.5.2.

°*kalpa* m. rule for the udder (of the *agnihotra* cow), prescribed for a sacrificer who may subsist on milk drawn from a single under as his *vrata* food (*ekastanavrata* Bh. Śr. XII.5. 18) Āp. Śr. X.16.15; similarly, from 2 (*dvi*°), 3 (*tri*°) and 4 (*catur*°) udders Bh. Śr. XII.4.5; 5.10, 13 (*upasad* of *Soma*).

°*vibhāga* m. graded milking as above X.9.15.

स्तम्बयजुर् (हरण) *Stambayajur* n. (*haraṇa*) n. "*mantra* of the bunch of grass"; rite of cutting grass with a *sphya* and throwing them outside the altar and the accompanying *mantra* Āp. Śr. II.1.4 (*Darśa*); explained as loose earth mixed with cut up grass comm. on Āp.Śr. l.c. Also at *Soma* in which it is thrown from the *uparava* to the *āgnīdhra*. Cf. C.H. 75.

स्तरणी *Staraṇī* f. strewing of the *barhis* Bh. Sr. XII.6.8. See *paristaraṇa*.

स्तुत *Stuta* mfn. "praised"=*stotra* B. Śr. XIV.9.

°*doha* m. "milking", i.e. the *mantra* which marks the end of a *stotra* (*bahiṣpavamāna*), uttered by the sacrificer (*stutasya dohaṁ vācayati*) B. Śr. l.c.

°*śastra* n. *stotra* and *śastra* Āp. Śr. XIV.8.3.

स्तोत्र *Stotra* (√*stu*, cl.2 "to praise") n. chant, composed of verses, mainly taken from the RV, which is chanted in ritual service, in contradistinction to the *śastra* (q.v.). S° always precedes a *śastra* Āśv. Śr. V.10.1. It is a chant to which one of the innumerable melodies (*sāman*) is set, and *stobhas* are added, and chanted in various forms (*stoma*). All s° are chanted by the *Udgātṛ*, the *Prastotṛ* and the *Pratihartṛ* (the 3 choristers), and sometimes the sacrificer joins them Āp. Śr. XII.17. 11-12. Except the *bahiṣpavamāna* all s° are chanted inside the *sadas* near the *audumbarī*, and during the chanting the *Udgātṛ* sits facing the north, the *Prastotṛ* facing the west and the *Pratihartṛ* facing the east (see plan 3).

In all *Soma* s° are spread out in the 3 *savanas* of the *sutyā* day. In *Agniṣṭoma* there are 12 s°, the 1st at each *savana* is called *pavamāna* and the rest *dhuryas*, arranged as follows : in the *prātaḥsavana*, *bahiṣpavamāna*, 4 *ājya*° (the first being called *kṣullaka vaiśvadeva*) also called *dhuryas*; in the *mādhyandinasavana*, *mādhyandinapavamāna* (also called *grāva*), the 1st *pṛṣṭhya*, the 2nd *pṛ*° (or *vāmadevya*), the 3rd *pṛ*° (or *naudhasa*), the 4th (or *kāleya*); in the *tṛtīyasavana*, *ārbhava* (or *tṛtīya*) *pavamāna*, *agniṣṭoma* (or *yajñāyajñīya*). See also *paryāya*, *viṣṭuti*, *sāman*, *stobha*, *stoma*. A s° is brought forward by the *Adhvaryu*. See *upākaraṇa*.

stotrīya m. name of the *tṛca* which belongs to a *stotra* but recited by one of the *hotrakas* at the beginning of the corresponding *śastra* (in the 1st *śastra* of the *Hotṛ* it is called *pratipad*) Āśv. Śr. V.10.13.

स्तोभ *Stobha* (√*stubh*, cl.1 "to praise") m. musical interjections : *hāu*, *hāi*, *hum*, *ho*, *ohā*, *ī*, *ū* interpolated into a *sāman* (q.v.). It is defined as addition to the letters of a chanted *ṛc*, and composed of *varṇas* other than those of the *ṛc* (*adhikaṁ ca vivarṇaṁca*) Mī. IX. 2.39. These are necessary to accomplish a *sāman*. Cf. Śab. on Mī. IX.2.29

स्तोम *Stoma* (√*stu*, cl.2 "to praise") m. form of chanting the *stotras* in which the verses are increased by repetition to a certain number. Therefore a s° is known by a number, e.g. *trivṛt stoma* (threefold=9), *pañcadaśa*° (15), *saptadaśa*° (17), *ekaviṁśa*°(21) *caturviṁśa* (24), *triṇava*° (27), *trayastriṁśa*° (33), *aṣṭācatvāriṁśa*° (48). All the *stomas*, except 24, can be arranged in two or more different varieties called *viṣṭuti* (q.v.), and each *viṣṭuti* is performed in 3 turns, *paryāya*, consisting of a triplet, some of which are to be repeated more than once so that the desired number can be obtained. In *Agniṣṭoma* only the first 4 *stomas* are used. The first *ājyastotra* consisting of 3 verses (a,b,c) (RV. VI.16.10-12) is a *pañcadaśastoma*, i.e. 15 verses are to be produced in 3 turns (each turn consisting of 5 verses) :

1st *paryāya* : a a a b c
2nd p° : a b b b c
3rd p° : a b c c c

This is the *pañcapañcinī viṣṭuti*; for the other 2 *viṣṭuti*s Eggeling SBE. XXVI, 308-09; for details of *stoma*s Chinna 92-96. See also *kuśa*.

°*bhāga* m. name of a *mantra* (TS. IV.4.1), recited by the *Hotṛ* with which he gives his permission (*prasava*) to chant the *stotra* Āp. Śr. XIV.8.2; in pl. name of the bricks for altar laid with the muttering of *mantra* XVII. 3.5 (*Cayana*).

°*yoga* m.=(*stotra*) *upākaraṇa* (q.v.) Cf. Eggeling SBE XXVI, 311.

stomāyana n. name of 4 animals offered in *Soma* (*savanīyapaśu*) K. Śr. IX.8.7=*kratupaśu*.

स्थाणु *Sthāṇu* m. bolt or pin (*khaḍaka* n. comm) to which a chariot wheel is fixed K. Śr. XIV 3.12 (or a post (*Vāja*)

स्थान *Sthāna* n. position of voice : *mandra* (soft), *uttama* (high, sharp), *madhyama* (middle) Āśv. Śr. IV 13.6; 15.10. All recitations before the *ājyabhāga* and at the *prātaḥsavana* are in *mandra* (loud but soft) before the *sviṣṭakṛt* and at the midday *savana* in *madhyama*, and in the remainder and at the third *savana* in *kruṣṭa* (sharp) Āp Śr. XXIV. 1 12-14; *mandra*, *madhyama* and *uttama* Āśv. Śr. I.5.25-28. But in *Soma* these are different: *mandra*, *mandratara*, *upāṁśu*, *upāṁśutara* and *ucchaiḥ* Āp. Śr. X.4.11 (differentiated by the position of voice coming out of breast, *uras*, throat, *kaṇṭha* and head, *śiras* comm. on ib.).

स्थाली *Sthālī* f. earthen dish or bowl used for holding rice grains Āp. Śr. I.7.5 (*Darśa*), chaff of grain VIII.8 12 (*Varuṇapraghāsa*). Vai. Śr. XI.9 mentions : *āditya*°, *āgrayaṇa*°, *ukthya*°, *caru*°, *dhruva*°.

°*pāka* m. pot-boiling; husked grains, cooked on the *dakṣiṇa* fire and mixed with butter, and used as oblation to the *pitṛ*s Bh. Śr. I. 7. 6 9. (*Darśa*) See also Gṛhya section.

स्थूणा *Sthūṇā* f. bamboo pillars of the *sadas* Āp. Śr. XI.10.5; having wood-knots pointing to the east, of the *havirdhāna* shed B. Śr. VI.25= *sthāṇu* (of the *Vāja*) L. Śr. V.12.9.

°*rāja* m. central (*madhyama*) and the main column of the *prācīnavaṁśa* Āp. Śr. X.3.4.

स्पन्द्या *Spandyā* (=*syandyā* from *syanda*, "flowing" SW) f. a rope with which the *mahāvedi* is encircled by connecting it to the *śaṅku*s (pegs), fixed at the 4 corners Āp. Śr. XI.4.15.

anuspandyam ind. along the *spandyā*= *pṛṣṭhyā* line (probably because the *pṛṣṭhyā* was marked by a *spandyā*) B. Śr. VI.22.

स्फ्य *Sphya* n. a wooden implement, shaped like a sword, made of *khadira* wood K. Śr. I. 3.33, 39; one *prādeśa* in length Vai. Śr. XI.7. It is used for various sacrificial acts: to symbolically ensure the safety and unhindered performance of a sacrifice; to perform all acts pertaining to the *vedi* (*Darśa*) Bh. Śr. II.2.5, to draw an outline of the *vedi* Āp. Śr. I.8.8 and other lines (*lekhā*) 25.14, to remove the upper layer (*tvac*) of the *vedi* II.2.4, to use it as a support of a pan III.8.5 (*Darśa*). In *Soma* the *Adhvaryu* holds it erect (√*stabh* or √*stambh*, cl 5 or 9) when he issues *praiṣa* to the *Āgnīdhra* Bh Śr. XII.2.15. Also held by the *Āgnīdhra* while he makes the *pratyāśrāvaṇa*. The *mahāvedi* also is prepared optionally with it 4.20. It is one of the *yajñāyudha*s TS. I. 6 8.2-3.

स्रक्ति *Srakti* f. corners of the *vedi* (of the *Piṇḍapitṛyajña*), 4 in number, directed to 4 principal quarters Āp. Śr. VIII.13.2-3. The *prācīnavaṁśa* has openings (*āroka*) on its 4 corners X.5.3.

स्रुच् *Sruc* f. name used for the large offering spoons : *juhū*, *upabhṛt* and *dhruvā*, also the *agnihotrahavaṇī* (B. Śr. III.4), each made from different kinds of wood, of one arm's length (or 1 *aratni*) having a bowl on the barkside (*tvagbila*), shaped like an elephant's lip or a crow's tail (*vāyasapuccha*) or a swan's beak (*haṁsamukhaprasecana*) Bh. Śr. I.16.6, with a slight variation Āp. Śr. I.15.12, K. Śr. I.3.37 & comm on 36, Vai. Śr. XI.7. It is made of gold or wood at *Varuṇapraghāsa* Āp. Śr. VIII. 5.29. The *āghāra* (one of the two) offered with it is called *srucya* IV.9.5.

स्रुव *Sruva* m. a small dipping spoon, as distinguished from the *sruc*, used mainly for ladling out the clarified butter or milk from the pot into the *sruc*. It is made of *khadira* wood, 1 *aratni* long, having a round bowl (*puṣkara*) measuring in diameter a thumb's joint, and without a beak K. Śr. I.3.32, 38; or as long as a *juhū* Vai. Śr. XI.7. Used at the *Agnihotra* K. Śr. I.3.36 comm. One of the 2 āghāras performed with it is called *srauva* Āp. Śr. IV.9.4.

स्वधा *Svadhā* ind. sacrificial exclamation, used in connection with the *āhutis* for the manes Āp. Śr. I.8.3-4. At the *Piṇḍapitṛyajña*, *svadhā namaḥ* instead of *vaṣaṭkāra*, and *ye svadhāmahe* instead of the *yājyā* of the *Hotṛ* are used. Similarly, it is used in *āśrāvaṇa*, *pratyāśrāvaṇa* and *sampraiṣa* VIII.15.11. But countermanded by the *Bahvṛcas* and *Vājasaneyins* ib. 12.

स्वधिति *Svadhiti* m. f. knife with blades on 2 sides, used for cutting up the sacrificial animal Āp. Śr. VII.14.10.

स्वयमातृण्णा (इष्टका) *Svayamātṛṇṇā* (*iṣṭakā*) f. name of the "self perforated" bricks (probably porous stones) Āp. Śr. XVI.13.10; 3 of these are placed in the centre of the 1st, 3rd and 5th layers of the fire altar (*Cayana*).

स्वर *Svara* m. tone or accent pitch of the vedic texts, specially of the saṁhitās : *udātta* or accute (raised), *anudātta* (not raised) or grave and the third, *svarita* (provided with tone ?) or circumflex. The *mantras* in the ritual are to be pronounced in tones as given in the saṁhitās or in the brāhmaṇas (*bhāṣikasvara*) K. Śr. I.8.16-17. But actually all *mantras* are to be pronounced in monotone ib. 18 (*tāna*= *ekaśruti*).

Of the brāhmaṇas, only the Taittirīya and the Śatapatha are accented. Cf. Whitney Grammar 28-34.

स्वरसामन् *Svarasāman* m. name of the 3 days before and after the *viṣuvat* of the *Gavāmayana* (the last 3 days of the first and the first 3 days of the second half of the year) Āp. Śr. XXIII. 3.9.

स्वरु *Svaru* m. splinter of wood (*śakala*), which is obtained when the *yūpa* is being hewn from the tree trunk. But only the first piece, cut (*avatakṣaṇa*) off the trunk, is called s° Āp. Śr. VII. 3.3. The first one will be used in all animal sacrifices K. Śr. I.7.17 comm, VI.1.13 comm. cf Mī. XI.3.8-12. The s° is put into a coil of the girdle twisted round the *yūpa* (*Paśu*).

स्वाहा (कार) *Svāhā* ind. (*-kāra* m.) sacrificial exclamation, pronounced at the end of a *mantra* which accompanies an offering of clarified butter from *sruc* into the fire (*pūrṇāhuti*) Bh. Śr. V.11.1, 3 (*Ādheya*).

°*kṛti* f. name of the 11th preliminary oblation of *Paśu* Āp. Śr. VII.20.4, K. Śr. VI.6.20.

स्विष्टकृत् *Sviṣṭakṛt* (*su*+*iṣṭa*+*kṛt*) mfn. "maker of good offering", an epithet ascribed to Agni, for it is he who makes a sacrifice perfect (ŚBr. I.5.3.23). If any sacrificial food is offered to any deity, *Sviṣṭakṛt* Agni should invariably get a share of it I.7.3.7. It is interesting to note that Agni came to be identified with the different local deities : Śarva (of the eastern people), Bhava (of the *Bāhīkas*), Paśūnāṁpati, Rudra. All other names being "inauspicious" he is called simply *Sviṣṭakṛt* I.7.3.8 & Eggeling's note on it. Name of a secondary oblation offered to Agni after the principal one. The offering should consist of cut off portions from each of the several remnants of the *havis* K. Śr. III.3.26-27. This *āhuti* should not come in contact with other *āhutis* ib. 29 (*Darśa*); also at *Paśu* Āp. Śr. VII.25.14; replaced by an oblation to Agni *Kavyavāhana* VIII. 15.20 (*Mahāpitṛyajña*). For other appellations of Agni, Eggeling SBE XLI, 159-60.

ह Ha

हरण *Haraṇa* (√*hṛ*, cl.1 "to take") n. act of removing loose earth and cut up grass from the (*dārśikī*) altar by the *Āgnīdhra* after the *Adhvaryu* has cut up the grass, trimmed the surface and done the *parigrāha*. The rubbish is to be thrown on the *utkara* B. Śr. I.11.

pātra° n. act of fetching utensils K. Śr X.6.24.

हवनी *Havanī* f. offering spoon (comm *juhū*), with which clarified butter is offered K. Śr. X.2.5.

हविर्ग्रहणी *Havirgrahaṇī* f. K. Śr. II.3.33=*agnihotrahavaṇī*.

हविर्धान *Havirdhāna* n. "oblation receptacle"; name of the 2 vehicles on which the *soma* plant, a *havis*, is placed, on the day before *sutyā* for pressing out juice(*anas, śakaṭa*); *haviḥ somo dhāsyate anayoḥ*. This is done after the *agnipraṇayana*. The carts are washed, yoked, placed side by side in the *mahāvedi*, one at the distance of 1 *aratni* to the south of the *pṛṣṭhyā* (*dakṣiṇa*°), and the other at the same distance to the north of the *pṛṣṭhyā*. The southern h°, which is reserved for the *Adhvaryu*, is larger than the northern h° belonging to the *Pratiprasthātṛ*. The shafts of both remain facing east. They are made of *varaṇa* wood K. Śr. I.3.36 comm. & VIII.3.21-22 comm. The carts are covered with mats.

°*maṇḍapa* (abbrev. *havirdhāna*) m. n. a shed constructed within the *mahāvedi* to the east of *sadas* in which the h° carts are garaged; erected on 12 or 8 posts with 2 or 4 beams, covered with (triple) *chadis*, and enclosed by a mat cover. A *rarāṭī* (garland) is suspended in the front. A door on the east and another on the west are so fixed that visibility is not obstructed (*sāṁkāśina*). The shed is a little higher in the east than in the west. Cf. Āp. Śr. XI.7-8; for various rules C.H. 87-91. See plan 3.

हविर्यज्ञ *Haviryajña* m. a class of sacrifice in which offerings of *havis* : milk, butter, rice, barley and similar materials take place, as distinguished from *Soma*. Also called *iṣṭi*. Like *Soma* it has 7 *saṁsthās* : *Agnyādheya*, *Darśapūrṇamāsa*, *Paśubandha*, *Cāturmāsya*, *Sautrāmaṇī* as well as *Pākayajña* L. Śr. V.4.22. Cf. Āp. Śr. XXIII.10.8.

हविष्कृत् *Haviṣkṛt* m(fn.)"maker of *havis*"; it occurs in a *praiṣa mantra* : *haviṣkṛde3hi* (the summons is addressed to the divine h° TBr. III.2.5.8), repeated thrice by the *Adhvaryu* to the person (also called *haviṣkṛt*) who prepares the materials for oblation, i.e. separates the grains from husks by pounding them. The call varies according to the caste of the sacrificer Āp. Śr. I.19.8 (*Darśa*). The sacrificer's wife should pound grains Bh. Śr. I.22.10. The call may be used when necessary Āp. Śr. XXIV.1.43, and may occur in *Soma* Mī. XII.2.11.

हविस् *Havis* n. any oblatory material that is poured as an oblation into the fire, e.g. barley, rice or similar other things K. Śr. I.9.1; things prepared with them : *puroḍāśa*, *caru* etc. ib comm; even milk (Bh. Śr. I.1.2), clarified butter, limbs of animal (to be offered as oblation) are included. There are 5 types of h° : *auṣadha*, *payas*, *paśu*, *soma* (cf. *havirdhāna*), *ājya* B. Śr. XXIV.1.

हारियोजन (ग्रह) *Hāriyojana* n.(*graha*)m. name of a *soma* libation taking place after *śaṁyu* (Āśv. Śr. VI.11.8) for the purpose of yoking the horses of Indra for his departure from the sacrifice K. Śr. X.8.1-3. C.H. 383.

हिंकार *Hiṁkāra* m. sacrificial exclamation of the word : *him*, which marks the opening of a *sāman*, repeated thrice by the *Hotṛ* Āp. Śr. XXIV.11.5; by the *Udgātṛ* who replaces h° by *hūm ā* 2 (all the choristers join together) XIII.15.8.

abhihiṁkāra m. technical name for the repetition of *him* (3 times), followed by the *vyāhṛti* : *bhūrbhuvaḥsvaro3m* (the latter is also called *japa*), done by the sacrificer Āśv. Śr. I.2.4.

abhihiṁ-√kṛ to do (recite) *him* on (a churned fire) Āp. Śr. XXI.7.6 (*Dvādaśāha*).

In the sense of *āhāva* (*śaṁsāvom*) Vt. Śr. XX.16.

हृदयशूल *Hṛdayaśūla* m. See *śūla*.

होतृ *Hotṛ* (√*hu*, cl.3 "to sacrifice") m. "pourer of oblation"; one of the 4 principal priests to whom the RV. belongs. He recites the *mantras* (of RV.) to invoke the gods. His special duty is to recite the stanzas of the RV., i.e. *śastras*. He performs all those acts for which no other person has been specifically mentioned Āśv. Śr. I.1.14. He sits facing the east, to the north of the northern *śroṇi* of the *vedi*. He has a *dhiṣṇya* just on the *pṛṣṭhyā* line (see plan 3). His functions along 3 other priests have been referred to RV.X.71.11. In pl. his assistants are indicated. *Caturhotṛ* designates priests in general. *Saptahotṛ* : *Hotṛ*, *Maitrāvaruṇa*, *Brāhmaṇācchaṁsin*, *Potṛ*, *Neṣṭṛ*, *Āgnīdhra*; the *Grāvastut* is sometimes considered as the 8th h°.

hotraka m. assistants of the h°, 6 persons in total (*Hotṛ* being left out), see the *saptahotṛ* list. They partly correspond to the *camasins* (q.v.) Āp. Śr. XII.23.4, and are entitled to drink *soma* twice from their own cups 25.21. At the morning pressing 5 h° are mentioned as the *Acchāvāka* appears only at the third pressing C.H. 213; at the midday 6 h° B. Śr. XXI.22; at the third pressing they correspond to 7 principal *camasins*. But h° who participate in a *śastra* recitation are : *Maitrāvaruṇa*, *Brāhmaṇācchaṁsin* and *Acchāvāka*. See *śastra*.

hotrā f. (pl.) (1) *hotrakas* B. Śr. ib, Āp. Śr. XII.23.14.

(2) functions of 7 priests : *Hotṛ*, *Maitravaruṇa*,

Brāhmaṇācchaṁsin, *Acchāvāka*, *Potṛ*, *Neṣṭṛ*, *Āgnīdhra* PBr. XII. 13.5.

(3) *mantra*s recited by the *Hotṛ* Āp. Śr. XXIV.2.5.

hotrīya mfn.*dhiṣṇya* of the *Hotṛ*, situated on the *pṛṣṭhyā* Āp. Śr. XI.14.4, where limbs of the victim are offered by the *Pratiprasthātṛ* VII.26.9.

होम *Homa* ($\sqrt{}$*hu*, cl.3 "to sacrifice") m. act of pouring or throwing an oblatory material (*havis*) into fire; the oblatory material is clarified butter, when no other material is mentioned, offered into the *āhavanīya* with a *juhū* K. Śr. I.8.38, 44-45. It may constitute the main feature (*pradhāna*) of a sacrifice Āp. Śr. VI.4.12 while a *homa* in *prayāja* and *anuyāja* are *aṅga* XXIV.2.31, cf. K. Śr. I.2.4. Again there can be 2 categories of h° (1) *tiṣṭhad*° performed in a standing position, belonging to *yajati* class (called *yāga*), accompanied with *vaṣaṭ*, *yājyā* and *puro'nuvākyā*; (2) *upaviṣṭa*° offered in a sitting position, belonging to *juhoti* class (called *homa*) accompanied with *svāhā* K. Śr. I.2.6-7.

PART TWO : GRHYA SECTION

अ A

अंसाभिमर्शन *Aṁsābhimarśana* n. See *Jātakarman.*

अक्षत *Akṣata* (*āḥ*=pl.) m. barley; °*dhānā* grains of barley, powdered (°*saktu*), used for cooking the mess of food ĀśvGṛ. II.1.2-3 (*Sarpabali*).

अक्षय्य (स्थान) *Akṣayya* (*sthāna*) mfn. a *mantra*, containing the wish that the offerings be imperishable, which is pronounced by the sacrificer at the time of *piṇḍa* offering : May what has been given at this *śrāddha* to our father N. N. of N. N. *gotra* be imperishable (*Pārvaṇaśrāddha*). The phrase may be replaced by : May it approach the fathers (*Ekoddiṣṭa*) ŚGṛ. IV.2.5. Cf. Oldenberg SBE XXIX, 109.

अगार *Agāra* n. a house.

°*sthūṇā* f. (*virohaṇa* n.) blossoming of the shoots on a post in a house; considered as an ill-omen (*utpāta*) ĀpGṛ. XXIII.9.

maṇḍalāgāra n. a round apartment in which the *Sīmantonnayana* rite is performed HGṛ. II.1.3; also *Puṁsavana* 2.2.

अग्नि *Agni* m. the fire for domestic rite is only one (as distingushed from the *śrauta*); called *aupāsana* ĀpGṛ. I.12 comm; for installation cf. *ādhāna*, generation *araṇipradāna*; see also *sūtikāgni*.

°*pradakṣiṇa* mfn.circumambulation of the fire at the marriage ceremony. The bridegroom leads the bride three times round the fire (and the water pot) in such a manner that their right sides are always turned towards the fire (*pradakṣiṇa*), opposite of *prasavya* ĀśvGṛ. I. 7.6, ŚGṛ. I.13.13, PGṛ. I.5.1; 7.3, GGṛ. II. 2.8, HGṛ. I.20.5, ĀpGṛ. V.1, 7. For the *mantra*s uttered at the time see *Vivāha*; cf. *Aśmārohaṇa*.

°*samādhāna* n. KāGṛ. XLV.1-2. See *ādhāna*.

अग्नौकरण *Agnaukaraṇa* n. act of pouring portions of the cooked food (for the brahmins) and *ājya* into the fire, done in *Pārvaṇa*° and *Māsiśrāddha*s (q.v.), but not in *Ekoddiṣṭa* BGṛ. III.12.6.

अङ्कलक्षण *Aṅkalakṣaṇa* n. a figure or mark branded on cattle, a rite, performed on the new moon day after the *phālguna* fullmoon ŚGṛ. III.10.1.

अङ्गार *Aṅgāra* m. n. burning embers, drawn from the sacred fire for warming the *ājya* HGṛ. II.3.7

अजिन *Ajina* n. skin (black coloured for the brahmins ĀpDh. I.3.3 etc.), worn by an initiate as an outer (*uttaram*) garment ĀpGṛ. X.11 (*Upanayana*).

अञ्जन *Añjana* n. anointing of axle of a chariot by the newly married girl with clarified butter ŚGṛ. I.15.3 (*Vivāha*); salve brought from the *Trikakud* mountain (*traikakudam*) HGṛ.I.11.5 (*Upanayana*). See also *abhyañjana, sambhāra*.

°*kośa* m. a salve box, used by a bridegroom and a bride for anointing each other ŚGṛ. I. 12.4 (*Vivāha*); for the ceremony PGṛ. I.4.14. ŚGṛ calls the rite *samañjana*, which, according to Oldenberg SBE. XXIX, 33, is done by a third person.

अधःशय्या *Adhaḥśayyā* f. sleeping on the ground, prescribed for the married couple from the *sthālīpāka* day through three nights (*trirātra*, q.v.), a period of sexual continence ĀpGṛ. VIII.8.

अधिदेवन *Adhidevana* n. a site for the game of dice, played at the rite for *śvagraha* ĀpGṛ. XVIII.1.

अधोनिवीत *Adhonivīta* mfn. mode of wearing the sacrificial cord below (round) one's neck; worn by the relatives (*amātya*) in the funeral procession ĀśvGṛ.IV.2.9. See *upavīta, prācīnāvītin* (Śrauta) & *yajñopavītin*.

अनध्याय *Anadhyāya* m. interruption of study of the vedas, occasioned by various omens, e.g. blowing of wind, a fall of meteor, earthquake and by innumerable other reasons : eating at the *Śrāddha*, death of one's preceptor or of a fellow student, presence of a dead body or of a *caṇḍāla* in the village etc. PGṛ. II.11.

=*uparama* m. holiday on the 14th days of every fortnight, the *amāvāsyā* and the *aṣṭakā* days ŚGṛ. IV.7.

अनवलोभन *Anavalobhana* n. rite for the prevention of miscarriage in which the husband in the shade of a round apartment inserts the sap of an herb into the right nostril of his wife ĀśvGṛ. I.13.1, 5-7 (=*lopana*, comm); said to have been mentioned in the upanișad (Cf. Bṛ Up. VI.4.24, MaxMüller SBE XV. 222). See *Garbharakṣaṇa*.

अनवानम् *Anavānam* (√*ve*, cl.1 "to weave") ind. a mode of uttering *mantras*, done without taking breath, i.e. without a pause ĀpGṛ. XXI.9 (*Māsiśrāddha*). Cf. *ṛgāvānam* (Śrauta).

अनाप्रीत *Anāprīta* (√*prī*, cl.9 "to please") mfn. "not pleased", said of a cup or platter which has not been used before ĀpGṛ. XIV.14 (*Puṁsavana*); used for fetching waters BhGṛ. I.22 (*Kṣipraṁsavana*).

अनुगुप्त *Anugupta* mfn. "concealed", said of waters brought with a covering for *Ādhāna* GGṛ. I.1.9.

अनुपेत *Anupeta* mfn. one who has not received ("not led to") the *Upanayana* initiation; he is debarred from performing the *Pākayajña*, but allowed to perform *kāmyā* (special wishes), *bali* rites ĀpGṛ. VIII.3-4.

अनुप्रवचनीय *Anupravacanīya* mfn. m. a rite relating to the study of the veda (with a teacher) called *Anupravacana*, performed after the recitation of the *sāvitrī* as well as after other portions of the veda ĀśvGṛ. I.22.10 (comm : after the recitation of the *mahānāmnīs*, the *mahāvrata* & the upaniṣad); after the study of the other texts GGṛ. III.2.48-49. cf. ŚGṛ. II. 8.1. Synonym : *anuvācana* II.7.

अनुप्रवचनीया *Anupravacanīyā* f. food for A°, to be begged ĀśvGṛ. I.22.8.

अनुस्तरणी *Anustaraṇī* f. See Śrauta section; also a goat ĀśvGṛ. IV.2.4, 6. See also *Antyeṣṭi*.

अन्तर (वासस्) *Antara* (*vāsas*) n. a lower garment (to cover the loin, comm), must be fresh—*ahatam* ĀpGṛ. XII.8 (*Samāvartana*)=*antarīyam*, worn during the studentship HGṛ. I. 9.10. (*Upanayana*). See also *brahmacārivāsas*.

अन्तर्दिवाकीर्त्य *Antardivākīrtya* m. (fn.) a village in which a *caṇḍāla* resides (*divākīrti* m. Mn. V.85), the place where the study of veda is to be interrupted PGṛ. II.11.4 (*Anadhyāya*).

अन्त्येष्टि *Antyeṣṭi* f. funeral rite, one of the *saṁskāras* of the gṛhya rites; the description in the Gṛhyasūtra, with minor variations, closely follows the *śrauta* rite of A° (q.v.) ĀśvGṛ. IV.1-4 *Udakakarman* (q.v.) PGṛ. III.10.

अन्नप्राशन *Annaprāśana* n. rite of the first feeding of the child with cooked food; performed in the 6th month from the birth ŚGṛ. I.27.1, ĀśvGṛ. I.16.1, PGṛ. I.19.1 etc. or when he is teething KāGṛ.XXXIX.1. The father prepares a food of goat's meat or partidge's, or of fish or boiled rice, if he is desirous of obtaining strength etc. The food is mixed with curds, honey and ghee, and given to the child to eat. He offers oblation in fire. The remnant is eaten by the mother ŚGṛ. I.27.1-11. Cf. also ĀśvGṛ. I.16.1-6 (the rite for a girl without *mantra*), PGṛ. I.19.1-13, HGṛ. II.5.1-3, ĀpGṛ. XVI.1-2.

अन्वष्टका *Anvaṣṭakā* f. post-*aṣṭakā*, the day after the *Aṣṭaka* (the 9th day ĀpGṛ. XXII.9 or the 10th KhGṛ.III.5.1) on which a rite to the manes is performed in the paradigm of the monthly (*māsi*) *Śrāddha* ĀpGṛ. XXII 12 or of the *Piṇḍapitṛyajña* ŚGṛ. III.13.7, PGṛ. III.3.10. Also called *Anvaṣṭakya* ĀśvGr. II.5.1. The A° follows each of the 3 or 4 *Aṣṭakās*. The fire is established and round it a shed (*pariśrita*) is erected and *barhis* is strewn thrice. The articles of offering are laid on the ground: boiled rice, boiled rice with sesamum (*kṛsara*), *pāyasa*, *dadhimantha* and *madhumantha*. To the Fathers are offered a portion of these foods except *madhumantha*, and to the female ancestors, in addition to these, are offered wine (*surā*) and the scum of boiled rice (*ācāma*). Portions of food are also placed into the pits (*karṣū*), 2 or 6 in number; the eastern pits are meant for the Fathers and the western pits for the female ancestors. Food should be offered to 9 or to any uneven number of brahmins.

The brahmins are served with cooked beef (of a cow), which was kept aside from the immolated cow of the *Aṣṭakā* ceremony (Āp Gṛ. XXII.11) ĀśvGṛ. II.5-1-12. PGṛ. mentions offerings of the left rib and the left thigh, and *surā*, *ācāma*, collyrium, salves and garlands for the female ancestors III.3.10-11.

अन्वाहार्य *Anvāhārya* m., "fetched after"; (1) a supplementary rite, performed after the principal sacrifice; or the *Nāndīmukhaśrāddha* which precedes every domestic rite GGṛ. I. 1.5 comm, but the assertion seems to be doubtful.

(2) n. a mess of food, as is offered to the priests after the *Darśa* Oldenberg SBE XX, 14.

(3) n. a monthly *Śrāddha*, performed immediately after the *Piṇḍapitṛyajña* GGṛ. IV.4.3-4.

अपचिति *Apaciti* (*apa-√ci*, cl.3 "to pay respect" AV. I.10.4, Pāṇ. VII.2.30) f. *argha* reception, performed in honour of a *snātaka* and others ĀpGṛ. XIII.2-3. See *Argha*.

अपरपक्ष *Aparapakṣa* m. the other side or portion of the month, i.e. the dark half, *kṛṣṇapakṣa* (consisting of 15 lunar days or *tithis*) ĀpGṛ. I.9.

अपराजिता *Aparājitā* (*diś*) f. the northeast quarter ŚGṛ. IV.6.2.

अपवर्ग *Apavarga* (*apa-√vṛj*, cl.7 "to tear off"; "to fulfil") m. completion of a ceremony ĀpGṛ. I.6=*karmā*° ŚGṛ. I.2.1.

अपूप *Apūpa* m. a cake, with which the brahmins are fed ĀpGṛ. XVII.13. *apūpaṁ catuḥśarāvaṁ* (*śrapayati*) a cake of 4 cups or platters ĀpGṛ. XXI.12 (*Aṣṭakā*); baked on 4 or 8 potsherds like a *puroḍāśa* HGṛ. II.14.4.

अपूपाष्टका *Apūpāṣṭakā* f. See *Aṣṭakā*.

अब्दपूर्ति *Abdapūrti* f. a ceremony performed every month on the birthday of a child for one year and on the yearly birthday, mentioned in ŚGṛ. I.25.10-11, GGṛ. II.8.19-20, though not by the term. A *homa* is performed to Agni and Indra, to Heaven and Earth, then to the *tithi* and *nakṣatra* GGṛ. l.c. After *Nāmakaraṇa* a *homa* is performed every month for one year as in the *Jātakarman*, and at the end of the year flesh of a goat and a sheep are offered to Agni and Dhanvantari, and the brahmins are fed KāGr. XXXVI.12,14.

अभिघारण *Abhighāraṇa* n. act of sprinkling *ājya* over the mess of food ĀpGṛ. VII.4 (*Sthālīpāka*). See also *upaghāta*, *upastaraṇa*.

(*praty*) *abhighāraṇa* n. a second sprinkling ŚGṛ. I.13.16.

अभिनिष्ठान *Abhiniṣṭhāna* (*abhi-niḥ-√sthā*, cl. 1 "to bring to an end") m. technical term of *visarga* (used by the old teachers, comm) ĀpGṛ. XV.9=°*niṣṭāna* (*√stan*, cl 1), a sound which dies out ĀśvGṛ. I.15.5. cf Pāṇ. VIII. 3.86.

अभ्यातान *Abhyātāna* (*abhi-ā-√tan*, cl. 8 "to spread at") m. "aiming at", name of a *mantra* (PGṛ. I.5.10) which procures victory, used in a subordinate oblation ĀpGṛ. II.7. cf. TS. III.4.6.1.

अभ्रि *Abhri* f. a scraper or shovel, used for digging pits for the pillars (bamboo) of a house HGṛ. I.27.1.

अमावास्या *Amāvāsayā* f. GGṛ. I.5.7. See Śrauta section.

अम्बरीष *Ambarīṣa* m.n. a pan on which the domestic fire is lighted ŚGṛ.I.1.8, and carried for the installation of fire GGṛ. I.1.15.

अरणिप्रदान *Araṇipradāna* m. n. rite of handing over the *araṇis* to the sacrificer by the *Adhvaryu* after producing fire by attrition and installing it; on receiving the a°, the sacrificer and his wife keep the *uttara*° and *adhara*° on their laps respectively (cf. K. Śr. IV.7.22, Āp. Śr. V.8.7). This rite is optional in the domestic rite for installation of fires PGṛ. I. 2.5; it shows that fires may also be produced by attrition in the domestic rite.

अरुन्धती *Arundhatī* f. the star Alcor, belonging to the Great Bear, shown to the bride ĀpGṛ. VI.12 (*Vivāha*).

अर्घ *Argha* (*√arh*, cl.1 "to deserve") m. a reception ceremony, performed in honour of a bridegroom by his father-in-law, or of a newly married couple on their return to the bridegroom's house. On these 2 occasions the *madhuparka* (q.v.) and cows (also called *m*°) are offered to them as deserving guests ĀpGṛ. III.3-8, ŚGṛ. I.12.10. Cf. Oldenberg SBE XXIX, 34.

Another reception ceremony is performed in honour of the guests who are called *arghya* (persons worthy of or entitled to *a*°) PGṛ. I. 3.1, ŚGṛ. II.15.1. Six are enumerated : *ācārya* (teacher), *ṛtvij* (officiating priest), *rājan* (king), *priya* (friend), *snātaka* and *vivāhya* (comm, *vara*=father-in-law or bridegroom, Harihara on PGṛ, but *śvaśura* ĀpGṛ. XIII.19, ĀśvGṛ. I.24.4). Paternal and maternal uncles are also included ĀśvGṛ. ib. The rite is also called *Madhuparka* I.24.33.

The guest is offered a seat (*kūrca* or *viṣṭara*), waters for washing feet (*pādya*), *arghya* waters simply called *arghya* HGṛ. I.12.14 , waters for rinsing mouth (*ācamana*), *madhuparka* and a cow. The last one is so important that it is enjoined that there can be no *madhuparka* without flesh. These are offered with an announcement by the host : "*Argha* waters for washing feet" or "Here is the cow". The guest consumes thrice the food offered to him, and he gives the remainder to a person he likes. The rite is to be performed whenever a guest visits the house or once a year ĀpGṛ. XIII.2-20, HGṛ. I. 12.8-13; 14, GGṛ. IV.10.1-26, PGṛ. I.3.1-31, ĀśvGṛ.I.24.1-33, ŚGṛ. II.15-16.

(अन्) अर्थावेक्ष *(An) Arthāvekṣa* mfn. one who (a sacrificer) does not care for worldly desires, i.e. a sacrificer must not be influenced by any interest while choosing the brahmins in a *śrāddha* feast ĀpGṛ. XXI.2.

अर्धर्चशः *Ardharcasaḥ* ind. a mode of reciting the *sāvitrī mantra* (TS. I.5.6.4), in which the recitation is done half verse by half verse by the teacher at the *Upanayana* ĀpGṛ. XI.10. See *pacchaḥ*.

अवकीर्णिन् *Avakīrṇin* (*ava*-√*kṛ/kir*, cl.6 "to throw off") mfn. a student (*brahmacārin*) who has violated his vow of continence by having sexual intercourse during *brahmacarya* PGṛ. III.12. 1, K. Śr. I. 1.13, TĀr. II.18. He has to perform an expiatory rite called *gardabhejyā* (q.v. in Śrauta) in the manner of *Pākayajña* H.Dh. IV, 112.

अवदान *Avadāna* n. (1). cut off portions of the sacrificial food, taken out by a ladle (*sruc*); sprinkled with *ājya* and finally sacrificed GGṛ. I. 8.7; or cutting up the dough into 2 parts ĀpGṛ. VII.4, 8.

(2). cut off portions of the limb of a cow, cooked and mixed with the mess of cooked food, and sacrificed to Agni, Rudra, Śarva, Paśupati, Ugra, Aśani, Bhava, Mahādeva, Īśāna PGṛ. III.8.6 (*Śūlagava*); cut off portions of the omentum, 11, 5 or 3 in number PGṛ. III.11.6-7 (animal sacrifice), ĀśvGṛ.I.11.12. Cf K. Śr. VI.7.6.

अवनेजन *Avanejana* (*ava*-√*nij*, cl.3 "to wash") n. ablutions of hands PGṛ. II.6.19 (*Samāvartana*); washing of the snakes by pouring water to them ib. 14.11. (*Śravaṇā*). *avanikta* n. act of washing by pouring water ib. 13.

अवभृथ *Avabhṛtha* m. completion of a ceremony by pouring out water from a vessel on the *barhis* at the (*Pārvaṇa*) *Sthālīpāka* ĀśvGṛ. I. 10.25. See also Śrauta section.

अवर (अन्न) *Avara* (*anna*) n. rice grains of inferior quality, not to be used for the *Pākayajña* ĀpGṛ. VIII.3.

अवस्नाता *Avasnātā* f. a woman who has taken her bath, i.e. attained puberty; *an*° said of a girl who has not attained puberty; she is allowed to pound the *nyagrodha* shoots ĀpGṛ. XIV.11 (*Puṁsavana*).

अवाचीनपाणि *Avācīnapāṇi* mfn. one who offers *piṇḍas* to the manes with his hand turned downwards HGṛ. II.12.3.

अशौच *Aśauca* n. impurity arising out of the death of a person, in which case the relatives should not cook food during the night when they have just returned after cremation. For three nights they shall not eat mineral or ordinary salt. There shall be no distribution of gifts and the study of veda when one of the *mahāgurus* (parents, teacher who performed *Upanayana* and taught the vedas) dies. The same restriction applies for 10 days after the death of a *sapiṇḍa*, of a *guru* who is not *sapiṇḍa*, of unmarried female relations; for 3 nights after the death of other teachers, of relation who is not a *sapiṇḍa*, of married female relations, of a child that has no teeth, of a still-born child; for one day after the death, of a fellow pupil and of a *śrotriya* of the same village ĀśvGṛ.IV.4.14-27. According to PGṛ. III.10.4 it lasts 1 to 3 nights. Parents become impure when a child below 2 years dies ib. 2; burial permitted in this case ib. 5.

अश्मारोहण *Aśmārohaṇa* n. (1) rite of treading on a millstone, while the bridegroom leads the bride thrice round the fire (*agnipradakṣiṇa*); he makes her tread on the stone, kept to the north of the fire, in each round. He says : Tread on this stone; like a stone be firm. Overcome the enemies; tread the foes down ĀśvGṛ. I.7.7, ŚGṛ. I.13.12, PGṛ. I.7.1, GGṛ. II.2.3, HGṛ. I.19.8, ĀpGṛ. V.3,7 (*āsthāpana*), KāGṛ. XXV.28.

(2) A new born child is laid on a stone HGṛ. II.3.2 (*Jātakarman*).

(3) An initiate is made to set his right foot on a stone to the north of fire ĀpGṛ. X.9 (*āsthāpana*) at the *Upanayana*.

अष्टका *Aṣṭakā* f. rite of the 8th *tithi* of the dark fortnights of the 4 months (or any month after fullmoon ŚBr. VI.4.2.10) of the *hemanta* and *śiśira* seasons (*mārgaśīrṣa*, *pauṣa* or *taiṣa*, *māgha* and *phālguna*). This is a rite for the dead ancestors; recognized as *A*° *śrāddha*, generally 3 in number, ŚGṛ. III.12.1, PGṛ. III.3, KhGṛ. III.3.27 etc. to be performed on the 8th day of the dark fortnight of *mārgaśīrṣa* (called *āgrahāyaṇī*), *pauṣa* (*taiṣa*) and *māgha*; 4 with the option of 1 ĀśvGṛ. II.4. 1-2.

A° can be compressed into 3 days : the 7th, 8th and 9th of the dark half of *māgha* or even into a single day: the 8th of *māgha* BGṛ. II. 11.1-4. The rite on the last mentioned day is the only *A*°, called *Ekāṣṭakā*, recognized by

HGṛ. II.14.2, and with certain variations by BhGṛ. II.15.

The *sūtrakāra*s differ also in the matter of deities : Viśvedevāḥ, Agni, Sūrya, the *pitṛ*s, *paśu*s etc. ĀśvGṛ.II.4.12, although the rite is exclusively meant for the *pitṛ*s (Cf. the commentators).

Similarly, the offerings vary : for the 3 *A*°, cooked vegetables (*śāka*) in the first, flesh (omentum) in the middle one (*mādhyāvarṣa*, q.v.) and cakes (*apūpa*) in the last. In the same order of the rite : *apūpa*, flesh and *śāka* PGṛ. III.3.3, KhGṛ III.3.29-30; 4.1.

Various kinds of grains, cake, rice, animal can be offered Kauś. S. CXXXVIII.2. There is also a wide variety of animals : deer, buffalo, rhinoceros, boar, hare, pigeon if a cow or a goat or a ram is not available; even some thickets or grass for cows may be offered BGṛ. II.11, 51-61.

The A° has a preparatory day (the 7th of the dark fortnight): a *homa* is performed in the evening and a dinner given to the brahmins. On this day a cake of 4 cupfuls of rice is baked or a *puroḍāśa* is prepared, the *ājyabhāga*s are poured over the fire, and then a part of the cake is offered into the fire. The rest of the cake divided into 8 parts, is offered to the brahmins. On the *A*° (next) day a cow is slaughtered after *upākaraṇa*, 5 *ājya* oblations are offered; the omentum is cooked, and after *upastaraṇa* and *abhighāraṇa*, is offered in a *palāśa* leaf. Boiled rice and cooked flesh of cow (*māṁsaudana*), *piṣṭānna* and oblation of clarified butter are offered. The *Sviṣṭakṛt* rite and offering of the *piṇḍa*s are done as in the monthly *śrāddha*. Curds may also be offered in the manner of the *apūpa* offering, optionally ĀpGṛ. XXI.10-13; XXII.1-10 (ĀpGṛ calls it *Ekāṣṭakā*). Then follows *Anvaṣṭakā*.

apūpa° *A*° of cake; the rite performed on the 8th day of the dark fortnight after the *āgrahāyaṇī* GGṛ. III.10.9, in which *apūpa* is offered.

The word *A*° is derived from *aṣṭan*, only in the sense of a rite in which the manes are deities (*aṣṭakā pitṛdaivatye* Pāṇ. VII.3.45 vārttika. Cf. H.Dh. IV, 353-58. See also *Anvaṣṭakā*, *Ekāṣṭakā*, *Śrāddha*.

अष्टाकपाल *Aṣṭākapāla* mfn. said of an *apūpa* baked on 8 potsherds like a *puroḍāśa* ĀpGṛ. XXI.13 (*Aṣṭakā*).

असम्भवेप्सु *Asambhavepsu* m. (fn.) one who desires (*īpsu*) that his wife should not have sexual intercourse (*a-sambhava*) with others ĀpGṛ. XXIII.3; see *ādhārikā*.

असि *Asi* m. a sword ; its point (*agra*) is placed on the head of a bride by her father or brother ŚGṛ. I.13.1 (*Vivāha*).

अस्तमितोदित *Astamitodita* mfn. See *paurṇamāsī*.

अस्थिसंचयन *Asthisaṁcayana* n. rite of collecting the bones, done after the 10th *tithi* from the death or on a *tithi* with an odd number, of the dark fortnight; collected in urns having male or female sex marks according to the sex of the deceased. The performers go round the cremation spot three times in *prasavya* direction, and sprinkle milk mixed with water on it with a *śamī* branch; gathering begins with the feet first, head last; bones are purified with a winnowing basket, and the urn is put into a pit; a lid is placed over the urn (*kumbha*); without looking back they go away and bathe in water and perform a *śrāddha* ĀśvGṛ. IV.5.

अहत (वासस्) *Ahata* (*vāsas*) n. "uninjured, unwashed", i.e. new, fresh garment, worn by the bride ĀpGṛ. IV.8.

अहुत *Ahuta*(mfn) a class of *Pākayajña* (q.v.), in which oblation is "not sacrificed", i.e. the sacrifice is performed with the *bali* offerings.

ahutāda mfn. the Maruts who are said to be "eaters of non-sacrifices", i.e. to whom a *bali* offering is made instead of *ājya* oblation PGṛ II.15.3.

आ Ā

आकर्षफलक *Ākarṣaphalaka* n. a board of *udumbara* wood, shaped like a snake, 1 arm long PGṛ. II.10.17 & comm, with which sesamum seeds are sacrificed (*Upākaraṇa*).

आख्यात *Ākhyāta* n. "said"; a verb ĀpGṛ. XV.9.

आग्रयण *Āgrayaṇa* n. the domestic rite, performed by one who has not set up the *śrauta* fire (*anāhitāgni*) ĀpGṛ. XIX.6, also by an *āhitāgni* ĀśvGṛ. II.2.5. The purpose of the domestic *Ā*° is same as the *śrauta Ā*° *iṣṭi*.

A mess of cooked food (*sthālīpāka*) is offered to the deities of the *śrauta* rite with Agni *Sviṣṭakṛt* as the 4th. The sacrificer fills his mouth with rice grains, swallows them, sips water. After rolling a ball of rice (*piṇḍa*) of the said cooked food he throws it up on to the central beam (*stūpa*) of the dwelling house ĀpGṛ. XIX.7; cf ŚGṛ. III.8, PGṛ.III.1, GGṛ. III.8.9-24, KhGṛ. III.3.6-15 etc. *Ā*° is described in most of the Gṛhya texts immediately after the *Āśvayujī*. Obviously, both the *śrauta* and *gṛhya Ā*° are agricultural rites.

आग्रहायणी *Āgrahāyaṇī* f. belonging to the month of *agrahāyaṇa*; name of a rite performed on the fullmoon day of *mārgaśīrṣa* HGṛ. II.17.1 comm. See *Pratyavarohaṇa*.

आघार *Āghāra* m. libation of clarified butter (*ājya*) ĀpGṛ. II.5. See Śrauta section.

आचमन *Ācamana* (*ā-√cam*, cl. 1 "to sip") n. sipping of water from the palm, before sacrifice begins GGṛ. I.1.2, thrice and water wiped off twice 2.5; must be done in a sitting position. The ceremony is often followed by touching various limbs of body I.2.7, 8, KhGṛ. I.1.9. For elaborate rules for *ā*°, developed in the Smṛtis ĀpDh. I.5.15.2-11, Mn. II.58-62 etc.

ācamanīya n. water for sipping HGṛ. I.12.14, offered as *argha*. See *madhuparka*.

आचान्त *Ācānta* mfn. one (an initiate) who has sipped water HGṛ. I.4.13.

ācāntodaka mfn. one who has sipped water, and drunk a little, and also has worn a sacrificial cord becomes eligible for performing a rite GGṛ. I.1.2.

आचाम *Ācāma* m. scum of boiled rice, used for mixing with the chaff (*phalīkaraṇa*) and water as *bali* offering to Rudra GGṛ. I.4.31; the scum is also offered to the female ancestors ĀśvGṛ. II.5.5 (*Anvaṣṭakā*).

आचारिक *Ācārika* n. customary rites, performed at the marriage ceremony KāGṛ. XXV.7. See also *āvṛt*, *grāmavacana*, *janapadadharma*.

आजि *Āji* m.f. a running match (RV. I.116.15; IV.41.8), in which the runners run until they lose their breath HGṛ. II.20.11 (*Utsarjana*).

आज्य-भाग *Ājya-bhāga* m. libations of *ājya*, offered to the deities ĀpGṛ. IV.10 (*Vivāha*). Two libations of *ā*°, offered on the fire II.6.

°*lepa* m. salve of *ā*° ŚGṛ. I.16.5 (*Vivāha*).

°*saṁskāra* m. rite of purification of *ājya* before its use in the sacrifice. ĀpGṛ. I.22 describes it : *ā*° is melted (*vilāpya*) and poured (*nirupya*) into the °*sthālī* over which 2 *darbha* purifiers are laid. *Ā*° is put on the embers (*aṅgāra*) drawn from the domestic fire, and lustrated by burning grass blades, and a firebrand is moved (*paryagnikaraṇa*) round it thrice. Then *ā*° is taken out of the fire, embers are pushed back to the fire, and thereafter *ā*° is purified 3 times with the purifiers. The purifiers are thrown into the fire. See also GGṛ. I.7.24-28. *Utpavana* is another method.

आढारिका *Āḍhārikā* f. a centiped, pounded alive and powdered; its powder is inserted by the husband into the vagina of his wife as a preventive charm against her illicit sexual relation ĀpGṛ. XXIII.3.

आतिथ्य *Ātithya* n. "proper for a guest"; a rite of hospitality in which a cow is slaughtered in honour of the guest ĀpGṛ. VII.26. See *gorālambha*.

आदर्श *Ādarśa* m. a mirror, which is looked at by a student ĀpGṛ. XII.11 (*Samāvartana*); also held by the bride in her left hand ŚGṛ. I.12.7 (*Vivāha*).

आधान *Ādhāna* n. setting of the domestic fire, is to be performed at the time of one's marriage (*dārakāle*), or of the partition of the ancestral property (*dāyādyakāle*) ŚGṛ. I.1.2-3, PGṛ. I.2.1-2. The fire is fetched from the house of a *vaiśya*, who is rich in cattle (*bahupaśu*) or from the house of a person, who, whatever be his caste, has performed many sacrifices GGṛ. I.1.16 (*bahuyājin*), or it may be produced by attrition.

See also *agni*, *araṇipradāna*, *parameṣṭhikaraṇa*.

आनर्तन *Ānartana* n. dancing, performed 4 times by 4 or 8 women, who are not widows, after they have been regaled with food and wine ŚGṛ. I.11.5 (*Vivāha*).

आपूर्यमाणपक्ष *Āpūryamāṇapakṣa* m. the increasing side, i.e. the time of increasing moon, auspicious time of marriage ŚGṛ. I.5.5.

आप्यायन *Āpyāyana* n. act of swelling or strengthening the sense organs (*prāṇān*) of a slaughtered cow by sprinkling water on the carcase (*āpyāyya*) HGṛ. II.15.5 (*Śrāddha*). See also Śrauta section.

आभ्युदयिक *Ābhyudayika* (*abhi-ud-√i*, cl.2 "to rise") n. a *Śrāddha* (q.v.) rite to the ancestors, with a view to obtaining prosperity ŚGṛ. IV. 4.1;these rites are performed on such occasions as the birth of a son, marriage of a son or daughter, *Cūḍākaraṇa*, *Nāmakaraṇa* etc. See *Śrāddha*.

(अन्) आम्नातमन्त्र *(An) Āmnātamantra* (*ā-√mnā*, cl.1. "to mention") mfn. deities for which no *mantra* has been mentioned; they are to be worshipped by uttering only *svāhā* ŚGṛ. I.9.18.

āmnāya m. the vedic texts which are learnt by repetition, i.e. sacred tradition GGṛ. I. 6.12.

आयुष्य *Āyuṣya*. n. See *Jātakarman*.

आरग्वध *Āragvadha* m. a piece of wood : Cathartocarpus fistula, used as faggot (*samidh*) ĀpGṛ. XVIII.7 (*Sarpabali*).

आराम *Ārāma* m. a garden (literally, resting place), for the consecration of which a rite is performed ŚGṛ. V.3.1.

आवसथ *Āvasatha* m. dwelling place HGṛ. I. 12.8.

āvasathya m. fire belonging to the dwelling place PGṛ. I.2.1 = fire for the domestic rites (*āvasathyādhāna*). see *Ādhāna*.

आवहमान *Āvahamāna* (*ā-√vah*, cl.1 "to lead near") mfn. those who bring a bridegroom near, said of the relatives ŚGṛ. I.6.4.

आवाप *Āvāpa* m. insertion of rites between the general expiation and the oblation to Prajāpati ŚGṛ.I.9.12, PGṛ. I.5.6. Cf. Oldenberg SBE XXIX, 28.

आवाहन *Āvāhana* n. invitation to the manes at the *Śrāddha*, but not performed at the *Ekoddiṣṭa* ŚGṛ. IV.2.5; done at the *Ābhyudayika* 4.11. Cf. Oldenberg SBE XXIX, 109.

आवृत् *Āvṛt* f. (pl) (1) "turning"; said of those ceremonies which are performed without *mantras*, and customary among the people, i.e. popular rites, which are to be learnt from the womenfolk, for all *gṛhya* rites ĀpGṛ. II. 15; cf.Haradatta comm. The ceremonies of the *Jātakarman*, *Annaprāśana* etc.for girls are performed without *mantra* (*āvartā*) ĀśvGr. I. 15.10;16.6. See Śrauta section.

आश्वयुजी *Āśvayujī* f. a rite, performed on the fullmoon day of *aśvayuja*, the month of *āśvina* (under the constellation of *asvayuj*, Pāṇ. IV. 3.36). The householder wearing a new garment, adorns his house, cooks a mess of food and offers to Paśupati. In his joined palms he offers speckled butter *pṛṣataka* (milk mixed with butter) ĀśvGṛ. II.2.1-3; also oblations of clarified butter to the Aśvins ŚGṛ, IV.16; the rite is called *Pṛṣātaka* : *pāyasa* is cooked and a mixture of curds, honey and ghee, both offered to Indra, Indrāṇī, the Āśvins etc. He partakes of a portion of the sacrificial food.

आसादन *Āsādana* (*ā-√sad*, cl.1 "to lay down") n. act of putting down the sacrificial food or utensils near the fire ŚGṛ. I.3.4.

आस्थापन *Āsthāpana* n. rite of placing foot on a stone, to be done twice ĀpGṛ. V.6, 9 (*Aśmārohaṇa*) in the marriage.

(यथा) आस्यम् (*Yathā*) *Āsyam* ind. offering of the sacrificial food to each god according to his mouth, i.e. according one's due portion or share ĀpGṛ. XX.4 (*Śūlagava*).

आहार्य *Āhārya* mfn. "fetched"; the domestic fire which is fetched (not produced by attrition) from a *śrotriya*'s house (as distinguished from *manthya*) ĀpGṛ. V.18.

आहिताग्नि *Āhitāgni* mfn. a person who performs worship to the domestic fire called *aupāsana* HGṛ. I.26.3.

an° mfn. one who has not set up the *śrauta* fire; such a person is allowed to perform *Āgrayaṇa* (q.v.) ĀpGr. XIX 6.

आहुति *Āhuti* f. offering of oblation into the fire ĀpGṛ. II.7.

इ I

इण्व *Iṇva* n. a wooden plate, used for protecting hands when holding a hot pan ĀpGṛ. XXIII. 7. Cf. *darbheṇva*, *khārīṇḍva* (Śrauta). *Iṇḍva* n. 2 pads of *muñja* grass, used as protection of hands for carrying the *ukhā* containing fire ŚBr. VI. 7. 1.25, K. Śr XVII. 2.4 (*Cayana*).

इतिहेति *Itiheti* m. a prattler (?) ŚGṛ. IV.12.11.

इध्म *Idhma* m. fuel log ĀpGṛ. II.5.

citi f. pile of logs on which a deadbody is cremated ĀśvGṛ. IV.2.14.

इन्द्रयज्ञ *Indrayajña* m. a rite dedicated to Indra

performed on the fullmoon day of *prauṣṭha-pada* (August-September) in which milk rice (*caru*), cakes and 2 *ājya* oblations to Indra and Indrāṇī are offered; and after eating a portion of the sacrificial food the sacrificer offers a *bali* to the Maruts PGṛ. II.15.

इन्वका *Invakā* f. *Mṛgaśiras*, a star ĀpGṛ. II.16; III.4.

ई Ī

ईशानबलि *Īśānabali* m. See *Śūlagava*.

उ U

उच्छिष्ट *Ucchiṣṭa* (mf) n. remainder of the sacrificial food, given away to a well-disposed person by the student HGṛ. I.13.8 (*Madhuparka*). The sacrificial remainder is used as fee at the *Pārvaṇa Sthālīpāka* ĀśvGṛ.I.10.27.

उतूल *Utūla* m. a slave; a rite is performed to prevent him from running away from the master's house by sprinkling master's urine round him (°*parimeha*) PGṛ. III.7.1. Name of a tribe in the northwest India Oldenberg SBE XXIX, 350.

उत्तरीय *Uttarīya* n. upper garment, worn by a student during his studentship HGṛ. I.9.10 (*Upanayana*). See *antara (vāsas)brahmacārivāsas*.

उत्तान (हस्त) *Uttāna (hasta)* mfn. "palm up", the position of the bride's right hand, held by the bridegroom with his right hand in palm down position. This is the mode of holding hands at the marriage ceremony ĀpGṛ. IV.11. Various forms are prescribed for different purposes : to seize only the fingers (of the wife) except the thumb for obtaining birth of only daughters 12, the thumb (of the wife) for sons 13. cf. *Pāṇigrahaṇa*.

उत्थान *Utthāna* n. rite of getting up from child-bed. On the 10th or the 12th day after child birth, the parents wash their heads, wear new clothes; the father cooks a mess of food on the *sūtikāgni* and offers oblations to the *tithi* of the child's birth, 3 *nakṣatras* etc. ŚGṛ. I.25.

उत्पवन *Utpavana* (*ud-√pū*, cl.9 "to cleanse") n. purification of the *ājya* with 2 *kuśa* blades (*pavitra*), which are held down by the sacrificer over the *ā*° (contained in a pot), and moved by him from the west to the east ĀśvGṛ.I.3.2-3. Cf. ŚBr. I.3.1.22. More elaborately described ŚGṛ. I.8.14-21. For a different procedure see *ājyasaṁskāra*.

उत्पात *Utpāta* (*ud-√pat*, cl.1 "to fly up") m. "thrown up"; a sudden unusual event boding calamity; considered as an ill-omen, e.g. earthquake (Cf. AV. XIX.9.7); or even such a trifle as seeing the footprint of a dove on the household hearth etc. is an *utpāta* which is to be averted by offering oblations ĀpGṛ. XXIII.9.

उत्सर्ग *Utsarga* m. releasing a cow at the *Madhuparka* instead of killing it, and in that case a meal is prepared with other meat HGṛ. I.13. 11, 14. See also *Vṛṣotsarga*.

उत्सर्जन *Utsarjana* (*ud-√sṛj*, cl.1 "to set free, to abandon") n. rite of suspension of vedic studies for a certain period, performed on the fullmoon day of *pauṣa* or *māgha* BGṛ. I.5. 163 (but it varies) to mark the conclusion of the vedic study. Formerly, the rites : *Upākaraṇa* (q.v.), the beginning, and the *Utsarjana*, the conclusion of the vedic study, were performed on different dates and in different months, but later with the decline of the vedic studies they came to be performed one after another, H.Dh.II (2), 807=*utsarga* ĀśvGr. III.5.13=*samāpana* ĀpGṛ. VII.1=*uparama* ŚGṛ. IV.7.1. The rite is similar to *Upākaraṇa* ĀśvGṛ. III.5.13, boiled rice is offered instead of *ājya*, ib. 20-22. The teacher and pupils go to a river (or out of the village, turning faces either to the east or north GGṛ. III.3.15). Water oblations (*tarpaṇa*) are offered to the gods, vedas, metres, *ṛṣis* etc., then the *sāvitrī* is recited 4 times. The cessation of study is announced loudly by proclaiming *viratāḥ sma* PGṛ. II.12. Then a holiday (*anadhyāya*) follows as in the *Upākaraṇa*. Even in those days there were people who defied the rules. Aṣṭāvakra condemns those delinquents of his time : *yadā tu tasmin kāle na kecanotsargam anutiṣṭhanto dṛśyante tadā kiṁ kurmaḥ kam upālabhemahi. śāstrārthastāvad yathā asmābhirvarṇitaḥ* MGṛ. I.5.1 comm.

The cessation of study can be occasioned by various incidents. There is a long list of such incidents in ŚGṛ. IV.7.

उद् *Ud* (cl.7) to wet the initiate's head with water, done by the teacher by pouring warm water into cold (*unatti*) ĀpGṛ. X.5 (*Upanayana*).

उदककर्मन् *Udakakarman* n. libation of water, poured out with joined palms for the deceased but not for a child under 2 years; performed just after the cremation by all relatives to the 7th or 10th degree. Wearing the sacred cord in *prācīnāvītin* fashion they plunge into water facing the south. They offer libation with the words : N.N. ! this water to thee. They come out of water and sit down on a spot covered with grass, and they are entertained with ancient tales. Thereafter they return to the village led by the youngest without looking back PGṛ. III.10.1-23.

According to ĀśvGṛ. IV.4.10 this libation is to be offered once to the deceased by mentioning his *gotra* and personal name. Then they come out of the water, put on other clothes, wring out the wet clothes once and lay them away with their skirts to the north, and sit down until the stars appear and return home.

उदकाञ्जलि *Udakāñjali* m. joined palms (of a teacher) filled with water, poured again into the joined palms of an initiate ĀpGṛ. X.12.

°*sparśana* n. touching of water, a rite performed at the *Godānavrata* according to the *sāmavedins* ĀpGṛ. XVI.16, GGṛ. I.2.5 sqq, KhGṛ. I.1.7-10. See *Udakakarman*.

उदक्या *Udakyā* f. a woman in her courses ŚGṛ. IV.7.47.

उदगयन *Udagayana* n. the northward course of the sun to the north of the equator, a propitious time for performing the domestic rites ĀpGṛ. I.2.

उदूह *Udūha* (*ud-√ūh*, cl.1 "to remove, to push upwards") m. a broom, made of *palāśa* or *śamī* wood, with which the ground (*avakāśa*) of a house is swept ĀpGṛ. XVII.1.

उद्धूपन *Uddhūpana* n. rite of fumigation of a new born child (male child according to Mātṛdatta comm) with small grains mixed with mustard seed, which are thrown on the embers of the *sūtikāgni* HGṛ. II.3.7.

उपक्लृप्त *Upakḷpta* (*upa-√kḷp*, cl.1 "to prepare"; "bring near") mfn. said of sacrificial implements which are arranged near the fire GGṛ. II .9.3 (*Cūḍākaraṇa*.).

उपगमन *Upagamana* n. sexual intercourse, which is, according to some teachers, consummated by pronouncing *mantras* either on all occasions or on the first occasion after the wife's menstruation HGṛ. I.25.3-4.

उपघात *Upaghāta* (*upa-√han*, cl.2 "to hit at") m. "picked up" portions of the sacrificial food with a *mekṣaṇa*, offered into fire; this is called *u*° *homa* in which *abhighāraṇa* and *upastaraṇa* of the sacrificial food do not take place GGṛ. I.8.2 (*Darśa*).

darvy° act of picking up done with a *darvī* PGṛ. II.14.13 (*Śravaṇā*).

उपनयन *Upanayana* (*upa-√nī*, cl. 1 "to lead near") n. rite of initiation of a boy (belonging to the castes of *brāhmaṇa*, *kṣatriya* and *vaiśya*) in which he symbolically is led near his teacher HGṛ. I.5.2 or, probably, he is ushered by initiation into the next stage of life, from adolescence to youth. It is a rebirth ŚBr. XI. 5.4.12. The rite is associated with the studentship. The prescribed age of the boy for the rite varies, for a *brāhmaṇa* : the 7th or 8th year HGṛ. I.1.2 or the 8th year from the conception (*garbhāṣṭama*) ĀpGṛ. X.2, ŚGṛ. II.1.1; for a *kṣatriya* : the 11th year; for a *vaiśya* the 12th year. The time also varies : spring, summer and autumn for *brāhmaṇa kṣatriya* and *vaiśya* respectively ĀpGṛ. X.4, HGṛ. I.1.4, ĀpDh. I.1.1.

An initiate wears 2 garments, one for the lower part of his body (*antaram vāsas*), and the other for upper part (*uttarīya*); made of hemp, flax, deer-skin (*ajina*); or of wool (*āvika*) PGṛ. II.5.16; a dress of skin of a black deer, *ruru* deer and cow for the 3 castes respectively ĀśvGṛ. I.19.8; also of linen (*kṣauma*), hemp (*śāṇa*), cotton (*kārpāsa*) GGṛ. II.10.8.

A staff (*daṇḍa*) is an essential element for the rite; its material and size vary according to the caste of an initiate ĀpGṛ. XI.15-16, ĀśvGṛ. I.19.13; 20.1, ŚGṛ. II.1.21-23.

Equally important is the girdle (*mekhalā*), worn by the initiate which has been allued to RV. III.8.4 (used as a *mantra* in the rite ĀśvGṛ. I.20.8, PGṛ. II.2.9, BhGṛ. I.8). Strangely, however, none of the *sūtrakāras* mentions the *upavīta* as a part of U°. *Yajñopavīta* has been mentioned only by BGṛ. II.5.7-8.

On the otherhand, the initiate participates in the rite already wearing the sacred thread before the ceremony commences HGṛ. I.2.6, BhGṛ. I.3, MGṛ. I.22.2.

The rite has been described elaborately in ĀpGṛ. X-XI, HGṛ. I.1-2. The variations in the detail and in the order of the rite are innumerable. The teacher shaves the head of an initiate, who has worn a new garment or antelope's skin. The initiate takes hold of his teacher's hand, and the latter offers a *homa* into the fire. The teacher sits to the north of the fire and the initiate in front of him. The teacher pours water into the folded palms of the initiate and his own; thereafter he tells the boy to look at the sun, and asks his name, *gotra* etc. The teacher places his hands over the boy's shoulder, and touches his heart. Then follows the rite of putting logs into the fire, accompanied with *mantras*, by the initiate. The initiate worships Agni, and embracing the feet of the teacher asks him to recite the *sāvitrī*. The teacher gets hold of the upper garment of the initiate, and recites the *sāvitrī*, first, *pāda* by *pāda*, then hemistich by hemistich and finally the whole verse. A three-plaited girdle is tied round the initiate, and a staff is given to him. Then the initiate goes through the village to beg food, first of his mother or a woman. He should not be refused. With this alms he may cook his food and eat with the permission of his teacher ĀśvGṛ. I.19-22, ŚGṛ. II.1-6; PGṛ. II.2-6 etc. He will also put logs into the fire daily.

The concept of *brahmacarya* which is associated with the studentship occurs in ŚBr. XI. 5.4.

Synonymes of U°: *upāyana* KāGṛ. XLI.1, *mauñjībandhana*, *baṭukaraṇa*, *vratabandha*, Ādityadarśana comm. on ib. Cf. *upasampadā*, *pabbajjā* Upasak Monastic terms. See also *dīkṣā* (Śrauta).

उपयमन *Upayamana* **mfn.** "serving as a support", i.e. layer of *kuśa* grass on which the *ājyasthālī* is placed PGṛ. I.1.4. Cf. *upayamanī* (Śrauta).

(2) n. literally, rite of seizing a girl near, i.e. marriage rite PGṛ. I.9.1 but comm on ib. says *upayamana kuśānādāya*, having taken up the *kuśa* blades. Cf. Oldenberg SBE XXIX, 286.

उपरतशोणिता *Uparataśoṇitā* f. woman (the wife) whose menstrual flow (literally, blood) has ceased after the beginning of the course GGṛ. II.5.8.

उपरम *Uparama* **m.** cessation of the vedic study ŚGṛ. IV.7.1 = *anadhyāya* (q.v.).

उपलेपन *Upalepana* **n.** act of smearing the *sthaṇḍila* with cowdung ĀśvGṛ I.3.1, ŚGṛ. I. 5.3 (*upalipta*).

उपवसथ *Upavasatha* m. fasting GGṛ. I.5.13.

aupavasthika mfn. fast day food, which is consumed by the sacrificer so that he may be powerful GGṛ. I.6.1-3.

उपवास *Upavāsa* m. fasting, prescribed for the newly married couple ĀpGṛ. V.19; *upoṣita* is a person who has fasted for being eligible for a sacrifice VII.17.

उपवीत *Upavīta* n. See *yajñopavītin*.

उपसमाधान *Upasamādhāna* n. act of putting wood into the fire ĀpGṛ. IV.10 (*Vivāha*).

उपस्तरण *Upastaraṇa* n. act of spreading *ājya* under an oblation ŚGṛ. I.13.16, ĀpGṛ. VII.4 (*Sthālīpāka*). Sipping of water before eating the *madhuparka* food also serves as a substratum ĀśvGṛ. I.24.13.

उपस्थ *Upastha* m.n. vagina (of the wife), touched by her husband who is about to cohabit ŚGṛ. I.19.2 (*Garbhādhāna*).

उपस्थान *Upasthāna* n. shrines for the images of gods inside a house PGṛ. III.4.9.

उपहार *Upahāra* (*upa-√hṛ*, cl.1 "to bring forth") m. offering of *bali* oblations, e.g. cakes to the deities KāGṛ. L. 1-2.

उपाकरण *Upākaraṇa* (*upa-ā-√kṛ*, cl.8 "to bring near") n. (1) a rite which marks the commencement of the session for the vedic study Āśv Gṛ. III.5.1, ŚGṛ. IV.5.1; performed annually (*vārṣika*), in the rainy season ĀśvGṛ. ib. 19. But time varies. Cf. PGṛ. II.10, KhGṛ. III.2.14-15, HGṛ. II.18.2 etc. Deities also differ.

Two *ājyabhāgas* followed by oblations to Sāvitrī, Brahmā, Śraddhā etc. are made. Then with the accompaniment of *mantras* barley powder (*saktu*) mixed with curds is sacrificed (ĀśvGṛ. ib. 4-12). Then follows a holiday (*anadhyāya*) of varying duration ŚGṛ. IV.5.17, Mn. IV.119, PGṛ. II.10.23. For details of the rite H.Dh. II(2), 807-815. See also *Utsarjana*.

(2) act of touching an animal (as in the *śrauta*) with the blades of grass before the victim is sacrificed in a rite for the deceased PGṛ. III.11.2; touching a cow, the victim ĀpGṛ. XXII.3 (*Aṣṭakā*).

adhyāya° vedic study ĀśvGṛ. III.5.1,= *adhyāyopākarman* PGṛ. II.10, VasDh. XIII. 1; the whole of veda (Kṛṣṇa YV) and *kāṇḍa*° the study of the sections of TS., according to Haradatta comm on ĀpGṛ. VIII.1.

उपानत् *Upānat* (*upa-√nah*, cl. 4 "to tie near") f. a pair of shoes, used by a student ĀpGṛ. XII.11=*upānadyuga* ĀśvGṛ. III.8.1 (*Samāvartana*).

उलप *Ulapa* m. a kind of soft grass (RV.X.142. 3), strewn in a line from the entrance of the bridegroom's house to the bedroom KāGṛ. XXVIII.1.

उल्का *Ulkā* f. a firebrand, held by a person when the snakes are entreated to keep away PGṛ. II.14.11 (*Śrāvaṇīsthālīpāka*).

उशीर *Uśīra* m.n. fragrant powder. See *sambhāra*.

उष्णीष *Uṣṇīṣa* m.n. a turban, wound round the head of a student PGṛ. II.6.25 (*Samāvartana*).

ऊ Ū

ऊबध्य *Ūb(v)adhya* n. undigested food in the stomach (of a cow), besmeared with blood, thrown into the fire or buried in a pit PGṛ. III.8.12, ĀśvGṛ. IV.8.26 (*Śūlagava*). Cf RV. I. 162.10. See also *ūvadhyagoha* (Śrauta).

ऋ Ṛ

ऋत्विज् *Ṛtvij* m. officiating priest; the *Brahman* is the only officiating priest at the *Pākayajñas* GGṛ. I.9.8, and the sacrificer himself is a *Hotṛ* 9; the assistance of *Brahman* is optional except at the offerings to Dhanvantari and of *Śūlagava* ĀśvGṛ. I. 3.6.

ए E

एकाष्टका *Ekāṣṭakā* f. *Aṣṭaka* par excellence (Caland PBr 92), a rite for the *pitṛs* performed on the 8th day of the dark fortnight (*vyaṣṭakā*) after the fullmoon, and which falls under the *jyeṣṭhā* constellation, specially of the month of *māgha* (AV. III.10.5) ĀpGṛ. XXI. 10, HGṛ. II.14.2. See *Aṣṭakā*.

एकोद्दिष्ट *Ekoddiṣṭa* n. See *Śrāddha*.

एध *Edha* (*√indh*, cl.1 "to kindle") m. fuel log (RV. I.158.4)=*samidh*, fetched from a forest to kindle a separate fire after the extinction of the fire of *Upanayana* ĀpGṛ. XI.22.

एरका *Erakā* f. a sort of sacrificial grass ĀpGṛ. XII.3.

औ Au

औदक *Audaka* mfn. water carrier, who sprinkles the bridegroom and the bride with water GGṛ. II.2.15.

औपकार्य *Aupakārya* (*upa-√kṛ*, cl.8 "to provide, to prepare") n. preparatory acts which are done before a ceremony begins ĀpGr. XXI. 11.

(the evening of the day before *Ekāṣṭakā* day).

औपवस्त्र *Aupavastra* n. food suitable for the fasting day KāGṛ. XLVI.2.

औपसद *Aupasada* m (fn) the domestic fire, with which the *Pākayajñas* are performed KāGṛ. XLVII.1-2. (*upasad=āvasatha*, comm).

औपासन (अग्नि) *Aupāsana* (*agni*) m. fire for sitting near, i.e. the sacred domestic fire, kept from the marriage ceremony by the householder, and the sacrificer is called *āhitāgni* by worshipping this fire HGṛ. 1.26.1-3. Cf PGṛ. I.9.1. See *Ādhāna*.

क Ka

कक्ष *Kakṣa* m. a wood ? RV. VI.45.31; underwood, burnt in the forest as an optional rite for *Aṣṭakā* ŚGṛ. III.14.5, ĀśvGṛ. II.4.9.

कपिञ्जल *Kapiñjala* m. a bird (partridge); its flesh is offered to the child at *Annaprāśana* PGṛ.I.19.8.

कपुच्छल *Kapucchala* n. tuft of hair on the backside of the head (hanging like a tail ?) GGṛ. II.9.18 (*Cūḍākaraṇa*).

कपुजा *Kapujā* f. lock of hair KāGṛ. XL.2(*Cūḍākaraṇa*)= *sikhā*.

कपुष्णिका *Kapuṣṇikā* f. tuft of hair on both sides of the head GGṛ. II.9.12 (*Cūḍākaraṇa*).

करद् *Karad* m. ? n. ? a formula, uttered by the husband when he touches the vagina of his wife before sexual copulation KāGṛ. XXX.5.

कर्मंकर *Karamakara* m. labourer (mentioned alongwith *dāsa*); On the path they use for running away from their master's house a rite is performed ĀpGṛ. XXIII.7.

कर्षू *Karṣū* f. a trench or pit, 2 or 6 in number, in which the *piṇḍa*s for the manes are placed ĀśvGṛ. II.5.6, 7 (*Anvaṣṭakā*); in length 1 *prādeśa*, east-west, in breadth 4 fingers, and situated at the distance of 4 fingers from one another KāGṛ. LXV.3.

कल्प *Kalpa* (√*kḷp*, cl.1 "to be adapted to") m. rule for the manner of acting (RV. IX.9.7), i.e. ceremonials. It is said that the knowledge of the ceremonials only does not make a student eligible for *snātaka*hood; he must learn the vedas with its 6 *aṅga*s PGṛ. II.6.7 (*Samāvartana*).

paśu° rules for the animal sacrifice ĀśvGṛ I.11.1. Also the rite *Paśu* °(q.v.) See also *tantra* (Śrauta).

कांस्य *Kāṃsya* n. a brass vessel into which *madhuparka* is poured ĀpGṛ. XIII.10.

काम्य *Kāmya* mfn. "desirable"; those rites which are performed out of the desire of benefit; it is an alternative of the śrauta *kāmyā iṣṭi* Āśv Gṛ. III.6.1; women can perform it ĀpGṛ. VIII.4.

°*śrāddha* m. see *Śrāddha*.

काष्ठकलाप *Kāṣṭhakalāpa* m. bundle of firewoods, collected by a student daily during his studentship HGṛ. I.8.2.

कितव *Kitava* m. gambler ĀśvGṛ. II.7.11.

कुटि *Kuṭi* f. a hut ĀpGṛ. XIX.14 (*Śūlagava*); 2 k° where the deities are invoked XX.1,3.

कुण्डल *Kuṇḍala* m. two ear-rings, given to a student at *Upanayana*, and he holds them over the fire, pours *ājya* oblations over them into the fire, washes and wears them HGṛ. I. 10.6-7; 11.1.

कुप्तु *Kuptu* f. domestic oven (*cullī*, *bhrāṣṭra*, comm); a dove's footprint on it is a bad omen ĀpGṛ. XXIII.9. See *utpāta*.

कुम्ब *Kumba* m.n. the broad end (shaped like a pot) of the log used as *śamyā*.

prācīna° mfn. such *śamyā* turned towards the east; thus northwards turned k°=*udīcīna*° HGṛ. I.2.2-3.

कुश *Kuśa* m. sacred grass, commonly known as *darbha* (Poa cynosuroids), used for strewing round the fire in 3 or 5 layers ŚGṛ. I.8.1-2, for sprinkling water round the fire 3 times with 2 blades ib. 17. Also used as *pavitra* and held over a vessel into which water is decanted for preparing the *prokṣaṇī* waters ĀpGṛ. I.20.

°*bhitta* n. layer of k° for receiving the hair ŚGṛ. I.28.7 (*Cūḍākaraṇa*).

°*sūnā* f. a network of k°, 4 in number, on which *bali* offerings are made, and blood of the sacrificed animal is poured ĀśvGṛ. IV. 8.22,27 (*Śūlagava*).

कूब(व)र *Kūb(v)ara(i)* mfn. a pole of a cart GGṛ. III.4.31, K.Śr. XII. 4.11.

कूर्च *Kūrca* m. n. a bundle of grass, used as a seat by a student ĀpGṛ. XIII.2 (*Samāvartana*).

कूर्मपित्त *Kūrmapitta* n. gall of a tortoise, put on the wife's lap if the householder desires his son to become valiant PGṛ. I.14.5 (*Puṁsavana*); a dish filled with water, Harihara comm.

कृसर *Kṛsara* m. mess of boiled rice mixed with sesamum seeds, covered with ghee, cooked on a dish (*sthālīpāka*), to be looked at and eaten by the wife GGṛ. II.7.9, 11 (*Sīmantonnayana*). This meal is offered to a barber 9.7 (*Cūḍākaraṇa*). This is an oblatory material at the *Anvaṣṭakā* ĀśvGṛ. II.5.2.

केशवपन *Keśavapana* (√*vap*, cl.1 "to shave") n. rite of shaving, in which an initiate's hair is shaved (*pravapati*) by his teacher (later, however, by a barber); the shaved hair is collected by the initiate's mother into a vessel filled with a lump of bull's dung, and she strews barley grain over the dung; the hair finally is disposed of at the roof of an *udumbara* tree or in a tuft of *darbha* grass ĀpGṛ. X.8 (*Upanayana*).

°*vinayana* n. act of separating hair, to be cut and made into tufts on the head (*vinīya*) ĀpGṛ. XVI.6 (*Cūḍākaraṇa*).

केशान्त *Keśānta* m. =*Godāna*, the rite of shaving hair and beard at the 16th year PGṛ. II.1.7.

कौटुम्ब *Kauṭumba* mfn. any object which belongs to the household (*kuṭumba*), to be fetched before one mounts a chariot ĀśvGṛ. II.6.10.

क्षपण *Kṣapaṇa*(√*kṣap*, cl.1 "to be abstinent") n. interruption (temporary) of the veda-study for a period of 3 days and 3 nights both at the *Upākarman* and *Utsarjana*, and for 1 day and 1 night at the *Aṣṭakās* ŚGṛ. IV.5.17; done by reciting the *sāvitrī* 4 times PGṛ. II.12.3-4. Cf. Mn. IV.119.

क्षार (अन्न) *Kṣāra* (*anna*) n. pungent food, unacceptable as sacrificial food for the *Pākayajñas* ĀpGṛ. VIII.3.

क्षिप्रंसुवन *Kṣipraṁsuvana* n. a rite by which quick delivery is sought ĀpGṛ. XIV.13=*Kṣipraprasavana* HGṛ. II.2.8. See *Soṣyantīkarman*.

क्षुद्रसूक्त *Kṣudrasūkta* n. short hymns of RV (X. 129-191), of which an *anuvāka* is to be recited by an initiate at the time of his vedic study ŚGṛ. II.7.21.

क्षुर *Kṣura* m. razor, made of iron or copper (*loha*° ŚGṛ. I.28.7, *āyasa*° GGṛ. II.9.17), used for shaving hair at *Cūḍākaraṇa*, *Godāna* ĀpGṛ. XVI.9.

ख Kha

खर *Khara* mfn.m. a mound of earth, 6 in number, built to the south of *karṣū* (q.v.), and on which fire is set up for offering *piṇḍas* to the manes KāGṛ. LXV.4-6 (*Anvaṣṭakā*). See Śrauta.

ग Ga

गणकाम *Gaṇakāma* mfn. a teacher who is "desirous of obtaining *gaṇa*"; he should recite the *mantra* RV. II.23.1 SGṛ. II.2.13. (*Upanayana*) G° is translated as host of adherents, Oldenberg SBE XXIX, 63, which is, however, not clear. G° probably means a clan, and it refers to the primitive clan initiation.

गर्भरक्षण *Garbharakṣaṇa* n. rite of the protection of the embryo, performed on the 4th month of pregnancy, in which 6 oblations from the mess of cooked food are offered ŚGṛ. I.21.1-2. See *Anavalobhana*.

गर्भाधान *Garbhādhāna* n. rite of impregnation, performed before the sexual intercourse which takes place on the 4th day of the marriage; generally known as *Caturthīkarman*. But treated as a separate rite BṛUp. VI.4.13, 19-22. Cf H.Dh.II(1), 201-02. As the marriageable age of a girl was lowered C° was pushed aside, and its place was taken by G°, performed as a separate rite long after the marriage.

गर्भाष्टम *Garbhāṣṭama* m. the eight year of a child reckoned from the date of conception, i.e. the 7th year of birth in which the *Upanayana* is performed ĀpGṛ. X.2. Cf. similar other reckonings, *garbhaikādaśa*, the 11th year; *garbhadvādaśa* ĀśvGṛ. I.19.1-7. See *Upanayana*.

गृह्य *Gṛhya* mfn. (pl.) relatives of a bride, "dwelling in the house", a term used to distinguish the bridegroom's representatives who are called *āvahamāna* ŚGṛ. I.6.4.

गोत्रनामन् *Gotranāman* n. name of the clan of bridegroom, to be declared by the relatives of the bridegroom before asking a girl in marriage ŚGṛ. I.6.4.

°*sambandha* m. relation between a brahmin and the sacrificer through a common *gotra* (=*sagotra*); such a brahmin is debarred from the feast ĀpGṛ. XXI.2 (*Māsiśrāddha*).

asagotrā f. a bride not having the same *gotra* of her husband HGṛ. I.19.2.

गोदान *Godāna* (√*dā/do*, cl.6 "to cut") n. rite of shaving hair or beard of a boy, performed in his 16th year. In this rite whole hair is clean shaved without leaving locks (*śikhā*), in contrast to the *Caula* or *Cūḍākaraṇa* rite ĀpGṛ. XVI.12, 15, ĀśvGṛ. I.18.6. G° is identical with *Cūḍākaraṇa* ŚGṛ. I.28.19, and *Keśānta* PGṛ. II.1.7, but according to KāGṛ. XLIV.2 it follows the pattern of *Jātakarman*.

°*vrata* n. vow connected with G° ĀpGṛ. XVI. 14, for the *sāmavedins* GGṛ. III.1.

गोयज्ञ *Goyajña* m. rite for obtaining a thriving condition for cows, in which boiled rice with milk is offered GGṛ., III.6.10; performed in the paradigm of the *Śūlagava* PGṛ. III.8.15.

गोरालम्भ *Gorālambha* m. slaughtering of cow, done on 3 occasions : reception of guests, rites to the *pitṛ*s and in marriage ĀpGṛ. III. 10 (apparently, ĀpGṛ leaves out the *Śūlagava*); in honour of the deceased PGṛ. III. 10.49. In the *Aṣṭakā* its omentum (*vapā*) is cooked and offered; with its meat *māṁsaudana* is prepared and offered. A portion of the flesh is kept aside to be served at the dinner for the brahmins in the *Anvaṣṭakā* (next day) ĀpGṛ. XXII.3-5 (Sudarśana comments : *vapāhomānte gorviśasanaṁ kārayitvā anvaṣṭakābrāhmaṇabhojanavyañjanārthaṁ māṁsam avaśiṣya*). At the marriage a cow is slaughtered by the bride's father in honour of the guest III.6 and of the bridegroom; and of the newly married couple after their return to the husband's house ŚGṛ. I.12.10, of a student at the *Samāvartana* ĀpGṛ. XIII.15-17 (this is called *apaciti* ĀśvGṛ. I.24.8). The ritual of beef eating is too repugnant to the feelings of Sudarśana (ca 1550 A.D.) who warns the devout by saying that the cow slaughter is considered one of the improprieties (*anācāra*) of the *Kali* era, and therefore the practice is to be abandoned now (on ĀpGṛ. XIII.16). See also *matasna*, *śūla*, *hṛdaya*.

गोष्ठ *Goṣṭha* m. cow pen, where the remainder of *pṛṣadājya* mixed with water is poured out ĀpGṛ. XV.4 (*Jātakarman*).

ग्रामवचन *Grāmavacana* n. instructions of the village (community), which are to be followed at the wedding besides what is laid down in the ritual texts PGṛ. I.8.11; at the wedding and funerals, it is enjoined, *grāmaṁ prāviśatāt* : let ye, resort to the village, quoted from the authority, and therefore on these two occasions the authority lies with the village 12-13 (*grāmapramāṇam*).

Oldenberg SBE XXIX, 285 reads *praviśatāt* and takes it in the sense of entering the village, literally. But this would hardly make any sense since in those days people lived in a village. ĀpGṛ. I.1 states that all domestic ceremonies are derived from custom (and not from the śruti). Cf. *āvṛt*.

In the same sense *grāmadharma*, *janapadadharma* (q.v.) ĀśvGṛ. I.7.1.

ग्रुमुष्टि *Grumuṣṭi* m. a great (=*guru*) handful of sacrificial grass. *darbha*° ĀpGṛ. XX..11.

ग्लप्स *Glapsa* m. a bunch (of *udumbara* fruit), used at the *Sīmantonnayana* for parting hair ĀpGṛ. XIV.3, ĀśvGṛ. I.14.4;=*grapsa* PGṛ. I.15.4.

च Ca

चतुरवत्तिन् *Caturavattin* mfn. a sacrificer who takes four *avadāna* portions of the sacrificial food : from the middle and the east side GGṛ. I.8.6.

चतुरस्र *Caturasra* mfn. "four-cornered", a quadrangle, the shape of a *sthaṇḍila* ŚGṛ. I.7.2. See *caturaśra* (Śrauta).

चतुर्थविसर्ग *Caturthavisarga* m. abandonment of the fourth generation; the rule that only three higher generations are entitled to get *piṇḍa* on their attaining the realm of manes after *Ekoddiṣṭa*; the 4th generation, *pra-pra-pitāmaha*, though one of the *pitṛs*, is to be omitted at the regular *Pārvaṇaśrāddha* ŚGṛ. IV.2.8. Cf. Oldenberg SBE XXIX, 109.

चतुर्थीकर्मन् *Caturthīkarman* n. rite of consummation of marriage, performed on the 4th day (whence the name) by the husband after observing the period of continence for 3 nights (*trirātra*, cf. *adhaḥśayyā*); this is considered a part of the wedding ceremony.

After removing the staff (*daṇḍa*), the husband offers a *homa* ĀpGṛ. VIII.9-10, with 8 oblations to various deities ŚGṛ. I.18.3; he offers a *sthālīpāka* to Prajāpati, pours the remainders into a waterpot from which he sprinkles water on the head of his wife. She eats the mess of cooked food. The husband besmears her body or the region of her heart with *ājya* ĀpGṛ. VIII.10, GGṛ. II.5.6. After the rite sexual intercourse can take place, and after each of her monthly courses ŚGṛ. I.18-19, ĀpGṛ. VIII.9-13, PGṛ. I.11, GGṛ. II.5, HGṛ. I.23.11; 24.1-8. The rite indicates that the bride attained puberty at the time of marriage. Cf. H.Dh.II(1), 202-04. See also *Garbhādhāna*.

चरु *Caru* m. ŚGṛ I.3.3; °*sthālī* f. GGṛ. I.3.8. See Śrauta section.

चातुष्प्राश्यपचन *Cātuṣprāśyapacana* n. cooking of the food for the 4 officiating priests, done at the *Ādheya*; the ceremonies connected with it are to be followed at the time of setting up of the *āvasathya* (domestic) fire PGṛ. I.2.4.

चात्र *Cātra* n. a spindle, filled with thread, used for parting the hair upwards PGṛ. I.15.4 (*Sīmantonnayana*).

चित्य *Citya* mfn. piled up fire-altar (*Cayana*); if it is touched one should discontinue reading the veda GGṛ. III.3.34. Cf. *anadhyāya*.

चूडाकरण *Cūḍākaraṇa* n. rite of preparing the locks on the child's head ŚGṛ. I.28.1; also called *Caula* ĀpGṛ. XVI.3. The tonsure ceremony is performed in the 3rd year (or the time can vary according to the caste), for a girl without *mantra* ĀśvGṛ. I.17.19. The utensils are filled with various grains; the child sits on the mother's lap; the father moistens the child's head with warm and cold water and curds, and shaves with a copper razor; the mother puts its hair in bull's dung. The number of locks of hair to be kept may be 1 or 3 or 5 BGṛ. II.4, or according to the family custom PGṛ. II.1.22, or according to the number of the *pravara* ĀpGṛ. XVI.6. KāGṛ mentions that the Vasiṣṭhas keep locks (*kapujā*) on the right, the Atris on both sides, the Bhṛgus have their heads clean shaved, the Aṅgirasas have 5 locks or a line of hair XL. 2-6. See also *kapucchala*. ŚGṛ. I.28.1-17, Āśv Gṛ. I.17.1-19, PGṛ. II.1.1-25, GGṛ. II.9.1-29. (°*karman*) HGṛ. II.6.1-20.

चैत्ययज्ञ *Caityayajña* m. rite dedicated to a sanctuary near a village in which *bali* is offered; if the *caitya* is at a distant place the *bali* is put in a leaf of *palāśa* which serves as a messenger (*palāśadūta*) ĀśvGṛ. I.12.1-2.

C° is explained as, *citte bhavaḥ*, i.e. this rite is performed if one has promised to a deity that he would offer him an oblation on fulfilment of his particular desire Nārāyaṇa comm on ib. Cf. Oldenberg SBE XXIX, 178.

चैत्री *Caitrī* f. rite performed on the fullmoon day of *caitra* ŚGṛ. IV.19=*Īśānabali* ĀpGṛ. XIX.13. See *Śūlagava*.

चौल *Caula* n. See *Cūḍākaraṇa*.

छ Cha

छत्र *Chatra* m. n. parasol, one of the things held by a student ĀpGṛ. XII.11 (*Samāvartana*).

छन्ना *Channā* (√*chad*, cl.1 "to cover") f. roof of a house; when erected, is touched by uttering *mantra* HGṛ. I.27.8.

छवि *Chavi* f. hide (of an ass), worn by an *avakīrṇin* (q.v.) in the *Gardabhejyā* (Śrauta, q.v.) PGṛ III.12.6. Cf. *adhīvāsa*, *kṛṣṇājina* (Śrauta), *ajina* (Gṛhya).

ज Ja

जनपदधर्म *Janapadadharma* m. customs of the country, which along with the customs of village (*grāma*°), are multiform, and are to be followed at the wedding ĀśvGṛ. I.7.1. See *ācārika, āvṛt, grāmavacana.*

जन्मतिथि *Janmatithi* m. birthday (lunar) ŚGṛ. I.25.5; a rite performed to such a day every month ib. 10.

जन्य *Janya* mfn. m. belonging to *jana* (people RV. IV.55.5; IX.49.2); friend or companion of a bridegroom (RV.IV.38.6), who fills up a cup with "firm water" (water which does not dry up), and another holding a whip or goad (*prajana*) stands near the fire GGṛ. II.1.13-14. (*Vivāha*)

जय *Jaya* m. victory, the name of a *mantra* TS. III.4.4 which, when used in a subordinate oblation, is supposed to produce victory PGṛ. I.5.7, ĀpGṛ. II.7.

जरायु *Jarāyu* (from ?√*jṛ*, cl.1 "to waste away") n. the outer skin of the embryo (as distinguished from *ulba*), which is caused to come out of the womb by sprinkling water on the mother accompanied with *mantras* ĀpGṛ. XIV.15 (*Puṁsavana*).

जातकर्मन् *Jātakarman* n. rite for the newborn child, both male and female (for the latter, performed without *mantra* ĀśvGṛ. I.15.10) ŚGṛ. I.24.1. For a son a cake on 12 *kapālas* to Vaiśvānara is offered TS. II.2.5.

It is composed of several elements, and the sūtras differ considerably over the sequence and details of these elements.

aṁsābhimarśana n. touching the shoulders of the child who is taken on the lap and kissed by the father with the *vātsapra* hymn ĀpGṛ. XV.1; with the *v°* *mantra* and another *mantra* "be stone, be an axe" ĀśvGṛ. I.15.3, PGṛ. I.16.8, 16, or the father puts an axe on a stone, a piece of gold on the axe, and then these things are turned upside down and thereafter the child is held on them HGṛ. II.3.2.

āyuṣya n. rite for obtaining longevity of a child by muttering *mantra* near his right ear or navel before the navel string is cut PGṛ. I. 16.3, 6; or at the time of feeding the child with honey and butter ĀśvGṛ. I.15.1, ŚGṛ. I.24.4 (but the rite is not specially mentioned there).

deśābhimantraṇa n. addressing and touching the spot where the child is born PGṛ. I.17.17, HGṛ. II.3.8; also called the touching (*abhimarśana*) of the earth (*pṛthivī*) ĀpGṛ. XV.5.

nāmakaraṇa n. rite of name giving; two names, one secret name known to the parents, another for common use. Patañjali refers to the custom that the parents give name to their newborn son in a closed room or space (*saṁvṛta avakāśa*) Mbh. I.1.3.1 on *yathā laukikavaidikeṣu*.

The date of name giving is a matter of controversy : the secret name on the day the child is born, and the ordinary name on the 10th day ŚGṛ. I.24.5-6; the order is reversed Āśv Gṛ. I.15.4-8; the name given on the birth day is to be used on the day for naming, or optionally a second name may be given KāGṛ. XXXVI.3-4. 2 names, but dates not specified HGṛ. II.4.11-14; only one name on the 10th day of the birth of the child ĀpGṛ. XV.8, PGṛ I.17.1.

On that day the child is bathed and dressed. Names should be composed of 2 or 4 syllables; beginning with a sonant; containing a semi-vowel; prefixed with *su*; or composed of 2 parts, a noun and a participle, e.g. Devadatta. Names for girls are to contain an odd number of syllables, ending in *ā* (PGṛ), *dā* (GGṛ II.8.16). Cf. H.Dh.II(1), 238-54.

nighrāpaṇa or *pañcabrāhmaṇasthāpana* n. rite of breathing over the child from 5 directions by 5 brahmins who say : *prāṇa* (up-breathing) from the east, *vyāna* (back-breathing) from the south, *apāna* (down-breathing) from the west, *udāna* (out-breathing) from the north and *samāna* (on-breathing) looking upwards (by the 5th one) PGṛ. I.16.10-15; even the father can do it if the brahmins are not available ŚGṛ. I.24.2. Cf. ŚBr. XI.8.3.6.

mātaramabhimantraṇa n. rite of addressing the mother with the verse—"thou art Iḍā, the daughter of Mitra and Varuṇa; thou strong woman hast borne a strong son. Be thou blessed with strong children, thou who hast blessed us with a strong son" by the father PGṛ. I.16.19; with the verse : "may no demon harm thy son etc." HGṛ. II.4.2.

medhājanana n. rite for generating intelligence. The word *vāk* (speech) is muttered over his right ear ŚGṛ. I.24.9; 2 ears ĀśvGṛ. I.15.2; by feeding the child, before the navel string is cut off, with honey and ghee with the accompaniment of *vyāhṛti* PGṛ. I.16.3-4, HGṛ. II.4.9, GGṛ. II.7.20.

stanapradāna n. rite of giving the breast to the child by the father who washes the breasts of the mother and gives them with *mantras* PGṛ. I.16.20-21.

snāpana n. rite of bathing the child on its day of birth ĀpGṛ.XV.4, HGṛ. II.3.10.

homa (or *phalīkaraṇa°*) m. oblation of mustard seeds mixed with rice chaff offered with the joined palms into the fire (the *sūtikāgni* which replaces the domestic fire, *aupāsana* PGṛ. I.16.23) for 10 days from the date of the child's birth ĀpGṛ. XV.6-7. Cf. HGṛ. II.3. 7. The rite is not mentioned in ĀśvGṛ & ŚGṛ. Cf. BṛUp.VI.4.24-28, H.Dh. II(1), 228-54.

जीवपुत्रा *Jīvaputrā* mfn.f. woman whose sons are all alive ĀpGṛ. VI.11; see *puṁsū*.

जीवितावभृथ *Jīvitāvabhṛtha* m. *avabhṛtha* bath of the life, i.e. death, since the a° occurs at the end of sacrifice to indicate its conclusion GGṛ. I.3.13.

ज्ञातिकर्मन् *Jñātikarman* (√*jñā* cl.9 "to know") n. rites performed by the near relatives (female) at the wedding GGṛ. II.1.11.

त Ta

तण्डुल *Taṇḍula* m. grains of any variety, used as sacrificial food ŚGṛ. I.3.10.

तन्त्र *Tantra* n. ĀśvGṛ. I.10.26. See Śrauta section.

तर्क *Tarka* m. inquiry into the meaning of the rituals, to be considered a part of the veda PGṛ. II.6.5.

तर्पण *Tarpaṇa* (√*tṛp*, cl.4 "to be pleased") n. water libation which "satiates" the *ācārya*s GGṛ. III.3.12 (*Upākaraṇa*); offered, after studying the vedas, to the deities, *ṛṣi*s, the manes etc. ĀśvGṛ. III.4. Cf. ŚGṛ. IV.9 & 10 in which, however, it is not clear what is the occasion for t°. Cf. Oldenberg SBE XXIX, 120.

तानूनप्त्रिन् *Tānūnaptrin* m. one who has performed the rite directed to *Tanūnaptṛ*; if such a person dies his fellow performers will observe *anadhyāya* for 3 nights PGṛ. II.11.8. Cf. Oldenberg SBE XXIX, 324.

ताम्बल *Tāmbala* mfn. m. stated be synonym of *śaṇa* with which a *raśanā=mekhalā* (q.v.) is made GGṛ. II.10.10 (*Upanayana*).

तित्तिर *Tittira* m. a partridge, whose flesh is used as food for a child at *Annaprāśana* ĀpGṛ. XVI.2; prescribed for those who are desirous of the lustre of Brahman (*brahmavarcasa*) ŚGṛ. I.27.3.

तिल *Tila* m. sesamum seeds, used generally as one of the ingredients of *piṇḍa* (q.v.) ĀśvGṛ II.5.2.

तीर्थ *Tīrtha* n. a sacred river (bathing place) ĀpGṛ. V.26; or a water reservoir (*bhūmiṣṭha*, comm) into which a student takes his ceremonial bath at the end of his study XIII.1 (*Samāvartana*).

तूर्यन्ती *Tūryantī* f. said to be a wild plant which blossoms at midday; its flowers are yellow, and leaves white; laid down at the feet of one's wife to secure quick delivery of child ĀpGṛ. XIV.14 & comm (*Puṁsavana*).

तृप्तिप्रश्न *Tṛptipraśna* m. the question whether the brahmins or guests are satiated with the *Śrāddha* meal, formally asked by the performer of *Śrāddha*, and also at the *Ekoddiṣṭa* ceremony ŚGṛ. IV.2.5. Cf. Mn. III.251.

तेजनी *Tejanī* f. mat or couch made of straw or reeds PGṛ. I.5.2 (*Vivāha*).

तैजस *Taijasa* (from *tejas* n. sharpness, splendour) mfn. consisting of hard metal, a vessel ĀśvGṛ. IV.7.10.

तैषीपक्ष *Taiṣīpakṣa* m. the fortnight (that precedes) the fullmoon of the month of *tiṣa* (December-January), the time for performing the *Utsarjana* rite HGṛ. II.18.8.

त्रिरात्र *Trirātra* n. the three nights during which the newly married couple should refrain from sexual intercourse (*brahmacarya*), though they are to sleep together on the same bed on the ground (*adhaḥśayyā*, q.v.); the sleeping place being interposed by a staff (*daṇḍa*) of *udumbara* wood, anointed with perfumes and wrapped round with a garment or thread; the staff is removed on the 4th night with appropriate *mantra*s ĀpGṛ. VIII.8-10.

त्रिवृत् *Trivṛt* mfn. three-fold; said of a *mekhalā* (girdle), made of *muñja* grass (*mauñjī*) twisted in 3 folds ĀpGṛ. X.11 (*Upanayana*).

त्रेणी *Treṇī* f. having white spots (variegated) at 3 places, said of the *Śalalī* bristle ĀpGṛ. XIV.3 (*Sīmantonnayana*), XVI.6 (*Cūḍākaraṇa*).

त्वग्बिल *Tvagbila* mfn. a ladle (*darvī*), "having the cavity on the bark side"; having a handle measuring 1 *aratni* BhGṛ. I.1 (*Upanayana*). Cf *haṁsamukhaprasekā* K. Śr. I.3.37 & comm.

द Da

दक्षिणा *Dakṣiṇā* f. sacrificial fees; a vessel full of grain, or only a bull ĀpGṛ VII.16, 18; a vessel filled with food, cooked or uncooked, or filled with fruit is the lowest, while the highest is unlimited; for instance, one Paijavana gave 100,000 cows as fee at the *sthālīpāka* to Indra and Agni GGṛ. I.9.10-12.

दण्ड *Daṇḍa* m. a wooden staff, held and carried by an initiate in *Upanayana*; its material varies according to the caste of the initiate; of *palāśa* wood for a *brāhmaṇa*. *nyagrodha* having a tip at the down-turned end for a *kṣatriya* (=*rājanya*), *badara* or *udumbara* for a *vaiśya* or any wood irrespective of caste ĀpGṛ. XI. 16-17, ĀśvGṛ.I. 19.13; 20.1. The size also varies ŚGṛ. II.1.21-23 (*Upanayana*).

Another staff, perfumed, and wrapped with a garment, is placed between the bedstead of the newly married couple as a symbol of continence (Cf. *trirātra*) ĀpGṛ. VIII.9-10 (*Vivāha*).

दधि *Dadhi* n. curds, consumed by the newly married couple ŚGṛ. I.17.1 (*Vivāha*).

°*mantha* m. porridge of flour (*saktu*) mixed with curds ĀśvGṛ. II.5.2 (*Anvaṣṭakā*).

दन्तधावन *Dantadhāvana* (°*prakṣālana*) n. act of cleansing the teeth by a student with an *udumbara* twig PGṛ. II.6.17 (*Samāvartana*); the tooth-cleaner is addressed with a *mantra* ib. 32.

दर्भ *Darbha* m. sacrificial grass (*kuśa*), strewn round the fire ĀpGṛ. I.12, offered to the manes with southward pointed blades ib. 14, used for wiping the sacrificial implements ib. II.1.

°*piñjalī* f. a bunch of d° with which the hair is parted thrice GGṛ. II.7.5, (*piñjūla*) PGr. I. 15.4, °*pūñjīla* ĀpGṛ XIV. 3 (*Sīmantonnayana*).

°*stamba* m. tuft of grass on which the cut up hair of an initiate is disposed of ĀpGṛ. X.8 (*Upanayana*).

darbheṇva n. a web or network (*iṇva*) of d°, which is placed over the head of a bride IV.8 (*Vivāha*). See *iṇva*.

दर्वी *Darvī* f. a spoon, made of *udumbara* wood HGr. II.15.7 (*Śrāddha*). °*homa* m. I.3. 1-2. see Śrauta section.

दशा *Daśā* f. skirt of a lower garment (*antaram vāsas*) of a student, to which 2 earrings are tied before an oblation is offered ĀpGṛ. XII.9 (*Samāvartana*).

दायाद्य (काल) *Dāyādya* (*kāla*) m. division of inheritance, the time when the domestic fire is kindled ŚGṛ. I. 1.4, PGṛ. 1.2.2.

दारगुप्ति *Dāragupti* f. rite performed for guarding one's wife from her paramour HGṛ. I.14.6. See *asambhavepsu*, *āḍhārikā*.

दास *Dāsa* m slave ĀpGṛ. XXIII. 7. See *utūla*, *karmakara*.

दुहितृमत् *Duhitṛmat* mfn. a person who has only daughters; he receives a gift of 100 cows with a chariot ŚGṛ. I. 14.16, PGṛ. I.8.18, as a compensation from the bridegroom for marrying a girl who has no brother. Cf. Oldenberg SBE XXIX, 39.

दृषद्पुत्र *Dṛṣadputra* m. a small (upper) millstone (=*upalā*, comm), used for grinding the *nyagrodha* shoot ĀpGṛ. XIV. 11 (*Puṁsavana*).

देवर *Devara* m. brother-in-law, who is to the widow a representative of her dead husband; he causes her to rise from the funeral pyre ĀśvGṛ. IV.2.18. Cf. *patittha* (Śrauta section).

देहली *Dehalī* f. threshhold (wooden) of a door, on which a bride should not stand on her arrival at the bridegroom's house ĀpGṛ. VI. 9.

ध Dha

धाना *Dhānā* f. See *sambhāra*.

ध्रुव *Dhruva* m. "fixed"; the pole star, shown to a bride ĀpGṛ. VI.12.

न Na

नग्निका *Nagnikā* f. "naked girl", i.e. one who has not attained puberty, said to be the best bride GGṛ. III. 4.6, HGṛ. I. 19.2. But comm on MGṛ. I.7.8 takes the word n° in the literal sense, and explains that even an ugly girl can look beautiful by means of toilet and garments but a naked girl (*vivastrā*) cannot.

The preference for the child marriage is obviously a later development otherwise the *trirātravrata* becomes redundant. See also *malavadvāsā, Caturthīkarman, Garbhādhāna.*

नवनीत *Navanīta* n. "newly brought", i.e. fresh butter ŚGṛ. I. 28.7 (*Cūḍākaraṇa*).

नवप्राशन *Navaprāśana* n. rite for eating the new fruit of the harvest, performed by a person who has not set up the *śrauta* fire PGṛ. III. 1 = *Āgrayaṇa*.

नवस्वस्तर *Navasvastara* m. bed of fresh grass on which the entire family sleeps at the *Pratyavarohaṇa* ĀpGṛ. XIX. 9.

नापित *Nāpita* m. barber who shaves hair and receives gift ŚGṛ. I. 28.24 (*Cūḍākaraṇa*).

(स) नाभि (*Sa*) *Nābhi* mfn. persons having the same "navel (womb)", i.e. of the same uterine relation (RV. IX. 89.4) ĀpGṛ. XX.18 (*sapiṇḍa*, comm).

°*kṛntana* (√*kṛt*, cl. 6 "to cut") n. act of cutting the umbilical cord of the newborn baby GGṛ. II. 7.17 (*Jātakarman*).

°*deśa* m. navel of a bride, touched by a bridegroom HGṛ. I. 21.4 (*Vivāha*).

नामकरण *Nāmakaraṇa* n. See *Jātakarman*.

निकक्ष *Nikakṣa* m. armpits, shaved ŚGṛ. I. 28.18 (*Godāna*).

निपरण *Niparaṇa* (*ni*-√*pṛ*, cl. 3 or 9 "to fill") n. act of putting down the *piṇḍa*s for the deceased KāGṛ. LXIII. 14.

नियोजन *Niyojana* n. act of "yoking" (tying) an animal to a *palāśa* branch PGṛ. III.11.2. Cf. K. Śr. VI. 3.27.

(आ) निर्दश (ता) (*Ā*) *Nirdaśa* (*tā*) f. the period until the 10th day (*ānirdaśa*), i.e. a period of 10days (from the day a child is born) during which the *phalīkaraṇa homa* is performed Āp Gṛ. XV. 7 ((*Jātakarman*).

निवीतिन् *Nivītin* mfn. one who wears the sacerd thread round the neck HGṛ. II.19.3.

निवेशन *Niveśana* (*ni*-√*viś*, cl.6 "to enter, to come to rest") n. a resting place in a house (*agāra*) ĀpGṛ. XVII. 13 (*Vāstupratiṣṭhā*).

निष्क्रमण *Niṣkramaṇa* n. moving out of the house with the newborn child. A minor rite performed in the 4th month (after birth) in which the father causes the child to look at the sun PGṛ. I. 17.5,6; mentioned as *candradarśana*, performed on the 3rd *tithi* of the third fortnight after the birth of a child. The child is bathed by the father in the morning, and dressed by the mother. The mother passes the child to the father who hands him back to the mother. Then the father makes a libation of water with his joined palms turning his face to the moon GGṛ. II. 8.1-7. KāGṛ. mentions *ādityadarśana* XXXVII and *candradarśana* XXXVIII

निष्ट्या *Niṣṭyā* f. the *svāti* star, Arcturus ĀpGṛ. III. 5 (*Vivāha*).

निह्नवन *Nihnavana* n. rite of begging "pardon" or seeking "evasion" from the *pitṛ*s after offering them the *piṇḍa*s into the pits. The sacrificer lays his hands with the insides turned upwards on the pits, and says "Adoration to you, O Fathers etc." GGṛ. IV.3.17-20, KhGṛ. III. 5.24 (*Anvaṣṭakā*). See Śrauta section.

नीचदक्षिण *Nīcadakṣiṇa* mfn. a person who pays small fees to a priest; the priest should refuse to accept assignments from him ĀśvGṛ. I 23.14. Cf. Oldenberg SBE XXIX, 196.

प Pa

पच्छः *Pacchaḥ* ind. *pāda* by *pāda*, a mode of reciting the *sāvitrī* (TS. I.5.6.4), done by a teacher who recites it at the *Upanayana pāda* by *pāda* preceded or followed by the *vyāhṛtis* (as distinguished from the *ardharcaśaḥ* method) ĀpGṛ. XI. 10.

पञ्चब्राह्मणस्थापन *Pañcabrāhmaṇasthāpana* n. See *Jātakarman.*

पञ्चमहायज्ञ *Pañcamahāyajña* m. five great sacrifices (which are called *sattras* ŚBr. XI. 5.6.1), performed after the *Samāvartana* or *Vivāha* PGṛ. II.9=*Pañcayajña* ĀśvGṛ. III.1 consisting of (1) oblations into the fire, a sacrifice to gods (*devayajña*), (2) *bali* offerings, a sacrifice to the beings (*bhūtayajña*), (3) *piṇḍa* offerings to the manes (*pitṛyajña*), (4) study of the vedic texts, a sacrifice to *Brahman* (*brahmayajña*), and (5) giving away to men, a sacrifice to men (*mānuṣayajña*); these rites are performed daily.

पञ्चावत्तिन् *Pañcāvattin* mfn. a sacrificer, belonging to the family of Bhṛgu, who takes 5 *avadāna*s from the sacrificial food, 3 from the middle and 1 each from the east and the west sides of the food GGṛ. I. 8.6.

पतितसावित्रीक *Patitasāvitrīka* m. a person who has lost the right of learning the *sāvitrī*, and is, consequently, ostracized from the social and religious life owing to his failure to get initiated at proper age ŚGṛ. II.1.9-13 (*Upanayana*). The lost sacrament may, however, be regained and the study of vedas resumed by performing the *Vrātyastoma* (see Śrauta section) PGṛ. II.5.43.

पत्नी *Patnī* f. the wife of a sacrificer performs a minor role in the gṛhya rite. According to the comm. She cannot on her own pour oblation into the fire, although she holds the oblatory material in her hand ĀpGṛ. V.6. According to some authority she may offer morning and evening oblations into the domestic fire, since a wife is called the sacrificer's house GGṛ. I 3.15

(*preta*)° ĀśvGṛ. IV.2.16-17. See Śrauta section.

patnyaudana m.n. a portion of rice taken from the mess of food, offered to the wife of Rudra HGṛ. II.8.7. (*Śūlagava*)

परमेष्ठिकरण *Parameṣṭhikaraṇa* n. act of setting the domestic fire (*parameṣṭhin=agni*, comm), to be done by the eldest of the family after the death of the householder GGṛ. I.1.12. Cf. Oldenberg SBE XXIX, 13; XXX, 15. See *Ādhāna.*

परशु *Paraśu* **m. an axe on which a newborn baby is laid HGṛ. II.3.2.**

परिचरणीया *Paricaraṇīyā* **(mfn.) f. waters with which different acts are performed, fetched in the evening and morning before the setting of fire GGṛ. I.1.24.**

परिणय *Pariṇaya* **(*pari-√nī*, cl. 1 "to lead around") m. act of leading the bride thrice round the fire (*agnipradakṣiṇa*) and the water jar, done by the bridegroom who recites the** *mantra* : *amohamasi* ĀśvGṛ. I.7.6 (*Vivāha*). **This is one of the several acts that constitute the ceremony of marriage, hence the word is a synonym of *Vivāha*.**

परिदा *Paridā* **f. rite of granting protection to the wife who has given birth to a child** BhGṛ. I.23.

परिदान *Paridāna* **n. rite of "giving away the initiate in charge" (of Prajāpati ?) by his teacher who says : "Whose *brahmacārin* art thou ? The breath's *brahmacārin* art thou. Who dost initiate thee and whom (dost he initiate) ? To whom shall I give thee in charge ?" The last line is translated : I give thee to Prajāpati (Ka) ĀśvGṛ. I.20.8** (*Upanayana*). Cf. Oldenberg SBE XXIX, 189, H.Dh. II(1), 282.

परिधि *Paridhi* **m. enclosure of 3 sticks called** *śamyā* round the fire HGṛ. I.2.1.

°*saṁdhi* m. the joint of p° ib. 3. **See Śrauta** section.

परिपशव्य *Paripaśavya* mfn. PGṛ. III.11.3. **See** Śrauta section.

परिव्ययण *Parivyayaṇa* n. PGṛ. III.11.2. (round a *palāśa* branch instead of *yūpa*). **See** Śrauta section.

परिश्रित *Pariśrita* m.n. enclosure (shed), erected round the fire, having a door to the north side of the shed ĀśvGṛ. II.5.2 (*Anvaṣṭakā*).

परिषद् *Pariṣad* f. an assembly of men, to which a *mantra* is addressed as a charm for winning victory in disputes HGṛ. I.15.7-8.

परिषेचन *Pariṣecana* (*pari-√sic*, cl.6 "to sprinkle round") n. act of sprinkling waters round the fire, done in various directions, accompanied with *mantras* ĀpGṛ. II.3; but silently at the ceremonies to the manes (*pitṛs*) 4; at the marriage V.13, at the *sthālīpāka* VII.14. **See** ***paryukṣaṇa.***

परिसमूहन *Parisamūhana* n. ĀśvGṛ. I.3.1 (round the *sthaṇḍila*). See Śrauta section; see also *samūhana*.

परिस्तरण *Paristaraṇa* n. ĀpGṛ. I.12, ŚGṛ. I.8.2. See *agniparistaraṇa* (Śrauta section).

पर्णपुट *Parṇapuṭa* m. n. a basket, made of rolled up *palāśa* leaves, shaped like a funnel, into which a lump of boiled rice is put and hung up on a tree as an offering to Rudra ĀpGṛ. XX.7, HGṛ. II.9.5. (*Śūlagava*)

पर्यग्निकरण *Paryagnikaraṇa* n. act of moving a firebrand three times round the melted butter (*ājya*), contained in the *ājyasthālī*, placed over the fire. This is the lustration of the *ājya* in the rite of *ājyasaṁskāra* (q.v.) PGṛ. I. 1.2, BhGṛ. I.3. Cf. Śrauta section.

पर्युक्षण *Paryukṣaṇa* (*pari*-√*ukṣ*, cl. 6 "to sprinkle round") n. act of sprinkling round the fire as is done in the *śrauta* rite ŚGṛ. I.3.17. See also *pariṣecana*.

पलाशदूत *Palāśadūta* m. a leaf of p°, used as a messenger for carrying *bali* of *piṇḍa*s to the *caitya*; the *piṇḍa*s are put into the leaf ĀśvGṛ. I 12.2 (*Caityayajña*).

°*śākhā* f. a branch of p°, driven into the ground, and used instead of *yūpa* at the domestic animal sacrifice PGṛ. III.11.1.

पवित्र *Pavitra* n. purifiers, made of 2 *kuśa* blades, used for purifying waters ĀpGṛ. I.20, for *ājya* ŚGṛ. I.8.21.

पशुकल्प *Paśukalpa* m. animal sacrifice performed either as a part of the *Aṣṭakā* GGṛ. III. 10.18-36; IV. 1-22, of *Śrāddha* to the manes HGṛ. II. 15.1-14 or as an independent rite ĀśvGṛ. I. 11.1-15. In any case it is a copy of the *Nirūḍhapaśubandha* (See Śrauta). Cf. *Anvaṣṭakā*, *Śūlagava*.

पाक *Pāka* m (fn) "ripening, growing"; said of Kṣetrapati, the lord of fields, to whom an offering of food is to be made very quickly because the god does not stay long (*pākaḥ devaḥ*) ĀpGṛ. XX.15 & comm. HGṛ. II.9.11. Cf. Oldenberg SBE XXX, 224, 291 (*Śūlagava*).

पाकयज्ञ *Pākayajña* m. "sacrifice with cooked offerings" ŚGṛ.I.1.1=*sthālīpāka* or *gṛhyasthālīpāka* PGṛ. I.1.1. The term p° is supposed to designate all the domestic rites in contradistinction to the *haviryajña* (the *śrauta* rites). Cf. Oldenberg SBE XXX, xv; ŚGṛ. I.1.15. Obviously, in imitation of the *haviryajña* and *Soma* the p° is also divided into 7 *saṁsthās*: *Aṣṭakā*, *Pārvaṇa* (=*Sthālīpāka*), *Śrāddha*, *Śrāvaṇī*, *Āgrahāyaṇī*, *Caitrī* and *Āśvayujī*. Cf. Oldenberg ib, ŚGṛ ib.

P° is also classified into 3 or 4 groups depending on the nature and purpose of the oblation offered: (1) *huta* oblation in the *Agnihotra*, (2) *ahuta* (not sacrificed), *bali* offering, (3) *prahuta* (sacrificed up), offerings to the manes and (4) *prāśita* (tasted), offering to a brahmin for tasting ŚGṛ. I.5.1; 10.7. *Huta*, *prahuta* (=*ahuta*) and *brahmaṇihuta* (=*prāśita*) ĀśvGṛ. I.1.2. P° is defined as a ritual connected with the wordly life (*laukika*) ĀpGṛ. II.9, in which *Brahman* is the only priest and the sacrificer performs the office of the *Hotṛ* GGṛ. I.9.8-9.

पाठा *Pāṭhā* f. the plant (Clypea hernandifolia), which is strewn round with 21 barley grains by a wife for winning over her husband's love; its root is secretly tied to the husband's hand for subjugating the co-wife (*sapatnībādhana*) Āp Gṛ. IX.5-6, 8.

पाणिग्रहण *Pāṇigrahaṇa* n. rite of seizing the bride's hand at the marriage ĀśvGṛ. I.9.1. The bridegroom with his right hand, palm down, holds the bride's right hand, palm up ĀpGṛ. IV. 11. The word is a synonym of *Vivāha* since the rite is one of the basic ritual elements of V°. Cf. *pariṇaya*.

पात्र *Pātra* n. sacrificial utensils, placed in pairs turned upside down on the sacrificial ground after strewing sacrificial grass to the north of the fire ĀpGṛ. I.16, before use they are raised up and sprinkled with the *pavitra*s ib. 19.

°*prokṣa* m. sprinkling of p° I.19.

पायस *Pāyasa* m.n. a meal of rice cooked in milk, offered as oblation Āśv Gṛ. II.5.2. (*Anvaṣṭakā*)

पार्वण *Pārvaṇa* m. rite performed on the *parvan* (joint) days which consists of an offering of a mess of cooked food ĀpGṛ. VII.23. See *Sthālīpāka*.

°*śrāddha* n. See *Śrāddha*.

पार्श्व *Pārśva* n. the rib (left) of a cow, offered at the *Anvaṣṭakā* in the manner of the *Piṇḍapitṛyajña* PGṛ. III. 3.10. See also *sakthi*. Cf. *jauhava* (Śrauta).

पिण्ड *Piṇḍa* m. lump of food, mixed with meat or boiled rice or, alternatively, boiled rice with sesamum seeds etc. for the manes, offered with the hands turned downwards, into 2 or 6 pits at *Śrāddha, Anvaṣṭakā* etc. ĀśvGṛ. II.5, HGṛ. II. 12.3, GGṛ. IV. 2.13.

Also lumps of earth, 8 in number, used for testing the quality of a bride ĀśvGṛ. I.5.5 (*Vivāha*).

पित्र्याणि *Pitryāṇi* n. *Śrāddha* rites belonging to the *pitṛs*, performed in the dark fortnight ĀpGṛ. I.7.

पिष्टान्न *piṣṭānna* n. pounded grain, cooked in milk, used as oblation and food for the brahmins ĀpGṛ. XXII.6 (*Ekāṣṭākā*).

पीठचक्र *Pīṭhacakra* n. a chariot with a seat, drawn by cows, used for carrying a dead body at funeral ĀśvGṛ. IV.2.3.

पीयूष *Pīyūṣa* m.n. beestings of a cow, offered in sacrifice for protection of cows ŚGṛ. III.10.3.

पुंसवन *Puṁsavana* (√*su*, cl.5 or 2 "to press out" or "generate") n. literally, a rite for obtaining the birth of a male child; performed in the 2nd month of pregnancy PGṛ. I. 14.2 or in the 3rd ĀśvGṛ. I.13.2 or when pregnancy is visible (*puṁsuvana*) ĀpGṛ. XIV.9. The wife fasts for 3 days and after that her husband gives her to eat a meal of curds mixed with 2 beans and barley. She is asked what she is eating, and she replies thrice : *puṁsavana* (procreation of male child). A pounded herb is inserted into her nostril in a round apartment or a *nyagrodha* shoot pounded by girls who have not attained puberty ĀśvGṛ. I.13.1-7, ĀpGṛ XIV. 9-11. Alternatively, the gall of a tortoise is put on her lap PGṛ. I.14.5. = *Puṁsuvana* ĀpGṛ. XIV.9.

पुंसू *Puṁsū* f. a woman who has given birth to male child (*pum*) only; and all of her children should be alive (*jīvaputrā*). One of her children is placed on the lap of a bride (at the bridegroom's house) ĀpGṛ. VI.11.

पुण्याह *Puṇyāha* n. auspicious day on which the domestic rites are to be performed ĀpGṛ. I.2.

पुनराधान *Punarādhāna* n. re-establishment of fire HGṛ. I.26.22. See Śrauta section.

पुरुपशु *Purupaśu* mfn. rich in animal (cattle), said of a *vaiśya* in whose house the domestic fire is lighted and brought for installation ŚGṛ. I.1.8.

पूर्त *Pūrta* (√*pṛ*. cl.3 "to fill") (mfn.) n. perfected; meritorious work, e.g. digging well, feeding brahmins etc. ĀśvGṛ. II. 5.13.

पूर्वपक्ष *Pūrvapakṣa* m. the first part of a lunar month, i.e. the bright fortnight ĀpGṛ. I.2.

पृषदाज्य *Pṛṣadājya* n. "speckled butter"; *ājya* mixed with curdled milk, used as oblation for the manes ĀśvGṛ. IV. 1.18-19; also as food by an initiate at the *Upanayana* HGṛ. I.4.10.

पृषातक *Pṛṣātaka* m.n. a mixture of clarified butter and curds, offered at the *Āśvayujī* rite ŚGṛ. IV. 16.3; whence the rite itself is called P° GGṛ. III. 8.1.

पौर्णमासी *Paurṇamāsī* f. the day of fullmoon, the time (*kāla*) of which may be reckoned in 3 different ways : *sandhyā*, the time when the fullmoon rises at the "meeting" of day and night, *astamitoditā*, when the moon rises after sunset and *uccaiḥ*, when the moon stands high in the sky at sunset GGṛ. I 5.7, 10. Cf. Oldenberg SBE XXX, 26.

प्रणीता *Praṇītā* f. name of waters, used at *Vivāha* ŚGṛ. I.8.8; the pot for p° is called °*praṇayana* HGṛ. I. 1.20. See Śrauta section.

प्रतिवचन *Prativacana* n. reply of an initiate in response to his teacher's question (*praṣṭa*) ĀpGṛ. XI.2 (*Upanayana*).

प्रतिश्रुत *Pratiśruta* (*prati*-√*śru*, cl. 5 "to promise") n. assent to give away the daughter in marriage by the bride's father ŚGṛ. I.7.1.

प्रत्ता *Prattā* (for *pradattā*) f. a bride who is given away (by her father) in the marriage PGṛ. I.4.15, ĀśvGṛ. IV. 4.23. *aprattā* f. unmarried woman (not given away) ib. 20.

प्रत्यगाशिस् *Pratyagāśis* mfn. m. name of the *mantras* which contain "wishes (benefit) turned inwards", i.e. to the initiate, repeated by him ĀpGṛ. XI.4 (*Upanayana*).

प्रत्यवरोहण *Pratyavarohaṇa* (*prati-ava*-√*ruh*, cl. 1 "to descend again") n. a rite which marks the ceremonial descent of the entire family from a high cot or couch, which was used from the fullmoon of *śrāvaṇa* for fear of snakes ; considered a part of the snake rite ŚGṛ. IV.17.1; sometimes mentioned as a separate rite, performed on the fullmoon day of *mārgaśīrṣa*, i.e. the month of *agrahāyaṇa*; whence the other name of the rite *Āgrahāyaṇī* HGṛ. II.17.1, PGṛ. III.2.1. It can be per-

—formed at the begining of each of the 6 seasons BGṛ. II.10.

By muttering *mantras* the family come down from the high bedstead and lie down on a new layer of straw or grass (*navasvastara*), the father to the south, the mother to his north and the others one after another from the eldest to the youngest. A *sthālīpāka* for Īśāna, and another for Kṣetrapati are offered ĀpGṛ. XIX. 8-14. On this occasion the house is replastered, a new roof added and the floor levelled. Milk-rice (*pāyasa*) is offered to the snakes and *mantras* are muttered while the members of the family lie down on the layer ĀśvGṛ. II.3.1-3. Cf. PGṛ. III.2.5-16, ŚGṛ. IV. 17.

प्रदक्षिण *Pradakṣiṇa* m.n. circumambulation, a movement round an object in which one's right side or hand is always kept turned to the object, as distinguished from the *prasavya* movement. Before the *homa* the bridegroom and the bride go round the fire (*agni*°) at *Vivāha* ĀpGṛ. V. 1; while strewing grass round the fire I.4.

प्रवक्तृ *Pravaktṛ* (*pra*-√*vac*, cl. 2 "to proclaim, to teach") mfn. m. a teacher of the vedas, in whose honour a cow is slaughtered and its omentum cooked ĀpGṛ. XIII. 20 (*Samāvartana*).

प्रवण *Pravaṇa* m.n.? declivity, slope (RV. I.119.3 etc) of a sacrificial ground, which may be inclined either towards the east (*prācīna*°) or the north (*udīcīna*°) or the northeast (*prāgudak*°) HGṛ. I.1.9.

प्रवर्त *Pravarta* m. earring (according to comm), 2 in number, worn by a student at *Samāvartana* ĀpGṛ. XII.9.

प्रवाहय् *Pravāhay* (*pra*-√*vah*, cl.1 caus.) –to carry away a bride in a palanquin (*śibikā*, comm), after unfastening her *yoktra*, to the bridegroom's house ĀpGṛ. V. 13, HGṛ. I.22.1.

प्रष्ट *Praṣṭa m.=praśna* questions asked by a teacher to an initiate: his name, *gotra*, teacher's name etc. ĀśvGṛ. I 20.8; the dialogue between the teacher and the initiate Kauś. S. LV. 9-18 (*Upanayana*). This word is either ungrammatical or a vedic pecularity ĀpGṛ. XI. 2 comm.

प्रसव्य *Prasavya* ind. m. n. movement round an object keeping it always on one's left side, as distinguished from *pradakṣiṇa*. This is done in the *Śrāddha* rites ĀpGṛ. I.9, ĀśvGṛ. IV.7.12.

प्राचीनावीतिन् *Prācīnāvītin* mfn. performer of a *Śrāddha* rite who wears the sacred cord (*upavīta*) in a reverse order (see Śrauta section) ĀpGṛ. I.8.

Alternatively, a person wearing the *upavīta* in the *yajñopavītin* fashion, but performing the Ś° rites with his left hand, or with right hand seized by his left hand will be considered a p° ĀśvGṛ. IV.7.13. This method of p° is elaborated further as: if the hand with which the rite is performed and the shoulder over which hangs the sacred cord be either both right or both left the person is a p° Nārāyaṇa comm on ĀśvGṛ. ib.

प्राजन *Prājana* m. a whip or goad, which is held by one of the companions (*janya*) of a bridegroom GGṛ. II.1.14 (*Vivāha*).

प्रातराश *Prātarāśa* m. morning meal, i.e. the breakfast of a student before performing a rite called *uddīkṣaṇikā*, the giving up of the *dīkṣā* ŚGṛ. II.12.1. Cf Oldenberg SBE XXIX, 78-9.

प्रादुष्करण *Prāduṣkaraṇa* n. act of setting the fire in blaze for sacrificing the morning oblation before or after the sunrise GGṛ. I.1.28.

प्राशित *Prāśita* (mfn.) n. "eaten oblations"; a type of oblation, offered in *Pākayajña* (q.v.), which is tasted by the brahmins ŚGṛ. I.10.7. Also one of the 4 types of *Pākayajñas*.

प्रास्थानिक *Prāsthānika* n. ceremony performed at the time of departure of the bridegroom to the bride's house KāGṛ. XXIII.1 (*Vivāha*).

प्रोक्षणी *Prokṣaṇī* f. water for sprinkling, poured into *sruva*, purified (*saṁskāra*) like *ājya* PGṛ. I.1.4, or as is done in *Darśa* but in silence Āp Gṛ. I.19.

प्रोष्य *Proṣya* (*pra*-√*vas*, cl.1 "to go abroad") ind. rite performed on return of the householder from abroad PGṛ. I.18.1. Cf. *viproṣya* the return after a journey GGṛ. II.8.21.

प्रोष्ठपद *Prauṣṭhapada* m. month of *bhādra* (August—September) relating to the *nakṣatra proṣṭhapada* ("foot of a stool") PGṛ. II.15.1. See *Indrayajña*.

फ Pha

फण *Phaṇa* m. a stick or comb, shaped like a snake's hood, which is offered to the serpents ŚGṛ. IV.15.7 (*Śrāvaṇī*).

फलीकरण (होम) *Phalīkaraṇa* n. (*homa* m.) oblation of chaff of rice (mixed with mustard), offered thrice ĀpGṛ. XV.6 (*Jātakarman*).

ब Ba

बन्धु *Bandhu* m. family (=*kula*) ĀpGṛ. III. 19, 20.

बर्हिस् *Barhis* n. sacrificial grass (see Śrauta section), cut off near the roots for the rites to the manes GGṛ. I.5.17.

बलि *Bali* m. gift, offering; used always with √*bhṛ* (cl. 1 or 3 "to carry") RV. I.70.9; V.1. 10 etc., but later with √*hṛ* (cl. 1 "to take") rite of offering (°*haraṇa* n.) the remnant of the sacrificial food to the gods, domestic deities, men, birds and other animals and even to the inanimate objects, e.g. water-pot, door-post; b° is offered on the ground, wiped and cleaned. This occurs in the *Vaiśvadeva* ŚGṛ. II.14, ĀśvGṛ. I.2; *Sarpabali* ĀpGṛ. XIX.2. Cf. GGṛ. I.4.5-15.

It is enjoined that the householder should not eat alone, the food is to be cut up and offered to dogs, dog eaters and birds; one should remember the verse RV.X.117.6: in vain the fool gets food ŚGṛ. II.14.22-26.

°*haraṇī* f. a spoon for offering b° ĀśvGṛ. II. 1.2.

बिल *Bila* n. bowl of a ladle ŚBr. VI.5.2.20.

upabilam ind. upto the hole, i.e. upto the brim HGṛ. I.1.23; a vessel having brims is called *bilavat* ib. 24.

बौढ्यविहार *Baudhyavihāra* m. rite of distribution (*vihāra*) of *palāśa* leaves (=*bauḍhya*, Mātṛdatta comm), forming a part of the *Śūlagava* for propitiating Rudra and his hosts and for averting evil from the cattle and the fields. The leaves are made into a basket (*parṇapuṭa*), and lumps of boiled rice are put into them and offered in oblation HGṛ. II.9. 1-5 (*Śūlagava*). Cf. ĀpGṛ. XX.5.

ब्रह्मचर्य *Brahmacarya* (√*car*, cl. 1 "to wander, move") n. literally, state of wandering in *Brahman*; but technically, the state of continence and penance observed by a religious student (°*cārin* RV. X.109.5) after his initiation (*Upanayana*). He puts on an antelope skin, wears long hair, collects fuel, begs, learns and practises penance AV. XI.5.3-10. This period may last 48 years for 4 vedas (*veda*°) or 12 for each veda or until one has learnt one or more vedas PGṛ. II.5.13-15. This period of b° is opposed by Mī. I.3.3 & Śab. on the ground that a householder being initiated in the 8th year (Cf *garbhāṣṭama*) and having passed 48 years in b° cannot marry until he is 56, and this will run counter to the vedic injunction that the 3 sacred fires are to be consecrated by one who has a son and whose hair is still black. Cf. H.Dh. II(1), 350-51, V.I. on b°

The word also designates sexual continence (Cf *trirātra*) ĀpGṛ. VIII.8.

ब्रह्मचारिवासस् *Brahmacārivāsas* n. the upper and lower garment worn by a student and taken off at the end of *brahmacarya* HGṛ. I.9.10.

ब्रह्मन् *Brahman* m. priest for the domestic rite. See *ṛtvij* (Gṛhya).

brahmasadana n. the seat of B° HGṛ. I.1.22.

ब्राह्मण *Brāhmaṇa* m. a person belonging to the brahmin caste; they are fed at the end of almost all domestic rites, paid fees for their participation in the rite ĀpGṛ. VII.15, 16, PGṛ. I.15.9. Feeding of the brahmins is said to be equivalent to the offerings to *Brahman* (*brahmaṇihutāḥ*, a class of *Pākayajñas*) Āśv Gṛ. I.1.2. At the *Śrāddha* rites and feast the larger their number is, the greater is the reward IV.7.2.

ब्राह्मणावेक्ष *Brāhmaṇāvekṣa* mfn. m. "seen by the Brāhmaṇa texts"; said of the domestic rituals (*Pākayajña*) which are claimed to be based on the ritual prescribed in the Brāhmaṇa texts ĀpGṛ. II.10 & comm.

भ Bha

भद्रपीठ *Bhadrapīṭha* n. soft chair on which the pregnant wife sits PGṛ. I.15.4. (*Sīmantonnayana*)

भसद् *Bhasad* ind. a mystical formula, uttered by the husband when he touches his penis at the time of sexual copulation KāGṛ. XXX.6. Cf *karad.*

bhasada n. vagina ib. 5.

भारद्वाजी *Bhāradvājī* f. name of a bird, whose meat is offered to the child PGṛ. I.19.7 (*Annaprāśana*).

म Ma

मज्जान *Majjāna* m. n. ? marrow of an immolated animal, offered to the manes KāGṛ. LXV.6 (*Anvaṣṭakā*).

मज्जुका *Majjukā* f. soup of the omentum of an animal, cooked on a dish and offered to the manes KāGṛ. LXII.4 (*Aṣṭakā*).

मणि *Maṇi* m. a gold pellet with settings (*upadhāna*) and strung on a thread (*sūtrota*), which is worn by a student ĀpGṛ. XII.8 (*Samāvartana*).

मणिका (अवधान) *Maṇikā* f. (*avadhāna* n.) rite of putting up a water jar on a pit in the dwelling house PGṛ. III.5.1.

मण्डल *Maṇḍala* n. circular space, marked by a line of water and having an entrance either on the east or the north; the teacher and his students enter the circle, and begin the recitation of the sacred texts ŚGṛ. VI.2.5-6; 3.1, 6.

मतस्न *Matasna* (du) n kidneys (or lungs RV. X.163.3 WR), taken out from the immolated cow, roasted along with the other limbs on the *udumbara* spits, sprinkled with *ājya* and offered to the brahmins, who should eat it HGṛ. II.15.5-8 (*Śrāddha*).

मत्स्य *Matsya* m. fish, offered as food to a child for obtaining speed (*javana*) ŚGṛ. I.27.4. (*Annaprāśana*)

मधुपर्क *Madhuparka* m. honey-mixture, either made of 3 substances (*trivṛta*) : curds, honey and clarified butter or 5 substances (*pāṅkta*) : water and ground grains in addition to the above; mixed in a brass vessel, then poured into a smaller one with a bigger covering, and finally offered as an *argha* to a *snātaka* and the *arghya*s along with a bunch of grass, water for washing feet, *arghya* waters, water for sipping HGṛ. I.12.10-14. The rite of reception (*argha*) is called m° in which flesh (of a cow) must be used ĀśvGṛ. I.24.33, ŚGṛ. II.15.2. Therefore a cow which is immolated in the rite is called m° cow ŚGṛ. I.12.10.

°*mantha* m. porridge made of flour mixed with honey; offered to the manes ĀśvGṛ. II.5.2 (*Anvaṣṭakā*).

मन्त्रसंबन्ध *Mantrasambandha* m. a brahmin who is related to the householder by *mantra* (teacher-student relationship). He is debarred from joining in the feast ĀpGṛ. XXI.2(*Śrāddha*).

मन्थ्य *Manthya* mfn. "churned", i.e. fire produced by attrition of the *araṇi*s ĀpGṛ. V.17.

मर्ग *Marga* m.=*mārga*, the path used by cows (*gavām*) ĀpGṛ. XX.12 (*Śūlagava*).

मलवद्वासा *Malavadvāsā* (mfn.) f. woman in "dirty" or "impure" clothes, i.e. in menstruation; after 3 nights she takes a bath to gain her "purity", and thereafter she can cohabit ĀpGṛ. VIII.12 (*Vivāha*). This indicates the custom of post-puberty marriage. Cf. *Garbhādhāna*, *Caturthīkarman* and also *nagnikā*.

महाभारत *Mahābhārata* n. name of the celebrated epic, to be uttered by a student at the end of his religious study, as a part of *tarpaṇa* to the famous teachers like Jaimini and the sacred texts. *Bhārata* n. is also mentioned ĀśvGr. III. 4.4.

मांस *Māṁsa* n. flesh (of cow), used as an offering in the rites to the manes HGṛ. II.13.4; the residue of the meat, used in *Aṣṭakā*, is used in the *Anvaṣṭakā* ĀpGṛ, XXII.11. See *Argha*, *gorālambha*, *madhuparka*.

māṁsaudana m. a sort of pilau, prepared by mixing cooked beef with boiled rice; used as oblation, and also as food eaten by the brahmins ĀpGṛ. XXII.5. (*Aṣṭakā*)

माघ्यावर्ष *Māghyāvarṣa* m. rainy season of *māgha* day, when *Anvaṣṭakya* is performed. But the meaning is doubtful. Cf. Oldenberg SBE XXIX, 103.

m° may designate a variety of the *Aṣṭakā* group of rites. See also *mādhyāvarṣa*.

माणवक *Māṇavaka* m. boy who has been initiated, and therefore has read the vedas GGṛ. II.10.7 (*Upanayana*).

मातरमभिमन्त्रण *Mātaramabhimantraṇa* n. See *Jātakarman*.

मातृयाग *Mātṛyāga* m. a *Śrāddha* ceremony dedicated to the mothers, preceding the rite to the fathers ŚGṛ. IV.4.3.

माध्यावर्ष *Mādhyāvarṣa* (corrupt form of *māghyāvarṣa*, according to Oldenberg SBE XXIX, 103) m. the middle of the year when a variety of the *Aṣṭakā* is performed; in this rite meat offering is compulsory (vegetables are allowed when meat is not available) HGṛ. II.13.3-4. Said to be the time for performing the 4th *Aṣṭakā* in which only vegetables are offered whence called *śākāṣṭakā* PGṛ. III. 3.13.

मार्जन *Mārjana* n. cleaning of body by sprinkling, done by the householder after he has eaten the sacrificial food PGṛ. II.14. 21 (*Śravaṇā*).See Śrauta section.

मासिश्राद्ध *Māsiśrāddha* n. ĀpGṛ. XXI.1. See *Śrāddha*.

मिन्दाहुति *Mindāhuti* f. an oblation for removing fault HGṛ. I.26.7 (*mindā* a physical defect, fault TS. III.2.5.4).

मीढुषी *Mīḍhuṣī* f. the "bountiful goddess" Oldenberg SBE XXX, 290; wife of Īśāna Āp Gṛ. XX.2 comm (*Śūlagava*).

मेक्षण *Mekṣaṇa* n. ladle with which the sacrificial food is sacrificed GGṛ. I.8.2, and thereafter thrown into the fire ib. 19. See Śrauta section.

मेखला *Mekhalā* f. girdle, made of *muñja* grass, twisted in 3 folds (*trivṛt*), tied round an initiate ĀpGṛ. X.11 (*Upanayana*), discarded behind a cow-pen (*vraja*) XII.4, and kept concealed at the root of an *udumbara* tree or in a tuft of grass (*darbhastamba*) ib. 5 (*Samāvartana*).

=*raśanā* f. made of *muñja*, *kāśa* or *tāmbala* (=*śaṇa*, comm) GGṛ. II.10.10 (*Upanayana*).

Cf. *kāyabandhana* Upasak Monastic terms.

मेधाजनन *Medhājanana* n. see *Jātakarman*.

मौञ्जी *Mauñjī* f. *mekhalā* (q.v.), made of *muñja* grass ĀpGṛ. X.11.

य Ya

यज्ञवास्तु *Yajñavāstu* n. rite of the sacrificial ground, performed with a handful of *kuśa* grass, dipped into *ājya*, sprinkled with water and thrown into the fire with a *mantra* addressed to Rudra GGṛ. I.8.26-29.

यज्ञोपवीतिन् *Yajñopavītin* mfn. one who wears the sacred thread over the left shoulder and under the right armpit at all domestic rites except the *Śrāddha* rites GGṛ. I.2.2, HGṛ. II. 10.7. Cf. *adhonivīta*, *prācīnāvītin*. See also Śrauta section.

yajñopavītinī f. a bride who wears the sacred thread in this fashion during the marriage ceremony GGṛ. II.1.19. The scholiast however explains that she wears the upper garment in this fashion, for women are not allowed to put on the sacred thread. Cf. H.Dh. II(i), 287-96.

यथालिङ्गम् *Yathāliṅgam* ind. according to the characteristics of a *mantra*; it is said that the ritual actions with regard to the particular materials are to be done according to the characteristics contained in the *mantra* Āp Gṛ. XIII.3.

यम *Yama* (√*yam*, cl.1 "to restrain") m. restraint observed by a *snātaka* as a religious conduct PGṛ. II.7.1. See *snātakavrata*.

यमसू *Yamasū* f. cow which brings forth twin calves ŚGṛ. III.10.4.

युग *Yuga* n. yoke, which is holed on the right side and put on a piece of *darbha* network over the head of a bride ĀpGr̥. IV.8.

योक्त्र *Yoktra* n. rope, with which the bridegroom girds (*saṁnahyati*) the bride ĀpGr̥. IV.8; it is removed before she is taken away from her father's house V.13 (*Vivāha*).

योनिसंबन्ध *Yonisambandha* m. relationship between a brahmin and a sacrificer by "womb", i.e. consanguinity; such a brahmin is not to be invited to the *śrāddha* feast ĀpGr̥. XXI.2. See also *mantra*°

र Ra

रजस् *Rajas* n. menstrual discharge ĀpGr̥. VIII. 13.

रशना *Raśanā* f.=*mekhalā* (q.v.).

राति *Rāti* m(fn.) a generous person, who collects the cut up hair, beard and nail of an initiate and puts them in a lump of bull's dung and finally disposes of them by saying, "I hide the sin of N.N. who belongs to N.N. *gotra* HGr̥. I.9.18.

°*kula* n. the family of r° from whom the initiate begs for alms I.7.17.

राष्ट्रभृत् *Rāṣṭrabhṛt* f. name of a *mantra* (TS. III.4.7), used for offering a subordinate oblation ĀpGr̥. II.7. (*Vivāha*); also the name of oblation PGr̥. I.5.7.

ल La

लक्षण *Lakṣaṇa* n. preparation of the ground for the sacred fire, which is done by fetching waters from a hidden place, sweeping (*parisamūhana*), smearing the ground with cowdung, drawing lines (*lekhā*), sprinkling water, strewing *darbha* (*paristaraṇa*), and finally setting up the fire on the *sthaṇḍila* GGr̥. I.1.9-10. Cf. ĀśvGr̥. I.3.1,

Also designates the characteristics of a bride, which are said to be difficult to ascertain Āśv Gr̥. I.5.4. See *piṇḍa*.

lakṣaṇin mfn. one who is an expert in ascertaining l° of a bride KāGr̥. XIV.3.

लवण *Lavaṇa* n. salt, the use of which as oblation in the *Pākayajñas* is forbidden ĀpGr̥. VIII.3; saltless food is to be eaten by the married couple during the period of sexual continence (*trirātra*) VIII.8.

लाङ्गलयोजन *Lāṅgalayojana* n. rite of harnessing the plough, a minor rite performed on an auspicious day, consisting of the offerings of curds, rice grains, fried grains to various deities and feeding the bullocks with honey and ghee PGr̥. II.13.

लाजहोम *Lājahoma* m. offering of parched grains (of rice) into fire by the bride; one of the important rites of the marriage ceremony recorded in all the texts. Her brother fills twice her joined palms (*añjali*) with l° mixed with *śamī* leaves; spreading under (*upastaraṇa*) and sprinkling over (*abhighāraṇa*) with *ājya* are also done in the *añjali*. Without opening her hands as if she is using a *sruc* spoon the bride pours it into the fire. Only HGr̥. I.20.3-4 mentions that the bridegroom offers it seizing her joined hands. Nārāyaṇa, Haradatta & Sudarśana (comms) support this view as, according to them, a woman cannot perform a sacrifice on her own. However, most of the *sūtras* hold the first view mentioned. ŚGr̥. I. 13.15-17, ĀśvGr̥. I.7.8-15, PGr̥. I.6, GGr̥. II. 2.5-10, HGr̥. I.20.3-4, ĀpGr̥. V. 4-6, KāGr̥. XXV.29-35.

लेखा *Lekhā* f. lines drawn on the *sthaṇḍila* on which the fire is placed; 3 to the east and 3 to the north ĀpGr̥. XVIII.10. Or, on the west a line running north to south is drawn on the ground, from the northern and southern points of this line two lines are drawn towards the east and in the middle three parallel lines to the east ĀśvGr̥. I.3.1; or, one line north to south and 3 parallel lines to the east from this line ŚGr̥. I.7.6-7. See *lakṣaṇa*, *sthaṇḍila*. Cf H.Dh. II(1), 209. Plan 9.

लेप (प्रहरण) *Lepa* m. (*praharaṇa* n.) offering of

the residue of sacrificial food and *ājya* by silently dipping the *barhis* into them, and throwing the *barhis* into the fire ĀpGṛ. VII.13 (*Sthālīpāka*).

(श्मशान) लोष्ट (*Śmaśāna*) *Loṣṭa* m.n. a clod of earth brought from a funeral ground (or a field *kṣetra*°), with which the characteristics of a bride are ascertained ĀpGṛ. III. 15-16 (*Vivāha*).

लौकिक (वाच्) *Laukika* (*vāc* f.) worldly words, which are not *mantras*, used for invoking the goddess Mīḍhuṣī (wife of Īśāna) ĀpGṛ. XX.2 (*Śūlagava*).

व Va

वंश *Vaṁśa* m. bamboo; said to be the central beam=*pṛṣṭha* of the dwelling house ĀpGṛ. XVII.5 (*Vāstupratiṣṭhā*).

वधूवासस् *Vadhūvāsas* n. garment worn by the bride, given away to a well-versed brahmin ĀpGṛ. IX.11 (end of *Vivāha*).

वपा (श्रपण) *Vapā* f. (*śrapaṇa* n.) rite of roasting the omentum of a cow (and its other limbs) with a spit of *udumbara* called °*śrapaṇī*; after spreading *ājya* under and sprinkling over the omentum, in a *darvī* or *palāśa* leaf it is offered to the manes into the fire in *Śrāddha* HGṛ. II.15. 6-8, in *Aṣṭakā* ĀpGṛ. XXII.4, in honour of a guest XIII.16.

vapoddharaṇa n. act of drawing out the omentum after immolating the victim PGṛ. III.11.4=°*utkhedana* with °*śrapaṇī* ĀśvGṛ. I. 11.10 (*Paśukalpa*).

वप्तृ *Vaptṛ* (√*vap*, cl.1 "to shave") m. a barber, who receives a razor from a student for shaving him ĀpGṛ. XII.3. (*Samāvartana*). But at the *Upanayana* the *ācārya* (priest) shaves him. Cf. *vapat* m. X.6, 7. See *keśavapana*.

वर *Vara* m. wooers who go to the bride's father to settle the marriage ĀpGṛ. II.16; they are friends of the bridegroom, and are versed in *mantras* IV.1 (*Vivāha*).

वरूथ्यदेशे *Varūthyadeśe* ind. in a protected (spot) ŚGṛ. I.3.3. Cf. RV. V.24.1; VIII.47.10.

वर्चस् *Varcas* n. a privy, where a *bali* is offered GGṛ. I.4.10.Cf. Pāṇ V.4.78 on the word.

वर्णक *Varṇaka* m.n. paint, poured out for the snakes ŚGṛ. IV.15.8 (*Śravaṇā*).

वसन *Vasana* n garment for covering an initiate, may be either of linen (*kṣauma*), or hemp (*śāṇa*), or cotton (*kārpāsa*), or wool (*ūrṇā*); for a *brāhmaṇa*, *kṣauma* or *śāṇa*, for a *kṣatriya*, *kārpāsa*, and for *vaiśya*, *ūrṇā* GGṛ. II.10.7-8, 12 (*Upanayana*). See also *antaravāsas*. Cf. *cīvara* Upasak Monastic terms.

वाजि *Vāji* m. line of hair or locks, optionally worn by Aṅgirasas KāGṛ. XL.6 comm. (*Cūḍākaraṇa*)

वास्तु (प्रतिष्ठा) *Vāstu* n. (*pratiṣṭhā* f.) rite of building a new house. The ground must be free from salinity, have trees, herbs, *kuśa*, and waters from all directions should flow to the centre of the ground and discharge to the east Āśv Gṛ. II.7.

Then follows the examination of the ground (*v*° *parīkṣā*) : a pit is dug knee-deep and filled with loose earth; if the loose earth rises above the pit, the ground is said to be excellent, but if the pit is levelled, the ground is of medium quality, and if the pit remains unfilled, the ground is to be rejected.

Or, another method may be adopted : a pit is dug; filled with water, and left overnight; if on the following morning water is found in the pit, the ground is considered excellent ĀśvGṛ. II.8.1-5. The ground should be white, red and yellow for *brāhmaṇa*, *kṣatriya* and *vaiśya* respectively; it is either a square or a rectangle, which is sprinkled with a *śamī* or *udumbara* branch 8.6-11. Between the bamboo posts single rooms are to be constructed ib. 13.

Earth from the pits, dug from left to right, is thrown on the building site, door-posts are fixed ĀpGṛ. XVII.3, 6. When the house has been constructed the householder carries fire in a dish inside the house, strews *darbha*, pours 4 potfuls of water ib. 9-10. A mess of food is cooked inside the house and offered to the brahmins ĀśvGṛ. II.9.9, and *ājyabhāga*, 4 oblations are offered, sprinkling round the fire and the house are done ĀpGṛ. XVII.12-13. ĀśvGṛ. II.7-9, ŚGṛ. III.2-4, ĀpGṛ.XVII. 1-13, (=*śālākarman*) PGṛ. III.4.

°*śamana* n. rite of appeasement of the building ground, done by sprinkling water containing gold, rice and barley, thrice round the ground with the hymn called *śantatīya* (RV. VII.35.1-5) ĀśvGṛ. II.9.6-7; or by performing a *homa* by night in an inner appartment of the house with the *vyāhṛti* and other *mantra*s HGṛ. I.27.9-10; 28.1-3.

वाह *Vāha* m. (du) two carriages (=*ratha*, chariot), drawn by horse or bull, used for carrying the newly married couple to the bridegroom's house ĀpGṛ. V.21-22 (*Vivāha*).

विघन *Vighana* mfn. clear, pure, said of the *caru* ŚGṛ. I.3.3; or thin Oldenberg SBE XXIX, 17.

विजट *Vijaṭa* mfn. loosened matted lock ŚGṛ. I.28.10 (*Cūḍākaraṇa*).

वितान *Vitāna* m.n. extension, i.e. establishment of 3 fires, done by taking the *aupāsana* fire to the forest for performing the animal sacrifice to Rudra PGṛ. III.8.3 (*Śūlagava*).

विधि *Vidhi* m. PGṛ. II.6.5. See *arthavāda* Śrauta section.

vidheya mfn. texts of the Brāhmaṇa, used at the sacrifice according to the rules (*vidhi*), one of the categories of the veda ib. See *tarka*.

विफाण्टित *Viphāṇṭita* (*vi-√phaṇ*,) cl.1-"to skim") mfn. n. decoction, obtained by "infusing" medicine with (boiled) water, with which the teacher sprinkles the student GGṛ. III.4.11.

विवाह *Vivāha* (*vi-√vah*, cl. 1 "to carry away") m. literally, rite of leading away the bride; marriage rite, one of the most important *saṁskāra*s, of which 8 types are enumerated : (1) *brāhma* in which a girl decked with ornaments is given away by pouring a water libation; (2) *daiva* such a girl given away to a *ṛtvij* while a *śrauta* rite is going on; (3) *prājāpatya* in which they (couple) fulfil the law (*dharma*); (4) *ārṣa* a man marries a girl after having given a bull to her father; (5) *gāndharva* v° resulting from a mutual agreement between the lovers; (6) *āsura* a man marries a girl after paying satisfaction money to her father; (7) *paiśāca* a man carries off a girl while her relatives sleep or are unmindful; and (8) *rākṣasa* a man carries off a girl forcibly killing her relatives and decapitating their heads ĀśvGṛ. I.6.

The *gotra* and *sapiṇḍa* exogamy are prescribed by GGṛ. III.4.4-5, HGṛ. I.19.2, and *savarṇa* endogamy is prescribed by HGṛ. l.c., MGṛ. I.7.8. All other sūtras are silent on these points.

A brahmin may marry 3 girls, one from his own caste and one each from the *kṣatriya* and *vaiśya*; a *kṣatriya* 2, one *kṣatriya* and the other *vaiśya*, but a *vaiśya* has only one wife. Besides these any person of the above castes may have a *śūdra* wife, married without using *mantra*s PGṛ. I.4.8-11.

Marriageable age of a girl is not specifically mentioned. Though the word *nagnikā* (q.v.) may indicate pre-puberty marriage, *trirātravrata* (q.v.) and the consequential rite of *caturthīkarman* which mark the consummation of marriage firmly contradict the view of *nagnikā*. The rite can be held at any time ĀśvGṛ. I.4.2, and is performed in a shed outside the house (*bahiḥ śālā*) PGṛ. I.4.2.

A bride must possess auspicious physical characteristics, belong to a good family and possess good health; and so be the bridegroom ŚGṛ. I.5.6-10, ĀśvGṛ. I.5.1-3, ĀpGṛ. III. 18-19.

Various kinds of earth : *loṣṭa* and *piṇḍa* are proferred to the bride, who is asked to touch them, to ascertain her characteristics (*lakṣaṇa*) ĀśvGṛ. I.5.5, ĀpGṛ. III.15-16, or an expert (*lakṣaṇin*) is employed KāGṛ. XIV.3. The central features of V° are *pāṇigrahaṇa*, *homa*, *agnipradakṣiṇa* and *saptapadī*. There are several other rituals which precede or follow these. No one *sūtra* agrees in the matter of details and of the sequence of the rituals.

As a preliminary, wooers (*vara*) are sent to the bride's house ŚGṛ. I.6.1-4, ĀpGṛ. II.16: they are received as guests and a cow is killed in their honour. They settle the marriage. The bride's father declares his assent ŚGṛ. I. 7.1, and the bridegroom performs a sacrifice I.7-8. The bride is washed with wine by her female relatives GGṛ. II.1.10.

The bridegroom goes to the bride's house ŚGṛ. I.12.1, a shed is erected for the ceremony PGṛ. I.4.2, he gives her a mirror and a garment; they anoint (*samañjana*) each other ŚGṛ. I.12.4-8, GGṛ. II.1.18, PGṛ. I.4.12-14 or he washes her placing a piece of gold, a yoke hole and *darbha* network on her head, and ties a *yoktra* over her garment (*yoktrasaṁ-*

nahana) ĀpGṛ. IV.8. The bridegroom is given a reception (*Argha*) at the bride's house. He takes hold of her, and offers 4 oblations with the *vyāhṛti*, *jaya* and *abhyātāna mantras* ŚGṛ. I.12.11, ĀśvGṛ. I.7.3, PGṛ. I.5.3-11. The *sūtras* differ over the number of *āhutis* and *mantras*.

The custom of giving away the bride (*prattā*) by her father is mentioned PGṛ. I.4.15. They look at each other (*samīkṣaṇa*) ib. 16, ĀpGṛ. IV.4.

While leading the bride thrice round the fire and water jar (*agnipradakṣiṇa*) the bridergoom recites the famous *mantra : amohamasmi, sā tvam; sā tvamasi amoham; dyauraham pṛthivī tvam; sāmāham, ṛktvam; tāvehi, vivahāvahai. prajāṁ prajanayāvahai. saṁpriyau, rociṣṇū, sumanasyamānau jīveva śaradaḥ śatam*: "This (*ama*) am I, that (*sā*) art thou; that art thou, this am I; the heaven I, the earth thou; the *sāman* I, the *ṛk* thou. Come ! Let us marry. Let us beget offspring. Loving, bright, with genial mind may we live a hundred autumns" (Oldenberg SBE XXIX, 168) ĀśvGṛ. I.7.6, ŚGṛ. I.13.4, 13, HGṛ. I.20.2, with some variations PGṛ. I.6.3.

Then the bridegroom holds the right hand of the bride saying : I seize thy hand for the sake of happiness. If he desires only male child, he touches her thumb ĀpGṛ. IV.11-15, ŚGṛ. I.13.2, ĀśvGṛ. I.7.3-5, PGṛ. I.6.3, GGṛ II.2.16, HGṛ. I.20.1. (*Pāṇi*° or *Hastagrahaṇa*).

He performs a *homa* with parched rice grains (*lājahoma*), held in her hands, and she, led by the bridegroom, takes seven steps called *Saptapadāni* (q.v.), and thereafter their heads are sprinkled with water ĀśvGṛ. I.7. 20, PGṛ. I.8.5. He touches her right shoulder over the heart saying : *mama vrate te hṛdayaṁ dadhāmi, mama cittamanucittaṁ te astu. mama vācam ekamanā juṣasva, prajāpatiṣṭvā niyunaktu mahyam* : "Into my will I take thy heart; thy mind shall follow my mind; in my word thou shalt rejoice with all thy heart; may Prajāpati join thee to me" (Oldenberg SBE XXIX, 284) PGṛ. I.1.8. She is made to tread on the stone (*Aśmārohaṇa*). The bride is carried away in a vehicle to the bridegroom's house ĀpGṛ. V. 12, ĀśvGṛ. I.8.1. On entering the house she (or both of them) has to sit on a red bull's skin. Again a *homa* is performed by the husband while his wife takes hold of him. Thereafter, she observes silence until the stars appear ĀpGṛ. VI.8-11. She is shown the pole star (*dhruva*) and the alcor (*arundhatī*) ib. 12, and the ursa major (*saptarṣi*) ĀśvGṛ. I.7.22; or the pole star only, with the words : *dhruvam asi dhruvaṁ tvā paśyāmi dhruvaidhi poṣye mayi. mahyaṁ tvādāt bṛhaspatir mayā patyā prajāvatī saṁjīva śaradaḥ śatam* : Firm art thou; I see thee, the firm be thou with me, O thriving one ! To me Bṛhaspati has given thee; obtaining offspring through me, thy husband, live with me a hundred autumns" (Oldenberg SBE XXIX, 285-6) PGṛ. I.8.19. Even if she does not see the star she has to say : "I see" ib. 20.

After the marriage rite they are to avoid salt and pungent food and to observe sexual continence (called *brahmacarya*) for 3 nights. Cf. *adhaḥśayyā, trirātravrata*. Or the period of continence may be longer, 6 or 12 nights PGṛ. I.8.21.

For the consummation of marriage a rite is performed. See *Caturthīkarman*.

It is interesting to note that the diversity of the marriage customs of different areas has been recognized in ĀśvGṛ. I.7.1. See *janapadadharma*.

H.Dh.II(1), 527-41. See also *Gosava* (Śrauta).

विवाह्य *Vivāhya* mfn. m. one who has to be carried, i.e. the bridegroom KāGṛ. XXIV.1.

विष्टर *Viṣṭara* (*vi*-√*stṛ*, cl. 9 "to strew") m. a couch ("spread") of grass, offered to a guest at *Argha* PGṛ. I.3.5, at *Madhuparka* ĀśvGṛ. I.24.7, to the bridegroom KāGṛ. XXIV.8.

वीणागाथिन् *Vīṇāgāthin* m. a singer who sings with the accompaniment of a lute; 2 v° mentioned ĀpGṛ. XIV.4 (*Sīmantonnayana*). At the ceremony they should sing the first verse for the people of Sālva, and the second for the brahmins ib. 5. The wording of the song varies according to the texts.

Perhaps they were ancient ballad singers who composed popular ballads. See sālva.

वृषोत्सर्ग *Vṛṣotsarga* m. rite of releasing a bull, performed as a meritorious work on the full-moon day of *kārttika* or on a day of the *aśvayuja* (*āśvina*) month under the star *revatī*. One red-coloured or 1-, 2- or 3-coloured bull which is the finest of the herd and perfect in limb is chosen and decorated. An *ājya* oblation is offered, and a mess of cooked food to Pūṣan by reciting a verse to the deity. When the bull stands among the cows of the herd a verse is recited. With the milk of all cows *pāyasa* is cooked and the brahmins are fed with it. The bull is set free ŚGṛ. III.11, PGṛ. III.9.

वैवाह्य *Vaivāhya* mfn. m. related through marriage, i.e. the father-in-law PGṛ. I.3.1, ŚGṛ. II.15. 6. See *arghya.*

वैश्वदेव *Vaiśvadeva* m. offerings of cooked food to all gods (whence the name of the rite) Āp Gṛ. VII.27, ĀpDh. II.2.3.1. The food is sprinkled with *ājya* or curds or milk but not with oil or salt; the food may be cooked by the "pure men" of the first three castes, or even by a *śūdra*, who must observe personal cleanliness : hair trimming, nail pairing etc., ĀpDh. II.3.1. 4, 6; the rite is to be performed twice : morning and evening ĀśvGṛ. I.2.1.

व्यष्टका *Vyaṣṭakā* f. the first day in the dark half of a month ĀpGṛ. XXI.10. See *Aṣṭakā, Ekāṣṭakā.*

व्याहृतिहोम *Vyāhṛtihoma* m. an oblation of clarified butter, poured with the accompaniment of the v° *mantra* : *bhūḥ, bhuvaḥ, svaḥ* or *suvaḥ*, pronounced singly or together HGṛ. I.3.4; in the marriage 3 oblations called *mahā*° ŚGṛ. I.12.11-12.

The v° formulas are pronounced singly at the beginning or the end of the *pāda*s when the *sāvitrī* is repeated (*pacchaḥ*) at the *Upanayana* ĀpGṛ. XI.11. Also pronounced together (*Sīmantonnayana*) XIV.3. See also *sāvitrī.* Cf. *pratigara* (Śrauta).

व्रज *Vraja* m. cow-pen (n. RV. III.30.10; V.6.7), which is entered by a student before sunrise. He remains there for the whole day before taking his ritual bath (*snāna*) ĀpGṛ. XII.1-2 (*Samāvartana*).

व्रतादेशन *Vratādeśana* n. imposition of *vrata*, i.e. the observances which a student has to keep for a certain period of time before he is eligible to learn the vedic texts PGṛ. II.10.10. The preparation of a student for the *sāvitrī* verse is called *sāvitravrata* which lasts 1 year or 3 days, or the *sāvitrī* can be taught imme-diately after the *Upanayana* ŚGṛ. II.5.1-3. Then follows the *śukriya*° (purity or brilliance) lasting 3 or 12 days or 1 year or as long as the teacher pleases before the study of a course of veda called *anuvācana* II.7; 11.10. Thereafter come the *śākvara, vrātika* and *aupaniṣada vratas*, each lasting 1 year, before the study of the different parts of the Aitareya Āraṇyaka II.11.11-12. Rites beginning from the shaving of head upto *paridāna* are to be performed in v° ĀśvGr. I.22.20. For the v° belonging to the *sāmavedins* GGṛ.III.1.28-31. See H.Dh. II. (1), 370-73, *snātakavrata, vrata* (Śrauta).

°*visarga* m. cessation of v° at the *Samāvartana* PGr. II.10.10.

श Sa

शकलोत *Śakalota* (of doubtful meaning) n. ? explained as *śāluka*, lotus root, GGṛ. II. 4.8 & comm, which is thrown into the joined palms of a boy (*Vivāha*).

शकृत् *Śakṛt* n. cow-dung, one of the materials used for testing the characteristics of a bride ĀpGṛ. III.16.

शङ्कु *Śaṅku* m. peg, made of *vīratara* wood (= *vīraṇa* Andropogon muricatus), one of the implements used for parting the hair PGṛ. I.15.4 (*Sīmantonnayana*).

शङ्खिन् *Śaṅkhin* mfn. a boy suffering from the *śaṅkha* disease (*graha*) (?); the patient utters cries like the sound of a conch (*śaṅkha*) Āp Gṛ. XVIII.3 & comm. See also *śvagraha.*

शम्या *Śamyā* f. wooden yoke pin, used for marking the boundary of the domestic fire ĀpGṛ. II.2. See Śrauta section.

शराव *Śarāva* (etymology unknown) m.n. shallow cup or dish, made of earth, with which water is drawn in the direction of the river's current; and water is sprinkled on the wife who is about to give birth to a child ĀpGṛ. XIV.14 (*Puṁsavana*).

vrīhi°, Ś°, 4 in number, with which rice is measured for preparing a cake (*Aṣṭakā*). See *apūpaṁ catuḥśarāvam.*

शलली *Śalalī* f. quill of a porcupine, containing white spots at 3 places (*treṇī*), with which hair of the wife is parted ĀpGṛ XIV. 3

(*Sīmantonnayana*); needle-shaped bristle of a *śalya*, comm on ib. Also used at *Cūḍākaraṇa* for combing hair of the boy XVI.6. It is held by the bride in her right hand as a protection against widowhood ŚGṛ. I.12.6 (*Vivāha*).

शलालु *Śalālu* n(?). unripe *udumbara* fruit (or its varieties : *kharapatrodumbara, piśācodumbara*, comm); made a bunch (*glapsa*) of its fruit and used for parting the wife's hair ĀpGṛ. XIV.3 (*Sīmantonnayana*), and for combing the boy's hair XVI.6 (*Cūḍākaraṇa*).

शवान्न *Śavānna* n. funeral food, which is either bought or received from others, after the death of a person, and eaten by the relatives; but such food is not to be eaten by a *snātaka* PGṛ. II.8.4; III.10.26.

शाक *Śāka* n. vegetables, used as oblation at one of the *Aṣṭakās* (q.v.) ŚGṛ. III.12.2.

śākāṣṭakā f. a fourth *Aṣṭakā* performed in the *mā(dh)ghyāvarṣa* in which vegetables are offered PGṛ. III.3.13. cf Oldenberg SBE XXIX, 345.

शाखा *Śākhā* f. See *palāśa°*.

शामित्र *Śāmitra* m. ĀśvGṛ. I.11.2. See Śrauta section.

शालाकर्मन् *Śālākarman* n.=*Vāstupratiṣṭhā* (q.v.).

शास *Śāsa* (√*śas*, cl. 2 cf. *viśas*, Śrauta section) m. a butcher's knife, which is held by the host in his hand when he announces thrice : "a cow" to the guest PGṛ. I.3.26 (*Madhuparka*).

शिक्य *Śikya* n. strings, suspended to a pole for hanging a jug and a spoon for *bali* ĀśvGṛ. II. 1.2.

शिखा *Śikhā* f. a tuft or lock of hair worn on the head after tonsure; the number of such locks depends on the number of the *ṛṣis* in one's *pravara* list or on the family usuage ĀpGṛ. XVI.6-7, or arranged according to the *gotra* GGṛ. II.9.25 (*Cūḍākaraṇa*).

शिखाजट *Śikhājaṭa* mfn. m. one (a student) who ties the lock of hair on his head in a knot HGṛ. I.8.11.

शुङ्गा *Śuṅgā* f. sheath or calyx of a bud (that looks like two testicles : *vṛṣaṇa*), used as *paridhi* instead of the *śamyā* ĀpGṛ. XIV.10 (*Puṁsavana*).

शूर्पकुष्ठा *Śūrpakuṣṭhā* f. mouth or neb of a winnowing basket, by which the bride sacrifices *lāja*, the 4th oblation, into the fire PGṛ. I.7.5 (*Vivāha*).

शूल *Śūla* m.n. spit of *udumbara* wood with which the heart, kidneys of an immolated cow are roasted HGṛ. II.15,6 (*Śrāddha*). See also *vapāśrapaṇa*. Cf. *śūla*, Śrauta section.

शूलगव *Śūlagava* (also called *Īśānabali*) m. ox in the spit, a rite in which the flesh and other limbs of an ox are offered to Rudra. It is mainly a domestic animal sacrifice, performed in the paradigm of *Nirūḍhapaśubandha*. *Śūla*= Rudra who holds a spit (*śūlin*) ĀśvGṛ. IV.9.1 comm. It is stated that the bull is to be set free, for the people are opposed to the sacrifice of an ox KāGṛ. LII.1. comm. A cow may, as an alternative, be sacrificed as implied by the designation of rite PGṛ. III.8.5 (*Śūlagava*).

The rite is performed in autumn or spring, outside a village after midnight or early in the morning (but time varies) ĀśvGṛ. IV.9.2, 12-13. A bull is slaughtered, and its omentum is offered to Rudra. There is one unchiselled (*ataṣṭa*) *yūpa*. The procedure of animal sacrifice is followed. *Bali* or blood filled in 8 vessels, made of leaf, is offered to the 4 quarters, followed by Agni *Sviṣṭakṛt* offering. Uncooked offerings are not brought into the village. The rest of the victim and its skin are buried into the ground. ĀśvGṛ. IV.9, PGṛ. III.8, BhGṛ. II.8-10.

श्मशान *Śmaśāna* n. cemetery where the dead-body is to be burned, the place from which the waters flow off to all sides ĀśvGṛ. IV.1.15 & comm; also the place where the gathered bones are to be deposited ib. 11. comm. Cf. Oldenberg SBE XXIX, 237. The ground should be of the length of a man with upraised arms, of the breadth of 1 *vyāma*, of the depth of 1 *vitasti*; the place must be open on all sides, fertile in herbs, inclining towards the south or southeast or southwest IV.1.6-15. For urn burial of bones see *asthisaṁcayana*. Cf. *śmaśāna* Śrauta section.

श्रवणाकर्मन् *Śravaṇa (ā)karman* n. ŚGṛ. IV.15, PGṛ. II.14. See *Śrāvaṇīsthālīpāka*.

श्राद्ध *Śrāddha* n. (*śrat*-√*dhā*, cl. 3 "to have faith or faithfulness, belief or confidence") cf. *śratte dadhāmi* RV. X.147.1; the word *śraddhā* designates a deity RV.X.151.1-5; also II.26.3, VII.32.14 etc; *śrāddhin* mfn. one who has eaten the ś° dinner Pāṇ V.2.85.

Ś° is a group of rites, apart from the *Aṣṭakās*, for the manes, and classified into :

1. *Ekoddiṣṭa*, performed for one person;

2. *Pārvaṇa*, performed for 3 generations on a *parvan* day, i.e. on the *amāvāsyā* day of a month, particularly in the dark fortnight of *bhādrapada*;

3. *Māsi*° performed every month (in the dark half, in the afternoon ĀpDh. II.16.4-5) ŚGṛ. IV.1.1, but taking the same procedure as the *Pārvaṇa*°, described in ĀśvGṛ. IV.7.1;

4. *Sapiṇḍīkaraṇa*, performed one year after the death of a person or on the 12th day from the death;

5. *Ābhyudayika*°, *śrāddha* rite for prosperity, celebrated to mark some good happenings as the birth of a son, *Nāmakaraṇa*, *Cūḍākaraṇa*, marriage etc.;

6. *Kāmya*°.

Learned brahmins serve as representatives of the manes at the Ś° rites and join in the feast The larger their number the greater the reward Āśv Gṛ. IV.7.2. Cf. Oldenberg SBE XXIX, 106.

आभ्युदयिक *Ābhyudayika*° (*abhi-ud-√i*, cl. 2 "to go up, rise") n. rite relating to prosperity, in which offerings are made to the ancestors on the occasions of rejoicing. The rite is performed in the morning; the number of the brahmins must be even; the *darbha* must be straight, the sacrificer wears his sacred cord in the *yajñopavīta* fashion (not in the *prācīnāvīta* fashion); all actions are done from the left to the right (*pradakṣiṇa*); *svadhā* is not used; instead of sesamum, *yava* grains are oblatory material. On these points Ā° differs from all other forms of *Śrāddhas*. The sacrificer sits facing the east or the north, and with the permission of the brahmins invokes the Fathers having cheerful faces (*nāndīmukhāḥ*); this clearly brings out the nature of the rite. He says, 'May, the *Nāndīmukhās* be pleased'; offers *arghya*. When he asks the brahmins about the dinner he says '*sampannam*' (was it well done ?); to which they reply *susampannam*' ŚGṛ. IV.4.1-15. Only briefly mentioned ĀśvGṛ. II.5.13-15, GGṛ. IV.3. 35-37.

एकोद्दिष्ट *Ekoddiṣṭa* n. a *Śrāddha* rite in which one (deceased) person is intended, in contrast to *Pārvaṇa*° or *Māsi*° in which 3 paternal ancestors are invoked. The rite is performed through one year for the *preta* after his death. Thereafter, the *preta* attains the realm of the Fathers (*pitṛ*) by the *Sapiṇḍīkaraṇa*, and consequently he is entitled to receive the *piṇḍas* in the *Pārvaṇa* (cf. *Caturthavisarga*). In E° only one *arghya* and one *piṇḍa* are offered; there is only one *pavitra*.

There is no offering of cooked food and *ājya* into the fire (*agnaukaraṇa*), no invitation to the brahmins to represent the Viśve devāḥ, no *āvāhana*, no cakes, no utterance of *svadhā*, no incense (*dhūpa*), no light (*dīpa*); the question on satisfaction at the dinner is asked with the word *svaditam* (did it taste well ?), to which the brahmins reply : *susvaditam*. The brahmins say, "May the food approach the deceased" ŚGṛ. IV.2.1-8, BGṛ. III.12.6.

On the 11th day after the death one should feed brahmins of uneven number, and kill a cow; offer *piṇḍas* PGṛ. III.10.48-50.

काम्य *Kāmya*° n. a *Śrāddha* rite performed in order to obtain a special reward ĀśvGṛ. IV. 7.1.

पार्वण *Pārvaṇa*° n. ĀśvGṛ provides the same rule for all types of *Śrāddha*. A good number of brahmins are invited. The larger the number the greater the reward. They must be of high reputation. Water and *darbha* seats are given to the brahmins who act as representatives of the Fathers. Water is poured into 3 vessels which are covered with *darbha* blades, and *tila* (sesamum) seeds are poured into them. The rites are performed from the right to the left (*prasavya*).

He offers *arghya* water to the Fathers with the part of his left hand between the thumb and the forefinger or with his right hand, held by his left (see *prācīnāvītin*), and proclaims "This is your *arghya*, O father and O grandfather, and O great-grandfather". He hands over the *arghya* water to the brahmins, and recites *mantras* when it is poured out. With the remaining water he moistens his face. The first vessel into which *arghya* water was poured should not be removed till the end of the rite. He offers the gifts of perfumes, garlands, incense, lights and clothes to the brahmins. He eats some food of the *sthālīpāka* (prepared for the *Piṇḍapitṛyajña*), and having smeared it with ghee, with the permission of the brahmins, he sacrifices it into the fire.

With the remainder of the food other food is mixed, and it is served to the brahmins at the dinner. They are asked whether the food was perfect, and to which they reply in affirmative. Now he prepares lumps from the remnant of this food and *sthālīpāka*, and offers the rest of food to the brahmins. The lumps are put down on the ground. The remnant of food is strewn on the ground, the brahmins are dismissed with the word "*om svadhā*" ĀśvGṛ. IV.7-8, ŚGṛ. IV.1.

मासि *Māsi*° n. the monthly *Śrāddha* is, according to Haradatta comm. (ĀpGṛ XXI.1), the model (*prakṛti*) of all *Aṣṭakās* and other *Śrāddhas*; a succinct account is given in ĀpGṛ. XXI.1-9. The brahmins who are not related to the sacrificer by consanguinity, or by common *mantra* through teacher-student relationship are invited and fed. A portion of the food cooked for this dinner is taken out, and from this 7 food oblations are offered to the Fathers : 2 each to father, grandfather, great-grandfather and 1 to the *pitṛs* in general; 7 *ājya* oblations are also to be offered. He touches the food and gives it to the brahmins to eat. After the dinner when the brahmins are going away, he goes after them and circumambulates them. He strews grass, distributes the *piṇḍas* for the male and female ancestors as in the *Piṇḍapitṛyajña*, pours water, worships the ancestors, again pours water thrice round the *piṇḍas*, from the right to the left; sprinkles the vessels. He cuts off portions (*avadāna*) from all food and eats at least one morsel of it. This rite has been elaborately treated in HGṛ. II.10-13. See *Sapiṇḍīkaraṇa*.

श्रावणी (स्थालीपाक) *Śrāvaṇī* f. (*sthālīpāka* m.) rite of cooked offering like *Pārvaṇa*°, performed on the fullmoon day of the month of *śrāvaṇa* (July-August) after sunset ĀpGṛ. XVIII.5-6 (*Sarpabali*); offered either on the *dakṣiṇāgni* or the *aupāsana* by an *anāhitāgni* HGṛ. II.16.2 (*Śravaṇā*)=*Śravaṇakarman* ŚGṛ. IV.15=*Śravaṇākarman* PGṛ. II.14. A mess of cooked food and a cake on 1 *kapāla* are prepared. The cake is smeared with butter and along with the cooked food is offered to Agni, the fullmoon of *śrāvaṇa* etc. Out of the jar which is filled with fried barley grains he draws some barley, and with it offers *bali* to the snakes to ward them off (the divine snakes). In this way the offering should be performed every day at night with the grains till the time of the *Pratyavarohaṇa*. He now ascends the high couch (bedstead).

श्रुत *Śruta* mfn. n. "heard"; knowledge (communicated from generation to generation); learning, a quality par excellence, which surpasses all other qualities of a brahmin, and a learned brahmin should not be passed over ŚGṛ. I.2.3-4.

श्रोत्रिय *Śrotriya* mfn. m. one who is well-versed in the *śruti* (vedas) ĀpGṛ. V.18.

श्वग्रह *Śvagraha* m. "dog-seizer" said to be a dog demon, attacked by whom a child, his victim, behaves like a dog (hydrophobia ?); one of the maladies of a child, to be cured by a rite : the patient is covered with a net and led to the gambling-place (*adhidevana*) of a gambling-hall (*sabhā*); and the dice are cast; the patient is sprinkled with curds and salt, morning, noon and evening, accompanied with *mantras* ĀpGṛ. XVIII.1. See also *śaṅkhin*.

श्वपच *Śvapaca* m. one who cooks dogs; obviously, the low caste people are meant. Food is thrown for them on the ground ŚGṛ. II.14. 22 (*Vaiśvadeva*).

स Sa

संसद् *Saṁsad* f. an assembly ĀśvGṛ. II.6.11.

संसर्जन *Saṁsarjana* (*sam-√sṛj*. cl. 6 "to send forth together") n. act of mixing together warm and cold water by pouring on the head of the boy ĀpGṛ. XVI.8 (*Cūḍākaraṇa*).

संस्तूप *Saṁstūpa* m. heap of the household sweepings, where a *bali* is offered to the host of *Rākṣasas* GGṛ. I.4.11.

(अ) संस्यूत (*A*)*Saṁsyūta* (*sam-√sīv*. cl. 4 "to sew together") mfn. said of rice grains which are not chewed but swallowed PGṛ. II 14.25 comm. (*Śrāvaṇīsthālīpāka*); grains which do not form a coherent mass Oldenberg SBE XXIX, 331. Cf. *sam-√sīv* SW.

संस्रव *Saṁsrava* (*sam-√sru*, cl. 1 "to flow together") m. remainder of *sthālīpāka*, poured into a waterpot, out of which it is sprinkled on the bride's head by her husband PGṛ. I. 11.4 (*Caturthīkarman*).

saṁsrāva m. remainder of water, poured on the head of a bride ŚGṛ. I.16.7, HGṛ. I. 24.2 (*Vivāha*) See also *saṁsrāva* Śrauta section.

सक्थि *Sakthi* n. (left) thigh of a cow, offered at the *Anvaṣṭakā* in the manner of the *Piṇḍa-pitṛyajña* PGṛ. III.3.10. See *jauhava* (Śrauta).

संगव *Saṁgava* m. morning; one of the 5 divisions of a day; the time when one can take a wife HGṛ. I.19.3; explained as one *nāḍikā* before and one *nāḍikā* after sunrise comm. on ib. Cf. Oldenberg SBE XXX, 186. See Śrauta section.

संचयन *Saṁcayana* n. ĀśvGṛ. IV.5.1. See *Asthi*°.

संज्ञपन *Saṁjñapana* n. act of killing a cow HGṛ. II.15.4 (*Aṣṭakā*). See Śrauta section.

सटोद्धरण *Saṭoddharaṇa* n. rite of "raising up" the braid of hair (*saṭā* f.) and hairdressing (*anulepana*) of a virgin (betrothed, *vāgdattā* comm) KāGṛ. XXXI.6.

सद्यःकृत्तोत (वासस्) *Sadyaḥkṛttota* mfn. (*vāsas*) n. a piece of cloth which has been spun (√*kṛt*, cl. 6 "to cut") and woven (*ūta* from √*vā*/*ve*, cl. 1/4 "to weave") on the same day (*sadyaḥ*); this garment is worn by the initiate on the day of initiation ĀpGṛ. X.10 (*Upanayana*). On the 4th day after U° his teacher takes this garment for himself and the initiate puts on another garment XI.26. See also *antara*°, *brahmacārivāsas*, *vasana*.

सनि *Sani* m.f. begging or alms obtained by begging (gift RV. VI.70.6) ĀpGṛ. XXII.13.

संधि *Saṁdhi* m. juncture of the wall and the post inside a house PGṛ. III. 4.10 (*Vāstupratiṣṭhā*). See also *paridhi*°.

संध्या *Saṁdhyā* f. (1) juncture of day and night (twilight) GGṛ. I.5.2. See *paurṇamāsī*.

(2) "twilight" service, performed by the initiate in which he silently mutters the *sāvitrī* turning his face to the northwest until the stars appear ŚGṛ. II.9.1.

संनाम *Saṁnāma* (*sam*-√*nam*, cl. 1 "to bend together") m. alteration of *mantra* (*mantra*°) ĀpGṛ. II.8=*ūha* (Śrauta). Cf. *saṁnamana* (Śrauta).

सपत्नीबाधन *Sapatnībādhana* n. a rite by which the co-wives are subjugated, performed by a wife who strews thrice 7 barley grains around the plant called *pāṭhā* (Clypea hernandifolia), which is set upright next day; she ties its root to his hand furtively, and she embraces her husband ĀpGṛ. IX.5-8.

सपिण्डीकरण *Sapiṇḍīkaraṇa* n. rite of reception to get the deceased (*preta*) admitted into the community of the *pitṛ*s (manes), who are entitled to the *piṇḍa* offerings; one of the *Śrāddha* rites, performed at the end of a year after death or in the 4th or the 6th or the 11th month or on the 12th day BhGṛ. III.17 or after 3 months ŚGṛ. IV.3.2. Of the 4 pots of *arghya* water mixed with sesamum and scents, 3 pots are offered to the 3 *pitṛ*s and the 4th to the deceased (*preta*). Four lumps (*piṇḍa*) of flour are prepared.

The first lump for the *preta* is put on the three other. In the same way the pots containing *arghya* water are arranged. In a similar manner the rite for the mother, a brother and a wife who died before her husband is performed ŚGṛ. V.9. Cf. H.Dh. IV, 520-25.

सप्तपदानि *Saptapadāni* (also called *abhyutkramaṇa* or *parikramaṇa*) n. (pl.) rite of seven steps (*saptapadī*); the most important rite in the marriage ceremony in which the bridegroom makes the bride step forward from the west with her right foot to the north of fire in a northeastern or northern or eastern direction. The bridegroom recites 7 *mantra*s with each step of the bride : *iṣa ekapadī, ūrje dvipadī, rāyasposāya tripadī, mayobhavyāya catuṣpadī, prajābhyaḥ pañcapadī, ṛtubhyaḥ ṣaṭpadī, sakhā saptapadī bhava. sā māmanuvratā bhava. putrānvindāvahai bahūṁste santu jaradaṣṭayaḥ* : May you take one step for sap (*iṣ*), two for juice (or vigour, *ūrj*), three for the thriving of wealth, four for comfort, five for offspring, six for seasons, be friend with seven steps. Be devoted to me. Let us have many sons who may reach old age ĀśvGṛ. I. 7.19, (with a slight variation) ŚGṛ. I.14.6, PGṛ. I.8.1, ĀpGṛ. IV.16-17 etc.

सभा *Sabhā* f. a gambling-hall where the dice are played, and a boy attacked with *śvagraha* is laid on the dice ĀpGṛ. XVIII.1.

समारोहण *Samārohaṇa* (*sam-ā*-√*ruh*, cl. 1 "to ascend") n. a rite of causing the fire to "enter" the body of the sacrificer or the 2 *araṇis* or another piece of wood when one goes out on a journey by suspending the functions of the sacred fire. For causing the fire to enter the body, one's hands are warmed on the *gārhapatya*; for the *araṇis*, by warming them on the fire, and another piece of wood by warming it ŚGṛ. V.1.1-4. Cf. Oldenberg SBE XXIX, 133. See *samāropaṇa* (Śrauta).

समालम्भन *Samālambhana* (*sam-ā-√labh*, cl. 1 "to take hold of") n. act of touching a wife who is in childbed, prohibited for 10 days after her confinement GGṛ. II.7.23. This period is considered impure (*aśauca*).

समावर्तन *Samāvartana* (*sam-ā-√vṛt*, cl. 1 "to turn back") n. rite for the return home of a student from his teacher's house on completion of the vedic study ĀśvGṛ. III.8.1; also designated by the terms *snāna* ĀpGṛ. XII.1, PGṛ. II.6.1, *āplavana* GGṛ. III.4.7, both meaning a ceremonial bath taken on completion of the study, and after *snāna* he is declared a *snātaka*; this is the central part of S° (*vedam adhitya snāsyan* ĀpGṛ. l.c., *vedān samāpya snāyāt* PGṛ. l.c.). The ceremonial bath is not a part of *Vivāha*, Medhātithi on Mn. III.4.

The materials required for the rite are : a jewel, 2 earrings (*kuṇḍala*), a pair of garments, an umbrella, a pair of shoes, a staff, a turban, a garland, eye-salve, ointment ĀśvGṛ. III.8.1. He enters a cow-pen (*vraja*), having a door covered with hide so that sun does not shine upon him; he puts logs on fire and offers *ājyabhāga* oblations; sits over a mat, and is shaved by a barber, bathes in lukewarm water, or according to ĀpGṛ. XIII.1 in a *tīrtha* and cleans his teeth; discards the *mekhalā* and wears new clothes, shampoos his body. anoints himself, applies eye-salve to his eyes, puts on 2 earrings, the jewel, and fastens the garland round his neck. He looks into a mirror, steps into the shoes, takes the umbrella and the staff. He keeps silent till the stars appear. He is now a *snātaka* duly discharged from the studenthood, and may go wherever he likes. He is now allowed to marry. ĀpGṛ. XII.1-14; XIII.1-2, ŚGṛ.III. 1.1-18, ĀśvGṛ. III.8-9, PGṛ. II.6.1-32, GGṛ. III.4.7-34, HGṛ. I.9-11, KāGṛ. III.1-11. Cf. H Dh.II(1), 405-15.

समावेशन *Samāveśana* (*sam-ā-√viś*, cl. 6 "to enter together") n. sexual intercourse, performed in the last part of the 4th night (after marriage) ĀpGṛ. VIII.10. See *Caturthīkarman*.

ṛtu° sexual intercourse after the menstrual period, the 4th to the 16th day, considered the most favourable time for procreation ib. 13 (=*ṛtugamana* IX.1). See also *upagamana*.

समीक्षण *Samīkṣaṇa* (*sam-√īkṣ*, cl. 1 "to look at") n. rite of causing the bridegroom and the bride to look at each other, done by the bride's father PGṛ. I.4.16 (*Vivāha*).

समूहन *Samūhana* (*sam-√ūh*, cl. 1 "to sweep together") n. act of wiping with wet hand thrice round the fire, done by the sacrificer ŚGṛ. I. 7.11.

संपात *Saṁpāta* m. remnant of *ājya* sticking to a ladle, poured over the bride's head GGṛ. II. 3.7. Cf. Śrauta section.

संप्रेषण *Saṁpreṣaṇa* n. directions, given by the priest to the initiate for observing the *brahmacarya*, e.g. "Eat water. Do the service. Put on fuel. Do not sleep in the day time" (*saṁpreṣyati*). GGṛ II.10.33-34 (*Upanayana*). Cf. ĀśvGṛ. I.22.1. Cf. *saṁpraiṣa* (Śrauta).

संबाध *Sambādha* (*sam-√bādh*, cl. 1 "to press together") m. female sexual organ ĀpGṛ XXIII.3. See *āḍhārikā*.

संभार *Sambhāra* (*sam-√bhṛ*, cl. 1 "to bring together") m. a collection of things required for a rite : unground (*saṁpuṣkā*) grain (*dhānā*), parched rice grain (*lāja*), collyrium (*añjana*), ointment (*abhyañjana*), fragrant powder (*sthagara* and *uśīra*). These are offered to the snakes ĀpGṛ. XVIII.10-11 (*Śrāvaṇīsthālīpāka*).

सर्पबलि *Sarpabali* m.=*Śrāvaṇīsthālīpāka*.

सर्षप *Sarṣapa* m. mustard seed, mixed with rice chaff (*phalīkaraṇa*), and offered thrice on the *sūtikāgni*, installed at the entrance of the confinement room; this offering is done by the father and all visitors who enter the room ĀpGṛ. XV.6 (*Jātakarman*).

साण्ड *Sāṇḍa* mfn. having testicles (not castrated), said of the bull immolated at the *Śūlagava* PGṛ. III.8.4.

सांतपन *Sāṁtapana* n. "heating", name of a penance (*kṛcchra* comm.) in which a *homa* and a water libation are offered to the Maruts, and one is to drink a concoction of cow-dung, urine of a cow, milk, curds, clarified butter and *kuśodaka* in one day; on the next day he fasts KāGṛ. VII.1-3. Mn. XI.211.

Also a method of producing fire by heating dried cow-dung powder, cotton waste with sun-ray through a stone KāGṛ XXV. 8 comm.

सामशब्द *Sāmaśabda* m. recitation of a *sāman* (literally, its sound) when heard, the recitation of Ṛgveda is to be interrupted. This incompatibility is due to the capricious manner of handling the RV texts in the Sāmavedārcika, Aufrecht Rigveda; 2nd ed. II, xxxviii quoted by Oldenberg SBE XXIX, 116.

साल्व *Sālva* m(pl). the Sālva people whose verse is sung by two lute players (*vīṇāgāthin*) at the command of the sacrificer ĀpGṛ. XIV. 4-5 (*Sīmantonnayana*).

The verse runs :

yaugandharireva no rājeti sālvīravādiṣuḥ.

vivṛttacakrā āsīnāstīreṇa yamune tava (Mantrapāṭha II.11.12).

Yaugandhari is our king, said the Sālva women, turning a wheel and sitting on your bank, O Yamuna. Immediately follows another verse for the brahmins mentioning the river near which the brahmins dwell : *soma eva no rājetyāhur brāhmaṇīḥ prajāḥ. vivṛttacakrā āsīnāstīreṇāsau tava*, Mantrapāṭha 13. The brahmins sing "Soma is our king". For variations of these verses Cf. ĀśvGṛ. I. 14.6-7, PGṛ. I. 15.7-8, HDh. II (1), 224.

Whether or not the Sālvas performed the *Sīmantonnayana*, the verse was once a part of some ritual of the Sālvas performed by the wheel-turning women. Later, it was incorporated into the *Sīmantonnayana*.

This wheel-turning ceremony is a particular form of the *Vājapeya* J. Przyluski, Ancient people of the Punjab (tr. by Chitrabhanu Sen; Calcutta, 1960), 53-54. According to a kārikā quoted in Kāśikā on Pāṇ IV. 1.173 the Yugandhara people (clan?) is a division (*avayava*) of the Sālvas : *udumbarāstilakhalā madrakārā yugandharāḥ. bhuliṅgāḥ śardaṇḍāśca sālvāvayavasaṁjñitāḥ.* Cf. Pāṇ IV. 1.173; 2.135, HDh. II(1), 224-5.

सावित्री *Sāvitrī* f. name of the *mantra* (*gāyatrī* verse RV. III. 62.10), sacred to Savitṛ : *tat saviturvareṇyaṁ bhargo' devasya dhīmahi. dhiyo yo naḥ pracodayāt* ; this *mantra* is imparted by the teacher, sitting to the north of the fire, facing the east, to the initiate facing the west (*sāvitryupadeśa*), preceded or followed by the *vyāhṛtis* (q.v.). This is recited first by a single *pāda* (*pacchaḥ*) : *oṁ bhūstat saviturvareṇyam; oṁ bhuvaḥ bhargo devasya dhīmahi; oṁ suvaḥ dhiyo yo naḥ pracodayāt.* Then by half-verse (*ardharcaśaḥ*) : *oṁ bhūstatsaviturvareṇyaṁ bhargo devasya dhīmahi ; oṁ bhuvaḥ dhiyo yo naḥ procodayāt.* Finally the whole verse : *oṁ suvaḥ tatsaviturvareṇyaṁ bhargo devasya dhīmahi dhiyo yo naḥ pracodayāt.* Alternatively, the *vyāhṛtis* can be added at the end of the verse as arranged (*Upanayana*) ĀpGṛ. XI. 9-11 & Sudarśana comm. Cf. BhGṛ I.9. The *vyāhṛti* and the *sāvitrī* assumed a mystical significance as indicated by their permutations and combinations. Cf. *pratigara* (Śrauta).

The recitation of s° in this manner has been referred to ŚBr. XI. 5.4.15. Cf. HDh. II(1), 300-04. See also *patitasāvitrīka*.

सिग्वात *Sigvāta* m. wind from the hem of a skirt (*sic* RV. III. 53.2); if it blows against a person who is going about on business it is addressed with a *mantra* ĀpGṛ. IX.3.

सीतायज्ञ *Sītāyajña* m. sacrifice to Sītā, the deity of furrow, performed on a ploughed field to secure protection of the crop. A mess of food is cooked with barley or rice grains, and offered to Sītā, Yajā (the goddess of sacrifice), Samā (the goddess of devotion), Bhūti (the goddess of welfare) PGṛ. II. 17.10, or to Sītā, Āśā, Araḍā and Anaghā GGṛ. IV. 4.29. A *bali* is also offered to the protectors (demons?) of the furrow (°*goptṛ*). Women also offer oblations PGṛ. II.17.

°*loṣṭa* m.n. a clod of earth taken out of a furrow III.2.7 (*Āgrahāyaṇī*).

सीमन्तोन्नयन *Sīmantonnayana* n. rite of parting the hair upwards (of a pregnant wife), performed at the first pregnancy in the 4th month of pregnancy ĀśvGṛ. I.14.1, ĀpGṛ. XIV.1 or in the 6th or 8th month PGṛ. I.15.3; also called *Sīmantakaraṇa* KāGṛ. XXXI.1, GGṛ. II.7.1. It takes place after *Puṁsavana* (and performed like it PGṛ. I.15.2) in the fortnight of the increasing moon when the moon is in conjunction with a *nakṣatra* having a male name Āśv Gṛ. I.14.2.

It is a social festival to keep the expectant mother cheerful. To the west of the establis hed fire the wife sits on a bull's hide with its neck to the east; the husband offers 8 *ājya* oblations while she takes hold of his hand. Then he parts her hair upwards three times with a bunch of unripe *udumbara* fruits (*śalālu*), a porcupine's quill (*śalalī*) having white spots at 3 places (*treṇī*) and 3 bunches of *darbha* grass accompanied with the utterances of *vyāhṛti*. Two lute players sing the songs of the Sālvas (q.v.) and the brahmins ĀpGṛ. XIV.5. Popular rites as instructed by an aged brahmin woman are to follow ĀśvGṛ.I. 14.8. This rite may also be performed in a round apartment (*maṇḍalāgāra*) HGṛ. II.1.3. Treated in ĀśvGṛ. I.14, ŚGṛ. I.22, ĀpGṛ.XIV 1-8, BhGṛ. I. 21 etc.

सीर *Sīra* m.n. a plough, touched by a brahmin at the first ploughing ŚGṛ. IV.13.4.

सुभैक्षम् *Subhaikṣam* n. "good alms", uttered by a teacher when he accepts the alms presented by the student HGṛ. I.7.16.

सुरा *Surā* f. wine, drunk by 4 or 8 women, not widows, who dance at the wedding ŚGṛ. I. 11.5.

सूतिकाग्नि *Sūtikāgni* m. the fire for the woman who has given birth to a child ŚGṛ. I.25.4; it replaces the *aupāsana* (the domestic fire) during confinement, and is kept near the confinement room; on it oblations of mustard seeds mixed with rice chaff, every day for 10 days, are offered for driving away the goblins by the husband or any visitor who wants to enter the room ĀpGṛ. XV.6-7; or the s° is used for warming dishes etc. HGṛ. II.3.5. On the 12th day after the birth of a child (or the 10th) when the mother and child take a bath this fire is removed and the *aupāsana* is brought again II.4.8.

सूत्र *Sūtra* n. thread, one blue and another red, spread in the wheel tracks of a chariot by which the bridegroom and the bride are to depart ĀpGṛ. V.24 (*Vivāha*). A thread is fastened round (*parivīta*) a staff (*daṇḍa*) which is placed between the beds VIII.9 (*trirātra*).

सोदरी *Sodarī* (mfn). f. the uterine relations ("of the same womb") of a bride, who pour out *lāja* into her hands; the *lāja* is offered into the fire (*homa*) ĀpGṛ. V.4 (*Vivāha*).

सोमप्रवाक *Somapravāka* m. *soma* herald ĀśvGṛ. I.23.21. See *Soma* Śrauta section.

सोमांशु *Somāṁśu* m. stalks of *soma*, pounded, and the powder is inserted into the nostril of the pregnant wife ŚGṛ. I.20.3, PGṛ. I.14.4 (*Puṁsavana*).

सोष्यन्तीकर्मन् *Soṣyantīkarman* (√*su*/*sū*, cl. 2/6 "to impel/to give birth") n. rite for the parturient (*āsannaprasavā* or *sūyamānā* KāGṛ. XXXIII.1 comm; *prasavaśūlavatī* PGṛ. I.16. 1 comm.); also called *Soṣyantīsavana* KāGṛ. l.c., *Kṣipramsuvana* ĀpGṛ. XIV.13, °*prasavana* HGṛ. II.2.8. The earliest references of the rite RV. V.78.7-9, also BṛUp. VI.4.23. It is performed by the husband for his wife who is in labour pain for accelerating the delivery. The *tūryantī* plant is placed at her feet; water is drawn in the direction of the current of a river in a cup which has not been dipped in water before (*anāprīta*); the husband touches the wife on the head or belly., sprinkles her with water accompanied with the *mantras*. More *mantras* may be recited if the *jarāyu* does not come out. ĀpGṛ. XIV. 13-15, HGṛ. II.2.8; 3.1, GGṛ. II.7.13-14, PGṛ. I.16.1-2, KāGṛ. XXXIII.1-3.

°*homa* m. oblations of *ājya* and strewing of grass, performed when the child is appearing GGṛ. l.c.

स्तनप्रदान *Stanapradāna* n. rite of causing the child to suck its mother's breast, one of the rituals of *Jātakarman*. After addressing the wife with *mantra* (*mātaramabhimantraṇa*) the husband washes the breasts of his wife, and gives them to the child to suck, the right one first PGṛ. I. 16.20-21, HGṛ. II.4.3-4; or causes her to give the right breast (°*pratidhāpana*) ĀpGṛ. XV.5.

स्तूप *Stūpa* m. top of the house (the main beam, *pṛṣṭhavaṁśa* comm) ĀpGṛ. XIX.7.

स्त्री *Strī* f. wife of the householder; she can participate in the worship of the domestic fire ĀśvGṛ. I.9.1,3, but not allowed to perform the *homa* except in the rite of special wishes (*kāmyā*) and *bali* ĀpGṛ. VIII.3-4. But it is also enjoined that a female should not offer oblation in the *Pākayajña* ĀpDh.II.15.18 and she cannot perform any religious act independent of her husband Mn. V.155. For rights of the wife H. Dh. II (1), 556. For the authority of womenfolk on popular and customary rites, see *āvṛt*, *sālva*, *Sīmantonnayana*, *Vivāha*.

स्थगर *Sthagara* n. See *sambhāra*.

स्थण्डिल *Sthaṇḍila* n. altar for the domestic rites;

a square, raised surface of sand or loose earth, measuring one *iṣu* (arrow) on all the sides, levelled, swept (*samūhana* or *pari°*), strewn with *darbha* (*paristaraṇa*), sprinkled with water. Six lines are drawn on it (*lekhā*), and the fire is placed on it ĀśvGṛ. I.3.I. The *Brahman* sits to the south, and *praṇītā* water is placed to the north of it ŚGṛ. I.8.6, 8. See plan 9. Preparation of s° H.Dh.II(1), 208-09.

स्थपति *Sthapati* m. "lord of place"; a chieftain, who may belong to any caste, as distinguished from a king (*rājan*, by caste *kṣatriya*). He is one of the persons who is eligible for *Madhuparka* ĀpGṛ. XIII.3

स्थालीपाक *Sthālīpāka* m. "cooking in pot"; name of a sacrifice, one of the divisions (*saṁsthā*) of the *Pākayajña*, in which rice or barley grains are cooked in a dish, and used as a sacrificial food. It is sacred to Agni, also called *Pārvaṇa°* for its first performance on the first fullmoon day after the marriage by the married couple and its continued performance on the *parvan* days of the full and newmoon by them throughout their lives.

The newly married bride on her arrival at her husband's house husks grains (4 handfuls for each deity ĀśvGṛ. I.10.6), cooks the food, sprinkles *ājya*, removes the food from the fire. She takes hold of her husband who offers the mess of food on the fire to the deities of *Darśa*. Portions of it (*avadāna*) are spread under (*upastaraṇa*) and sprinkled over (*abhighāraṇa*), and offered to Agni, Agni *Sviṣṭakṛt*. A brahmin is fed with the remnant of the food, and he receives a bull as present. ĀpGṛ. VII.1-19, ĀśvGṛ. I.10.

स्थूणा *Sthūṇā* f. a post of a house, dug in the centre of the building site ĀpGṛ. XVII.3.

dvāra° f. door-post ib.

स्थेया *Stheyā* (mfn). f. name of water, contained in a jar which is placed to the northeast of the fire, and circumambulated by the bridegroom and the bride ŚGṛ. I.13.9 (*Vivāha*).

स्नातक *Snātaka* m. a person who has taken the ceremonial bath on completion of his vedic study (*vedam adhītya snāsyan*) ĀpGṛ. XII.1, or even before finishing his study if permitted by his teacher ĀśvGṛ. III.9.4. The word *snāna* means the ceremonial bath which marks the end of studentship as well as the rite of *Samāvartana* HGṛ. I.9.1. Three types of s° are enumerated :

(1) *vidyā°* a *snātaka* by knowledge, i.e. one who has finished the study but before the expiry of the period of vow.

(2) *vrata°* a s° by *vrata*, i.e. he has completed the period of vow but before he has finished the vedic study.

(3) *vidyāvrata°* a s° who has finished both PGṛ.II.5.32-35, GGṛ. III.5.21-22. The last ranks the highest ib. 23. Anyone of the above categories can perform *Samāvartana* (q.v.). Snātakahood lasts till one marries, and thereafter he becomes a *gṛhastha*, householder.

°vrata n. observances of a *snātaka*. As long as a *snātaka* does not marry he has to follow certain code of conduct which is called *vrata* ĀśvGṛ. III.9.5, (*yama*) restraint PGṛ.II.7.1. He shall not bathe at night nor shall bathe naked, nor lie down naked. He shall not look at a naked woman except during sexual intercourse. He is not to run during rain, nor climb up a tree, nor go down into a well ĀśvGṛ. III.9.6-7. He shall not go to another village by night. He should call a pregnant woman *vijanyā*, an ichneumon (*nakula*) *sakula*, a *kapāla* (skull) *bhagāla*. He should not wear dyed (*vikṛta*) garment. He must be firm in his intentions, a protector of other's life and a friend of all PGṛ. II.7.1-18, for more elaborate rules ŚGṛ. IV.11-12. See also *vratādeśana*.

स्नापन *Snāpana* n. See *Jātakarman*.

स्रज् *Sraj* f. a wreath, worn on the head by a student ĀpGṛ. XII.11 (*Samāvartana*).

स्रस्तर *Srastara* m.n. a couch (or a layer of straw Oldenberg SBE XXIX, 132), spread on the floor, on which all the members of a family lie for one night ŚGṛ. IV.18.5, 12 (*Pratyavarohaṇa*).

स्रुव *Sruva* m. a spoon (see Śrauta section), held at the bottom in right hand and used as a vessel (*pātra*) for offering *ājya* oblations ŚGṛ. I.9.1, 3-4.

It is warmed, wiped with *kuśa* blades, sprinkled with water and warmed again before use PGṛ. I.1.3.

स्वस्त्ययन *Svastyayana* n. "auspicious progress"; the time which brings good fortune, i.e. the most (*°tama*) auspicious time for beginning a rite ŚGṛ. I.3.2.

स्वाध्याय *Svādhyāya* m. "lesson for self"; repetition or recitation of portions of the veda to oneself, to be done every morning ŚGṛ. I.4.1.

The rite (°*vidhi*) for recital : he goes out of the village to the east or north, has a bath in water, sips water, spreads *darbha* grass having the tufts directed to the east; he wears dry garment and the *yajñopavīta*, sits on the grass making a lap (cross-legged), turns his face to the east, holds the *pavitra* (*kuśa* blades) in his hands with the right hand on the top; he looks at the horizon or closes his eyes or in any other way gets ready to recite the text; the *vyāhṛti*s preceded by *om* is first pronounced, then follows the *sāvitrī*, first by single *pāda* (*pacchaḥ*), then by half-verse (*ardharcaśaḥ*), finally the whole. Now, the main recital begins. He finishes the recital by uttering *namo brahmaṇe* etc. ĀśvGṛ. III. 2-3.

ह Ha

हविस् *Havis* n. ĀśvGṛ. I.10.17. See Śrauta section.

हस्तग्रहण *Hastagrahaṇa* n.=*Pāṇi*°.

हुत *Huta* (√*hu*, cl.3 "to sacrifice") (mfn). m. one of the 4 kinds of *Pākayajñas* in which oblations of clarified butter are poured into the fire ŚGṛ. I.5.1: an oblation itself is called h° if made by the performing of the *Agnihotra* SGṛ I.10.7.

a° a rite in which a *bali* offering or *homa* does not take place PGṛ I.4.1 & comm. (a variety of *Pākayajña*).But See *ahuta & Pākayajña*.

pra° mfn. m. also a kind of *Pākayajña*, consisting of *homa, bali and prāśita* PGṛ. ib and the name of an oblation which is "sacrificed up" to the manes (i.e. *Śrāddha*) SGṛ I.10.7.

हृदय *Hṛdaya* n. the heart of an immolated cow, drawn out silently, roasted on a spit of *udumbara* (°*śūla*), sprinkled with *ājya*, and finally the brahmins are fed with it HGṛ. II.15.5-8 (*Śrāddha*). The *hṛdayaśūla* is also used in the domestic animal sacrifice ĀśvGṛ. I.11.15. See also Śrauta section.

°*deśa* m. the place of a bride's heart, touched by the bridegroom HGṛ. I.21.3 (*Vivāha*); of an initiate, touched by his teacher ĀśvGṛ. I.20.10. (*Upanayana*).

होतृ *Hotṛ* m. the priest, whose functions are performed by the householder himself. See *ṛtvij* (Gṛhya).

होम *Homa* m. act of pouring an oblation, specially, of clarified butter (*ājya*) into the fire; h° is an essential feature of the domestic rites. Preparation of the *sthaṇḍila*, purification of *ājya* (*ā*° *saṁskāra*), sweeping (*parisamūhana*) and strewing (*paristaraṇa*) always precede a h°. The offering ladle is warmed, wiped off with *darbha* grass, and again warmed, logs are put into the fire. Then the householder pours out *ājya* into the fire, and 2 *ājyabhāga*s are optional in the *Pākayajña*, and so is the *sviṣṭakṛt* oblation.

Oblation is poured by mentioning the deity and pronouncing *svāhā*. This is called *ājya*°. ĀśvGṛ. I.3.4-10, ŚGṛ. I.9.

homātikrama m. fault of passing over a regular *homa*, a transgression which calls for a *prāyaścitta* ŚGṛ. V.4.3.

होलाक *Holāka* m. ? a minor rite performed by maidens who are desirous of attaining good fortune; Rākā is the deity; also called Holākā, Rākā etc. KāGṛ. LXXIII.1.

APPENDICES

SACRIFICIAL IMPLEMENTS AND UTENSILS

PLATE I

Haug Collection

1. *dhruva*
2. *upabhṛt*
3. *juhū*
4. *agnihotrahavaṇī*
5. *camasa ?*
6. a similar goblet (*praṇītāpraṇayana*)
7. similar to no. 5
8. goblet
9. *sruva*
10. *antardhana*
11. similar to no. 6
12. *ṣaḍavatta*
13. *musala*
14. a-b probably *pūrṇapātra*
15. *ulūkhala*

16-17. shaped like a mortar; probably *ūrdhvapatra*

18. *sphya*

19-20. *upaveṣa*(?)=*dhṛṣṭi*; no. 20 is probably a *mekṣaṇa*

21. offering spoon

22-23. offering spoons; probably no. 22 is a *prasitraharaṇa*

24. part of no. 12
25. *araṇi* having 5 parts
26. missing
27. 3 pieces of stick, use unknown

PLATES II–III

Collection of the Pit Rivers Museum

1. *yoni*-shaped ladle used in *homa*, from Varanasi; presented by W. Crooke, 1893
2. same as above (probably *pariplu patra*)
3. *upabhṛt*
4. *dhruvā*
5. label missing
6. *pṛṣadājyagrahaṇī*
7. *agnihotrahavaṇī*
8. *pracaraṇī*
9. *juhū*

10. *vasāhomahavanī*
11. *sruva*
12. spoon for pouring ghee in *homa*, used in Varanasi; presented by W. Crooke, 1893
13. container for ghee; presented by W. Crooke, 1893
14. *praṇītāpraṇayana*
15. *prāśitraharaṇa*
16. *phalīkaraṇapātra* (preferably, *ṣaḍavatta*)
17. *iḍāpātra*
18. *ulūkhala*
19. *musala*
20. *mekṣaṇa*
21. *dhṛṣṭi* (cf. nos. 19 & 20 pl. I)
22. *sphya*
23. *śamyā*
24. *antardhāna*
25. *dṛṣad*
26. *upalā*
27. *śūrpa*
28. *anvāhāryasthālī*
29. *bharjanapātra*
30. *ājyasthālī*

Pl. 1

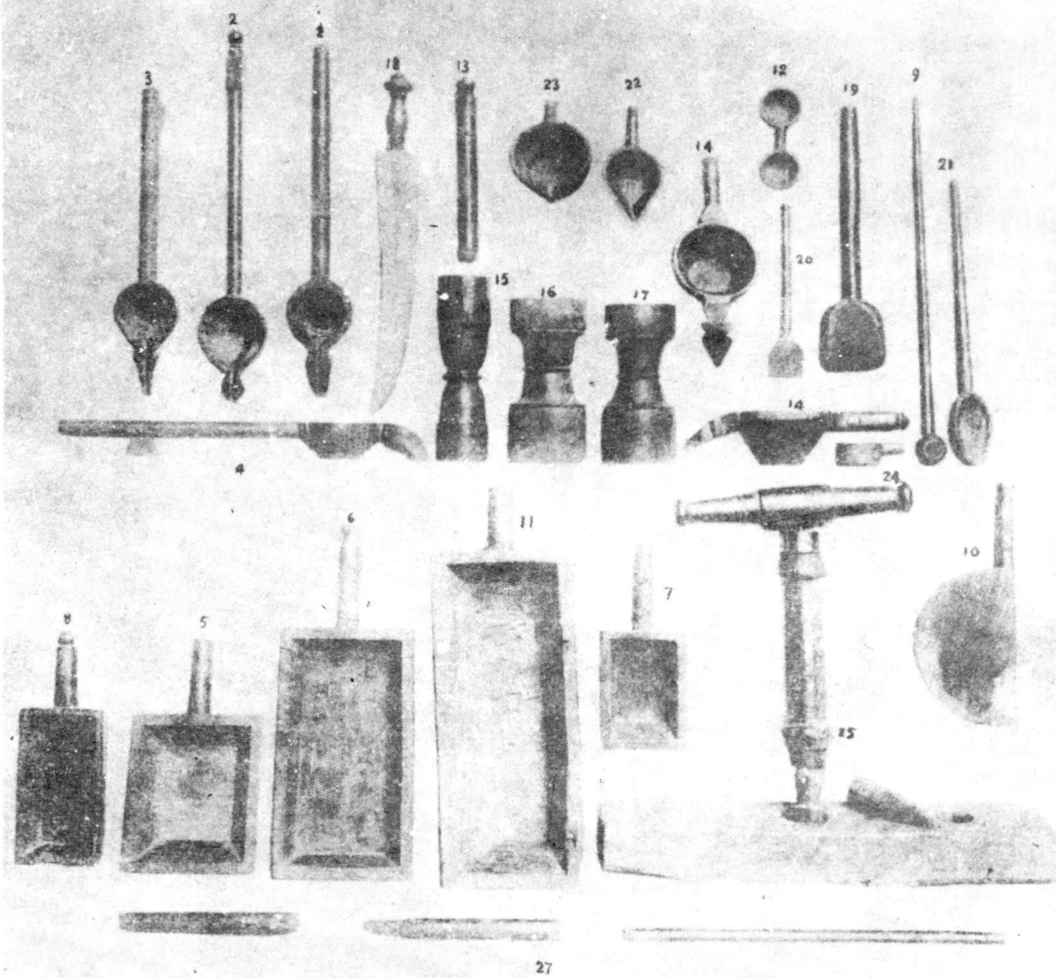

Phototypie Berthaud, Paris

Pl. II

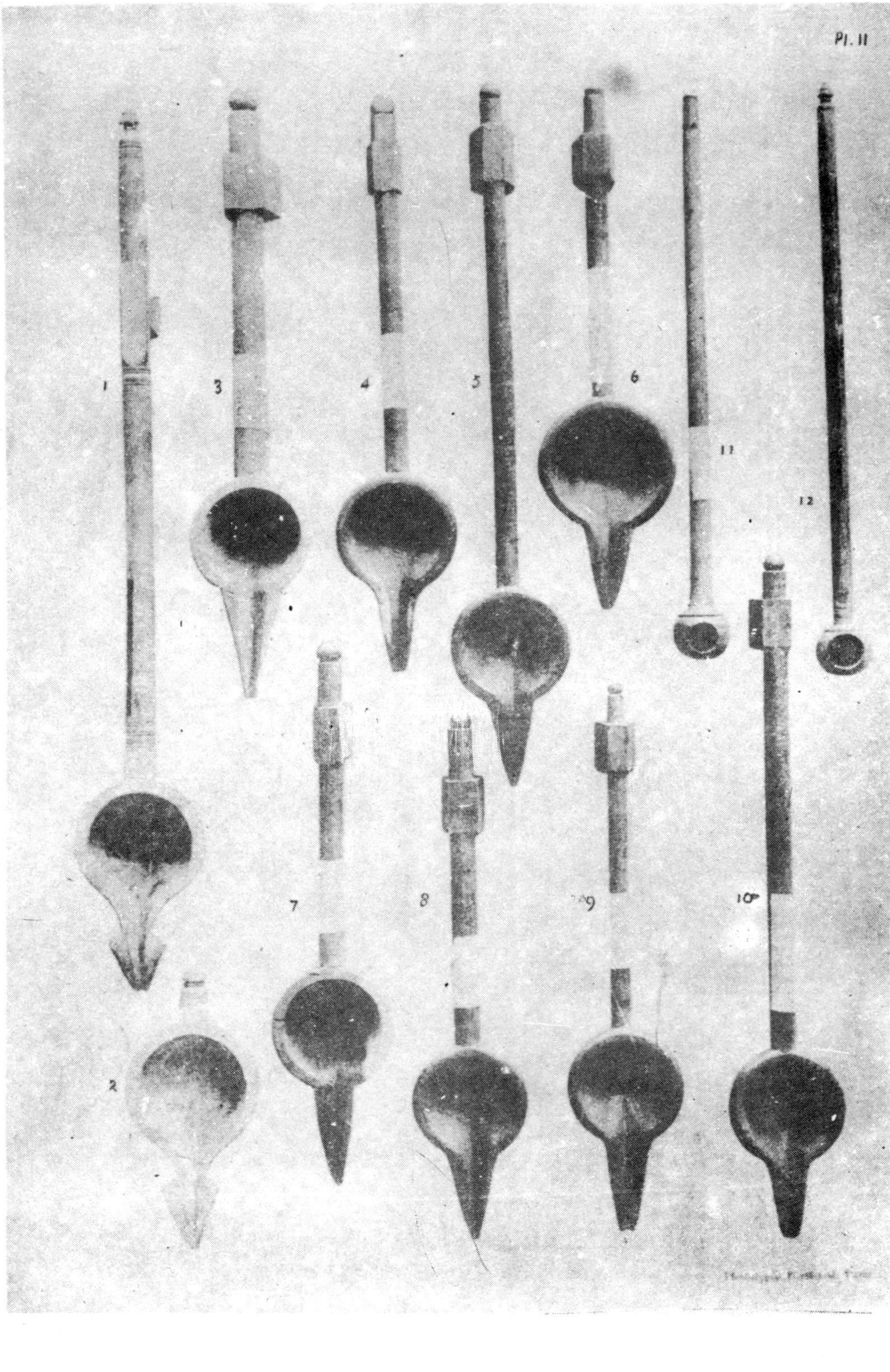

Pl. III

Plan 1

THE FIRST, THIRD AND FIFTH PRASTĀRAS OF THE ŚYENA (SUPARṆA) CITI

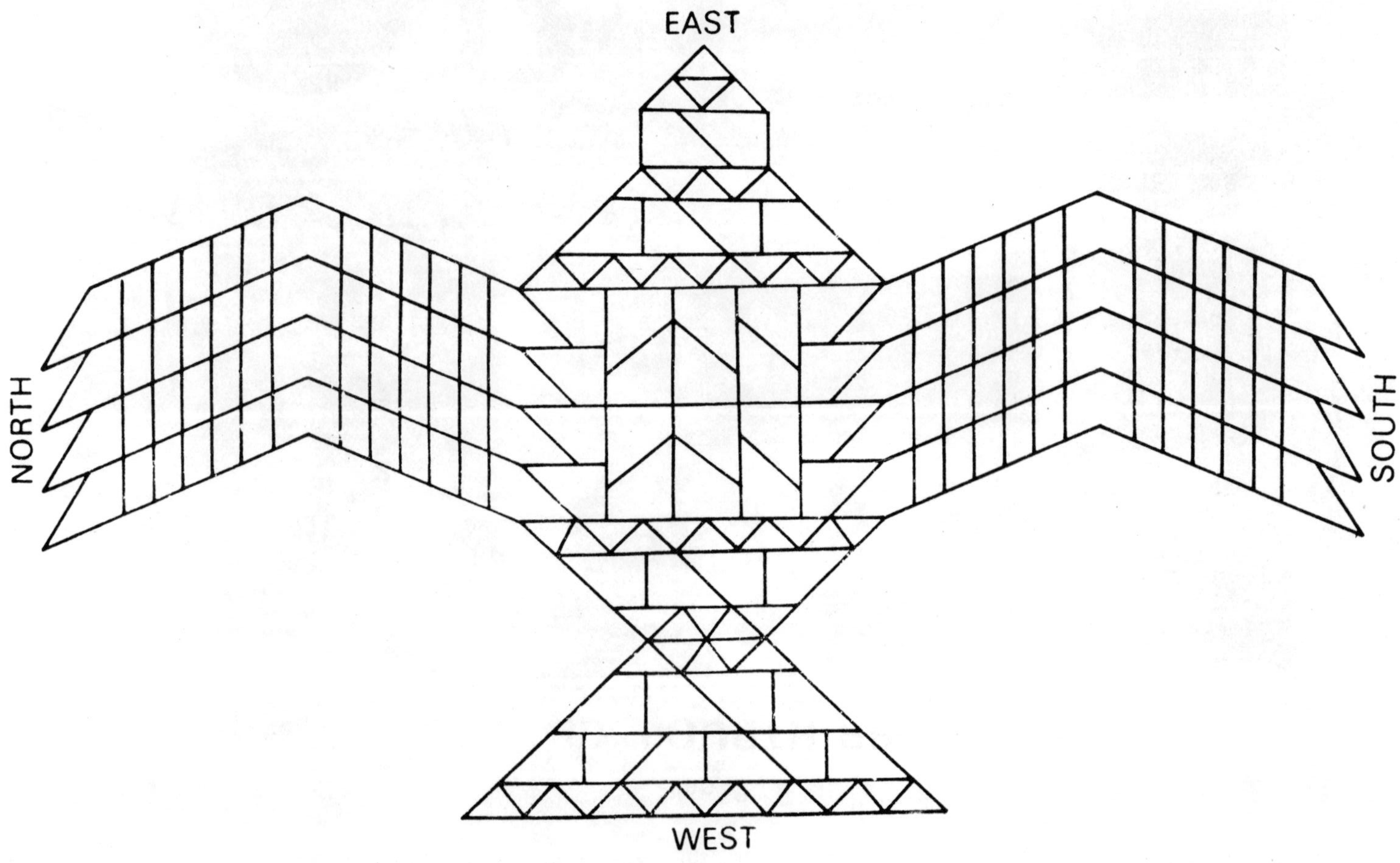

Plan 2

THE SECOND, FOURTH PRASTARAS OF THE SYENA (SUPARṆA) CITI

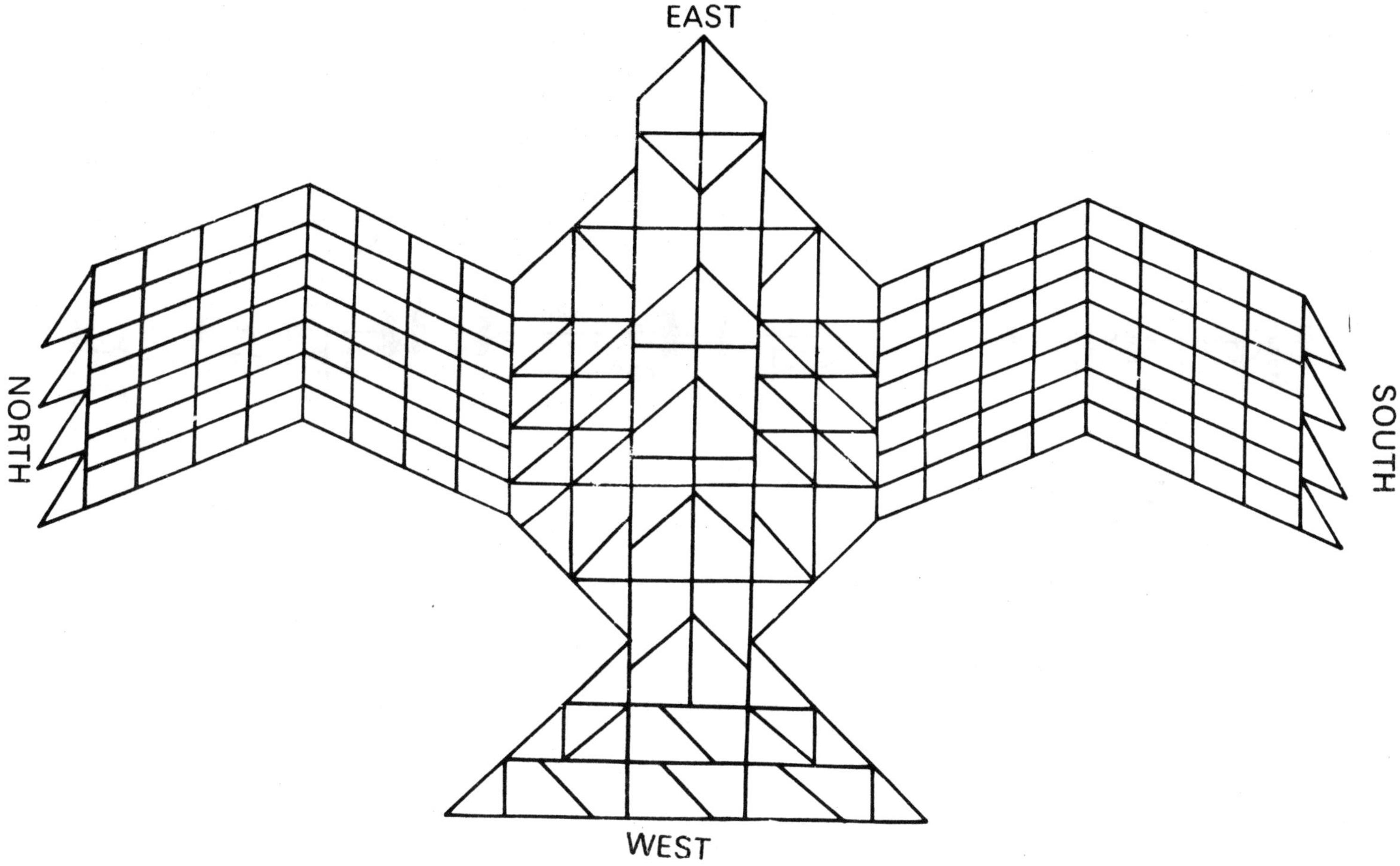

Plan 3

THE ARENA OF THE SOMA SACRIFICE

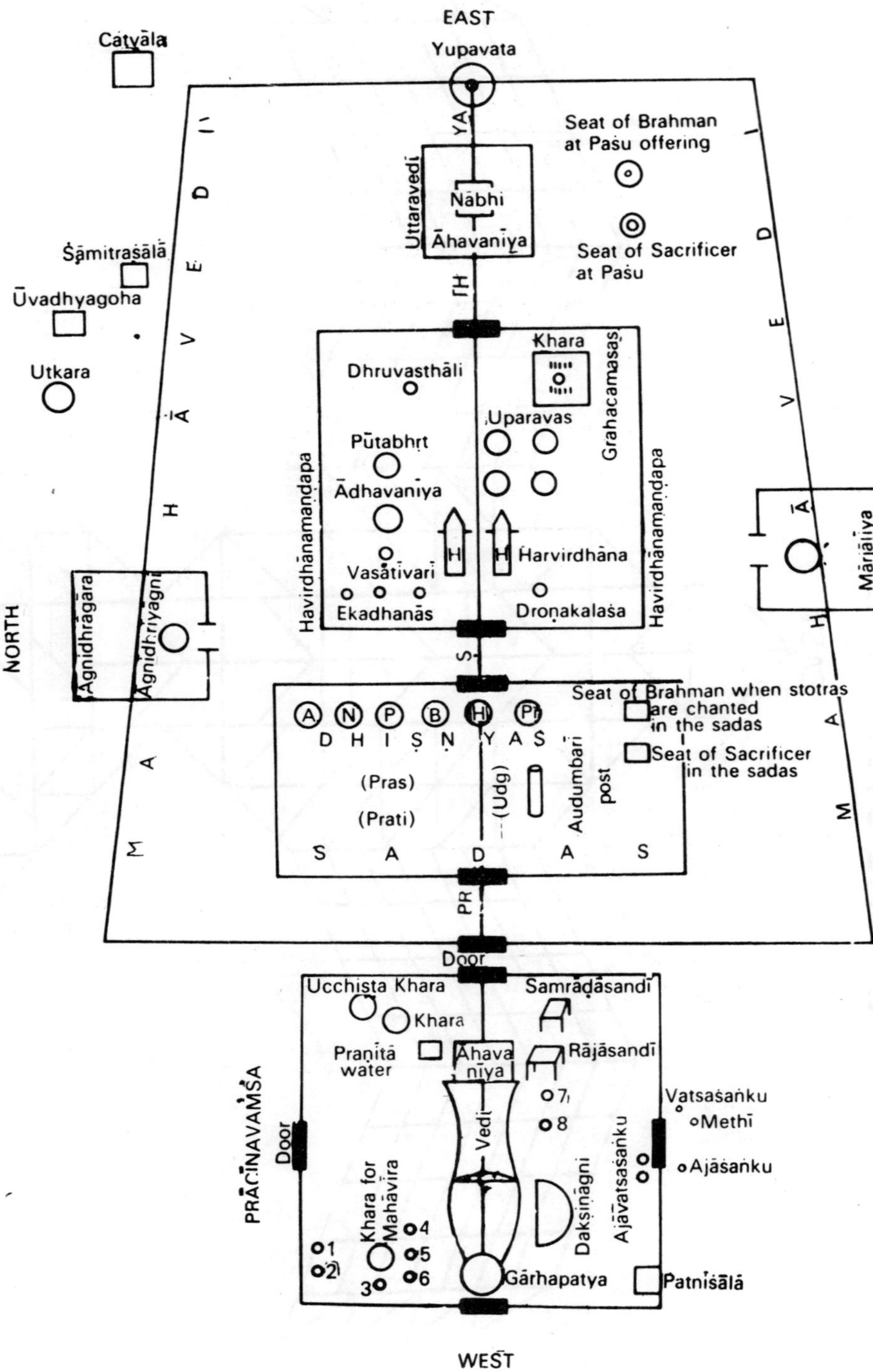

(A) Acchāvāka; (N) Neṣṭṛ; (P) Potṛ; (B) Brāhmaṇācchaṃsin, (H) Hotṛ
(Pr) Praśāstṛ, (Pras) Place of Prastotṛ; (Prati) Place of Pratihartṛ;
(Udg) Place of Udagātṛ when chanting

1. Seat of Pratiprasthātṛ; 2. of Āgnīdhra, 3 of Hotṛ
4. of Brahman; 5. of Sacrificer, 6 of Prastotṛ.
7. Place of Brahman, 8 Place of Sacrificer

Plan 4

VEDI FOR THE AGNIHOTRA, DARSAPŪRNAMĀSA AND ISTIS

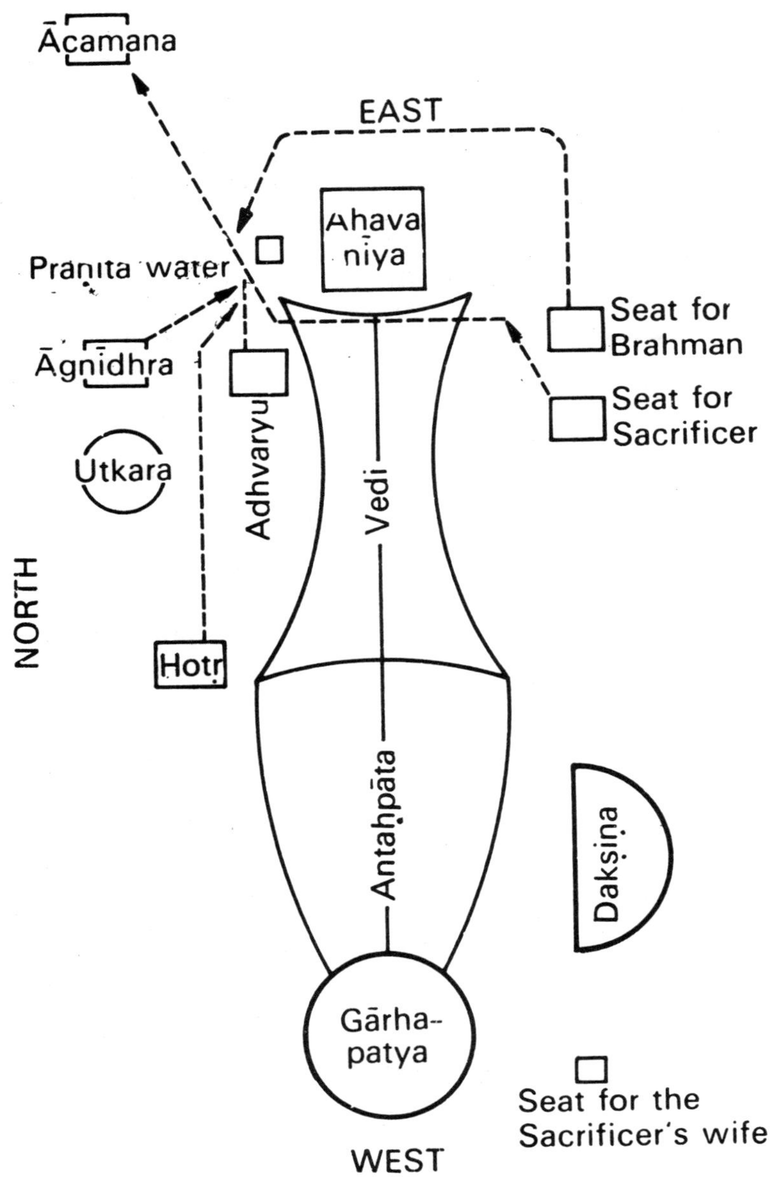

* Dotted lines indicate the samcaras of the Brahman etc.

Plan 5

VEDI FOR THE NIRŪḌHAPAŚUBANDHA

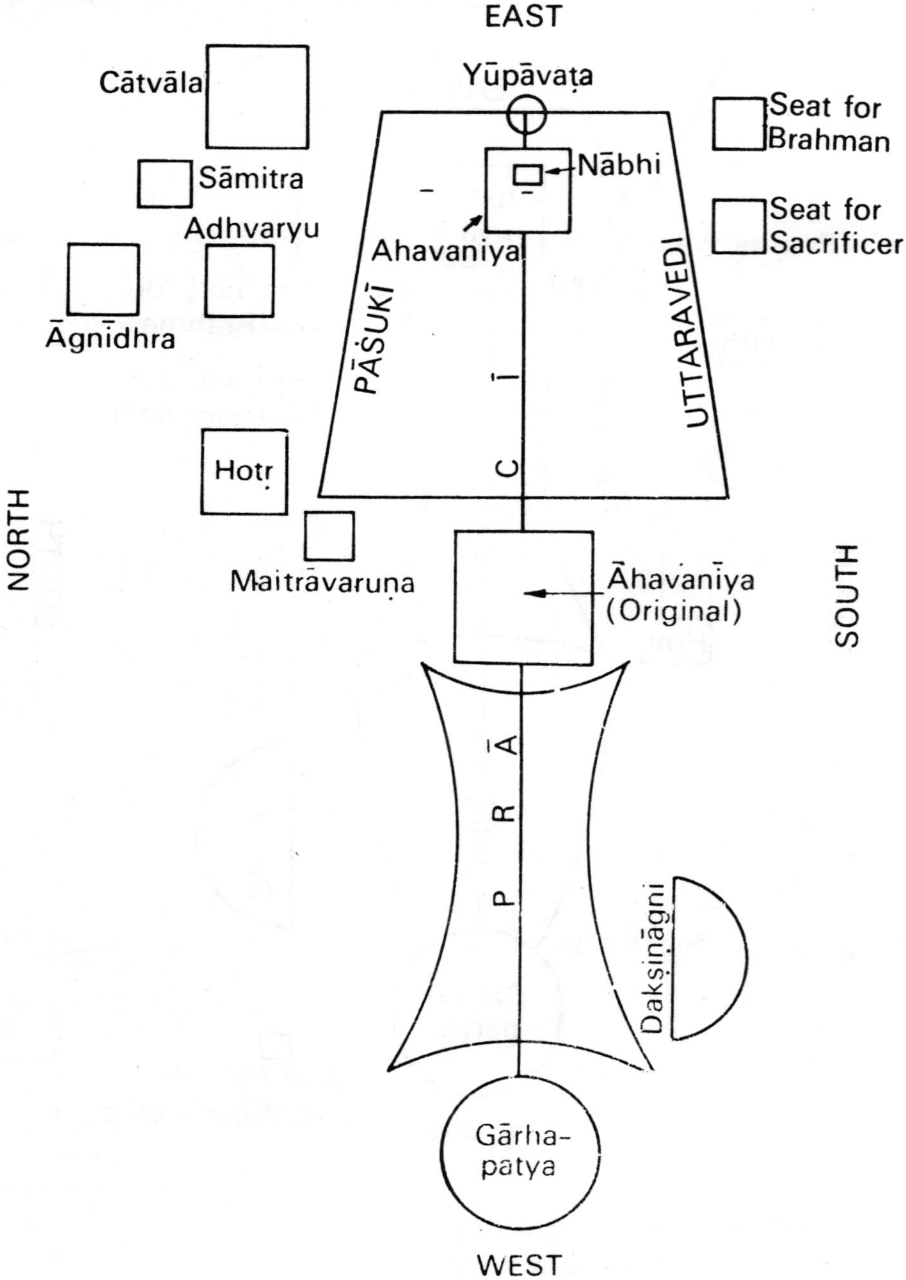

Plan 6

VEDI FOR THE VARUṆAPRAGHĀSA (CĀTURMĀSYA)

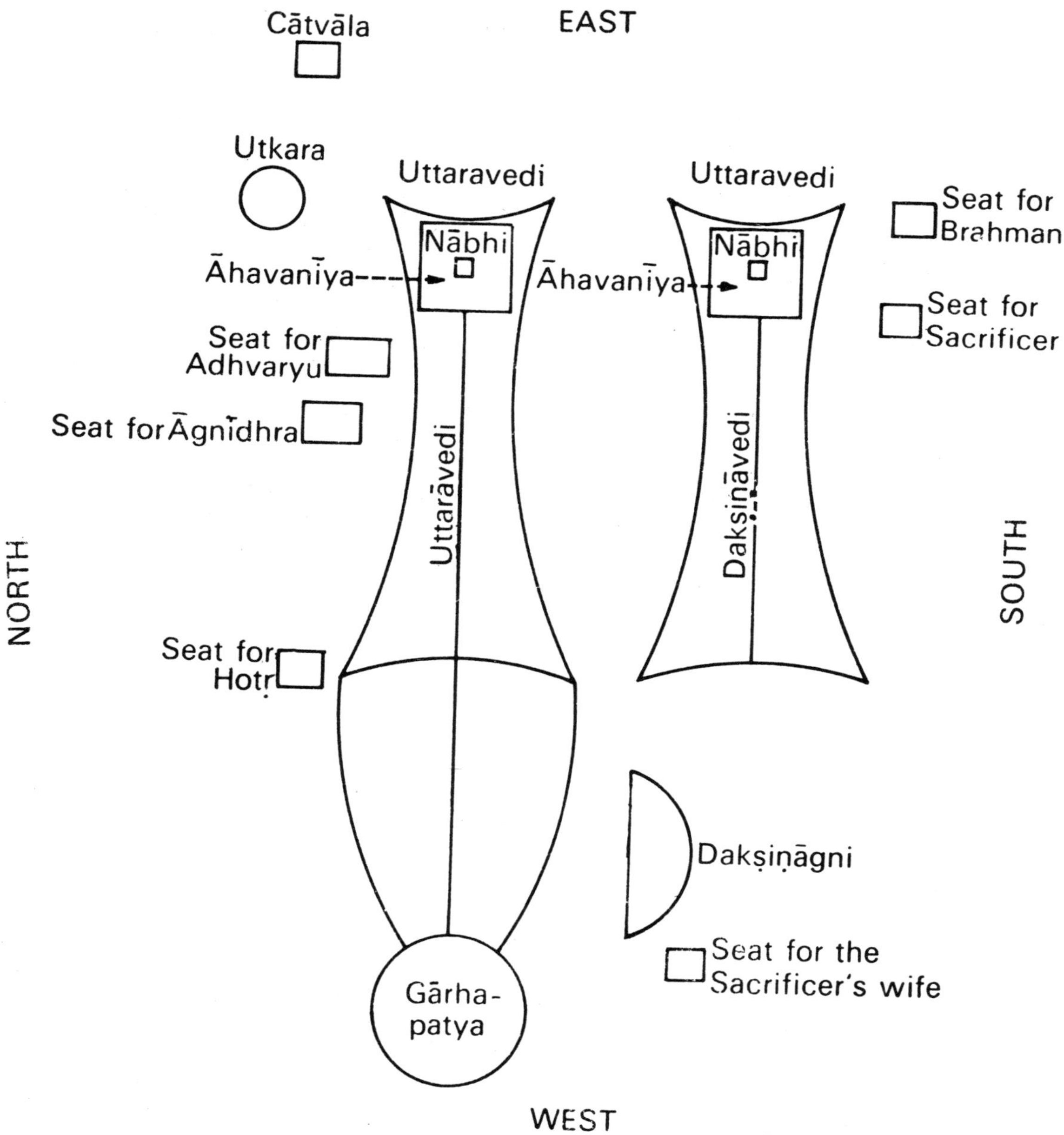

Plan 7

THE ARRANGEMENT OF KAPĀLAS

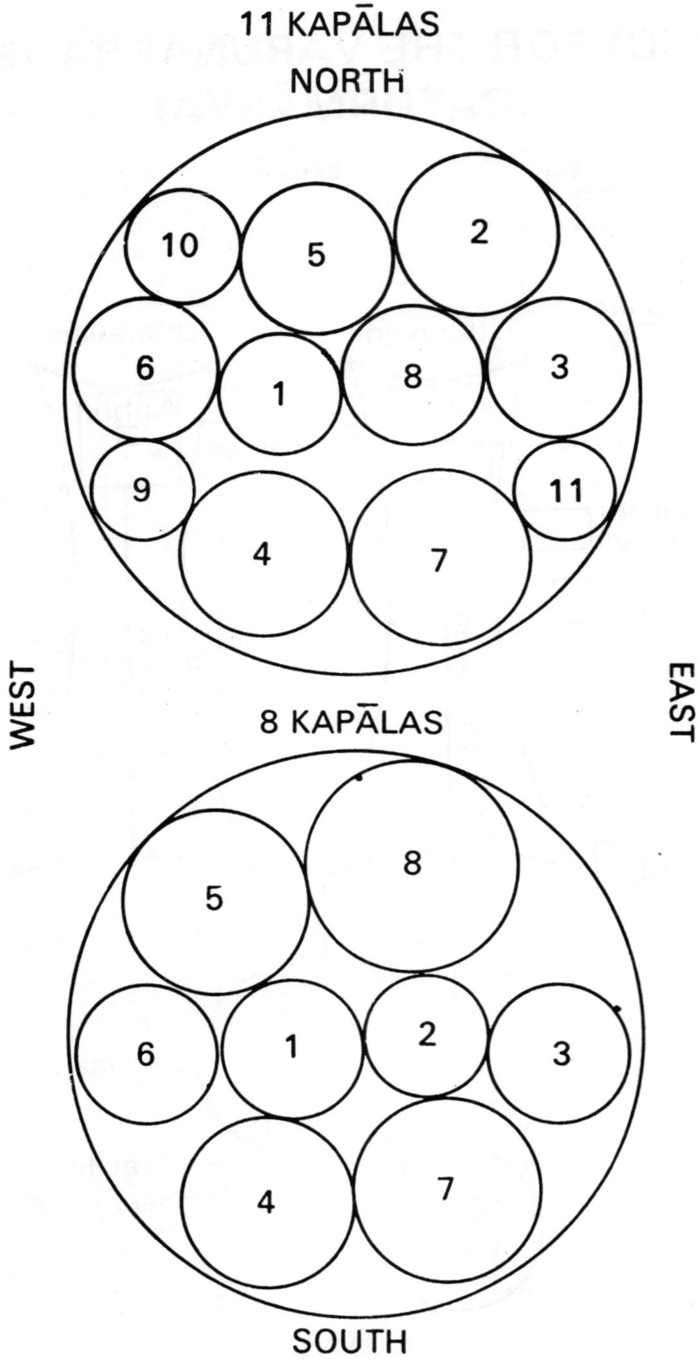

Plan 8

THE ARRANGEMENT OF 11 KAPALAS

(Another Variety)

NORTH

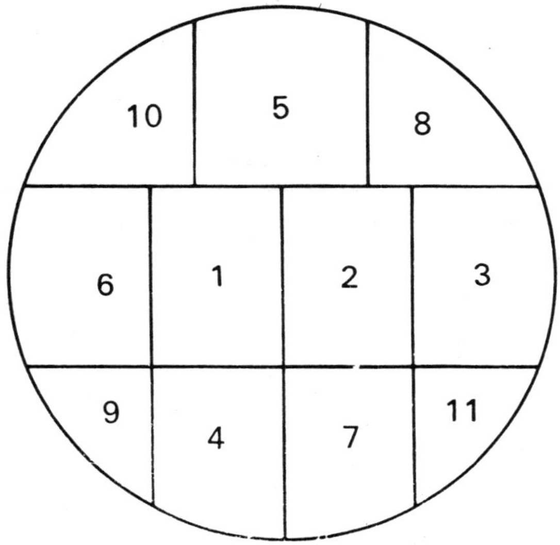

WEST

THE ARRANGEMENT OF 8 KAPALAS

(Another Variety)

EAST

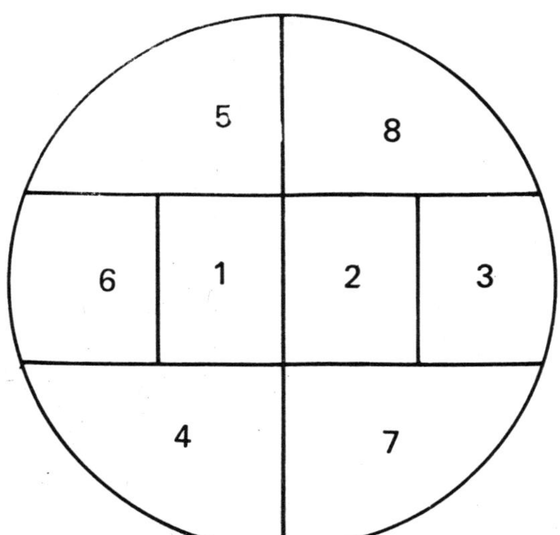

SOUTH

Plan 9

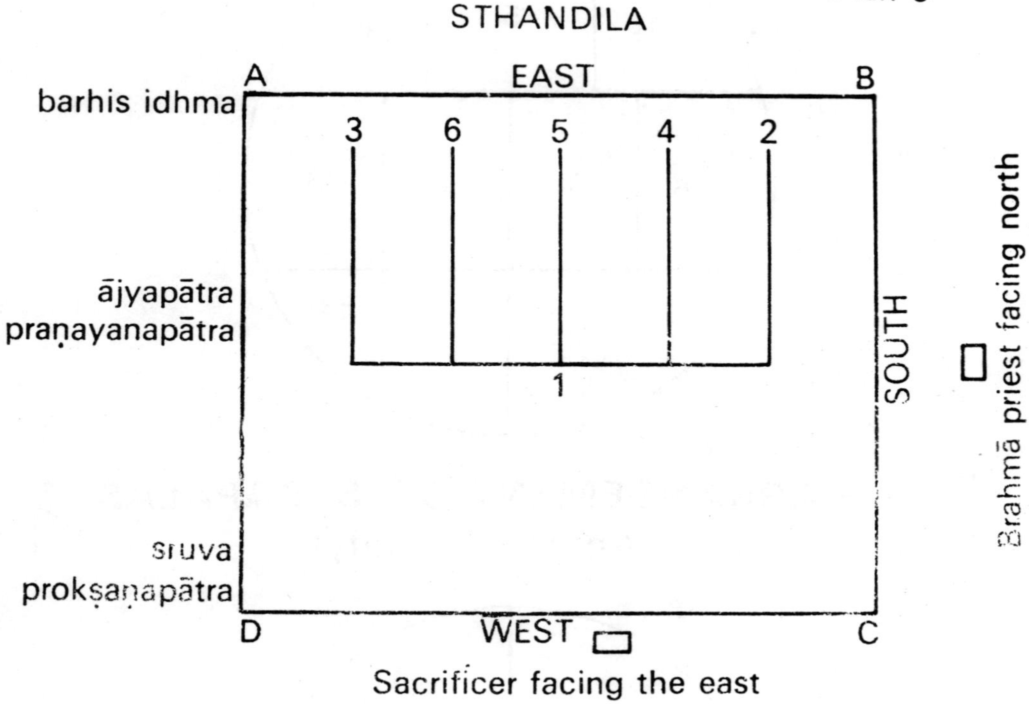
STHANDILA
A
EAST
B
barhis idhma
3
6
5
4
2
ājyapātra
praṇayanapātra
1
SOUTH
Brahmā priest facing north
sruva
prokṣaṇapātra
D
WEST
C
Sacrificer facing the east